The Potala Palace, Lhasa, Tibet
(*Courtesy* : Rajiv Mehrotra)

His Holiness the XIV Dalai Lama (*Courtsey* : S.N. Sinha)

The Spirit of Tibet :Vision for Human Liberation

The Spirit of Tibet
Vision for Human Liberation

Selected Speeches and Writings of
H H The XIV Dalai Lama

Editor
A.A.Shiromany

TIBETAN PARLIAMENTARY AND POLICY RESEARCH CENTRE
NEW DELHI
in association with
VIKAS PUBLISHING HOUSE PVT LTD
NEW DELHI

Published by
TIBETAN PARLIAMENTARY AND POLICY RESEARCH CENTRE
A-2/18, Safdarjung Enclave, New Delhi-1100 29
in association with
VIKAS PUBLISHING HOUSE PVT LTD
576, Masjid Road, Jangpura, New Delhi 110014
First Floor, N.S.Bhawan, 4th Cross,
4th Main, Gandhi Nagar, Bangalore-560 009

First Published 1996
© Friedrich-Naumann Foundation
ISBN 81-259-0210-4

Typeset and Printed at Neographics
1811, Gyani Bazar, Kotla, New Delhi-110003

FOREWORD

The occasion was the celebrations of the 2500th anniversary of Lord Buddha. Two figures appeared in Vigyan Bhavan, H.H. the Dalai Lama and the Panchen Lama. They were a radiant pair from the *Devaloka*. The enigmatic smile, the pure laughter of H.H. the Dalai Lama enraptured us all who were organisers, witnesses and participants in the 1956 celebrations.

The Late Sri Jawaharlal Nehru escorted H.H. the Dalai Lama throughout this visit with a protective and affectionate care which was deep and gently visible. If clouds of apprehension loomed in the inner landscape of both, there were no outward signs. The sight of H.H. the Dalai Lama was like a vision come true from ancient lore and the magic mysterious lands of beyond the snows.

Hardly had we recovered from the exhilaration of having encountered one so pure and unsullied that the news of his flight spread. We held our breath in prayer. After a most arduous journey he arrived in India in April 1959. He was greeted by Sri Jawaharlal Nehru with a telegram:

"My colleagues and I welcome you and send greetings on your safe arrival in India. We shall be happy to afford the necessary facilities to you, your family and the entourage to reside in India. The people who hold you in great veneration, will no doubt accord their traditional respect to your personage. Kind regards to you."

H.H. the Dalai Lama the human child and adolescent protected within the Patola Palace, no doubt political and spiritual leader, was suddenly with no territory and horizon and an uncertain future. His corporeal frame, as he says in his biography, experienced an awesome freedom in exile. Consequently his inner being and consciousness radiated to lands far and near to civilisation and cultures, which may or may not have heard of the potency of the energies held in bondage within a geographical region. And today it is H.H. the Dalai Lama, the Universal Being of unparalleled stature, delivering and teaching his message of Universal Responsibility through the universal acceptance of the value of altruism, compassion, love and non-violence as motivations for human action.

H.H. the Dalai Lama has spoken, addressed innumerable forums on countless occasions; has written and discussed issues, political, social, moral and spiritual for a vast spectrum of humanity, youth, old and young, easterners and westerners, scientists, philosophers, environmentalists, men of reflection and of action and those others the holders of power who decide destinies of political states. His capacity to reach out to each group and individual and to communicate simply and lucidly, direct and deep, is the measure of his greatness and universality of his presence. It is the clear light and purity of experience which transforms those who are touched and moved by his presence with or without words. He can transform the gross to the subtle, the *rajasic* to the *satvika*.

No residual record of words not even his, can replace or substitute the experience of the presence and the essence of this the Universal Being amongst us, the mere humans, fragmented within and without with the multiple bondages of our own making. And yet a collection of his 'speeches', 'addresses' and the responses he evoked from the International Press was necessary. The editor Shri A.A.Shiromany and the editorial board undertook a difficult and challenging task of collecting, sifting and classifying the material. This has been done most painstakingly. The result is a very valuable volume of the thoughts of H.H. the Dalai Lama.

A person who views life as a totality and is total himself can hardly make a clear-cut distinction between the purely physical mundane issues of politics from those of moral and ethical values. This is what resonates in his remarkable address on the occasion of receiving the Nobel Prize. He said,

"I am deeply touched .... I am very happy to be here with you today to receive the Nobel Prize for Peace. I feel honoured, humbled and deeply moved that you should give this important prize to a simple monk from Tibet. I am no one special. But, I believe the prize is a recognition of the true value of altruism, love, compassion and non-violence which I try to practise, in accordance with the teachings of the Buddha and the great sages of India and Tibet. I accept the prize with profound gratitude on behalf of the oppressed everywhere and for all those who struggle for freedom and work for world peace. I accept it as a tribute to the man who founded the modern tradition of non-violent action for change—Mahatma Gandhi—whose life taught and inspired me."

And again

"As a Buddhist monk, my concern extends to all members of the human family and, indeed, to all sentient beings who suffer. I believe all suffering is caused by ignorance. People inflict pain on others in the selfish pursuit of their happiness or satisfaction. Yet true happiness comes from a sense of inner peace and contentment, which in turn must be achieved through the cultivation of altruism, of love and compassion and elimination of ignorance, selfishness and greed."

As a sentient being, citizen of the World, his concern for environment and as Buddhist for all forms of life is sharp and clear and as the apostle of compassion, love and altruism his unshakable faith in non-violence and peace permeates through each page of the volume. Those who read and those who hear will, I am sure, be inspired to follow the path in thought and action and not only because a leader has spoken, but because the perennial truth and veracities of life have spoken through him.

May his presence illumine and radiate our paths.

New Delhi,   Kapila Vatsyayan
June 27, 1995

O Bhikshus and wise men,
Do not accept my words merely
out of respect for me,
But as gold is tested by being
melted, cut and burnished,
So, analyse what I have said
and only then accept it.

— Lord Buddha

INTRODUCTION

The story of Lhamo Thondup, anointed at the age of four, as Jamphel Ngawang Lobsang Yeshe Tenzin Gyatso, the 14th Dalai Lama, is unique for its portrayal of adventure, courage and kindness in the face of diabolical cruelty and crime against humanity. It is at once poignant and thrilling. It depicts the inevitable conflict between spiritual power and brute force, between truth and fabrication, and between love of humanity and hatred. With his genius of gentle love and compassion the Dalai Lama has turned this fearsome fiasco into a humanistic episode, a saga of non-violence, love and universal responsibility.

Ever since the Chinese communist forces, ironically called the People's Liberation Army, crossed the Tibetan border, it began a systematic repression and subjugation of a whole race of peaceful and peace-loving people. Tibet was then being administered by Prime Ministers and a Regency. The young Dalai Lama was assiduously pursuing his studies of Buddhist scriptures and disciplines under the strict supervision of his tutors. Tibet had begun to reel under the oppressive alien occupation and the State had become vulnerable without its formal Head, the Dalai Lama, who had yet to be enthroned. It was, therefore, decided to hold the investiture ceremony on November 17, 1950 and formally enthrone him as the temporal Head as well as the religious and spiritual leader of seven million Tibetan people at the age of fifteen, nearly three years ahead of the normal practice.

For almost ten years, the Dalai Lama had been seeing the desecration of his land, the temples and monasteries, and the degradation of his people, who were forced to work as labour gangs on road-building, factories and so on, on starvation wages. Even women and children were not spared. Well-to-do farmers were robbed of their belongings and farm products. They were dispossessed of their lands. Those offering a semblance of opposition were either shot dead or sent to concentration camps to be tortured and maimed. The Tibetans were not only deprived of their basic human rights, including the right to worship and freedom of speech, but reduced to a state of abject servility. More and more Chinese troops and settlers were brought in to alter the ratio of the Tibetan population and reduce them into a minority in their own homeland.

The chaotic conditions and bloodshed that were to overtake Tibet had already been prophesied by the Thirteenth Dalai Lama in his Testament before his death in 1933. It said: "It may happen that, here in Tibet, religion and government will be attacked both from without and within. Unless we guard our country, it will now happen that the Dalai Lama and Panchen Lama, the Father and Son and all the revered holders of the faith will disappear and become nameless. Monks and their monasteries will be destroyed, the rule of law will be weakened, land and property of government officials will be seized. They themselves will be forced to serve their enemies or wander the country like beggars. All beings will be sunk in great hardships and overwhelming fear; the days and nights will drag on slowly in suffering."

The prediction turned out to be prophetic. Some may wonder at the accuracy of the prophecy—the graphic description of the events, which were to take place in the land of the snows, a quarter of a century later—as something quite incredible. This is true particularly of those who may not be familiar with the Oriental spiritual concepts that lie at the root of Buddhism, namely, the theory of re-birth (incarnation), and the cumulative effect of Karma during previous states of existence.

Most people in the world, particularly in the West, with a pro-nounced materialistic background, may find it hard to comprehend or give credence to such prophecies. Others may consider the idea of incarnation, as superstition verging on blind faith or regard it with a certain amount of scepticism. Faith, being beyond the sphere of logic, cannot be justified or explained through logical examination. In the case of Tibetans, who are steeped in Buddhism, faith is a blending of religion, spirituality and mysticism, while for others it may be a mystery, something belonging to the realm of the unknown, unexplored or the occult.

For the Tibetans the institution of the Dalai Lama, including his re-incarnation, is an article of faith. They are one of the most intensely religious people the world has ever known. Buddhism flows in their veins and they regard the Dalai Lama as the manifestation of Buddha's compassion and patron deity, the Avalokitesvara. They have absolute and implicit faith in him and his word is law (*dharma*) for them. This faith is inherent in their religious beliefs and spiritual heritage handed down through generations over the centuries. It is deeply ingrained as an irrevocable belief inexorably held by them.

As a foreboding of the tragic events, late one evening in August 1950 in Tibet, they experienced an unprecedented series of tremors followed by deafening, rumbling thunder, accompanied by an unearthly orange glow of light. These thunderous explosions and a strange blinding light, juxtaposed against the dark sky, could be heard and seen as far as 300 to 400 miles away. It was reported that they were observed even in Calcutta. At first, some people thought it was an artillery exercise carried out by the army. It was later discovered that no such exercise had taken place. With no other scientific explanation being available, it was believed to be a presage of ominous and celestial phenomena. Many, however, considered this extraordinary occurrence as the harbinger of catastrophic events. Soon afterwards conditions in Tibet started to deteriorate.

News reached Lhasa that some 80,000 soldiers of the People's Liberation Army had invaded Tibet on October 7, 1950 and the Chinese Radio announced that "peaceful liberation of Tibet" had begun. The axe had fallen. In the course of the fight, a large number of Chinese soldiers lost their lives due to fierce resistance from the Tibetans. In addition to the direct casualties of war, the Chinese had also suffered due to lack of supplies and the harsh climate of Tibet. Many died of starvation and others succumbed to altitude sickness. But for the Tibetan army direct confrontation was bound to end in disaster, considering the enormous size of the Chinese forces. Besides, they were armed with the latest automatic weapons and artillery. Tibet had an army only of 8,500 officers and men. It was not adequately equipped or trained either. They were mostly utilized for doing police work, of preventing entry of unauthorized travellers. Its officers and men were hardy and brave, but they were quite unprepared to fight a war.

Though the young Dalai Lama was without any experience in governance or State administration, he realized the impracticability of fighting the overwhelming might of the Chinese forces. In an endeavour to avoid further bloodshed, he sought to stem the tide of the Chinese onslaught by sending out a number of appeals and delegations to the United Nations Organization, super powers like, the U.S.A., Great

Britain and even the neighbouring country of Nepal, in the hope of intervention. These countries were sympathetic but unwilling to render any assistance. The United Nations, at the instance of some its member countries, decided not to consider the question. With no help coming from any quarter, the Tibetan Government decided to start negotiations and sent a delegation to Peking in the hope of arresting the Chinese advance.

Even after prolonged discussions, the Chinese refused to acknowledge Tibet's independence in spite of the evidence and arguments advanced by the Tibetan delegation. They forced a Seventeen-point Agreement on the delegation, which assumed that Tibet was a part of China. One of the clauses stressed the need for driving out "imperialist aggressive forces from Tibet" although there was not even a trace of any such aggression. When the Tibetan delegation refused to sign the Agreement, they were threatened with dire consequences, and made to sign it under duress. On their inability to produce the Tibetan seals, the Chinese forged duplicate seals to validate the Agreement.

In the face of the impending Chinese invasion, the freedom fighters and Khampa warriors were preparing themselves to fight the invaders and to engage them in guerrilla warfare. The Dalai Lama in his autobiography says: "…… there was open warfare throughout Kham and Amdo. The freedom fighters, under the command of a man named Gompo Tashi, were increasing their numbers on a daily basis and becoming ever more audacious in their raids. The Chinese, for their part, showed no restraint. As well as using aircraft to bomb towns and villages, whole areas were laid waste by artillery barrage. The result was that thousands of people from Kham and Amdo fled to Lhasa and were now camped on the plains outside the city. Some of the stories they brought with them were so horrifying that I did not really believe them for many years. The methods that the Chinese used to intimidate the population were so abhorrent that they were almost beyond the capacity of my imagination. It was not until I read the report published in 1959 by the International Commission of Jurists that I fully accepted what I had heard: crucifixion, vivisection, disembowelling and dismemberment of victims was commonplace. So too were beheading, burning, beating to death and burying alive, not to mention dragging people behind galloping horses until they died or hanging them upside down or throwing them bound hand and foot into icy water. And, in order to prevent them shouting out, 'Long live the Dalai Lama', on the way to execution, they tore out their tongues with meat hooks."

The brazen atrocities committed by the Chinese forces in Tibet are unsurpassed in their gravity and scope, no other country is known to have been outraged on such a large scale in such an organized manner, in recent times anywhere in the world. The Chinese had begun the subjugation and conquest of Tibet in 1950 in complete disregard of international law and custom. They continued gradually to tighten their vice-like iron grip until they had squeezed out every vestige of human dignity and honourable existence from the entire length and breadth of Tibet. They were doing everything possible to demoralise and dehumanise the Tibetans by annihilating the racial and ethnic character of Tibetan people with a view to wiping out their separate identity as a nation and merging it with the Chinese mainstream. This was possible only by total negation of their national aspirations, religion and cultural traditions. In spite of brutal suppression, the embers of simmering resentment raging in the hearts of the Tibetans against the Chinese, occasionally and sporadically erupted in the form of open rebellion in various parts of Tibet. The indomitable will and spirit of the Tibetan people could not be subdued and their resolve to throw off foreign domination remained undaunted. Further repression only fanned and added fuel to the fire of their determination, ultimately culminating in "Tibetan people's national uprising" on March 10, 1959.

On an invitation from the Chinese General, the Dalai Lama had agreed to witness a theatrical performance in the auditorium inside the Chinese military headquarters in the first week of March 1959. The General wanted to keep the visit "strictly secret" and the Dalai Lama was asked to come without his usual retinue of senior abbots, courtiers and bodyguards. It was inconceivable for the Tibetans that the Dalai Lama should leave his palace and move about in public without proper escort. The Tibetans being apprehensive of the Chinese General's intentions, saw in his strange request a threat to the security of the Dalai Lama. Suspicion became rampant that the General would detain or kidnap His Holiness, isolate him from his advisors and followers and use him as a helpless instrument to advance the Chinese policies and designs in Tibet. The news spread like wildfire among the people of Lhasa and the surrounding areas. A vast crowd, estimated at over thirty thousand strong, surrounded the Dalai Lama's summer palace, the Norbulingka, meaning the Jewel park, and elected a committee of seventy leaders, demanding that on no account should the Dalai Lama be allowed to risk his life by visiting the Chinese camp. Khampa warriors had mingled with the crowd, armed with swords, daggers and rifles. The Tibetans made no secret of their hostility towards the Chinese and anti-Chinese manifestos were openly displayed and distributed. Faced with these demonstrations of open defiance, the Chinese grew nervous and set-up machine guns and trained their artillery on the Dalai Lama's palaces—the Potala, and the Norbulingka.

In the meanwhile the Dalai Lama continued to exchange letters with the Chinese General to assuage his feelings with a view to gaining time for averting a crisis. On the afternoon of March 17, the Chinese in their attempt to intimidate the Tibetans fired two mortar shells which harmlessly fell into a nearby pond. This brought matters to a head and the Kashag, the Tibetan cabinet, which was in session, decided to advise the Dalai Lama to leave Lhasa. The decision of the Kashag was immediately conveyed to him. They pleaded with him to leave before it was too late. He agreed to do so if that was their unanimous decision and if by going he could help his people and not merely save his own life. Soon after dark, minutes before 10 o'clock, the Dalai Lama, discarding his spectacles and disguising himself as a soldier in trousers, a long, black coat, slinging a rifle on his right shoulder, slipped out of a small gate in the remote corner of the Norbulingka. Accompanied by a couple of soldiers, he crossed the nearby Kyichu river, a tributary of the Brahmaputra. On the far side of the shore, he was met by a detachment of thirty Khampa guerrillas who were waiting with some horses. Here he was joined by his family members and other staff who had preceded him separately in small groups. Under the cover of darkness, the party swiftly headed south, past the lights of the formidable Chinese camp. Undetected they continued to proceed for eighteen hours with only brief halts, entering the guerrilla held mountains beyond Lhasa.

Two days later, even before they knew of the Dalai Lama's escape, the Chinese opened fire on the Jewel Park, reducing it to shambles. They shelled Lhasa and the neighbouring monasteries inhabited by nearly 10,000 monks, the largest in the world. This pounding continued for six months. By the lowest estimates, 87,000 Tibetans were killed, 25,000 arrested and imprisoned, tens of thousands wounded. However, a hundred thousand managed to follow the Dalai Lama, who crossed into the Indian territory. The Dalai Lama reached Tezpur on April 18 at about

7.30 in the morning while it was raining intermittently. From there he issued his first statement about the tragic events in Tibet and his escape to India. His avowed task here was to keep alive the hopes of the Tibetans in exile and restoration of human rights and democracy in their home-land.

Throughout his early years of training, the young Dalai Lama had been impressed upon the need for an altruistic frame of mind. He had been encouraged to practise the six perceptions of the Mahayana path, namely, generosity, morality, patience, perseverance, one pointed or meditative concentration and penetrative insight into the inherently void nature of reality. These six qualities were enjoined, for perfection, upon a Bodhisattva aspiring to ultimate enlightenment. These initiations gave the Dalai Lama an ever stronger sense of peace and happiness, culminating in what he describes as a "unique equanimity of mind".

Buddhism is a sophisticated and profound philosophy and strongly stresses rationality. In this sense it is very modern in its sensitivity and outlook. It has much to say on the nature of matter and on the brain and the nervous system. It can contribute a great deal to the modern world. Buddhism has been a tremendous source of strength to the mind and contributes a great deal in the development of mental faculties. The Dalai Lama himself says: "I feel that the Buddhist emphasis on love and patience has helped us considerably in coming through this difficult period of our history. It has helped us maintain a sense of clarity, strength and humour. Although almost a quarter of our population was killed by the Red Guards, the Tibetan people can still smile and laugh. They can still look to the future with eyes of hope. We call it *sem-zangpo*, the good heart. We have been treated very brutally. Many have died, many others have spent years in concentration camps under inhuman conditions. But as a people we still possess 'the good heart'."

Having pledged himself as a Bodhisattva to the salvation of all human beings from ignorance and sorrow, it was unthinkable for him to retaliate against his enemy by using violence. It became his commitment to return hatred with patience and violence with compassion. "In spite of the atrocious crimes that the Chinese have committed in our country, I have absolutely no hatred in my heart for the Chinese people. We should not seek revenge on those who have committed crimes against us. The hope of all men, in the last analysis, is simply for peace of mind. My hope rests in the courage of Tibetans and the love of truth and justice that is still in the heart of the human race."

It is this courage, combined with compassion and love, which characterises the role of the Dalai Lama in the preservation of the Tibetan religion, culture and tradition. But this is only a part of his overall scheme of things, for his concern includes the happiness and welfare of all humanity, aptly described by him as "universal responsibility", embracing all mankind as well as nature. He has come forward with constructive proposals for the solution of international conflicts, human rights issues and global environmental problems. He has been striving to create an awareness for the preservation of nature and natural resources, in order that a pollution free world may be inherited by the future generations. He has been going round the world, fervently appealing to the powers that be, for reduction in nuclear arsenal and creation of peace zones, which should include Tibet.

During the three-and-a-half decades of his sojourn in India, the Dalai Lama has propounded his philosophy of love, compassion and universal responsibility with untiring energy and dedication. In contemporary times he is regarded as the foremost exponent of non-violence and love, next only to Mahatma Gandhi, whom he regards as his mentor. The Nobel Prize Committee in their citation say that the 1989 Nobel Prize for peace was being awarded to the Dalai Lama as a tribute to the memory of Mahatma Gandhi, the apostle of peace and non-violence.

The Dalai Lama insists on achieving his objective through completely peaceful and non-violent methods, eschewing all forms of hatred and violence, without malice or rancour towards the oppressor or the wrong doer. Non-violence does not mean the mere absence of violence. It is something more positive and more meaningful than that. True expression of non-violence is compassion, which according to the Dalai Lama, is not a preserve of the sacred or the religious. It can be developed and nurtured without following any particular religion. The common factor among all religions is that, whatever the philosophical differences between them, they are primarily concerned with helping their followers become better human beings. Thus all religions encourage the practice of kindness and concern for others. Compassion is not a matter for contemplation for one's own "narrow individual happiness". True compassion is to develop a feeling of closeness to others to do something concrete for them.

In the course of the evolution of human civilization, there have been many upheavals, some caused by nature and others by man himself. Each one of these had a lesson to offer for those who cared to learn it. The fact that the Dalai Lama was uprooted from his native country, enabled him to interact with the world at large, to come in contact with the problems and realities beyond Tibet and to disseminate his message, his thoughts and philosophy. In the Buddhist view of life, the cycle of birth and death is characterised by suffering, physical pain, sickness and death, which are the consequences of our own actions in this and previous lives. The only way to break free from this bondage is to follow the path of morality and loving kindness while undergoing, at times, self-inflicted suffering. Tibet has come out all the purer from the fire it has gone through. The agony and suffering of the stoic Tibetans has not gone in vain. On the contrary, it has proved a blessing in disguise, for Tibet's loss is the world's gain, with the Dalai Lama having emerged as an outstanding crusader for the emancipation of human soul. His theory of universal responsibility is certainly a step forward in the service of humanity, which includes human as well as sentient beings. As a protagonist of peace and non-violence and a champion of human rights, today he stands out as one of the most popular and universally acknowledged world leader and is counted amongst a galaxy of luminaries like Martin Luther King Jr., Mother Teresa and Nelson Mandela, to name but a few.

About a lac of Tibetans, who have followed the Dalai Lama, in exile have eventually settled down into communities spread along India's mountainous northern frontier, among the hills of the southern state of Karnataka, and a number of other settlements dotted all over India. Through their adaptability, resourcefulness, intelligence and hard work, they have carved out for themselves a life of modest prosperity in the land of their adoption. But all Tibetans, including those born, brought up and educated in India, await the day when they will return to their homes on the other side of the Himalayan range of mountains.

At the hour of the Tibetan nation's gravest trial, it has been her greatest fortune to be blessed with a leader who truly exemplifies the ideals of wisdom and compassion that are the corner stones of the Buddhist faith. As an embodiment of the teachings of the Buddha, the Dalai Lama has steered ahead a struggle that is purely non-violent. Holding a shattered people together, he has led them on the path to democracy. Though abdicating his role as the head of the state, he has not for a moment neglected his responsibility towards his people, and has justified their trust in him by initiating democratic processes and instituting a democratic charter, a popularly elected representative legislature for the Government-in-Exile. His dynamic and charming personality, radiating an aura of self-confidence and gaiety, has kept alive the hopes and aspirations of his people and organised them to act in unison in their fight for the fundamental human rights of the people in their homeland. He has infused them with renewed vigour to achieve their cherished goal of joining their compatriots in the not-too-distant future. As their supreme spiritual leader and temporal head he has enabled them to sustain their faith in their religious beliefs, preserve their cultural identity and heritage, literature and traditional art. Forty-seven years after the first occupation of Tibet, the Tibetans are more determined than ever to regain their human rights, their fundamental freedom and political identity.

They are quite optimistic in their belief that Tibet is bound to be free from the shackles of the Chinese Communist regime and will once again be restored to its pristine glory of a free and self-respecting nation, wedded to Buddhist philosophy and a peaceful way of life; its people will once again enjoy their freedom of speech and worship, unfettered in the pursuit of their moral and spiritual attainments. Though firmly grounded in its traditions and culture, they fondly hope, Tibet will be a proud member of the comity of forward looking nations shedding its luster from the roof of the world, as its were.

"The Spirit of Tibet: Vision for Human Liberation" is the companion volume of "The Spirit of Tibet: Universal Heritage" published earlier. It covers his later years after he had settled down in India and had the time to contemplate in retrospect over the stormy events in his life following his flight from Lhasa. It begins with an interview by the Editor, followed by the Dalai Lama's articles, statements and interviews through which he set the record straight and cleared up some of the misconceptions appearing in the "The New York Times" and other newspapers which contained "patently false information about the situation in Tibet and the position of Tibetans in exile" (p.46). As an indefatigable fighter for the rights of his countrymen he has been raising his voice in world forums of democratic and freedom-loving nations for their sympathy and support to a just and humane cause. In his forthright utterances and writings he has been espousing the cause of Tibetans who look to him for support, sustenance and solace.

His writings and speeches have been thematically arranged. They portray intimate glimpses of the Dalai Lama's many faceted personality, his wide-ranging interests and his thoughts on subjects of global signifi-cance. He has emerged in modern times as a profound thinker and philosopher for establishing a non-violent and peaceful world order for the emancipation of human suffering. His prescription of peace and love has the potential for transforming individual human nature for cultivating a harmonious attitude of mutual understanding. It is his endeavour to resolve outstanding disputes which defy solutions, through discussion and dialogue, as opposed to conflict and confrontation.

The purpose of these volumes is to present the *magnum opus* of His Holiness the Dalai Lama's thoughts and philosophy at one place. His speeches and writings are a study in simplicity, nobility of thought, deep philosophical content, infinite compassion, universal brotherhood and above all his commitment to peace and non-violence. Incorporated in this volume is only a representative selection of his writings and speeches on various subjects. It is our hope that the reader will enjoy savouring through these pages replete with thoughtful and absorbing reading.

Let us join him in his endeavours for making this world a better place to live in with harmony and mutual goodwill. While it would be wrong on our part to submit to injustice and violation of our own rights, we would be equally remiss if we sat back and allowed blatant injustice and violation of the rights of fellow human beings without even registering our indignation and protest. Lack of will, courage or resources may well result in surrender before tyranny, but to be silent spectators while it is being perpetrated on our neighbours is tantamount to its tacit approval. Failure to challenge violation of humanity is undoubtedly to give gratuitous encouragement to its tormentors. Let all self-respecting and right-thinking men, therefore, lend their support to the worthy and humane cause for which the Dalai Lama is fighting, to his peaceful struggle against injustice and oppression wherever it exists, for the restoration of basic human rights—the right to self-determination, democracy, freedom of speech and worship—which have been denied to his countrymen in Tibet for almost half a century.

A. A. Shiromany

ACKNOWLEDGEMENTS

For material in this volume we owe our gratitude to:

The Private Office of His Holiness the Dalai Lama, Dharamsala;
The Department of Information and International Relations, Dharamsala.

Central Institute of Higher Tibetan Studies, Sarnath, Varanasi;

Bureau of H.H. the Dalai Lama, New Delhi;

The Library of Tibetan Works and Archives, Dharamsala;

The Foundation for Universal Responsibility, New Delhi;

The following newspapers and journals;

Asian Wall Street Journal, Auroville Today, (The) Guardian Weekly, Leader's Magazine, Maclean's, New York Times. South China Morning Past, Sunday, (The) Telegraph, Tibetan Review, (The) Times, (The) Times of India, and (The) Wall Street Journal.

We owe a deep sense of gratitude to Dr. (Ms) Kapila Vatsyayan, Academic Adviser, the Indira Gandhi National Centre For The Arts, New Delhi, for agreeing to write the Foreword to these volumes.

We are specially grateful to the Friedrich-Naumann Stiftung, and to the Regional Director, Dr. Jurgen Axer; Ms. Rebon Banerjee; and Mr. O.P. Tandon, Executive Director, TPPRC, for their support and encouragement.

For photographs we are grateful to Mr. Rajiv Mehrotra, Mr. S.N. Sinha, Mr. Vijay Kranti, Mr. Yog Joy, Mr. Nitin Upadhye, Ms. Francoise Guerin, Ms. Tsering Youdon, and for the cover design to H.H. the Dalai Lama's 60th Birthday Celebrations Committee, New Delhi.

Last but not the least, we are grateful to all friends and well wishers who have assisted us in making our venture a success.

The Friedrich-Naumann-Stiftung (FNSt), Federal Republic of Germany, is a foundation, a non-profit organisation for public benefit. It was founded in 1958 by the first post-war president of Germany, Theodor Heuss, and is named after the liberal statesman Friedrich Naumann (1860-1919). The FNSt is the Foundation for ideas on liberty and training in freedom. It promotes the liberal principle of freedom and human dignity in all sectors of society, both nationally as well as internationally, in industrialised as well as developing countries.

It is the goal of liberal policies that all citizens may live together freely in an open society; the civic society. Human beings need freedom in order to realise their full human potential. Liberal policies strive for co-operation in development through free international trade by helping to establish free and responsible civic societies in developing countries with a view to gaining world-wide victory of human and civil rights.

The Foundation is active in more than 75 countries. In the South Asian Region comprising of the SAARC countries it concentrates on the promotion of human rights and civic education, environmental protection, promotion of small and medium scale industries and of consumer advocacy. All these activities are carried out in co-operation with local, national and international NGOs, the emphasis being on self-reliance and the setting up of democratic institutions.

The Tibetan Parliamentary and Policy Research Centre (TPPRC) has been set up by Friedrich-Naumann-Stiftung with the purpose of strengthening the Tibetan diaspora in building up a healthy democratic working ethos under the aegis of the Assembly of Tibetan People's Deputies (Parliament-in-Exile) thorough a framework of legislative, executive and judicial institutions based on the concept of the Tibetan polity guided by *Saddharma*. The objective is to prepare the Tibetans in exile, particularly the young amongst them, for the assumption of responsibilities that would respond to their hopes and aspirations, with a view to generating human values and considerations commensurate with man's free will, equality, justice and non-violence. There is an imperative need to constantly remind the Tibetan diaspora of their national identity, culture and heritage and the global community of Tibet's unique contribution to the world of thought and culture. It is in furtherance of this objective that this volume, *The Spirit of Tibet: Vision for Human Liberation* and its companion volume *The Spirit of Tibet: Universal Heritage* (selections of His Holiness the Dalai Lama's speeches and writings), have been brought out.

EDITORIAL COMMITTEE

CONTENTS

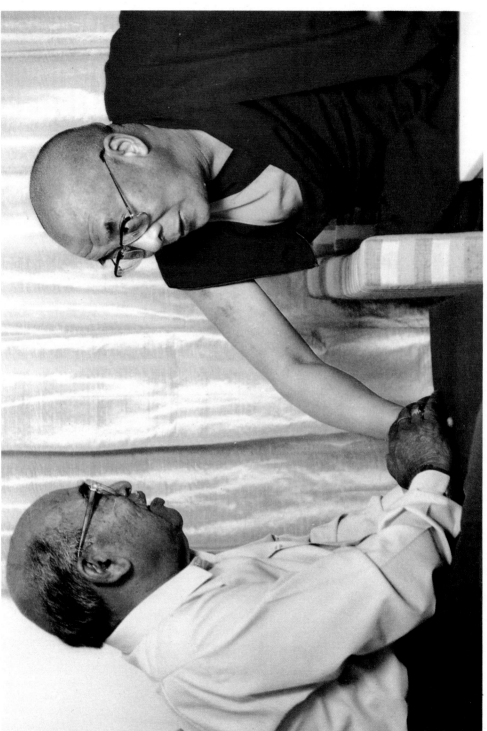

His Holiness and the Editor (*Courtsey* : Nitin Upadhye)

I
Interview By Editor

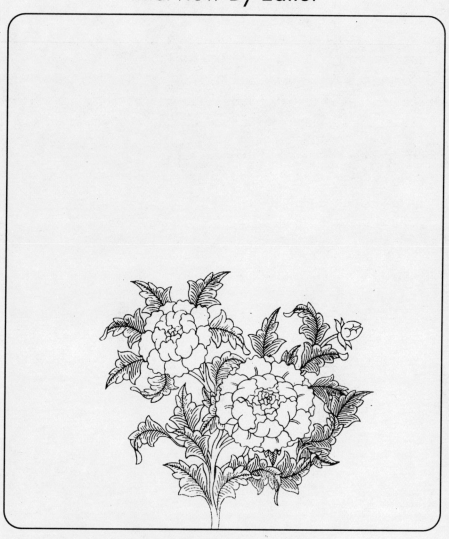

Chapter I
' INTERVIEW BY EDITOR

The God-King of Tibet, His Holiness the Fourteenth Dalai Lama, who had once lived in magnificent splendour in the thousand-chamber Potala Palace, now leads an austere life in India. After thirty-seven long years in exile and having renounced his kingship, he still rules over the hearts of millions of Tibetans and Buddhists settled round the globe. He regularly meets them in their settlements throughout India and abroad, helping them keep their morale high and sustain their faith in their religious traditions, cultural heritage and art. He is the epitome of their inspiration to keep up their non-violent and peaceful struggle for restoration of democratic rights, freedom of speech and worship in their homeland. As the slightly stooping figure, immaculately dressed in maroon ochre robes emerges with folded hands to greet the multitude of his followers, young and old, men, women and children, their faces glow and eyes glisten with tears welling up, beholding their beloved leader the Dalai Lama. They hold their breath in trying to contain their mixed emotions of elation and reverential adulation, while he speaks to them in his clear lucid style, his rich sonorous voice, carrying his devout followers from their mundane state to the realm of spiritual ecstasy. The incarnation of Bodhisattva, the Universal Being has a magnetic touch which enthralls them, for they know and adore him as their supreme temporal and spiritual leader, the sustainer and saviour of their souls. His seraphic smile charges the atmosphere, as it were, with his delightful personality. His good humour and jovial nature are infectious. The radiance of his dignified personage strikes home as his gentle smile breaks into pure child-like laughter which is as charismatic and charming as it is uninhibited. The delectable feeling of being face to face with him and hearing him in person is an exhilarating experience, to be cherished for its lasting, lingering impact. Being in his benign presence or having an audience with him seems to relieve them of their sorrow and agony they have gone through, inspiring them to forge ahead in their struggle with renewed vigour and determination; his lively discourses exude confidence and hope. He steels their hearts with fortitude to face the vagaries of life by his exuberance and gay abandon. His message of kindness, compassion and universal responsibility coupled with his concern for the welfare and happiness of all human and sentient beings, are in keeping with his role of "Ocean of Wisdom" and apostle of peace and non-violence.

His Holiness has settled down in the sylvan surroundings of Dharamsala, literally, the abode of Dharma, which has through usage acquired the meaning "transit camp for pilgrims". Situated in the picturesque valley on the foot-hills of the Dauladhar range of the Himalayas, the pilgrim camp itself has been bestowed with the hallowed ambience of a sacred city of pilgrimage by the presence of the Dalai Lama. The lush green undulating landscape, with a large variety of rich flora and forest, is dotted with graceful buildings of different colours, shapes and sizes, which have sprung up in the recent past. According to an age-old custom in Tibet the Dalai Lama was always given a warm, rousing reception whenever he set out from his palace in Lhasa or returned to the capital. In keeping with that tradition Dharamsala wears a festive look with flags, buntings and banners fluttering over house tops, trees and roadsides whenever the Dalai Lama goes out from or returns to the town in the course of his whirlwind tours. People in thousands sporting their traditional robes and bright, colourful costumes line up on both sides of the route and wait for hours to have a glimpse of their beloved leader.

Being a Buddhist monk of Mahayana tradition, the Dalai Lama is pledged "to the uplifting of all living and sentient beings" and according to it he "must actively work, lifetime upon lifetime, until all beings gain enlightenment".

The Dalai Lama replied to my questions readily without reservation or hesitation. His Private Secretary Mr. Tenzin G. Tethong, who was present during the interview, occasionally interpreted the thoughts of His Holiness whenever he fumbled for words or resorted to Tibetan speech.

Editor: *I am so happy that you have given me this opportunity of meeting you here in Delhi itself. In fact I was looking forward to going to Dharamsala. I may have to go there because possibly we cannot finish all the questions today for the second volume. Sir, what is your impression about the first volume ? Did you have time to see?*

H.H. the Dalai Lama : Oh! no I did not go through it all completely. Very good, very good. Thank you. Above all I appreciate the strong feeling you have [for the Tibetan cause]. I appreciate it.

E. *Thank you, Sir I had the good fortune of editing Gandhi for 34 years, from 1959 to 1993 and this is only God's grace that I am able to work on your speeches and writings. Sir, I had sent you this questionnaire earlier.*

H.H. Point by point you can ask, we can discuss.

Conflict between goodness and evil

E. *Yes Sir. We may begin with the beginning. This problem of conflict between right and wrong, between might and goodness; the forces of brute power always try to fight goodness, whereas the forces of goodness try to contain or control the evil elements— the evil forces. I was wondering, was it inevitable for China to attack Tibet. Could it not have been avoided by any chance or was it destined to be like that ?*

H.H. Actually many questions are involved in this. What is your question.

E. *Was the Chinese invasion inevitable ?*

H.H. I feel it was due to our own negligence, besides ignorance. Secondly, there was some kind of fear or uneasy feeling towards foreigners, particularly the Western countries. Somehow they say in the 1920's, 30's, 40's there was much negligence. So under those circumstances the Chinese invasion had become something inevitable. But if we go further back, say early this century, then I don't think this kind of invasion was unavoidable. If the Tibetans were alert and prepared themselves accordingly, then I don't think this invasion would have taken place .... I think the 13th Dalai Lama saw this very clearly. His testimony is very clear. He gave the warning, the purpose was that Tibetans should prepare themselves for any eventuality.

E. *But they had their inclinations towards spiritualism and religion. They were complacent about political developments.*

H.H.   Even politically the 13th Dalai Lama had given these warnings. This testimony is mainly political. Of course in the case of Tibet, Tibetan political sovereignty and spirituality are interconnected. So you see in the description of the Tibetan political situation, their spirituality was bound to be involved. But in the testimony the 13th Dalai Lama had made it very clear—after he had given the warning Tibetans should have prepared themselves in every respect, including their army. It was not totally non-violent. But in principle, I think no doubt, it was non-violent. In a particular sense, he saw the necessity of military preparedness and he mentioned it.

E.   *I have quoted in my first volume from that testimony. But I could not lay my hands on the later part of the testimony which says that the Tibetans will find their way home and the sun of happiness will ultimately shine for them. Will it come true? Will the Tibetan people find their happiness, will they ultimately succeed in going back to Tibet? I am told that is what the second part of the Testament says.*

H.H.   No, no. I can't remember that in very great detail. But my impression is that if we had prepared ourselves or if we had taken the challenge seriously or wisely then there was possibility of having happiness, prosperity and peace for another 100 years. That is what he had mentioned. It is not that after this tragedy had taken place at a later period happiness will come. It is the other way round. After all those warnings if the people had taken heed and prepared themselves properly, for another 100 years there would have been happiness and prosperity and so on.

E.   *He actually could foresee future very clearly.*

H.H.   Of course. As Buddhists we believe that he had some kind of clear feeling about the future.

E.   *Vision?*

H.H.   Yes, vision, there is no doubt. But even from the 'non-believers' viewpoint he was far sighted and very intelligent. He was able to see well ahead of times. If the preparations were made right from the beginning this invasion would not have taken place. But after they had neglected the warning the situation became so bad that the invasion became inevitable.

E.   *I can see that, Sir, because from the days of Rama, from the days of Mahabharata the conflict between goodess and evil has been going on. I want to ask you Sir, when you came to India in 1959, in those trying conditions, along with a large number of your followers, you had to settle them down in India. What were your feelings when you arrived here in India ? How did you feel ?*

H.H.   At that time we were quite hopeful that within a few years time we could return [to Tibet]. But at the same time we were prepared for the worst. Actually, to be practical, we planned in the field of education and rehabilitation at least for decades. We prepared long term plans, but mentally at that time we were very hopeful. We did not expect or think of more than three decades. But at that time in the early days after 1959, one thing that gave me a sense of security, some sense of relief, was that I had already been to India in '56', '57'. So that was a comforting factor. I knew many Indian leaders like Jawaharlal Nehru and other freedom fighters. In fact Jayaprakash Narayan made a lot of promises; 'If something goes wrong inside Tibet then you are not alone. India is with you.' But actually when the 10th March came nothing came from India [by way of help]. In 59 when I came, I already knew this country and the leadership. I knew there were lovers of freedom, of solidarity. So, I felt it was something like another home. That kind of feeling I had. I think it was one of the great feelings.

E.   *The difficulties you faced in India ? Of course the Government of India gave you their moral support. They also did something for the education of the Tibetan people and gave grant for settling them down, some land on low price ?*

H.H.   On lease. Some kind of lease. It was all with the assistance of the Indian Government. But in the early period our top priorities were resettlement and education. Resettlement because most of the Tibetans were farmers or nomads, ordinary people. And I think one very important point is that we really wanted to settle as a community or like a colony. The Government of India agreed. All the assistance was provided by the Indian Government and the

State Governments. They gave land or made the land available.

E.   *Even then, it was hard work.*

H.H.   Pandit Nehru personally took interest and responsibility. He wrote
        letters to all the States to make land available to Tibetans for their
        settlements. And in the educational field also Pandit Nehru
        personally took special interest. Actually, at that time the Govern-
        ment of India set up one organization or society, namely, the
        Tibetan School Education Society, I think at that time that is what
        it was called. Now it is called Central School for Tibetan
        Administration. In the beginning it was the Society.

The Chinese Aggression

E.   *That we have in the first Volume. Pandit Nehru was a great
        admirer of yours, Sir, as most Indians are. He was an honest man
        who sincerely tried for India China friendship—'Hindi Chinese
        Bhai Bhai', and initiated the idea of Panchasheel. But things did
        not turn out as he wanted them to be. The Chinese aggression
        could not be foreseen. Soon after your arrival the Chinese
        attacked India. You must have felt the same feeling about the
        Chinese aggression, which you had from 1950 to 1959 in Tibet.
        That must have been a great shock to you ?*

H.H.   I was not shocked by that because in early fifties around 52, some
        Chinese journal in Lhasa openly stated that the proposed libera-
        tion of Tibet is not for the Tibetans alone, but was part of a larger
        aim. World revolution was very much in their mind. So their
        ultimate aim was India, no doubt.

E.   *They had it in their mind already and had planned it that way ?*

H.H.   Not only planned they in fact specifically and categorically
        mentioned this on a few occasions. Tibet was only a stepping
        stone for them.

E.   *For attacking India ?*

H.H.   For greater aggression on other areas worldwide. At that time
        they had very impressive designs in their mind. That was their
        basic idea. Firstly, the aim of Marxist ideology is for the benefit
        of all human beings, particularly the working classes, that means,

less privileged and weaker sections of the society. And in that National boundaries are not important. Their aim was working class people of the entire world.

E.   *That is all right in principle. What are they actually doing in practice in China itself ?*

H.H. That is right.

E.   *In practice what are they doing to their own people ? They are not able to breathe freely.*

H.H. The shortcoming of Marxism is that its aim is very good. I feel in social economic theory, the Marxist theory is the only theory which involves morality or moral ethics. You know, Capitalism only talks about how to make profit, nothing else. The Marxist ideology does no such thing but says how to distribute, how to use money equally which is more beneficial for the community at large. But its shortcoming comes when they implement it, there is too much emphasis on hatred, completely ignoring compassion. So once they had started their movement, all their energy was spent on the destructive side, elimination of landlords through class struggle because of lack of compassion. Poor people still remained poor. Once the revolution is achieved, they destroy all other classes of exploiters, and once that is achieved they have nothing to offer to the poor people. That is because of lack of compassion. Another factor which is not necessarily part of Marxist system, but Soviet system, in which due to their particular circumstances once that system is established, first of all you have strict rationing system.

In 1918, 1919 in the Soviet Union, the Bolshevik minority, as also in the Czaristic tradition there was the police state. In early stages of Soviet Revolution led by Bolshevik forces there were so many internal as well as external hostilities. There was suspicion and spying which have now become a part of their system. With the result that all the communist countries follow the same pattern. That has destroyed the basic idea of human welfare. That system had destroyed the basis for human touch, human family every-where. Now they see suspicion everywhere even between husband and wife, parents and children and between brothers and sisters.

Role of non-violence

E.　*In the Communist system power gets concentrated into a few hands, few people who wield power want to remain in power. That is why they suppress their own people. In view of this, do you think that non-violence is the only force to guard against all violence and conflict in society. That is, the non-violence of the strong, of the brave, because timid people, weak people or people who are afraid cannot claim to practice non-violence. That is what Gandhiji used to say.*

H.H.　That depends more on whether somebody has truth on his side or not. Look at the Tibetan side, or the conflict between the Chinese and the Tibetans. As far as power is concerned China has no reason to fear from Tibet but because they do not have truth [on their side] they are so sensitive about the Tibetan issue. And on our side, though physically very weak, we have truth, not in the sense that some people have the emotional feeling that 'God is with me', 'Truth is with me, so everything will be all right'. Not in that sense, but in the real sense because truth is on the side of Tibetans.

　　　Therefore, although we are physically very weak, we have more confidence. I think the Chinese side has less confidence. If you speak in terms of strength the Tibetans are the ones who are the weaker side. Therefore, they are more desperate, there is more tendency towards violence. From the weaker side there is more possibility of indulging in violence because they are in a desperate situation. Here I think it is mainly due to truth, faith, spirit and compassion which are very important. Because our cause is just and also because I think of power or strength in terms of inner strength. It is our strong conviction that our cause is just. We have more self-confidence, more inner strength, as a result the practice of non-violence goes very well with us. On the other hand there is a very powerful nation but deep down there is no self-confidence. Although officially they claim Tibet as part of China but when they go deep into more details they don't find any solid grounds or firm conviction.

E.　*Of course, truth is on our side.*

H.H.   So they indulge in more violence. On our side we have the inner strength.

E.   *But non-violence requires infinite patience, faith and self-sacrifice for long term objectives. These three things you are providing in ample measure. People in the world, however, wonder how you are able to organize your people and ....*

H.H.   And also in my case in terms of long term friendship with the Chinese, with the people of China. If we involve ourselves in bloodshed or indulge in violence or killing of Chinese then it is only natural that from the Chinese side it will be very difficult to develop any kindness or sympathy towards those who may be said to be killing the Chinese. Therefore, now-a-days we are having more and more support and expression of solidarity and sympathy from the Chinese side. Not only from the Chinese who are outside, but also from those inside China. More and more people are showing their feelings of solidarity, concern and sympathy for Tibetans. I believe it is because we are sticking to non-violence. If we involve ourselves in killing the Chinese here and there, it will be very difficult to develop that kind of positive response from them.

E.   *Because the common man and the people in general inside China are also suffering. They don't have any freedom.*

H.H.   That is very true. Tibetans are not indulging in violence. Taking this into consideration, for many generations friendship has developed between Tibetans and the Chinese. There is another aspect in which the Chinese have been sharing oneness of feeling with the Tibetans, a sense of solidarity, namely, the Tibetans' resentment to or unacceptance of a totalitarian system. Secondly, the Tibetans' aspiration for freedom and democracy. These are the ideas that the Chinese share with Tibetans and therefore support them. Many of the Chinese who are in this democratic movement had from the very beginning contacts and good understanding with Tibetans.

E.   *But it requires a lot of self control. You have no rancour even against the Chinese and want them to be happy although they have done so much harm to your people and committed atrocities on them. Is it also possible that the Chinese invaded Tibet because of the problem of over population in China and that they had designs of aggrandizement, of spreading their empire in the garb of Marxism, rather than having genuine concern for the welfare and happiness of the Tibetan people? Actually they had this expansionism, at the back of their mind behind their Marxism. What do you think ?*

H.H.   I don't think it is Marxism. The Chinese, including the former Soviet Union in reality, are more concerned with nationalism rather than Marxism. It is true that in the guise of spreading internationalism, they had this expansionist idea.

E.   *They wanted new areas for settling down their population. This is expansionism actually.*

H.H.   That is right. Even when you look at the historical records, for centuries the Chinese had this tendency to keep on expanding.

Violence and Nuclear Proliferation

E.   *How to control the prevalence of violence everywhere? In India and other countries there is too much of violence, too much hatred and anger. Then the nuclear proliferation and armament. How can these be controlled and people persuaded for creating an effective world opinion against indulgence in violence and terrorist activities? How to go about it ?*

H.H.   This is very complicated. Of course on the one hand these things happen because people are not able to control their mind, their inner spirit. But at the same time many of these things happen because of circumstances, the environment and other factors.

E.   *Are we standing on the brink of a nuclear war? Although everybody is against nuclear war, even now France and China continue to conduct their underground nuclear tests. Is it not a dangerous game they are playing? Are they not playing with fire ?*

H.H.   But elsewhere they are destroying and reducing the nuclear warheads. As a matter of fact the continuation of nuclear tests by

France is a different case. But generally there is a reduction in nuclear weapons.

E. *Sir, isn't there need for creating a very strong public opinion against these nuclear tests and accumulation of warheads. What can we do about it? We must create strong public opinion everywhere against this nuclear activity.*

H.H. By aspiring or trying to achieve complete denuclearization. Through that process one could also talk about banning of nuclear tests.

E. *No, I am talking about creating a strong world opinion against these tests.*

H.H. We have to make an effort to create a totally denuclearized world. And if we continue that process the nuclear test will be automatically banned. They will not take place. On the other hand now at the moment there are five nations, including the United States and Russia, who are still maintaining many of these nuclear warheads and then they are condemning a country like France.

The Economic Situation

E. *Sir, I wish to ask about the economic disparity, the gap between the haves and havenots. These are the main causes leading to various forms of conflicts. Dissatisfied and disgruntled sections of society give expression to their resentment through violence and all kinds of conflicts. There is need for economic development as well as providing equality of opportunities. The gap between rich and the poor is too much.*

H.H. Yes, absolutely. Look at the United States. One of the reasons for a lot of crimes there today is lack of economic equality.

E. *That is right, so what should we do ?*

H.H. Revolution. I think at least in the socialist countries though some mistakes have been committed there, but in one aspect they are more equitable in giving free education and free health [care]. In moral and even in practical terms, unequal distribution is not right and that is the source of many problems. Something must be done to overcome this. You see the gap between rich and poor at global level, in southern and northern zone and even within the countries like United States, the richest country, biggest country, there is a big gap between the rich and poor, as in India also. Of course it is a poor country, but at the same time some individuals are very rich and majority remains very poor, and there are a lot of beggars. So this is not only morally wrong, but if this continues it will cause all sorts of social evils and problems. We have to reduce that.

E. *Gandhiji had a solution to this. He advanced the theory of trusteeship.*

H.H. What is that ?

E. *Trusteeship means that the entire assets of an individual are not his own, they belong to the society, and held in trust for the community. Suppose somebody has a large estate, palatial buildings and huge farms and so on, these should be held in trust for others. That they are not for the benefit of some privileged individuals alone but for all the people concerned in the area. Trusteeship theory has far reaching economic implications by way of equitable distribution of wealth. If implemented properly trusteeship can substantially reduce the gap between the rich and the poor.*

Role of Religion

E. *Sir, there is too much religious intolerance today and there are too many conflicts not only between the followers of two religions but also those belonging to two sections of the same religion, say, the Shias and Sunnies, the Protestants and the Catholics and so on. This has been going on from the days of the Hundred Years of War of Roses. Religion is one factor leading to conflicts and violence between various sections of society. My feeling is that if we were to be without religion we would probably be more pious because then their would be no dogmatism.*

H.H. I feel if the different religions have nothing else to contribute but only conflict, violence and dissension, then we have the right to abandon religion because in that case it is not serving any good purpose. But that is not entirely correct, because as human beings we have many mental problems due to lack of responsibility, lack of awareness and compassion. In developing or nurturing the mental faculties of human beings religion has a very important role to play. What we need is to have religions but we must try to develop good things that religion is capable of and do away with negative thinking responsible for various faults and short-comings in religious matters. Once there is a greater awareness among the people about the different religious traditions and closer communication, better understanding among different religions can be achieved. That is what I am trying to promote. Harmony among the different religious traditions and promotion of awareness about the potential of various different major religions is very important.

E.   *Sir, in the medieval ages kings used to fight for their principalities. One king used to attack another. Now-a-days major conflicts are between the protagonists of different religions, or between two sects of the same religion. That is a great tragedy although religion is supposed to create an awareness of human mind and for the development of human qualities of goodness, compassion and so on. Instead of that the dogmatism which has come into play in religion is responsible for endless conflicts between various people.*

H.H.   Actually, if you look carefully you will see that even if you take one particular religious tradition, majority of the people who are following that religion are not the ones who are creating all this trouble. They are satisfied with their faiths they have some belief, they have some hope and they go along and try to follow that religion. For example in India you can see millions of Hindus, Muslims and Christians living according to their own beliefs. They offer their prayers in the morning or on Sunday or some other day. Through their prayers and offerings they get some kind of satisfaction and support for their faith. Although they have a lot of problems and difficulties in their lives but prayer to their God gives them some kind of hope and sustenance. So you see millions of people are getting that. In South India I know in one village there are Christians, Muslims and Hindus who are living peacefully, the majority of them being believers live in harmony without any conflict.

E.   *But the religious heads, the Moulwi, the Pandit or the clergy, the people who control religion, particularly in a theocratic state, are mainly responsible for intolerance leading to conflicts.*

H.H.   This is the case not only in the religious matters but in every human sphere, obviously politics also. Now look at the Congress. During the British regime Congress was the only political party which really had fought for independence in India on the principles of self-determination and self-discipline. Now it is the same party, same ideology, but because the quality of people who are in the Congress has degenerated you have the present problems. There also it is not necessarily caused by the majority but by a few individuals who are brilliant but they are without a heart. If you go deep into the root causes it is the human brain, human intelligence, like in religious matters. If human beings do not do things properly and in the right way then it is better for them not to be there at all. There are several thousand species of mammals like tigers, lions, who look terrible and eat flesh and attack one another. But they attack only when necessary, when they are hungry. In Hyderabad there is a big open zoo and within the walled fence there are some tigers, lions and a few deers also. I asked the keeper if there is any danger to the deers. They say if you feed the tigers regularly and their stomach is full they do not attack the deers living in the same premises. So that is the animal world. We human beings go beyond our needs. I am staying in this hotel. Just this morning I was thinking, 'Why all these luxurious things?' Here you have more than what you need. In the bathroom they have all these beautiful marbles. I think if somebody had the means and money he may even go in for diamonds and other precious things for decoration. What is the use, it is just the same stone. There are many other things. I am really pained. These are all unnecessary things that human beings accumulate. You see the same thing in dress and food. Human beings go beyond what is necessary and then exploit other people. When we need a lot of superfluous things exploitation comes. As a result human beings are the ones who suffer the most and who have to undergo unnecessary hardships and unhappiness. Therefore, if human intelligence goes with good heart then human life is really worthwhile. Human beings can not only develop genuine peace of mind, happiness for themselves but also can extend their help to other animals, including the whole world. Human beings can take care of the other animals if some disaster takes place. Animals can't do anything, human beings can. So, from that point of view, the same thing applies to religion. Generally speaking there is real possibility that human beings can make life good and worthwhile or precious. Although human beings have many faults but at the same time they have the potential to make positive contribution in a very extensive manner in a big and substantial way. Similarly in the case of religion there may be some shortcomings but it has the potential to contribute to the good of humanity. Then only there is some justification for survival of humanity, but on the basis of an effort according to human nature, with gentleness, with compassion and with a sense of community in the right direction, with right guidance. Then I think humanity will not only be happy but also helpful for the whole world. But if it goes wrong I prefer some kind of nuclear blast and the whole world exploded. No more worry!

But from the Buddhist viewpoint there will be another life and another set of problems. So it is better to face today's problems and man can make effort [in the right direction].

E.   *Sir, I am told time is up for today's meeting. I will seek another interview because I have not finished my questions. May be I will come to Dharamsala or anywhere wherever it suits you.*

H.H.   I will let you know the date and the time.[1]

Why This Violence?

E.   *In spite of all the plenty that we have in the world we find suffering every where! What can an individual do to mitigate the suffering of his fellow beings? How can he help them? We feel sorry for the violence that is raging around us, but we are helpless spectators. If there is violence in Kashmir, we can only read about it and feel*

[1] The first half of the interview was held on November 22, 1995. What follows transpired on March 31, 1996.

sad, but cannot do anything to stop it. Why this violence? What should we do?

H.H.   Many problems and sufferings which we are facing can be basically of two categories. One, the man-made problems and the other the natural calamities or the ordinary suffering in some shape, that I would say is not man-made. I think perhaps it is due to carelessness of some individuals involved, but we can consider this as a natural problem.

In this case, if we have more sense of responsibility, and more spirit of harmony then we can arrest this problem and we can save our neighbour and a poor family. You can share at least a smile and provide them with your genuine sympathy and even help them materially. You may not be able to do much, but you can share their suffering and you can guide and support them. Then the Kashmir problem is a man made problem, which due to political reasons is created intentionally. Such problems will have to be solved in due course according to set procedures. Now look at Bosnia, like Kashmir problem is also created by man. Very often human actions get out of control. Then some times the only alternative is to use force.

E.   *Yes, and as individuals we feel helpless. We can help our neighbour in a way, we can help our community or some persons who we know need help. But that can be on a very small scale in the vicinity of our area, because our field of activity is not very large.*

H.H.   The proper way is to shape a new kind of attitude in the society. In this country, as I have noticed in other countries, people when they are arrogant, the other people tend to give in to these people, who try to please them. Then, the moment they see somebody is honest and humble they look down upon him, take advantage of him. This is very sad.

Struggle Between Evil and Goodness

E.   *Sir, you are a person who has many Godly qualities, God given gifts. You have studied and meditated for the welfare of humanity. How long will this struggle between evil and goodness continue?*

H.H.   Yes, it is going to continue, because we are there in this world.

E.   *Yes, the world is bound to be there. So will the struggle between the forces of evil and goodness continue?*

H.H.   I think from the Buddhist point of view, within each individual, day and night, his positive emotions and negative emotions are always in conflict. The evil forces and the positive forces are always pitted like that. There is a reflection of this, which is manifested in the human society. Somewhere there is a negative force, and somewhere there is a positive force. So long as this remains, this is going to continue. But of course, through education, and a certain system, we can reduce this.

E.   *The evil of an evil person can be reduced?*

H.H.   Yes, and sometimes we can neutralise it.

Rights and Duties

E.   *This also goes with your idea of* Universal Responsibility, *that in the entire world all the sentient and, human beings should be happy. That is what you are doing and working for their happiness, and if possible their prosperity. So more emphasis should be given on ones responsibilities rather than rights. Yet people today are insisting only on their rights, they do not think of duties, and the problem lies there.*

H.H.   Yes, but in a way one should also think of ones rights as well, and feel that rights and responsibilities are interlinked and interconnected.

E.   *But undue importance is being given today to rights. 'This is my right, I must have it'. But if you submit to the demands of everybody, some people may take undue advantage of you.*

H.H.   So let us do that, we do not insist on taking our rights, just keep on appeasing others, submitting to them.

E.   *Asserting your goodness.*

H.H.   Some individual general [religious] practitioners completely sacrifice their individual rights. They never bother about their privileges. If one gives up his individual rights, it is his business. We are talking of humanity in general. I do not think that it is very important for each individual to assert his individual right, but then what is wrong in it? What I feel strongly is that people are so obsessed by their own rights, that sometimes they go beyond their rights and they claim as their right, what actually is not theirs. So that kind of attitude without any sense of responsibility is dishonesty to mankind.

E.   *Then they do not think of their duties. Duties should also be performed in a society. I as an individual have some duties which I must perform.*

H.H.   Yes, these thoughts must go together, rights and responsibilities.

Future Vision of Tibet

E.   *Sir, I would like to know your views on the Future Vision of Tibet. You had said about ten years ago that Tibet will regain its own place of freedom, happiness and prosperity, that it would take 20-30 years. What do you think now? How much time it would take, the turn of the century?*

H.H.   I am hopeful even within this century or at the beginning of the next century. I am hopeful. Many changes are taking place very rapidly. The Communist totalitarian system is crumbling. Anything is possible. Generally speaking in a few years time things may change.

E.   *Let us hope and pray for that day when the Tibetans regain their freedom, because Tibet is the only country which has given spiritual teaching to the world. Although it had drawn its learning from India in the beginning, but after thousands of years of practice of Buddhism, non-violent and peaceful living, the Tibetans became the spiritual leaders of the world. That position they must again enjoy. That glory should be theirs, to spread light throughout the world, from the roof of the world.*

H.H.   When we were in Tibet in the past neither did we realise all that nor did we pay enough attention to the fact that Tibetans had this cultural heritage. After we have become refugees we have come in contact with many other people, wiser people. It eventually became quite clear. Tibetans are more friendly and easygoing people and so comparatively they have more peace of mind.

E.   *Not very worldly wise however. They do not care so much for their worldly possessions.*

H.H.   Not necessarily, it seems that because of their Buddhist training they keep themselves prepared to practise the concepts of contentment and concern for others.

E.   *What will be your future plans when you return to Tibet? What would you like to do? How would you like things to take shape?*

H.H.   As I have put it in one of my proposals, Tibet should be a zone of peace, not only externally, for there will be no military establishment any longer, but internally also through spiritual training. I call it internal disarmament and proper education. Tibetans traditionally are more compassionate people on the basis of their training, and proper development. So mentally there will be some kind of internal demilitarisation and external disarmament and then the natural environment of the country also will be quite peaceful. With all these things together I hope we can develop a genuine complete zone of peace. That is my dream. The government will have the democratic system of course, which means that Dalai Lama's institution will no longer be there and he will not continue as the Head of the Government.

E.   *But he will remain their principal advisor.*

H.H.   Yes, something like that, I do not know. I would just prefer to be an advisor.

E.   *A principal advisor like Gandhiji. Gandhiji had no official position, he was not even a four anna member of the Congress party, but Congress leaders used to rush to him for the Working Committee meetings. So, you will be for Tibet what Gandhiji was to India.*

H.H.   At that time the membership fee was four annas?

E.   *Yes, four annas were collected from every member of the Congress. That was in the thirties and forties. He was not even a four anna member. He met industrialists like Birlas and Tatas and told them to give money for Daridranarayan, that is, the poor starving millions. He told them: 'Being a Bania I have come to rob you', and they paid him up. Birla funded many schemes of Gandhiji. Even Jumnalal Bajaj was like that. Sir, will there be any problem in enforcing your religion, culture, traditional way of life in Tibet?*

H.H.   In the economic field for future Tibet I would prefer non-violent way of life which will suit them ideally. Obviously there we have no fishery, piggery, poultry, nor is there enough meat. Well it is not possible for the entire Tibet nation to be vegetarian, that is difficult.

E.   *That is not possible because you cannot grow many vegetables there.*

H.H.   Yes, but it is possible to transport them. With transport, we can bring vegetables to those areas where they do not grow. Still I refuse to believe that everyone would become vegetarian. But as a tradition, as in the past, when there is requirement a few animals can be sacrificed but there will be no export of meat.

Now in China they are making a programme of exporting meat, even to Hong Kong and it goes from Tibet, so have I heard. I do not think it is necessary to make that kind of programme about animals. It is better to have only a few for consumption. That is all right, but no special effort is to be made for this kind of programme. I feel that the non-violent system of economy is to be evolved.

There will be factories for making small knives, there will be no production of any weapons. Now the problem which I think is quite complicated is that we have to adopt a market oriented economy, otherwise there is no progress. At the same time right from the beginning we must put every thought and consideration for removing the possibility of gap between different people, and try not to have a big gap between the rich and the poor. That is, to have equality as in the socialist system. This is very complicated and yet very important.

Then there are industries and mining. Since there are a lot of minerals in Tibet it is important because we have to take out the minerals. But at the same time we have to be careful about mining these minerals without damaging the environment.

E.   *The rich cultural heritage is the product of the Orient, what can it offer to the West.*

H.H.   As I have mentioned earlier, through spiritual training and proper education, Tibet will genuinely be a peace loving, more compassionate country. And in this way we can help other human communities. At times I joke that Tibet can be a country where people can come and enjoy it as a holiday resort.

E.   *Yes, as a place of pilgrimage.*

H.H. Yes, people who have lost peace of mind and want mental peace or tranquillity, they can come to Tibet and spend some time in the beautiful natural environment having peaceful atmosphere. Then through special training of two or three weeks, it can serve their purpose. So they bring some dollars and we provide them with peace of mind, and friendly environment which has no shape or size, but money has concrete shape. This will be good business.

Spirituality and Materialism

E.   *Today the world has become so materialistic that spiritual values are on a discount. Due to this materialistic society, people give more importance to worldly possessions. In the Western countries they do not think much of spirituality, so that is what we have to trade with them. We have to give them spirituality in return for their materialism.*

H.H. Already there are some foreigners, among them are some Western tourists also, who visit Tibet even under the present circumstances and the tense atmosphere. There are a lot of Chinese soldiers with guns even then people do get some kind of peaceful experience. In future, when the whole atmosphere becomes genuinely friendly and peaceful for them, when there is no tension and on top of that, if there is some mental training— and through meditation and proper facilities we will be able to help many people.

In India and some other countries or areas where the basic human necessities are not yet available there is less genuine interest in spirituality. These people may take, as a tradition, some interest in spirituality but they may not be as serious as people in those countries where material things are in plenty. Yet they have begun to feel that material gain has its own limitations.

E.   *So they have started taking interest in spirituality.*

H.H. Not enmass but individually. There are people who have begun to realise that peace of mind is most important. For health also it is a very important factor. With more development where there are more scientific discoveries, they take more interest in spiritu-

ality. Of course this will not be world wide but in general there will
be a tendency towards realisation of the importance of peace of
mind. This feeling for spirituality and need for the peace of mind
has to come from within. You cannot buy it.

E.   *There is a tendency now amongst the Tibetan youth who have*
settled down in India, who are coming in contact with different
cultures and faiths, have taken to Western dress and style. Some
of them may marry outside their community. How is this fusion
between the two people going to affect their faith, religion, tradi-
tion and culture.

H.H.   I do not think things like dress, or hair style, are very important.
I know some young Tibetans, born in Switzerland and in some
other European countries, even in America or Canada, their
appearances are more Western, their hair styles are like those of
hippies, but their Tibetan spirit is very strong. I am really surprised.
I, therefore, always consider that the inner spirit is more important
than the outward appearances. The way some people are
dressed may be due to convenience. Generally young Tibetans
who live in foreign countries, due to environment, or because of
their daily contacts with people definitely change their appearances, but the essential part of their Tibetan spirit is quite strong.
What is really important is the essence rather than appearance,
or the ceremonial or the tradition part. So long as the essence is
intact it is alright. The appearances change as the time changes.
More important is the cultural aspect. It comes to the country from
time to time and as time passes by it changes. But as far as the
essence of Tibetan Buddhism is concerned, which has come from
India, in all important matters we entirely depend on Indian
writings. We usually take important quotation from a reliable
Indian master. But then the cultural aspect eventually develops its
own unique features. So some Westernised people today call
Tibetan Buddhists as Lama Buddhists which is something not true.

The inter-marriages however are on a very small scale.
Besides many of them may not inter-marry but they bring up
children of different nationalities and different appearances.

Corruption and Human Values

E.   *In India and in the world, the greatest problem today is the*
lowering down of moral values. Corruption is rampant in various

Moods of His Holiness during the Interview   (*Courtsey* : Nitin Upadhye)

Courtsey : Nitin Upadhye

Courtsey : Nitin Upadhye

Courtsey : Nitin Upadhye

Courtsey : Nitin Upadhye

Courtsey : Nitin Upadhye

fields of life. You have seen this in Hawala episode and various other instances. Corruption has entered life in a big way—how can an ordinary law abiding person like me survive in these conditions. I can either worship Saraswati, the Goddess of Learning or I can worship Laxmi, the Goddess of Wealth. I have not cared much for wealth, I have always had a craving for learning. Hence I am comparatively a poor man. This corruption is affecting everybody, people are getting demoralised with meagre salaries. What are we to do about it? How can this situation be overcome? These are very serious problems. I would like your guidance in this.

H.H.   What actually is happening now did not begin recently. The sources or the causes of these conditions have their roots in the past. This is because of sheer negligence in the past itself. It is difficult no doubt to change things, or to cope with them now. But we have got to do something. For some of the things which are happening these days like corruption and so on the Supreme Court has taken notice of them. Then the newspapers and media, should report without fear or bias. They should tell more home truths no matter how serious they are.

One good thing is that India is a democratic country, with an independent judiciary and freedom of speech and press. Besides, the spiritual leaders who are not spoiled ones should also come forward and speak openly. In order to ensure a good future long term plans are necessary. I always feel it will have to be based on proper education, with good academic teaching to form the character of the students.

Parents also should help, they have a great responsibility towards the society as a whole. Then, in the class teachers should build a good heart among the students and pay more attention to this. The average teachers particularly at the primary school level should act like parents, also as spiritual teachers, taking care of the children and also telling them, what is good and what is bad. In the classroom the teacher should set a good example, like parents do for their children.

E.   *So it requires long term planning, it cannot be solved in a day.*

H.H.   Yes, that is my feeling. Immediate measures may be taken like punishing the guilty and, making the wrong doings known to public.

In addition, information should be available to the voter about the candidates. The voter should not be deceived by beautiful lectures or speeches or by slogans.

E.   *People should not be allowed to buy votes, otherwise again those who are elected, will amass more wealth. As we have seen, there is a rat race for amassing wealth, rather than reducing the wants. Had we been in a village, one would have been satisfied with a small hut and since the fields there are nearby there would be no need for transport and so on. But this is not so in the cities.*

H.H.   Contentment is what is required. Contentment is of two types:

One kind of contentment is due to ignorance. Ignorance of the availability of things and so people do not want them. This is not real contentment. Another is genuine contentment, in which people know about different facilities and may have the means to obtain them but they are still contented. That is proper contentment. How to bring about that awareness.

E.   *Is the solution to that problem in proper education?*

H.H.   A sense of responsibility ... a sense of caring for others ... For example, if somebody is able to develop a sense of caring and sense of strong responsibility then such a person, even if he is well to do, but if he sees that besides him there is another person who does not have one square meal a day, then he will not indulge in those extravagant luxurious eating habits. In Bombay where I stay in an Indian hotel, in the five star hotels wealthy people consume foreign liquor, they spend huge amounts of money and at the same time, in front of the hotel there are several hungry, landless and homeless people.

E.   *This is the genuine difficulty of the city life. Inflation is going up by leaps and bounds. It is very difficult to cope up with these rising prices for an honest person who does not take money by underhand means. What can we do to reduce inflation.*

H.H.   I don't know. To deal with the economic situation of a country is very difficult and complicated thing. One must be fully aware of the exact internal situation in order to say something definite. If I knew I would certainly tell you. But I don't know.

Political Situation

E.   *What is your assessment of the political situation of India today? What is going to happen? Any thought given to it.*

H.H.   I have often been telling Indian audiences that even though India had obtained independence now for about fifty years, the spirit that existed during the independence struggle is still necessary today. I do feel that those Indians who are honest, fearless and selfless seem now to be relegated to a corner and pushed in the background. People of those qualities are not there, but the type of people who are around are using the opportunity for the sake of their own self-interests. So one does not know what is going to happen. Then it also depends on the leaders of the different political parties who also have their responsibilities towards the society.

E.   *Will the political situation improve in the next few months: Will there be a stable government?*

H.H.   It is true, that at the present there is a grave crisis, due to scandals. At the same time public has become aware and perhaps the politicians may find it more difficult to deceive or manipulate things. I think, unless the people or country get a new experience they will find themselves in an embarrassing situation. It is like a surgery. Sometimes, something happens when surgery should take place. It is somewhat painful but then afterwards there is some improvement. So the important thing is that we should not be demoralised or discouraged or we should not develop any kind of diffidence. That is very important.

E.   *There should be no pessimism. We should look forward to a better future with optimism.*

H.H.   Like one [religious] practitioner, when his or her mental attitude some time becomes discouraging, it is very important to meditate or to think about suffering and the negative side of life. When we think too much of these things on those lines, we feel discouraged. Your mind becomes weak and you feel low, but that is also necessary in order to counter too much of pride. So this is about the negative thinking. When it is too much on your mind, then it is very important to think of positive side of things, about precious things, like precious body, Buddha nature and how wonderful and beautiful is Nirvana. Then you become courageous and your mood becomes enthusiastic. That is the way to strike a balance. When your mind is too much excited, think more of negative side and when you are too depressed, think positively of the positive side.

Similarly about the country. When you think the situation is hopeless and the country is going down hill then you should think more of the richness of the Indian philosophy and also the population and sheer size. There are many brilliant Indian thinkers who will take you slowly out of your depression. The brilliance of the Indian mind is manifested by many of the highly trained scientists and engineers. I definitely consider this country is the Arya Bhoomi, it had a great tradition and a glorious past and long history.

E.   *Historical background and our scriptures are a great spiritual heritage. They are of great importance.*

       What is your message to humanity in general and to India in particular.

H.H.   Did you see some of my booklets? They have my message.[1]

E.   *Sir, I am so grateful to you for giving me the opportunity of meeting you.*

It is with some hesitation that I write about the very personal and precious experience of my encounter with His Holiness the Dalai Lama. I have called it an encounter because the experience was quite breathtaking. At the very outset I was moved by his informal yet hearty welcome as he greeted me with a firm handshake with both hands. The spontaneity of his affectionate and open armed welcome, as he conducted me into his suite, holding my hand, had an endearing effect. His voice was vibrant and the deep resonance of his laughter filled the atmosphere with his holy presence. I was enchanted by his delightful personality and felt it was like a dream come true. His divinely smiling eyes and radiant face held me under their magnetic charm. He embraced

[1] The reader will find the message of His Holiness the Dalai Lama in the Chapters that follow.

me with his arm over my shoulders and then held my hand in his for a few precious moments, the sensation of the soft touch of his charismatic and benign grace permeating my entire being. I do not recall having been so full of joy and blissful contentment ever before. The intensity of his warmth was overwhelming, making my body light and transforming my senses to a state of exaltation. Those moments of elation and pure delight are the moments in my life worth preserving. I am venturing therefore to share them with the readers, for it is possible that my experience, however personal, may strike a responsive chord with those of others.

I leave it to the readers to form their own assessment and impressions about the man who, in spite of his exalted position in Tibet and Tibetan diaspora, prefers to describe himself as a simple Buddhist monk (*bhikshu*), and is living the life of a *karmyogi*, tirelessly striving to restore the dignity of man and liberate the human soul from bondage. The respect and reverence with which he is treated almost universally have not left in him even a trace of ego or pride. His simplicity is extraordinary, his humility genuine. The serenity and equanimity of his mind are unique despite the inhuman treatment meted out to his countrymen. He has, however, no illwill or anger in him even against those who have attempted annihilation of a whole race, its culture and civilization. This equipoise stems from his infinite compassion, kindness and love for all humanity. His commitment to non-violence is with him an article of faith, it is his creed rather than a matter of policy. I am strongly reminded of another prophet of peace and non-violence, and the words of yet another Nobel Laureate Einstein ring in my ears: humanity will scarcely believe that such a man had ever walked on this earth in flesh and blood! I wish and pray His Holiness lives at least for 125 years, as Mahatma Gandhi had once wished to live, for the salvation of human soul and service of humanity.

II
Political Situation

Chapter II
POLITICAL SITUATION

The Dalai Lama of Tibet is one of the most respected, loved and admired leaders of the world today. The spiritual and temporal leader of the Tibetan people and Buddhists settled throughout the world is essentially a man of peace, compassion and non-violence. He has been consistently advocating his policy of kindness and compassion in the face of grave provocation and unprecedented suffering and suppression of his people in Tibet. In his stewardship the Tibetans in exile have been organised in an active movement of human rights, eschewing all forms of violence which had won him the coveted Nobel Prize for Peace in 1989. Ahimsa, with him, is an article of faith, for his commitment to non-violence is complete and fundamental.

He has endeared himself through forthright and sincere exposition of his views, touching and appealing to people's heart and the mind by the simplicity, profundity and large heartedness of his advocacy of peace and love, universal responsibility and compassion for all human and sentient beings. His concern for restoration of human rights and liberation of human spirit from bondage transcends all religious, regional, national and political barriers. The deep philosophical content of his thoughts is profound and all pervasive. He has a remarkable capacity to remain unsullied by the vicissitudes of life, unaffected by the astounding adversities faced by his people. Always completely at peace with himself in perfect good humour, he transmits his message of hope and universal love with conviction and sound reasoning for their application in human relations, including political situations, in order to make this world a better place to live in, with peace and harmony. It is his endeavour to establish a just and peaceful world order free from conflict and violence.

In the writings and speeches of the Dalai Lama the readers will sometimes find a reiteration of his commitment to observing and upholding human values both in public and private life. His policy of kindness and compassion for all mankind is fundamentally based on his profound Buddhist philosophy for universal application. He believes in solving all problems through dialogue and peaceful negotiations as opposed to strife, friction and force. His pronouncements therefore, emanate from his religious perceptions, spirituality and philosophy of loving kindness, directed to reshaping human attitudes to achieve the twin objects of human happiness and world peace.

—Editor

1

JUSTICE AND SOCIETY[1]

A human society without laws aimed at establishing justice will find itself enmeshed in suffering. The strong will impose their will upon the weak, the wealthy upon the poor, the governing upon the governed. So justice is something very important within society. If we lose sight of it we ourselves will greatly suffer as a result.

Many of you in the audience are students of law. I think that your work will not be easy. At the moment the world atmosphere is not very just, both for individual nations and within the international community. But we Tibetans have a saying: 'If nine efforts fail, try tenth.' It makes me happy to speak with people seriously attempting to create a just world. If you really work for justice you will meet with a lot of failures and disappointments, yet this effort is still very important.

I am told that you have some interest in hearing something about our political situation. Since my visit to this country (U.S.A. 1979) is mainly religious, educational, social and non-political in nature, it is difficult for me to speak on politics. But then, sometimes one creates a dynamic impression by saying something, and sometimes one creates a significant impression by remaining silent. I think it is more useful here to remain silent. At the moment the Asian political situation is changing rapidly, and many things that now appear static in actual fact are not as secure as it is believed. My own view is to do what I can and to wait patiently, watching the situation. Who knows what may happen?

Most of you here are interested in law. Law, education, science, technology, politics, religion: all these things are meant to be means for benefiting the society, the living beings. Benefit here means to bring joy to them, to increase their happiness. There are both material and spiritual means to accomplish this end, but both aim at the same thing: happiness.

[1] A talk to the law students of Wayne State, U.S.A.

All human beings, despite cultural, social, political and racial differences, are essentially the same in that they all have an innate feeling of "I" and, based on that feeling, is an instinctive wish for happiness. This has been their main concern throughout the past, and will be so in the future.

Because of this truth I have no difficulty in sitting before you here and speaking with you. I come from Tibet which is far beyond the Himalayan mountains and you are students of law here in America; yet because of the presence of this basic human element in both of us I feel a sameness with you, like sitting with an old friend. Although we are meeting physically today for the first time, I sense a human brotherhood between us. On that basis it is possible to share a closeness. If we can really feel that closeness, then working together for a just and harmonious society becomes natural.

At present the world is suffering from great conflicts, such as those in the middle East, South-East Asia and so forth, on top of the general East-West confrontation problem. All of these arise from a lack of understanding of one another's human-ness. The answer to them is not an armaments race or a show of force, but an understanding of the common human quality that I spoke to you about. The solution is not technological or political, it is spiritual; a sensitive understanding of our common situation. Hatred and fighting cannot bring happiness to anyone, even to the perpetrator of these acts. Prosperity is born out of social harmony. Destruction and violence always produce misery. It is time for the world to learn to transcend differences of race, culture and ideology, and to regard one another through eyes which understand the common human feeling.

This would benefit the individual, the community and the nation. As all nations are now dependent upon one another economically, this human understanding must transcend the bounds of the nation and embrace the international community. If people everywhere are not allowed to strive for the happiness they instinctively want, they will be dissatisfied and will create problems for everyone. Unless we can create an atmosphere of genuine co-operation, a co-operation not brought about by threat of force but by heartfelt understanding, life will become ever more difficult. If we can satisfy people at a heart-level, peace will ensue. Without this basis of coexistence, if undesirable social, political and cultural forms continue to be imposed upon people, peace becomes difficult. Within the nations each individual must be made happy, and between nations there must be equal concern for the wishes of the smallest. I am not here saying that one system today is better than all others and that all should adopt that one; on the contrary, a variety of systems and ideologies is desirable as there is a variety of dispositions within a human community. This variety could enhance the collective happiness of mankind. Each national community should be free to evolve its own political and social system. But the basis of them all must be self-determination, both on an individual and a national level.

Questions and Answers

Q.   *In an interview that Your Holiness gave some years ago, you stated that you were certain that, although it might take 20 or 30 years, Tibet would regain her freedom. Do you still believe this? Under what conditions do you feel this liberation will take place?*

A.   Certainly! I now believe it more strongly than ever. Of course, it would be difficult to say exactly how liberation will come about. The determination of the Tibetan people inside and outside Tibet is the main basis of our hope; but the fact that China has been having continual international problems, particularly within Tibet—economic, social, and political problems—is equally encouraging in terms of Tibet's potential for regaining her rights.

   The Tibetan issue has, since 1959, been an extremely sensitive topic for the Chinese. They are always on the alert at any mention of Tibet. This proves their lack of confidence in their control.

Q.   *What sort of political and social policies would you advocate in the event of your return to Tibet?*

A.   In the early sixties a draft on the basic policies of the Tibetan Government was drawn up, but of course these are only tentative. Policies must be established in accordance with the will of the majority of the people, which in the case of Tibet means those who have remained in Tibet throughout the Chinese occupation.

Q.   *How difficult will it be to restore the country's religion, culture and way of life?*

A.   Restoring the religion will be extremely difficult, but, anyway, religion is the business of the individual. As for the culture, this will require much thought.

In the old tradition, religion and politics were combined. Here, the word "politics" does not have the same connotation as it does in the west. It just means the managing of temporal, or worldly activities. In theory, "temporal" implies activities which benefit only this life, whereas "religion" implies activities which bring eternal benefit. In other words, "temporal" implies the maintaining of a decent standard of living and "religion" implies the development of the mind. Since all human beings have both a body and a mind, it is theoretically ideal for these two activities to be combined.

In many countries a great deal of material progress has been made, yet the people of these countries still experience various forms of mental suffering. On the other hand, if a country is spiritually developed but has a poor material standard, like India for example, its people experience physical sufferings such as disease, hunger and so forth. If temporal and religious activities can be integrated within a governmental system it is certainly very good. Therefore, it is my belief, that, in order to make a system truly effective, its leader must be either a saint or a philosopher.

In Tibet this unification of temporal and religious affairs was attempted. Like all social systems, it had its shortcomings. On the one hand, the standard of living was not always satisfactory, and on the other hand, spiritual leaders sometimes became excessively involved in politics, thus directly or indirectly harming the purity of religion. When we return to Tibet we shall have to give a great deal of thought to this problem and act in accordance with the circumstances prevailing at the time.

National economic theories are far too complicated to be discussed here, but in short it can be said that, if a state wishes to claim that all its citizens are equal then it must ensure that each of them has an equal economic status. If there is no equality of wealth individual rights cannot exist in practice. A poor man can never compete with a rich man. Maintaining this equality is a delicate problem. It would be wonderful if this could be left to the integrity of the individual, just as a Buddhist monk is responsible for his own religious practice; but such a policy would never work. Here perhaps socialism has something to offer. Unfortunately, no ideological system is perfect; each has its good and bad points. In Tibet's case, we shall have to adopt policies suited to the unique nature of

the country's geography, to the mentality of her people, and to her
current circumstances.

Politically, the present world atmosphere is not at all good, not
at all healthy. It seems that attachment and hatred predominate in
every system. If we were to copy these policies it would neither be
possible to combine politics and religion nor would it be of benefit
to the Tibetan people. Politics should be an instrument to serve society
but these days this sometimes seems to be the reverse.

Q. *It is a common belief that political and spiritual activities are mutually
contradictory, yet the lineage of Dalai Lama is an obvious exception
to this. Does the answer to this lie within the form of Buddhism
practised by the Dalai Lama's, and if so, in what way?*

A. In Tibet, the entire government, involving thousands of people, was
based on the combination of this system. Perhaps such a system,
which would have been more difficult in many other places, was
feasible in Tibet because its religion is Mahayana Buddhism, which
places such strong emphasis on benefiting human beings, and thus
on the fulfilling of the needs of society. Our system has faults, yet I
believe that these aren't to be blamed on Mahayana Buddhism but
on the social structure.

Q. *Many political scientists assert that a religious government is not
workable in an industrial society. What are your views on this?*

A. I don't think that it is any more difficult to have this kind of government
in an industrial than in an agriculturally-based society. Religion is
entirely a mental attitude. It has nothing to do, essentially, with the
physical activities that may surround it.

Q. *What does Your Holiness think of the use of violence, such as
guerrilla activities and sabotage, as a political tactics?*

A. Violence is never good, and in the circumstances peculiar to Tibet
it is impractical and ineffective.

Q. *China claims that for many centuries she has enjoyed sovereignty
over Tibet. Yet Tibet has never recognized this sovereignty and, in
actual fact, lived in seeming independence. How does Your Holiness interpret the historical relationship of the two countries?*

A. From the religious point of view, the Tibetans always considered that the relationship was one of *guru* and patron. For centuries the court of China looked to the high Lamas of Tibet for spiritual leadership, and in return Tibetan Lamas frequently visited China to teach.

Politically, even as early as the time of the Great Kings of Tibet (6th to 8th centuries) the status of the two countries was equal. On one occasion, Tibet even invaded China and the emperor had to flee for his life. However, history always speaks in terms of past tense, whereas what counts is the present reality. If, right now, the Tibetan people are happy under the Chinese occupation and the majority of the Tibetan people are satisfied and agree to remain under Chinese domination, then there is no problem. Whether in the past Tibet was independent or not would be irrelevant. But the actual situation is that Tibetans are not in the least bit content with the Chinese occupation, culturally or materially. Since 1959 the Chinese have had a completely free hand in all activities in Tibet. They could have done anything they wished. By now, they should have at least been able to raise the standard of living of the people, but even this has not happened.

Q.   *At this point of time, does His Holiness still consider His government in exile to be the sole legal representative of the people of Tibet?*

A.   We needn't bother too much about being legal or illegal. Sometimes even if you are legal you might become illegal and if illegal you might want to become legal. What counts is that the majority of Tibetan are placing their hopes here, in this government. Because of this we have a tremendous responsibility. This is the darkest age in Tibet's 2100 years old history. I consider it a great honour and privilege to be carrying on the responsibility that my position entails.

Q.   *What are the functions of the government in exile and what has it achieved?*

A.   The government here is formed of various departments run by members who, largely, have been elected by the refugees. These departmental heads are consulted on any major issues that arise. They must carry out the functions of their offices and maintain a liaison with the people.

In refugee work, the principal tasks are educating the young and settling the adult. Our main responsibility, however, is the greater task of regaining the rights of the Tibetan nation, and for this all that can be done, under the circumstances, is being done.

Q. *Does Your Holiness receive reliable information on what is going on inside Tibet today?*

A. Certainly. This we consider to be absolutely mandatory. Here, we act in accordance with the wishes of the Tibetan people who are in Tibet, and so we must know what they are thinking.

Q. *Are there any guerrilla groups still fighting the Chinese within Tibet?*

A. It is very difficult for large, organized guerrilla forces to exist, but throughout Tibet there have been revolts from time to time out of desperation.

Q. *How many Chinese are in Tibet today and, of these, how many are soldiers?*

A. This is also difficult to say for certain. I would estimate that there are approximately a third of a million soldiers there. Just prior to the Lhasa Revolt of 1959 there were more than 120,000. Maintaining control of Tibet is requiring about two and a half times that number. On top of this, approximately 100,000 Chinese civilians have been brought in.

Q. *Escaping refugee have given reports of Tibetan women being forced to marry Chinese soldiers and Tibetan children being forcibly separated from their parents and sent to China for "education", the former to destroy Tibet as a blood race and the latter to destroy it as a culture. What has been the outcome of these activities?*

A. Both of these have failed. Most of the forced marriages have now been dissolved and the project has largely been abandoned.

As for the children taken to China, most of them eventually return to Tibet to work in various fields. At the beginning they have great determination and enthusiasm, but gradually they turn anti-Chinese. When they are in China they hear only Chinese talk—progress, development, happiness and so forth—but when they return to Tibet they see what is really happening. They become disenchanted and usually become key-persons in leading the resistance. Some get arrested, but most use their training to subtly work against the Chinese, making it difficult for the Chinese to capture them. They use the very education they received from the

Chinese to resist the Chinese, and so from the Chinese point of view the tactics has completely backfired. From our point of view it has been very successful.

Q. *What language is used in the education and governmental systems?*

A. In government offices, Chinese is spoken almost exclusively. In school Chinese is the medium in which most subjects are taught. Here the Chinese have adopted a rather cunning approach. Tibetan is taught, but if anyone shows more interest in it than Chinese, many "obstacles" arise for them in school and, later on, in their careers. Alternatively, if anyone shows more interest in Chinese their prospects become far better and they meet with no hindrances. In addition to this, the standard of education is very low, the main emphasis being on Mao's thought. Most schools are more like labour camps rather than educational institutions.

Q. *Does India need a Tibetan buffer-zone?*

A. I cannot answer this question definitely. I don't represent the Indian government or the Indian people. However, generally speaking, the relationship between India and Tibet is something that is very close historically and culturally. Buddhism came to Tibet from India, and with Buddhism came a great flow of Indian culture. In a cultural sense we Tibetans are students of India; they are our Guru, we their disciples. From that viewpoint we are historically close. Tibetans have been travelling to the Buddhist places of pilgrimage in India for centuries, despite the great distance and the hard and perilous conditions. Similarly, many Indians have frequented places of pilgrimage in Tibet, such as Mount Kailash, Lake Mansarovar and so forth. Despite the tremendous cold, thousand of Indian friends have continued to visit these Tibetan holy sites. So our cultural relationship was very close. On top of this Tibet's geographical border is enormous and is located in rugged Himalayan mountains. Any political problem in Tibet, therefore, naturally becomes a problem to India. From that perspective Tibet is very significant to India.

Q. *You often say that you are not against communism and find some good things in it. Could you please explain what do you mean with this statement?*

A. If there were no good points in communism, there would be no reason for the attraction of so many people towards it. Of course, there are many defects in terms of practical application.

One of the main reasons why I respect communism is that basically it is concerned with the majority, the lower class, the working man. Secondly, everybody needs something, but the needs of the lower class are urgent, a question of life and death. So here is a theory which is more concerned with the poor majority, those who are in urgent need. This is very good. The communist theory calculates on the basis of producer and consumer, and is against the masses producing and a small group consuming. So I feel that here the point they raise is valid.

In reality, unless there is economic equality, social and political equality is very difficult to achieve. I am not criticizing other systems and nations; I have no right to criticize. I firmly believe that each nation has a right to practise its own ideas. That's very important. So I am not criticizing others. But in many so-called democratic countries, the rich people always get the top places. There is equality in the constitution but due to a poor economic situation the poor cannot reach the political top.

Of course it would be ideal if everybody voluntarily dedicated himself to the community, like the former Prime Minister Desai appealing to the Indian landlords to give up their surplus land. To some extent there were very good results. But still, all beings are not pure. Unless there is some pressure, some people won't listen. This is the difficulty. If under such circumstances there is an organization which creates equality for everybody—I think it is good. But I am mainly referring to the original Marxism, not the practices in the present systems and nations. Here I myself sometimes get confused: China is claiming that Russia is not a true Marxist; Russia points out the same thing to Peking. So who is the true Marxist? I don't know. It is difficult to say. And now with the growth of European communism we also have French, Italian and Spanish communist systems.

Q. *Is it true that the People's Republic of China has recently invited you to return to Tibet? If so, under what conditions could you accept such an invitation?*

A. We Tibetans became refugees because of political reasons and not because we committed crimes in Tibet. The situation in Tibet was exceedingly difficult and we felt we could do more by leaving. In the twenty years since this decision was taken we have done a great deal in the field of preservation of Tibetan culture and the Tibetan identity. Tibetan culture has two aspects: the social culture of the nation; and the culture that revolved around the philosophical issues aimed at understanding basic human sufferings, such as birth, sickness, old age and death. We feel that as long as there is human suffering this culture is very useful and effective in bringing happiness to the minds of people. As for aspects of Tibetan culture that are not beneficial to man, things that are just leftover from the past, it is sufficient to preserve a record of these in books. It would not be possible to preserve a living tradition of these things, and there would be no value in attempting to do so. But the Buddhist aspect of the culture is very valuable.

Living as refugees in India we have done much more to preserve this than we could possibly have done from inside. I feel that until the time comes when the majority of Tibetans in Tibet are genuinely satisfied and truthfully made happy I can best serve my country and my people from the outside and as a refugee.

Q.   *In an article published in a Dutch periodical Your Holiness stated that you may be the last in the line of Dalai Lama. Is this true, and what does it mean?*

A.   May be the last, I don't know. Anyway, beings possessing the qualification to be Dalai Lama are always there. The incarnation of a Buddha or Bodhisattva always continues to manifest, not only in human form but sometimes as an insect, as an animal and so forth. Whether or not a particular being is given the title of "Dalai Lama" depends on whether or not such a process is beneficial. For example, long before the first Dalai Lama there were many other incarnations of the Bodhisattva Avalokiteshvara, such as Drom Tonpa and Kunga Nying-po; but these were not given the title of "Dalai Lama". The title "Dalai Lama" was actually first given to the Third Dalai Lama, Sonam Gyatso. They then traced back through two previous incarnation of this man to Gendun Drub, the disciple of Lama Je Tsong Khapa (founder of Yellow Hat School), and called him and his two successive incarnations the Lama, Gendun Drub, had clearly remembered his previous incarnation, which had been a Nepalese Lama by the name of Padma Dorje, but this previous incarnation was not given the title "Dalai Lama".

Anyway, I am not the best Dalai Lama, but also I am not the worst. Therefore it might be best to be the last.

Q. *Many people would interpret the end of the line of Dalai Lamas to mean the end of Tibet as an independent nation.*

A. Possibly, but this would be a wrong interpretation. I am far more concerned with the Tibetan issue than with the office of Dalai Lama as such. This is the responsibility of being a Dalai Lama. As long as the title "Dalai Lama" is useful for Tibet it will be continued. Should it become no longer useful, there would be little value in maintaining it. This is in reference to the Tibet question. On the other hand, I am also a Buddhist monk of the Mahayana tradition vowed to the uplifting of all sentient beings and according to this vow, I must actively work in the world, lifetime upon lifetime, until all beings gain enlightenment. This is the pledge of every Mahayana Buddhist. So I have these two responsibilities. As long as the title "Dalai Lama", is an effective tool in fulfilling them, it will be maintained. Thus, perhaps I am the last Dalai Lama; but then again, perhaps not. If it is of greater benefit to beings for me to reincarnate as, for example, a dog or a bridge, then as a Mahayana it is my duty to do so.[1]

---

[1] Here the allusion is possibly to a dog or a person who could act as a faithful friend, protector or a guide to help the pilgrim in finding the path or direction when lost in wilderness. A bridge could be one which would help in crossing a river or a gorge. It could also be a person who could act as a medium between the seeker and the sought. The ideal of Bodhisattva is to be of use to humanity in any form.

2

MISCONCEPTIONS ON THE TIBETAN ISSUE

Recently a flood of articles on Tibet has appeared in the *New York Times* and many other newspapers throughout the world. Many of these articles contained patently false information about the situation in Tibet and the positions of the Tibetans in exile. I feel therefore, that it is time I myself contributed a brief article towards clearing up some of these misconceptions.

Tibet is geographically, racially and culturally different from China. Historically, too, Tibet has always been an independent country, and has never been "an integral part of China". The very fact that it has to be referred to now as "part of China" is a clear indication of its separate independent status in past. If it had always been a part of China what was the need of changing the boundaries in the maps of Central Asia prepared after 1959?

Another indication of Tibet's independent status is the great pain taken by the Chinese Communists in explaining to the Tibetans the status of Tibet. They make a distinction between China and "The Middle Kingdom." They have been stressing to us that Tibet isn't part of China, but that it is under the Middle Kingdom just as China is. Tibet and China, they explain, enjoy equal status and both are parts of the Middle Kingdom.

Second-Class Citizens

After the signing of the 17-point "Agreement"[1] when the first Tibetan delegation, headed by Kalon T.T. Liushar, called on Mao Tse-Tung, the latter told Kalon Liushar: "Now that Tibet has returned to the motherland, Peking is your city, Shanghai is your city ..... ." To this, Silon Lukhangwa my then Prime Minister, later remarked in Lhasa: "We do not want Peking

[1] *Vide* "The Spirit of Tibet: Universal Heritage", p.5.

or Shanghai, give us back Chamdo." Chamdo, the third largest city in Tibet, was kept under military administration by the Chinese since their invasion till the establishment of the "Preparatory Committee for the Autonomous Region of Tibet."

In official documents, Tibetans enjoy the same rights as the Chinese, but when it comes to implementation the Tibetans are treated as second-class citizens in their own country. Tibetans have been forcibly recruited in labour gangs to construct roads, military installations and buildings. Hundreds of schools have also been built, but refugees who still manage to trickle out maintain that these cannot be called Tibetan schools as only a little Tibetan is taught in the beginning grades. The rest of the curriculum consist of Chinese language and history, basic arithmetic and manual labour. The thousands of kilometres of roads constructed since the Chinese takeover aren't of much use to the Tibetans since there isn't any public transportation.

Improvement has also been made in agricultural output, but according to refugees, at the time of harvest most of the grain is taken away by the Chinese as "Surplus Grain Sales", "State Grain Tax", "Commune Development Tax", "War Preparation Grain", etc., and the Tibetans are left with a meagre ration of between 90 to 120 kilograms of barley per person per year.

It is for these reasons that the Tibetan Communists who had been most enthusiastic in the beginning, not only started to become disillusioned by about 1956 but eventually many of them openly resented the Chinese actions in Tibet. The result was that most of the Tibetan Communists were dismissed from their official posts and quietly deported to China.

We admit that the social and Governmental system of the past in Tibet was neither faultless nor suited to the changing times. But Tibetans were prepared to change of their own accord. Even before 1959 I brought about some reforms, but the Chinese weren't happy when we started to do these on our own. They didn't give their blessings. They wanted to reap the maximum benefit out of the reforms that they were planning to carry out, and our own action was endangering this prospect. Tibetans in exile are all for gradual modernity and change. With these aspirations in mind, I promulgated in 1963 the draft of a Constitution for a future Tibet. I have also said in an official statement a few years ago that the rule of the Dalai Lama may or may not continue in future Tibet and that we might even adopt socialistic systems. We are therefore, not against change or reform.

There isn't any doubt that China has made tremendous progress since the Communist take over. The masses have also benefited from this. I admit that even in Tibet they have brought about many changes which were necessary, but which might not have been possible for us to carry out. But at what cost and sacrifice have they achieved this? In terms of human lives and freedom, that we cherish so sacredly, the sacrifices have been tremendous and terrible, to say the least.

What has happened very often is this. In order to meet certain targets and to please higher authorities, Chinese officials have adopted every means, fair or foul, and completely failed to take into account the sufferings and feelings of the people, who in most cases have to pretend that they are happy even when they are not.

And the most unfortunate part of this whole process has been that the high officials were quite oblivious to what had actually happened on the spot, and accepted unquestioningly the reports of their subordinates even when they contained absolutely untrue statements. For example, while a certain section of the population might have strongly resented the implementation of a project, the report might say that the people whole heartedly joined the PLA and the Party in its implementation.

About 50,000 Tibetans, including myself, who left the country in 1959, had already experienced nine years of Chinese rule in Tibet. All those years I tried to reach an amicable solution with them because the inevitable result otherwise would have been an open clash between the Tibetan people and the Chinese troops, in which case the former would unquestionably be in disadvantageous position. Unfortunately, the situation deteriorated so fast that all my efforts were in vain and the open clash did take place in March 1959, with predictable results.

Dividing to Conquer

The tragedy of Tibet is that a whole race, a people strongly opposed to foreign domination, has been subjugated, oppressed and gobbled up by China. This has happened not only to Tibet but also to Mongolia and Eastern Turkistan (Sinkiang). It may not sound right for me to speak of these two other countries, which are in a similar situation, but I happen to know the true feelings and the national aspiration of these people. Their feelings of resentment against Chinese domination are no less than those of the Tibetans.

To make it easier to devour the invaded nations, the Chinese try to cut them into pieces. They persist, for example, in dividing Tibet into two parts: Inner and Outer Tibet. Historical facts and existing realities mean nothing to them. In all their propaganda they only mean outer Tibet when they say "Tibet", or more officially, "The Autonomous Region of Tibet". This means the cutting away of about half of Tibet's territory, and about two-third of our population. In this part of Tibet—the Inner Tibet—we have the Amdo and Kham provinces, which traditionally were inseparable from the rest of Tibet. No Tibetan or learned scholar on Tibet can imagine Tibet or Tibetan without Amdo and Kham provinces. The whole of Tibet, without this mythical distinction, has suffered under the invasion by the Communist China and has been determined in its struggle against the unjust foreign domination.

In fact it was in the eastern part of Tibet, which the Chinese call Inner Tibet, that the initial sporadic revolts against the Chinese occupation took place. So much so that the Tibetan resistance movement has often been mislabelled as a Khampa resistance movement.

Even today, there are recent reports that desperate acts of fighting and sabotage have been carried out in these regions. Another clear indication of continued Tibetan resistance and failure on the part of the Communist Chinese to win over the Tibetans completely is the lack of any prominent Tibetan from among the younger generation to toe their line, a generation that the Chinese had ample time to groom and indoctrinate since 1950.

It is well known that the Chinese have made a similar arbitrary demarcation in the case of Mongolia as well.

The struggle to free ourselves was and is a Tibetan initiative and a Tibetan movement. In the process of our struggle we have welcomed external help whenever it didn't go against our basic goal, and have shunned it whenever it did. And because our struggle is just and we believe in it, it could not and cannot be abandoned even if no help came at all.

Some parties persist in calling the Tibetans in exile "a handful of reactionary cliques" (some have given the figure 15,000). To me this need never be a subject of controversy. India and all other countries where there are Tibetan refugees are open societies. The truth or falsehood of claims by "about 100,000 refugees" can easily be verified by visiting these places.

The world has seen how unpredictable and inconsistent the Chinese are through the vicissitudes in the lives of Liu Shaochi, Lin Piao, Teng Hsiao-Ping, and more recently the Gang of Four. These acts are unprincipled and conducted at the whims of few individuals. One can imagine how much the Tibetans have also suffered through such vicissitudes under the Chinese rule.

The Chinese have recently extended an "invitation" to the Tibetans in exile, including myself, to return home. When the offer became known a number of newspapers hinted that it might be "profitable" for me to return now. Some even informed its readers that some sort of secret and indirect negotiation was going on between my representatives and the Chinese leaders.

The Real Issues

These rumours confirm that people in the West have totally misunderstood the true nature of our struggle. The issue isn't whether the Dalai Lama and the 100,000 refugees would be able to return to Tibet. The reason we appeal to other nations isn't because we want to go back and the Chinese aren't allowing us in. It isn't that I long for some of the privileges I used to enjoy and am bitter with the Chinese for having reduced me to the status of a refugee. The Chinese have been asking us to return since the end of 1963. Most of their offers have been regularly broadcast on Radio Lhasa and through printed leaflets. There has been no response from our side on this issue because this isn't the real issue. The real issues are the feelings and welfare of the six million Tibetans still left in Tibet. Why should an alien rule be forced upon them? Why shouldn't they have the choice of holding their own beliefs, traditions, culture and identity?

If those six million Tibetans there are really happy and contented, we would be prepared to return and accept whatever status the majority of them are prepared to grant us. But first it should be established to the total satisfaction of all Tibetans in exile that the Tibetans in Tibet are completely satisfied with their lot. This is the only pre-requisite. There isn't any question of "secret negotiations" to make it possible for me to return.

So far what the Chinese have claimed either directly or through a few selected visitors hasn't succeeded in convincing us. Some of these visitors have always been uncritical admirers of the "Chinese Revolution". They make their living out of reporting first hand news from China and commenting on it. How can they be expected to say anything that would conceivably jeopardize their chances of obtaining more Chinese visas in future. Fortunately, some recent visitors have tried to give an objective accounts of their visits to Tibet and I hope there are more and more such visitors in future.

In spite of many difficulties, we have been getting information about the conditions in Tibet. We consider this to be of utmost importance, because we must act according to the wishes of the majority of our people.

In fact, it would be a reassuring sign to us if the Chinese government stopped being selective about whom to invite. It would also be encouraging if the visitors itinerary weren't confined to Lhasa and its immediate vicinity. Some recent visitors have claimed to have travelled "throughout Tibet". But none of them mentions the names of other places, nor did they describe those regions. It is rather difficult for us to take their words for it.

In short, what is needed is what I have constantly been demanding; an internationally supervised plebiscite both inside and outside Tibet to determine whether the Tibetans in Tibet are happy. The plebiscite should be conducted throughout Tibet and it should also include in its investigative body people who can understand and speak Tibetan, so that they don't need to depend solely on the Chinese interpreters. It might even include one or two Tibetans, who don't have to be selected or recommended by me. I am prepared to accept whatever verdicts and commendations such a plebiscite comes out with.

Asian Wall Street Journal, Hong Kong, 25-8-1977

3

TO CHINA : OPEN UP TIBET

The recent developments in China indicate that the present Chinese leaders are following a moderate and pragmatic policy in their domestic as well as foreign affairs. As a result of this overall change, a certain amount of liberalization and leniency has been introduced in Inner Mongolia, East Turkistan and particularly Tibet.

This policy is certainly welcome, but it is difficult for us at the moment to be overly optimistic about these changes. It is yet too early to form a definite judgment on this. We view these recent changes with suspicion; something we had learned from the Chinese with our experience of having lived with them for nine years and having felt the impact of their policies in exile for almost two decades now. Chinese policies and the dramatic political changes in China have often been too unpredictable.

Teng Hsiao-ping was recently quoted as having said in Japan: "If you have an ugly face, it is no use pretending to be handsome." I am impressed by this philosophy, particularly when it is adopted by a Chinese leader. This is definitely a correct and practical attitude, and if he means it sincerely it reveals his willingness to accept existing realities. There is always the danger for those who are powerful to be over-confident and be unaware of their faults or to intentionally ignore them. This, in fact, is one the sources of many problems that we are confronted with in the world today.

The Chinese, through their official organs, have been saying that all is well and normal inside Tibet; that the Tibetan people are happy and contented under their rule.

We are far from being convinced and we cannot accept this propaganda for obvious reasons. We have in our possession, information and reports to the contrary. Therefore, we have two versions about the conditions inside Tibet: the Chinese version and the Tibetan version. I do not insist that the people of the world blindly accept the Tibetan version as the truth. I am simply demanding that the Tibetan people be given the opportunity of freely expressing themselves. So far the tendency in the world has been to regard only the Chinese version as authentic. There is a double standard to it.

While the world press diligently follows what the Chinese leaders have to say about China or Tibet, and reports matters of even the least importance if they come from the mouths of the Chinese leaders, they do not give credence to the ridiculous Chinese versions of the international situation, American "imperialism", Soviet "revisionism" or Indian "expansion". Just the history of the past 20 years should make the people outside China realize the extent of distortion of facts that comes from the Peking organs. When the Tibetans tried to tell the world in the 60's that conditions were bad inside Tibet, the world, by and large, chose to call it refugee propaganda and accept the Peking version of a "socialist transformation" as authentic.

In the 70's, when sufficient evidence to support the previous refugee claims, has emerged, the world again turns to Peking for an official explanation. The new leaders in Peking now have to admit things were not rosy in the 60's as were printed at the time, but that is because the "Gang of Four" was handling it at the time. This again is perfectly acceptable explanation to the world.

I have repeatedly said that the nature of our struggle is not anti-communist, anti-reform or even anti-Chinese. It is also not whether those of us in exile can return to Tibet. Fundamentally, the real issue is the happiness and welfare of the six million Tibetans inside Tibet. We are carrying out our freedom movements in accordance with the wishes of our people there. The majority of them, especially the young, are not at all happy with the Chinese and are not willing to live under their domination. But they are unable to do anything as the whole country is like a vast prison.

And as is the case with prisons of any size, not very many inmates succeed in effecting their release themselves. So they depend on us and we in turn depend on world conscience to support our cause.

Why should an alien rule be forced upon six million unwilling people? Why shouldn't they be given the right to choose for themselves? If the majority of people in Tibet are really happy and willing to live under the Chinese rule, it would be foolish and unreasonable on the part of the 100,000 Tibetans in exile to stubbornly act contrary to their wishes. It would not be right morally. But we must first know for certain that the Tibetans are completely satisfied and happy. So far it is only the Chinese publicity organs and their recognized spokesmen in the West who claim that the Tibetans in Tibet are happy.

We do not have a single independent Tibetan support to this claim.

During the past 30 years there has been much propaganda about the tremendous progress made by China in virtually every field, contrary to what was actually happening in the country.

We now read that even the Chinese people are expressing their discontentment with the existing conditions and admitting failure to make adequate progress. If the Chinese themselves have suffered so much under their own leadership, one can imagine the extent to which the minorities have suffered, particularly the Tibetans, whose race, language, culture and way of life have no affinity whatsoever with the Chinese.

If the Tibetans are genuinely contented with the present state of affairs, there is a way in which the Chinese can easily convince us and the world of this. As I demanded in a statement on March 10, 1978, Tibet should be opened so that Tibetans within and without can freely visit each other.

If the rosy picture painted by the Chinese is authentic and they have nothing to hide, we should be given the opportunity to see it for ourselves in a free and unrestricted manner.

Such an opportunity will help us in "seeking truth from facts", a popular slogan in China today.

And in this context I welcome the recent Chinese consent to allow a group of Tibetans in India to visit their relatives in Tibet.

The ultimate decision about the future of Tibet must be made by the majority of the people there. This is democratic; this is reasonable; and this is just. In order to be able to make that decision the people must have the freedom to express themselves without fear. The world must remember that the 1959 Tibetan revolt against the Chinese was ruthlessly suppressed by labelling it as counter-revolutionary, while it was, in fact, a popular people's uprising against the oppression and foreign domination of Tibet by Communist China.

New York Times, 3-2-1979

4

CHINA AND THE FUTURE OF TIBET

During the past few weeks I have visited many parts of the United States and spoken at universities, colleges and religious institutions and small centres of learning. I have also had the opportunity to address several organizations concerned with world affairs and foreign policy. In almost every situation I have taken the liberty to speak on love and compassion. I firmly believe that the promotion of these qualities can contribute to modern society's need for a balance against excessive material preoccupation.

I have spoken at length on these topics not simply as a Buddhist, but from a clear universal recognition that except for superficial differences all humans are in essence the same in that we all want happiness and do not want suffering and on this basis engage in various techniques to bring this about. Recognition of our fundamental aim and agreement is important.

The press, the general public and numerous individuals I have met have also indicated a keen interest in Tibet, the Tibetan people and their future. It is obvious that developments in China during the past few years have contributed to this interest and caused speculations of a quick end to my exile.

Therefore I think that I should express my thoughts on the subject and my views on what may possibly lie ahead.

One who is not politically motivated can easily understand that Tibet is a separate country different from China. This thought comes quite naturally because Tibet was and is in fact different from China—racially, culturally, linguistically, geographically and historically. No knowledgeable person would for a moment think that Tibetans are Chinese.

Patron-Priest Relationship

In the past there existed a special patron-priest relationship between

China and Tibet; a relationship which was spiritual rather than temporal. In those times, the three countries, China, Mongolia and Tibet, were referred to as separate countries. You ask a Tibetan what his nationality is and his answer will be "Tibetan ". Similarly, when people discuss something Tibetan, it is always in the sense of something that is different and distinct from Japanese, Indian or Chinese. For example, when people talk about Tibetan Buddhism, it is never implied that Chinese Buddhism represents Tibetan Buddhism as well.

The word "China" is "Gya-nak" in Tibetan. Since the Tibetan word "Gya-nak" refers to a foreign land, it implies Tibet to be separate from China. The Chinese do not use this word. They use the vague term "our nation" and "motherland", instead of "China" in their official documents and publications in the Tibetan language. They explain to us that Tibet is not a part of Gya-nak (China), but that it is a part of Chung Kuo (Middle Kingdom), just as Gya-nak (China) also is! However, Chinese who are not politically oriented do not make this distinction for they refer to the Chinese language as Chung Kuo Hua (language of the Middle Kingdom). But politically motivated Chinese refer to it as Han Hua (language of Han) in order to justify their stand that Tibet is an integral part of the Middle Kingdom. Linguistic concoctions cannot hide the facts of life and history.

Because Tibet as well as Mongolia and East Turkistan are basically and historically different from China, the Chinese have established various autonomous administrative systems in these occupied areas. They also use the language of these countries along with Chinese, on their currency notes. Also, in the case of Tibet, because it was independent until 1950, the Chinese signed the 17-point Agreement with the Tibetan government. No other Chinese-occupied nationality has any such agreement, pact or treaty with China. Here again, the Chinese say that this is an "agreement" and not a "treaty", giving the unsatisfactory explanation that "agreements" are made only within a nation between the central and local governments.

It may be of interest that Sun Yat-sen, the father of the Chinese republic, considered Tibet, Mongolia, and Manchuria as foreign countries. Also, Mao Tse-tung, in the 1930s when he was carrying out his struggle and was not yet in power, supported Tibetan independence. Many years later, in 1954 when I was in China, Mao told me that while we were poor and backward, China would help us, but that after 20 years we (Tibetans) would be able to help them (the Chinese). On another occasion he told me that the Chinese personnel then stationed in Tibet would be withdrawn when the Tibetans could manage by themselves.

Even after 30 years of occupation by the People's Republic of China— and in spite of China's world-wide propaganda projecting the picture of Tibet as an inseparable and integral part of China—nobody says that he has been to "China" when he has visited "Tibet", or that the "Chinese" have taken to socialism when he means that the "Tibetans" have.

During these past three decades the Chinese have placed great emphasis on the unity of their nation and have boasted much achievement in that direction. Speeches on this have been made on numerous occasions at public meetings and official receptions. If we are to go by the number of times this theme has been stressed, the Chinese should have by now achieved a rock-like, unshakable unity. But this has not happened, for it is an artificial unity that is being imposed unsuccessfully on different nationalities, Tibetans being one of them.

To claim that Tibet is a part of the Chinese nation is both distorted and hypocritical. The Chinese seem to realise this, and one hopes therefore that they will change their policy and accept the reality of a Tibetan nation. If the Chinese really want understanding and friendship, Tibetans, Mongolians and East Turkistanis should be treated according to their real circumstances and given their inalienable national rights and fundamental freedoms in their own homelands.

The Chinese claim that they did not come to Tibet as imperialists or colonialists, but as "liberators". What sort of liberation is it that denies the people their birthright and the freedom to determine their own destiny themselves? Having deprived the Tibetan people of freedom, the Chinese talk about an imaginary "state of glorious happiness and progress" said to be existing in Tibet.

I am pointing out these facts not with any antagonism towards the Chinese. If one day all the countries of the world join together as one nation, I would welcome that, and Tibet would become a willing partner in such a movement. But as long as this does not happen, the six million Tibetans are entitled to all the rights that other free peoples have, including the preservation of their separate, unique identity and way of life. As long as the six million Tibetans remain under foreign military occupation, they will continue to struggle for genuine national liberation and for legitimate rights in their own country.

A Clear Account

I think it is important that we as Tibetans present a clear and factual account of the Tibetan situation. This is particularly necessary now when the present Chinese leadership is reported to be following a moderate and responsible path. It remains to be seen whether Chinese leaders are prepared to recognize realities as they really exist, or whether they will continue to direct facts in order to draw conclusions that serve only China's interests.

I have always firmly believed that unless we act according to the real existing circumstances we can never achieve our true aspirations. To my great disappointment, ever since the invasion of Tibet by the People's Republic of China, owing both to a lack of understanding of the actual situation, and often because the truth was intentionally ignored by the Chinese, there has existed most unfriendly relations between Tibet and China. This is an unfortunate state of affairs between two countries who have been neighbours for centuries. The Chinese took advantage of the Tibetans whenever possible, and as a result the Tibetans have grown ever suspicious of them.

Unions or federations can take place only when there is mutual agreement and mutual benefits flow from such arrangements. But they have to be disbanded or discontinued when it is realized that the people do not support them. The future of Tibet is not a matter of determination by the Chinese occupation force. Six million Tibetans obviously cannot be absorbed or integrated with China, and their identity cannot be destroyed.

Friendly relation between Tibet and China, which I dearly wish for, can be established only on the basis of equality, mutual respect and mutual benefit. I for one would gladly accept whatever destiny the six million people of Tibet choose for themselves in a climate of genuine freedom and peace. The free will of the Tibetan people is the only true basis for determining their destiny. Until it flourishes, there will be no peace in the hearts and minds of my people. With boundless faith in themselves and in the righteousness of their own cause they will wait for the day, which must come, when they can fully and freely enjoy their legitimate national rights and at the same time enjoy a relationship with China on a new basis of mutual benefit and respect.

The Wall Street Journal, 8-11-1979

5
PLACE OF ETHICS AND MORALITY IN POLITICS

Happiness is man's prerogative. He seeks it and each man is equally entitled to his pursuit of happiness; no man seeks misery. Justice and equality belong to man's prerogatives too, but ones which should derive their practice from altruism and which have not been corroded by the stations of power and wealth. In order to build such an altruistic motivation so that justice and equality may co-exist in truth, the creation of a staunch moral fabric for the social environment is a prerequisite. Concerned voices are being raised about this inherent vacuum in the moral foundation of today since this lack is the foremost deterrent to a just and equal world.

The entire social structure must not only undergo a dynamic metamorphosis, but the chief constituents of this structure, the caretakers of society—men—must re-evaluate the attitudes, principles and values in order that such a change is seriously effected. The sceptics might question the possibility of altering the social system, but are we not the makers of our own environment? Man has created his social dilemmas, and if any change is to be forthcoming, the power to do so lies with man alone.

Man and society are interdependent, hence the quality of man's behaviour as an individual and as participant of his society is inseparable. Reparations have been attempted in the past as contributions to lessening the malaise and disfunctional attitudes of our social world in order to build a world which is more just and equal. Institutions and organisations have been established with their charter of noble ideology to combat these social problems. For all intents and purposes the objectives have been laudable but it has been unfortunate that basically good ideas have been defeated by man's inherent self-interest.

Today, ethics and moral principles sadly fall in the shadow of self-interest particularly in the field of political culture. There is a school of thought which warns the moralists to refrain from politics, as politics is devoid of ethics and moral principles. This is a wrong approach since politics devoid of ethics does not further the benefits to man and his society and life without morality will make man no better than beasts. The political concept is not 'dirty', a common jargon associated with politics today, but the instruments of our political culture have tempered with and distorted the fundamental concepts of fine ideals to further their own selfish ends. Today, spiritual people are voicing their concern about the intermingling of politics with religion since they fear the violation of ethics by politics and, according to them thereby contaminating the purity of religion. This line of thought is both selfish and contradictory. All religions exist to serve and help man and any divorce from politics is to forsake a powerful instrument for social welfare. Religion and politics is a useful combination for the welfare of man when tempered by correct ethical concepts with a minimum of self-interest.

In the correlation between ethics and politics, should deep moral convictions form the guideline for the political practitioner, man and his society will reap far-reaching benefits. It is an absurd assumption that religion and morality have no place in politics and that a man of religion and a believer in morality should seclude himself as a hermit. These ideas lack proper perspective vis-a-vis man's relation to his society and the role of politics in our lives. Strong moral ethics are as concomitantly crucial to a man of politics as they are to a man of religion, for dangerous consequences are foreseen when our politicians and those who rule forget their moral principles and convictions. Irrespective of whether we are believers or agnostics, whether we believe in God or Karma, moral ethics is a code which everyone is able to pursue. We need human qualities such as moral scruples, compassion and humility. In recognition of human frailty and weakness these qualities are only accessible through forceful individual development in a conducive social milieu so that a more humane world will come into being as an ultimate goal. Self realisation that materialism does not foster the growth of morals, compassion and humility should be innately created. The functional importance of religious and social institutions towards promoting these qualities thus assumes a serious responsibility and all efforts should be concentrated sincerely in fulfilling these needs. Prejudice and bias should be forgotten and different religions should work in unity not only for the creation of these qualities in man, but also for an atmosphere of harmony and understanding. The world has become communicably smaller today and with respect to its limitations, no nation can survive in isolation. It is in our own interest to create a world of love, justice and equality, for without a sense of universal responsibility based on morality, our existence and survival is at a perilous precipice.

The qualities required to create such a world must be inculcated right from the beginning, when the child is young. We cannot expect our generation or the new generation to make the change without this basic foundation. If there is any hope it is in the future generation but not unless we initiate a major change in our present educational system on a world-wide basis.

A dynamic revolution is deemed crucial for instigating a political culture founded on moral ethics; such a revolution must be sponsored by the powerful nations for any such attempt by the smaller and the weaker nations is unlikely to succeed. If powerful nations adopt policies based on a bed-rock of moral principles and if they concern themselves genuinely with the welfare of mankind, a new path and a new ray of hope will emerge. Such a revolution will surpass all other attempts to achieve justice and equality in our world.

I feel very strongly about this subject on moral ethics and appeal to all humanists and those who share my concern to contribute in making our society and our world more compassionate, more just and more equitable.

Leader's Magazine, 1979

6

SPIRITUAL CONTRIBUTION TO SOCIAL PROGRESS

Material progress alone is not sufficient to achieve an ideal society. Even in countries where great external progress has been made, mental problems have increased, causing additional hardships. No amount of legislation or coercion can accomplish the well-being of society, for this depends upon the internal attitude of the people who comprise it.

Therefore, mental development, in company and in harmony with material development, is very important. Since the development of a healthy social attitude built around a sense of consideration and kindness for others is vital to society, the cultivation of kindness, love and compassion cannot be limited, as has often been the case, to religious believers. Rather, whether one is a believer or not, the value of kindness and consideration is appreciated by all and therefore should be cultivated by everyone.

Anger and hatred cannot bring harmony. The noble task of arms control and disarmament cannot be accomplished by confrontation and condemnation. Hostile attitudes only serve to heat up the situation, whereas a true sense of respect gradually cools down what otherwise could become explosive. We must recognize the frequent contradiction between short-term benefit and long-term harm.

Of Prime Importance

Regardless of race, creed, ideology, political bloc (East and West), or economic region (North and South), the most important and basic aspect of all peoples is their shared humanity—the fact that each person, old, young, rich, poor, educated, uneducated, male or female, is a human. This shared humanness and thus the shared aspiration of gaining happiness and avoiding suffering, as well as the basic right to bring these about, are of prime importance.

All of the means to bring these about—economic and political systems, ideologies, religious creed and so forth—are secondary. These should be utilised for the main purpose, and not allowed to become primary and thereby obstacles to achieving what should be primary—the well-being of society.

The various spiritual systems basically have the same message of making better human beings. Though they espouse different philosophies, we should not concentrate on these differences to the extent of losing sight of the common aim and result—improving human beings. From this point of view, the adherents to the many different religious systems should develop mutual respect. Each system has its own value suited to persons of different disposition and mental outlook. At this time of easy communication we must increase our efforts to learn each other's systems. This does not mean that we should make all religions into one but that we should recognize the common purpose of the many religions and value the different techniques that they have developed for internal improvement.

The benefits gained through internal improvements are not limited to religious practitioners. Both believers and non-believers gain from development of these attitudes fundamental to society. Still, even if believers and non-believers have this commonality, are Buddhism and communism, for instance, not basically at odds with each other? It is a reality of today's world that much of Buddhist civilization, stretching from the borders of Thailand to parts of Siberia, is under the sway of communist ideology. This area is inhabited by more than a quarter of mankind, the vast majority of whom are Buddhists.

Communism has not, however, been able to eradicate people's faith in Buddhism. It may seem shocking, but when one considers the experience of the past few decades and the trend of the foreseeable future, it may be wise to attempt a dialogue between Communism and Buddhism. Millions of people have suffered due to the estrangement of these two systems. When the Buddhists view the communists with suspicion and distrust and vice versa, the two only become more estranged and the possibility of either's effectively helping the persons in this region lessen.

Theoretically, original Marxism and Mahayana Buddhism, despite many differences, also have many basic points in common. The foremost is the emphasis on the common good of society. Therefore, the adherents of these two systems could develop respect for each other.

Also, among religions, Buddhism is atheistic in the sense that a creator God is not accepted; rather, Buddhism presents a view of self-creation, that one's own actions create one's life situation. In this light, it has been said that Buddhism is not a religion, but a science of the mind.

In Buddhism, it is explained that everything depends on one's own *Karma*. This means that one's life situation in the present depends upon one's actions and their motivations in the past and that one's future is thus capable of being moulded through engaging in salutary actions with a pure motivation. Similarly, in Communist or Marxist theory everything is said to depend on one's own labour.

Furthermore, Marxist economic theory is related with ethical principles in the sense that the prime concern is with the use of resources and wealth, not their mere accumulation. The emphasis is not on the accumulation of money but the proper use of it for the welfare of the needy majority. Likewise, in Buddhism the practice of considering the needs of other beings is stressed to such as extent that one sacrifices the welfare of the minority, and oneself, for the benefit of the majority of sentient beings. All practice is seen as a means for serving others.

The original thrust of communism was towards anti-exploitation and anti-corruption; it was not necessarily anti-religion. Some religious institutions had come to involve corruption; thus they had to be opposed. Likewise, although Marxism has good points, the implementations of some of its practice are corrupt and therefore have to be opposed. In this way, distinction must be made between systems and their practitioners.

In general, all religions are anti-exploitation and against social injustice. Buddha himself, in a revolutionary way, overcame rigid class boundaries, explaining a system of inner mental development that is open to persons from all walks of life.

Since the thrust of Marxist thought is not absolutely anti-religious, there is no point in religious persons viewing Marxism as anti-religious, creating tension and distrust. The commonality of many aims should and must be stressed. Similarly, Marxists, out of ignorance and lack of personal experience see religion as totally counterproductive, which is wrong. A real Marxist must discard narrow and dogmatic attitudes, and be open to the value of spiritual teachings.

Marxist Ideology Is No Answer

The reason for developing such an attitude is not the preservation of religion, but successful improvement of society. The experience of the last few decades has yielded sufficient evidence that the Marxist ideology is not a full answer for human society—it has its good and bad points.

If it were adequate for the development of human society, there would be no argument, as there would be no need for contribution from other systems. However, it seems that some of its followers have destroyed one privileged social class only to create another in its place. Mental and creative developments have stagnated and brought fear and mistrust in society. This shows the need for inner, moral development of a socially oriented attitude.

History has shown that no single political, economic or social ideology has been sufficient. So it seems worthwhile for the two great systems of this large expanse of the world to take point from each other. Certainly, Buddhist theory is not sufficient by itself for full socio-economic policy in this or the next century; it can take many points from Marxist, socialist and democratic systems. Similarly, those systems can benefit from many points in Buddhist theory, especially in terms of the development of socially beneficial attitudes. Such a partnership would help millions of people.

For the development of a peaceful, friendly human family or nation with a rich variety of faiths and political and economic systems, each of us has the responsibility to strive towards such harmony. There is no alternative.

The Wall Street Journal, 29-10-1981

MEETING-POINTS IN SCIENCE AND SPIRITUALITY

I have always believed that the ultimate aim of humanity is genuine happiness and satisfaction. That is what I believe and what I take as the basic starting-point. In order to achieve the maximum happiness and satisfaction, we need to understand everything that is connected with mankind and the quest for happiness, whether it be in the field of matter or in the spiritual field. Then, taking advantage of our knowledge of the different approaches, we have to find the right method to follow in order to achieve that aim.

The knowledge of external phenomena, and the application of that knowledge, is that which nowadays we call science. The approach and methods which focus primarily on internal phenomena consciousness or the mind—constitute another sphere of knowledge. Both have the same objective, the achievement of happiness and satisfaction, which are the intimate concern of every human being. Not only the objective, but the method is also directly related to human beings as it is the individual person who puts it into action. The scientist investigating external phenomena is still a living human being who wants happiness; whether it is his profession or not consciousness is also his concern. The spiritual person, whose interest lies in consciousness, or meditation, has to deal with matter. No one single way is sufficient, indeed if just one approach had been found to be so, the need would never have been felt to bring these disciplines together.

Both approaches are therefore very important, and I should like to say a few words to relate them to one another.

The fundamental view or philosophy of Buddhism is that of "dependent arising". When one talks about the view of dependent arising one means that things exist in dependence or that they are imputed depending on something or other. In the case of a physical phenomenon, one would specify that it exists in dependence on its parts, whereas non-physical composite phenomena would be described as existing in dependence either on their continuity or an aspect of their continuity. Consequently, whether it be external or internal phenomena, there is not anything that exists except in dependence upon its parts or aspects.

If one were to investigate to find a basis for the imputation in any given phenomenon since one would not find anything at all which actually is the phenomenon— no solid lump of anything that one could point one's finger at, which represents the phenomenon—then one says that phenomena exist through the imputation of the mind.

As phenomena do not exist independently of the imputing mind, one speaks of "emptiness", which means the lack of any intrinsic existence that does not depend upon the imputing mind. Since things do not exist just of their own accord, but in dependence on conditions, they change whenever they encounter different conditions. Thus, they come into existence in dependence on conditions and they cease in dependence on conditions. That very lack of any intrinsic existence, independent of cease and conditions, is the basis for all the changes that are possible in a phenomenon, such as birth, cessation and so forth.

It may be interesting to compare the scientific interpretation of the role of the observer or "participator" with the Buddhist view that observed phenomena do not exist merely as a mental image a projection or vision of the mind, but rather that they exist as separate entities from the mind. Mind and matter are two separate things. Matter is separate from the mind which cognizes it and denominates it. This means that with regard to all phenomena without exception, though they are not simply a creation or manifestation of the mind having no entity of their own yet their ultimate mode of existence is dependent on the mind that imputes them—the "imputer". Their mode of existence is therefore quite separate from the imputer, but their existence itself is dependent on the imputer. I feel that this point of view perhaps corresponds to the scientific explanation of the role of the observer. Though different terms are employed to explain them, their meanings are somewhat related.

On the surface, the dependent arising and emptiness explained above may seem to be quite contradictory. Yet if one analyses them on a much deeper level, one can come to understand that phenomena, on account of their being empty, are dependently arising or dependently existing, and because of that dependent existence, they are empty by nature. Thus one can establish both emptiness and dependent arising on one single basis, and thereby two facets which, on a general level, seem to be contradictory, when understood on a very profound level, will be seen to fit together in a very complementary fashion.

The mode of existence of phenomena is differentiated from their mode of appearance. Phenomena appear to the mind differently from their actual mode of existence. When the mind apprehends their way of appearing, believes in that appearance as being true, and follows that particular idea or concept, then one makes mistakes. Since that concept is completely distorted in its apprehension of the object, it contradicts the actual mode of existence, or reality itself. So this disparity or contradiction between "what is" and "what appears" is due to the fact that although phenomena are in reality empty of any intrinsic nature, yet they do appear to the ordinary mind as if they exist inherently, though they lack any such quality. Similarly, although in reality things which depend on causes are impermanent and transient, undergoing constant change, they do appear as though they were permanent and unchanging. Again, something that in its true nature is suffering appears as happiness. And something which is in reality false appears as true. There are many levels of subtlety regarding this contradiction between the mode of existence of phenomena and their mode of appearance. As a result of the contradiction between "what is" and "what appears", there arise all manner of mistakes. This explanation may have much in common with scientists' views of the difference in the modes of appearance and existence of certain phenomena.

Generally speaking, an understanding of the meaning of emptiness and dependent arising will naturally lead one to a deeper conviction in the law of cause and effect, where, as a result of different causes and conditions, corresponding fruits or effects, positive or negative, arise. One will then pay more attention to the causes and also be more aware of the various conditions. If one has a good understanding of emptiness or familiarity with it, then the arising of distortions, like attachment, hatred, and so on, in the mind will diminish, since they are caused by a mistaken view, mistaken in not correctly distinguishing between "what is" and "what appears". You can see for instance, from your own experience, how your feeling towards something that you observe will change, depending on your own state of mind. Although the object remains the same, your reaction will be far less intense when your mind is calm than if it is overcome by some strong emotional feeling, like anger. The actual

mode of existence of phenomena, the bare truth of existence, is emptiness. When one understands this, and appreciates the contradictory
nature of the appearance of phenomena, one will immediately be able
to realize this mistaken view to be untrue. Consequently all of the mental
distortions such as attachment, hatred, etc., which are based on that
misconception, a deception rooted in the contradictory nature of phenomena, will decrease in strength.

We might ask: how do the different levels of the consciousness or
mind that apprehends an object actually come to exist themselves?
Different levels of consciousness established are in relation to the different
levels of subtlety of the inner energy that activates and moves the
consciousness towards a given object. So, the level of their subtlety and
strength in moving the consciousness towards the object determines and
establishes the different levels of consciousness. It is very important to
reflect upon the relationship between the inner consciousness and outer
material substances. Many Eastern philosophies, and in particular
Buddhism, speak of four elements: earth, water, fire and air, or five
elements with the addition of space. The first four elements, earth, water,
fire and air are supported by the element of space, which enables them
to exist and to function. Space or "ether" serves, then, as the basis for the
functioning of all the other elements.

These five elements can be divided into two types: the outer five
elements and the inner five elements, and there is a definite relationship
between the outer and inner elements. As regards the element space or
"ether", according to certain Buddhist texts, such as the Kalachakra
Tantra, space is not just a total voidness, devoid of anything at all, but it
is referred to in terms of "empty particles". This empty particle therefore
serves as the basis for the evolution and dissolution of the four other
elements. They are generated from it and finally are absorbed back into
it. The process of dissolution evolves in the order: earth, water, fire and
air, and the process of generation in the order: air, fire, water and earth.
These four are better understood in terms of: solidity (earth), liquids
(water), heat (fire) and energy (air). The four elements are generated from
the subtle level to the gross, out of this basis of empty particles, and they
dissolve from the gross level to the subtle into the empty particles. Space,
or the empty particle, is the basis for the whole process.

The "Big-Bang" model of the beginning of the universe has perhaps
something in common with this empty particle. Also the most subtle, fine

particle described in modern physics seems to be similar to the empty particle. Such parallels do present something that I feel it would be worthwhile to reflect upon.

From the spiritual point of view of Buddhism, the state of our mind, whether it is disciplined or undisciplined, produces what is known as "Karma". This is accepted in many Eastern philosophies. Karma, meaning "action", has a particular influence upon the inner elements which in turn affect the outer elements. This, too, is a point for further investigation.

Another area in Tibetan Buddhism which may be of interest to scientists is the relationship between the physical elements and the nerves, and consciousness, in particular the relationship between the elements in the brain and consciousness. Involved here are the changes in consciousness, happy or unhappy states of mind, etc., the kind of effect they have on the elements within the brain, and the consequent effect that has on the body. Certain physical illnesses improve or worsen according to the state of mind. Regarding this kind of relationship between body and mind, Buddhism can definitely make a contribution to modern science.

Buddhism also explains, with great precision, the different levels of subtlety within consciousness itself. These are very clearly described in the Tantras, and research on these, in my opinion, would produce very beneficial results. Consciousness is classified, from the point of view of its level of subtlety, into three levels: the waking state or gross level of consciousness, the consciousness of the dream state which is more subtle, and the consciousness during deep, dreamless sleep, which is subtler still.

Similarly, the three stages of birth, death and the intermediate state are also established in terms of the subtlety of their levels of consciousness. During the process of dying, a person experiences the innermost, subtle consciousness; the consciousness becomes grosser after death in the intermediate state, and progressively more gross during the process of birth. Upon the basis of the continuity of the stream of consciousness is established the existence of rebirth and re-incarnation. There are currently a number of well-documented cases of individuals who clearly remember their past lives, and it would seem that it would be very worthwhile to investigate these phenomena, with a view to expanding human knowledge.

Tibetan Review, October 1983

8

THE TRUE FACE OF TIBET

Tibet, known to many as the Roof of the World, is a land which abounds in great natural beauty and clean, pure air. It is a heaven for those who wish to escape the tense, unhealthy surroundings often caused by modern "progress". For centuries, we Tibetans have lived in peace and at peace with our environment, in accordance with Buddhist tenets of love and compassion and by an admirable code of ethics and civility.

Today, I live in exile in India. I nevertheless wish to extend a warm welcome, on behalf of the Tibetan people, to those of you who are able to visit our country. At the same time, I am apprehensive due to the fact that many of you may not see or understand the real conditions in Tibet. For this reason, I wish to explain a few things concerning Tibet and its present state of affairs.

Tibet is distinguished by its extraordinary geography, the unique race and language of its people, and the rich culture they have developed over 2,100 years of recorded history. Approximately six million Tibetans populate our country, which covers around 2.5 million square kilometres, an area the size of western Europe. The so-called Tibet Autonomous Region, recently created by the People's Republic of China, comprises less than half of Tibet's actual territory.

Recent geological excavations in Tibet have discovered evidence of Tibetan civilization dating as far back as 4,000 B.C. In 127 B.C. Tibet's King unified the nation. Since then our country's relations with her neighbours, and particularly those with China, have seen both good and bad periods. But never, even in the worst of times, has the distinct identity of Tibet, or its people been threatened.

In the majestic beauty of Tibet's natural surroundings, the people developed their culture, which was deeply influenced by the Buddhist teaching of India. Though materially backward, Tibetan society was highly sophisticated in terms of mental and spiritual development. This brought about peace and harmony in the minds of our people and our communities. The faces of Tibetans who grew up and lived in this environment of the past, immediately reveal the natural calmness and spontaneity which is so frequently commented upon by visitors from around the world.

It is now over thirty years since Communist China forcefully occupied Tibet. In this period, our religion and culture has been destroyed and the people of Tibet have suffered tremendous physical and economic deprivation. But the greatest loss of all has been the loss of our people's freedom.

On occasion, tourists permitted to visit Tibet, have been able to see some degree of the destruction which has occurred. However, that which remains unknown to them, far exceeds the few visible signs apparent in the restricted areas they visit. To date, from information gathered over decades of research, it is estimated that some 6,254 monasteries have been destroyed in Tibet. In addition at least 1.2 million Tibetans have died as a direct result of the brutal occupation of our country by the Chinese. Our recent past has been most unfortunate, truly, the most tragic episode in our long history. Nevertheless, today Tibetans face an even greater threat; that of the complete assimilation and absorption of our land by the vast sea of Chinese, whose population has so drastically increased over the past two thousand years.

At the beginning of the 20th century, the Manchus were a distinct race, possessing a unique culture and heritage. Today, only 2 to 3 million Manchurians remain in their homeland, Manchuria, surrounded by 75 million Chinese settlers. In Eastern Turkistan (which the Chinese now call Sinkiang) the Chinese population has grown from 200,000 in 1949 to 7 million, over half of the total population of 13 million. Another clear example of Chinese colonization lies with (inner) Mongolia, where Chinese now outnumber Mongols by four to one (8.5 to 2.5 million). According to a recent Chinese newspaper, the area where I was born— the Kokonor region of north-eastern Tibet—now has a population of 2.5 million Chinese and only 700,000 Tibetans.

Indeed, while the Chinese claim to be giving special attention to the indigenous character of the so-called Tibet Autonomous Region (which comprises only central and western Tibet), they are in fact dispatching large numbers of young colonists both there and to the east and north-eastern regions of our nation.

Tibet's great natural wealth, and in particular its priceless religious images, paintings and icons, which adorned our monasteries and temples for some 1,300 years, has been literally shipped to China in endless truck convoys over the past quarter century. Even the walls of the monasteries have been broken down, the beams used for construction of Chinese homes, and the stone blocks shattered by artillery and dynamite. Among our greatest losses are the thousands of irreplaceable ancient Sanskrit, Pali and Tibetan texts, most of which, though preserved so well in the cold and dry Tibetan climate, were burned by the Chinese.

It is truly impossible to estimate the immense material loss which Tibet has suffered under Chinese occupation. Yet, to this day, China has the audacity and arrogance to publicly boast of having spent 7.2 billion yuans in developing Tibet over the past three decades! What it fails to mention, is the simple fact that this amount, whether it is accurate or not, includes the tremendous expense of maintaining approximately half a million Chinese troops and almost double this number of civilian personnel in Central Tibet alone.

By any social, moral religious or legal standards, the theft of one individual's property by another is universally condemned, so is the suppression of that individual's rights and natural freedom. Surely, when this same act of robbery and oppression is committed by one race against another it can only be considered a crime of immense magnitude.

I am pleased by the slight improvement of conditions which began in Tibet in 1979. Since then, the availability of food has improved, a small degree of freedom has been reintroduced in the economic field and the movement of individual Tibetans has become less restricted. I am also encouraged to note that China's leaders are today more open minded and moderate than in the past. I hope that they will try to better understand the real situation in Tibet and, based on that knowledge, adopt a policy that is both pragmatic and morally principled.

It is my belief that in human society the fulfilment of basic needs, such as food, shelter and clothing, alone are not sufficient. If you observe them it is clear that animals experience a sense of satisfaction when well fed, sheltered and kindly treated. But, for human beings, the freedom to hold and express personal views is without doubt an essential ingredient for genuine happiness. To a distinct people with a long history, a rich culture and a deep spiritual tradition like ours, freedom is an inalienable right which can never be replaced or assuaged by temporary improvements in economic conditions.

We Tibetans are not against the Chinese people. We believe that the Chinese equally have a right to their own happiness and prosperity but not at the expense of another nation and people. China does not possess any right whatsoever to decide the fate of the Tibetan people.

Recently China has begun to take a more detailed interest in the history of Tibet. This is good. Just as China's history is based on Chinese records, so, I would suggest, should Tibetan history be based on Tibetan records. Not a single Tibetan record states that Tibet has, at any time, been a part of China.

There have certainly been periods in the past, when the Mongols and Manchus wielded influence in Tibet. But is there a nation in the world which has not, at one period or another, been subjected to the influence of an outside power? Stronger nations have, and still do, exert their might to impose claims of sovereignty over weaker nations. But such claims have no basis and their actions cannot legally or morally confer genuine sovereignty. Furthermore, in the case of Tibet, the Tibetan people, to whom Tibet rightfully belongs, have never voluntarily agreed to become a part of China. I call upon the many serious and impartial scholars of international law to study and give their opinion on this aspect of Tibetan-Chinese relations.

It is my view that the issue of Tibet is not the concern of the six million Tibetans alone. Because of Tibet's age-old ties with its many neighbours and because of its continuing strategic importance, its fate has a direct and significant impact on that of the region and world. The future of Tibet is therefore not for the Chinese to decide as they please, in their own interest alone.

Throughout the history of mankind the use of force to solve material problems has proven inevitably ineffective. The outcome has been transitory at best. Such apparent solutions have never lasted for very long. A solution can be genuine and lasting only if and when it is to the full satisfaction of all the people concerned.

In the final analysis, it should be for the concerned people themselves, in the case the Tibetans, to decide under what conditions they really wish to live their lives.

New York Times, 24-8-1985

III
Interaction with Foreign Media

Chapter III
INTERACTION WITH FOREIGN MEDIA

is Holiness the Dalai Lama believes in justice and human determination. e says: "In History of man it has already been proved that the human ill is more powerful than the gun. And also, in the Tibetan case, Tibetan ation has more than 2,000 years' experience of dealing with China, ith India and Nepal, with other Mongols and human communities." ccording to him, "although this is the toughest period, I quite firmly elieve that the Tibetan people, their culture and Tibetan faith will survive, ill once again flourish" (p.87).

In one of his messages to Beijing he says: "It is my belief that in uman society it is not sufficient just to satisfy the basic needs such as food, nelter and clothing—freedom is essential and basic. For the Tibetan eople, freedom is an inalienable right". Being confident of his own terpretation of the situation, he called upon all "unbiased and impartial cholars of international law to give their opinion on this aspect of the ino-Tibetan relationship. China has the right to its own happiness and rosperity but not at the expense of another nation or people" (p.96).

The Dalai Lama feels that the method of resolving the China-Tibet roblem is certainly not through the barrel of the gun or the use of force. lor can the solution be found solely on paper. According to him, "It has be settled from within, from the heart: then the solution will be real and iluable"(p.83).

—Editor

1

THE GUARDIAN WEEKLY[1]

Q. *Could the Kalachakra (wheel of time) initiation help ease present tensions, since these ceremonies at Rikon are specifically dedicated to peace in the world?*

A. The initiation to the Kalachakra is one of the most important in Buddhism, for this Tantra takes everything into account—the human body and the mind, the whole external appearance, cosmic and astrological. That is a measure of the tantric discipline's importance. By practising it fully, it is possible to achieve enlightenment in a single life.

    We attribute a very special significance to it and really believe in its power to ease tensions. Initiation to the Kalachakra is particularly conducive to creating peace, mental peace and world peace. It requires, in addition, the creation of a mandala (meditational background), which is highly complex to work out and calls for long and involved preparation. Which is why it is so rarely conferred. In this sense also it is considered very important and this is the first time it is given in Europe.

Q. *In the world of today, can Buddhism provide answers to the existential problems of the human being who, in theory and in fact, has the power of life and death over his own planet?*

A. If you are referring to nuclear weapons, it is a complicated matter and it's something serious. It depends to a large extent on the human mind, on man himself. These terrible weapons cannot function on their

[1] His Holiness the Dalai Lama was interviewed by Claude Levenson and JeanClaude Buhrer shortly before the initiation of Kalachakra ceremonies at Rikon, near Winterthur in Switzerland, which is one of the largest settlements in Europe having nearly 5,000 Tibetans.

own, they require a man's finger to press the fateful button to become operational. The finger itself, as such, is in no position to make a judgement. It is controlled by the brain. The brain is controlled by awareness. So automatically, it goes through the heart. If, in this place, there is hatred, resentment and wrath, the person can go mad. In this way, the control exercised by love and compassion disappears and the finger is driven to make a gesture.

True peace, the peace within, has to be cultivated. Internal peace is an essential first step to achieving peace in the world, true and lasting peace. How do you cultivate it? It's very simple. In the first place, by realising clearly that all mankind is one, that human beings in every country are members of one and the same family. In other words, all these quarrels between countries and blocs are family quarrels and should not go beyond certain limits. Just as there can be friction, disputes between man and wife in a union, but within specific limits, as each party knows deep down in the heart that they are bound together by a far more important sentiment. Next it is important to grasp the real meaning of this brotherhood based on love and kindness.

Each religion of course has its own potential for contributing to the development of this attitude. There is, however, no doubt that Buddhism can also contribute much, especially by the teachings in the Mahayana. I'm convinced, I have always believed, and I believe today more than ever, that all spiritual values have a major role to play and a special responsibility in this sphere for contributing to genuine world peace.

Q. *You like to meet scientists in the course of your journeys. Are science and religion compatible? How do you see their relationship?*

A. I do in fact like to talk with scientists, have them explain to me their discoveries. It seems to me that Western science and eastern philosophy can join together to create a really complete and full-fledged human being. It is only in this way that man will emerge strengthened from his condition and become whole. At any rate, this is what I believe. For it's not enough to speak of God and Heaven, one must also think of others, be compassionate and think of alleviating the sufferings of others. True peace of the soul can be attained only at this price, even in a world of materialistic yardsticks, where it is absolutely essential to place the right values on the things of the mind. There could not possibly be matter without awareness. What in fact interests me is what is beyond matter and awareness, what really is important and what makes us what we are.

Q. *What sort of future do you see for the exiled Tibetan community. Don't you sometimes fear some contamination of ancestral values, especially among the younger generations who haven't known the former Tibet?*

A. Certain changes were inevitable. Over the past 26 years our small community living in exile outside Tibet has, under the circumstances, done a relatively good job of preserving our rich cultural heritage. If our younger generations have changed, wear their hair differently, their thinking and way of looking at things have not changed on the whole. Our community living outside Tibet is small, but free. In our own country, after the experiments of recent years, the system in place is aimed at destruction. It is premature to make a forecast about the future.

Q. *How do you feel about the Chinese?*

A. The Chinese ...... A very old nation, highly civilised and very cultivated, of course, and it seems to me, a nation that is sometimes very strange ..... By "civilised" I mean that you could get the impression they are very pleasant, very courteous and extremely kind people, people of quality, and yet there are terrible things happening in my country. We have suffered greatly as a result. Which does not prevent us from having compassion for the authors of these acts ....

Q. *There is plenty of talk abroad about Peking pursuing a more flexible policy in Tibet. What do you personally think of that?*

A. It is better to wait before adopting a definitive attitude. Since 1979, in China itself, things have perceptibly improved, which is very well. I think things are slightly better also for culture, the arts. And that's a good sign. As for basic liberties, it is very hard to judge for the moment.

In Tibet itself, in the interior of the country, famine no longer exists, and this is good news. During the two previous decades a good many people died of starvation or ill-treatment, victims of executions and extremely painful living conditions. Corroborative reports show that 1,200,000 of Tibet's 6,000,000 population have disappeared. Compared with that period, things are certainly better today and the

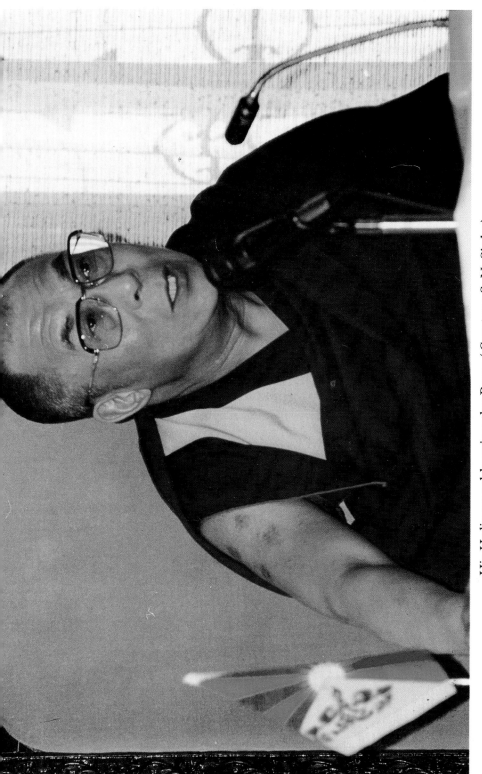

His Holiness addressing the Press (*Courtsey* : S. N. Sinha)

Norbulingka, Dharamsala (*Courtsey* : S.N. Sinha)

Chinese appear to be starting to show a little respect for Tibetan culture. That, too, is good.

Q. *Do you think that Buddhism and Marxism can co-exist?*

A. I have examined the question at length and very seriously, for it concerns millions of people from Thailand right up to Siberia. The ancestral faith remains very strong among the Buddhists. It seems to me that Buddhists do not easily allow themselves to be talked into abandoning their faith. There is today a sort of hostile attitude (to Buddhists) in countries governed by communists, and millions of people are suffering as a result.

Basically, Buddhism—Mahayana Buddhism, especially—and original Marxism have, I think, certain things in common. There could in fact be points on which a dialogue would be possible, but this presupposes a genuine open mindedness and a more realistic approach on both sides. Marxism is not a complete answer. Buddhism can give something more. In the economic field, Marxism could supplement Buddhism.

Q. *The Chinese authorities are going to celebrate 20th anniversary of the creation of what they call the autonomous region of Tibet. What significance does that have for you, for the Tibetans?*

A. For me, it's a very bitter anniversary .... I think, it's the same for most Tibetans. It's the beginning of enslavement. In a sense, it's the same for the Chinese as well, for while they are trying to celebrate this anniversary, they are also making a special effort to tighten their control over the whole of Tibetan territory. That means they know the Tibetans are not happy.

Q. *The Chinese keep telling all and sundry that you will be returning to Tibet this year. Are you thinking of doing that?*

A. At first, early in 1983, I did in fact express the hope of being able to go back to Tibet in 1985 so as to see for myself what was happening there. I thought that as certain changes have been noted since 1979, there would be a few improvements and that 1985 might be a good time to go there.

Unfortunately, at the end of 1983, many Tibetans were arrested, public executions took place and people disappeared without trace. When Hu Yaobang[2] went to Lhasa, he publicly apologised and

[2]General Secretary of the Communist Party of China

practically acknowledged the errors of the past; he also promised to follow a moderate, more realistic approach. But later, there was a recurrence of similar events, which means that nothing is certain, nothing has been definitively achieved.

Last year, the Chinese restated a certain number of conditions for a possible visit by me. So much so that I have no intention of going there. My person matters little. I am rather directly concerned with the fate of 6,000,000 Tibetans, 6,000,000 souls over there. The Chinese prefer to ignore all that and pretend to be concerned about the Dalai Lama. This is neither just nor correct.

The first time they invited me in 1980, I got the impression they thought the exiled Tibetan community was having trouble. They also seemed to believe that, in Tibet itself, as a result of political indoctrination and other methods the people would stop being loyal to the Dalai Lama.

In the circumstances, they thought it a good idea to invite me thinking that people would no longer come to pay their respects to me and that therefore it would be easy to manipulate me. At that time we sent a delegation to represent us. Spontaneously people came from everywhere to express their loyalty, their identity with me. This took the Chinese completely by surprise.

It is true, outside Tibet, we are only refugees. We have, on the whole, settled down fairly well and are doing our best to preserve Tibetan culture, educate our young people and maintain Buddhist perservance and teachings. So much so that today, authentic Tibetan culture and genuine Buddhism is to be found outside Tibet.

I feel that in their heart of hearts the Chinese don't really want to see me back in Tibet. In any case, I don't want to go back without the certainty that it could contribute something to Tibet. Since expressing this wish, I have received a large number of messages from Tibet itself warning me in particular not to come back under the present circumstances. I therefore consider it's better not to go back.

Q. *What are the Dalai Lama's conditions for his return?*

A. First and foremost, freedom for Tibetans to express their wish. Once this condition is met, I may return to my country with joy. As long as these people feel deep down in their hearts they are missing something, I think my place will be more useful outside. Even if in short, the recent past tends to prove that, because we are outside Tibet, Tibetan culture continues to survive on this planet. If we had remained over there, we would have been destroyed once and for all.

Q. *Do you think it possible to discuss these matters with the Chinese government and reach a gentleman's agreement?*

A. I hope so. In any case, the problem exists, whether or not it is openly acknowledged. It's there. Nobody wants it to drag on and on, neither we nor the Chinese. I feel the method, the way to resolve the problem is certainly not by guns or force. It cannot be solved either solely on paper. It has to be settled from within, from the heart: then the solution will be real and valuable. Of course. I'm always optimistic. Self-confidence, courage, determination and optimism are, in my view, essential for winning. Here, it is of paramount importance, as much for the human community as for the individual.

The Guardian, 21/22-7-1985

2

THE TIMES[3]

Q. *To most people outside, the life of the Dalai Lama was the most mysterious, the most exclusive existence on Earth. Would you tell us something of your life in the Potala, compared with life now in Dharamsala?*

A. When I was in the Potala Palace or at the Norbulingka, I had to sit with my tutors every day and have lessons. There were times when I did not want to listen or to have a lesson, but it was difficult to get out of it, as each day the time was fixed. On looking back, I now realise that my senior tutor was strict on time and even when there were 10 or 15 minutes to spare, he intended to use it for study. In that way there was a sense of isolation.

However, now when I recall those days, I am filled with admiration for my old playmates who entered into my games like children, refusing to accept defeat and competing with a will. Sometimes I used my position of Dalai Lama to try to bully them and felt angry when they wouldn't concede defeat! On the whole time passed easily, except when my teacher showed some kind of unpleasant attitude.

In the early part of my life, my third brother stayed with me. We usually played very risky games. I remember on one occasion we were hurling a kind of boomerang at each other and this time my stick hit my brother near the eye. He collapsed and started to bleed. It really scared me and the memory of his bleeding remains with me still. Stupid Dalai Lama. After some time, he left my place and went to school and only visited me every fortnight for a day and a half.

[3] Amar Jasbir Singh of *The Times*, London, met His Holiness at Rikon, Switzerland.

In Tibet, there is usually a holiday on each full moon and new moon. My other brothers and sisters visited me only occasionally. Whenever my mother came to call, she brought our native bread for me, which was a great treat.

My everyday life in Dharamsala is essentially the same. Each morning I start my day with religious practices such as prayer, meditation reciting something, reading religious texts and my own study, almost like homework. In the afternoon I give audiences, read papers regarding refugees, religious matters, the Tibetan situation. Then I never miss the early morning BBC Overseas Service.

Q. *It seems that the emphasis of your ministry is religious. Yet for Tibetans, you are their political ruler as well. Has the duality of your role as Dalai Lama been put aside and have you chosen only to wear your religious hat?*

A. When we talk of temporal or political headship it is associated with the Tibetan situation. Some people might take an interest in that, but there are many who show little interest in Tibet. Whereas when it comes to religion, Buddhism, there are no national boundaries. Although the majority of Tibetans are Buddhist, there are among them some Muslims and Christians and to them, as well as to those traditionally Christian countries, the message of the Buddha, the Buddhist way of approaching life and the search for enlightenment might be of some value. In the religious field, therefore, I can go straight to the heart of the matter and contribute in a more meaningful way.

As a Tibetan, however, there are around six million people in Tibet who trust that I shall not break faith with them or let their plight be forgotten. Morally speaking it is a heavy responsibility and it is my choice to bear it. After all, politics itself supposes a benefit to the people which, in itself, is an act of religion. In the Tibetan case, however, experience has shown that without political freedom, to maintain Buddhist practices has proved very difficult.

Q. *Tibetan refugee settlements, in an overpopulated and poor country like India, have been one of the few success stories in this age of displaced peoples. To what do you owe this success?*

A. With India we have very long historical link and more important the spiritual heritage has made the relationship very deep. What I usually call, heart to heart. Since 1959, when we arrived as refugees, the Government of India has contributed very generously for our rehabilitation. And then we have our own secretariat and various organisations which form a framework for administering the refugee centres and projects which relate to Tibetans. Wherever there are Tibetans, whether in Switzerland, England, America we try to maintain our identity and cultural heritage.

Q. *Your life in Tibet was very private—you were not often seen by the people. How much has your personal life changed in this respect— are you now more accessible?*

A. I think that when I was in Tibet, through religious teachings, there was close contact with the people. In another sense, of course, it was a very isolated position. My natural inclination is to be as straightforward and frank as possible. I have found that when everything is running smoothly there is a tendency to allow oneself to pretend that rituals and ceremonies show that all is well, even when there is something wrong.

Then when things become really desperate, you simply cannot pretend any longer and are forced to come closer to reality. In my personal experience, this tragedy has taught me a lot. I think the Dalai Lama has become more realistic. That's good. So nowadays, I try to act as informally as possible, and thus it is easy to be close to each other.

Q. *Have you left any family behind in Tibet? How have they fared?*

A. Yes, I do have relatives in Tibet. Some are in Lhasa, some are in my own native place Taktser. Of course there are restrictions, and no doubt it has something to do with them being my relatives, but some have got permission and visited me in Dharamsala.

Q. *Do members of your family play an important role in the running of your government-in-exile?*

A. I usually prefer not to have them in the main cabinet—Kashag. My sister runs the Tibetan children's village and has been very successful and helpful. Then my third brother is now working in the Tibetan medical institution in Dharamsala. Some of my family live in Dharamsala and some are abroad.

Q. *You are visiting Switzerland to give a teaching on the Kalachakra Tantra ("wheel of time"). Would you like to tell us something about it?*

A. Well, you know Kalachakra Tantra is respected by all the different sects in Tibet, i.e. Sakya, Kargyupa (Red Hat), Nying-ma-pa (Old Order), Gelugs-pa (Yellow Hat). Although sometimes there is a different interpretation, a different tradition within the orders, which has given rise to great debates, yet on the whole, Kalachakra itself is generally accepted by all schools of thought. Kalachakra initiation with the drawing of the great Mandala (sacred circle) needs a lot of preparation, and it is not possible for one or two people to perform it. Therefore it automatically becomes quite rare. We believe that Kalachakra Tantra reduces tension, is good for mental peace and therefore for world peace.

Q. *You have now been in exile for 26 years. In what way has being an exile affected you, and have you reconciled yourself to being one for your own lifetime?*

A. I personally think I am a very happy man. I really enjoy my way of life these days. Very fine. In general I believe that entire humanity is the same, and in that belief, I think of myself as belonging everywhere. I try to contribute wherever I can and to use my time as meaningfully as possible.

Q. *But are you reconciled?*

A. No problem.

Q. *Your Holiness, as the Dalai Lama you live by faith, by charity and, above all in your position, by hope. Can you tell us how you keep the flame alight?*

A. I believe in justice and in human determination. In the history of man it has already been proved that the human will is more powerful than the gun. And also in the Tibetan case, the Tibetan nation has more than 2,000 years experience in dealing with China, with India and Nepal, with other Mongols and human communities.

So although for us this is the toughest period, I quite firmly believe that the Tibetan people, their culture and the Tibetan faith will survive, will once again flourish. This I always believe.

The Times, London, 19-8-85

3

THE TIMES

Q. *In the British press there have been articles very critical about conditions in Tibet, which have confirmed the brutality of the repression by the Chinese. Are you tempted to say to the world "I told you so?"*

A. Oh, yes. As far as I can see, the important thing in world politics is that it has very little to do with justice. The only thing that counts is brute force unfortunately.

Q. *Why do you think the West has, during the 26 years of Chinese rule, chosen to ignore what was going on in Tibet?*

A. Well, of course, these things are difficult to say in a few words. But there are many factors, and perhaps one essential factor is distance.

Anything happening in the Soviet Union, for example, is sufficiently connected with the West for it to have an immediate impact. When it comes to China, people in the West regard the connection as essentially too remote, and of no immediate concern for them.

Another reason is that there are only six million Tibetans, whereas the other side has one billion Chinese. So naturally people are inclined to regard the bigger one as being more important.

For example, the West does not ignore what goes on in Afghanistan, or, say, somewhere like Cambodia, because it is happening now. But in the case of the Tibetan issue, it has been going on for a long time. When it first happened in 1959, nations, journalists and newspapers took some interest in Tibet. But now, gone is the dramatic impact.

Q. *Is it in the interests of the West to keep the two socialist blocks, China and Russia, apart? Do you think that has something to do with the West ignoring the Chinese occupation to Tibet?*

A. Yes, surely. By having better relations with China, they keep the emphasis on the Tibetan issue to the bare minimum.

Q. *Prime Minister Mrs. Margaret Thatcher makes a great deal of Russian involvement in Afghanistan, yet she is silent about China in Tibet. What do you make of it?*

A. Well, my feeling is that her silence is very unfortunate. From the viewpoint of a person who believes in the importance of justice and the rights, no matter how small, of every human being regardless of community or creed, the silent denial of the Tibetans is a very sad thing.

Q. *Do you think that Mrs. Thatcher could have come out more openly?*

A. I think so. Apart from the moral standpoint, the British Government, among the Western nations, has had the closest political relations with Tibet. There may be some confusion in present-day thinking, but Britain, above all, knows full well the political status of Tibet.

Q. *Do you think that Britain acknowledges Afghanistan as a sovereign independent state but considers Tibet's status as part of China?*

A. These things are very difficult to say. Very complicated matter.

In any case, since 1950-51 the Tibetan situation has changed, although I feel that morally speaking the Tibetans have always been a separate race and separate country. Even in the early part of this century, Tibet had privileges and the independent status to make direct treaties with foreign powers, including Britain of course. As a human being, I hope and pray that these past relations should not be completely dead.

Q. *Do you think that you could persuade Mrs. Thatcher to comment on Britain's treaty relations with Tibet?*

A. That's difficult to say. No, I have not asked—not practical. Unfortunately, today, one or two nations are doing something wrong, and as a result the weaker nations suffer. So also, we fit into that category.

Nevertheless, I feel a sort of inspiration in our own people's will, who remain, despite many tragedies, very determined. I always feel that things will change, will have to change.

Q. *There is this new dimension in British politics of China and Hongkong. Do you think that, in these deliberations, Mrs. Thatcher could raise the question of Tibet?*

A. Well, I think the legal question will be difficult for her to raise.[4]

   But the Tibetan issue itself, is still very much alive for two reasons. First, that region of the world is not at all stable, and strategically, the location of Tibet is very important.

   Second, the people of Tibet have undergone such untold suffering that they are extremely dissatisfied. So sooner or later that dissatisfaction will surely open up.

   Therefore, anyone, whether in government or private organisations, who may have an opportunity to deal with the Tibetan issue, should rethink and review their attitudes. This I believe.

Q. *Would you like to see the Queen before she goes to China next year, and do you think that she should have accepted such an invitation in view of the Tibetans' plight?*

A. I do not think there is any occasion to meet the Queen. Also there is not much to discuss or say. It is her own right to visit, to go wherever she wishes.

Q. *Might you consider sending her a message?*

A. I will see.

The Times, 20-8-1985

[4] The Simla Convention of 1914 which drew the much disputed Mc Mahon line defining the border between Tibet and India, was an agreement between Tibet, China and Britain and forms the modern basis for Tibet's ancient claim for independence.

4

SOUTH CHINA MORNING POST

Q. *You have made your home in India for the past 26 years, yet India, like Britain, has chosen not to define its treaty obligations to Tibet. What do you think of this?*

A. I feel that when the problem started, India was a young independent nation. This in itself was a major handicap and, if I may say so, there was some kind of confusion also involved.

As a result, when it came to the Tibetan problem the emphasis lay on short-term benefits, and it neglected to pay attention to the long-term ones.

In any case, I do believe that within India's own limitations, whatever it can do it will do. It is not only a question of recent treatise, but Indian and Tibetan relations are something unique and deep. Actually Tibetan culture and Tibetan dharma (religion)—that's India's heritage to us.

Q. *When Tibet was overrun and you were forced to come to India, Mr. Nehru did not openly say that Tibet was Independent of China. Do you think, on looking back, that in 1959 he ought to have been stronger in speech, if nothing else?*

A. Yes, I agree. But I think later he felt very strongly regarding Tibet, and expressed what he really felt deep down.

Q. *In view of India's treaty relations with Tibet, what is the reason for India not coming out openly in defence of an independent Tibet?*

A. Of course there are many difficulties as things have become very involved. But in the early 1960s, on one occasion, I expressed the view that Tibet did have direct contact with foreign countries and made treaties.

For instance, at the Simla Convention of 1914, Tibet was an equal partner in discussions and the treaty-making. So now, though

I cannot find the proper words through my poor English, you see the emphasis is on the treaty, but not much thinking about the country which signed the treaty. That is some kind of contradiction.

At that time, of course, Tibet was regarded as an independent country. Today things have changed. But if you ask me, the basic Tibetan nation still remains independent. Tibetan independence is always there.

Q. *Mr. Deng Xiaoping is reputed to have three, wishes before he departs the stage—settlement of the Hongkong issue, re-unification of Taiwan, and your return to China and the settlement of the Tibetan issue. Why does he want you to return to China rather than to Tibet?*

A. At the beginning, I feel, they thought they ought not to insist on the Dalai Lama remaining in Beijing or in China proper. At that time the Chinese felt that Tibetan refugees, and the Tibetan situation outside Tibet, were rather difficult, whereas the people in Tibet had undergone 20 years of their indoctrination and would therefore show a negative attitude towards the Dalai Lama.

Under those circumstances they only saw the return of the Dalai Lama as a benefit. Then things became clearer, and now they think that if the Dalai Lama returns and remains in Tibet, it may create problems for them. So better keep him in China proper.

Q. *When, in December last year, they invited you to go to China, they must have known that you would not accept such an invitation. So why did they do it?*

A. The Chinese Government believes that if they smile, the Dalai Lama will immediately return. It is that kind of impression, I think.

Q. *In your refusal to go to Peking you said the issue was not that of the Dalai Lama but the happiness of the Tibetan people. Since the status of the Dalai Lama is basic to Tibet, why did you say this?*

A. Basically, the Dalai Lama is an individual, and even the institution of the Dalai Lama came into being at a certain stage of Tibet's history. In the future it may disappear, but the Tibetan nation will always remain. Of course, at the moment the Dalai Lama is almost like a symbol of Tibet, and among the people I remain, if I may say so, still most popular.

Theoretically, there is the Tibetan nation as a nation, and the institution of the Dalai Lama as something different.

So you see, here I specially emphasise that the problem is not my own status or my own future. I do not worry about my future, but the basic problem of six million human souls in Tibet. That's the point.

Q. *If the Chinese improved conditions in Tibet, and showed that the Tibetan people quite liked being part of China, and it was only the Dalai Lama who was not prepared to acknowledge China's right to be in Tibet, what would you say to that?*

A. In fact, I listen to many messages in a written or verbal form. Some of the older people in Tibet express the wish to see me before they die. But on the other hand, the young and thoughtful people (who may also have the same wish) advise that, under the present circumstances, I should not return.

They do not want the Dalai Lama to be handcuffed and unable to speak in freedom on their behalf.

Q. *China's acquisition of Sikorsky Black-hawk military helicopters from the United States for Tibet, the continuance of the 250,000 strong Chinese garrison, and now sales of military hardware from Britain mean that the Chinese are strengthening their presence in Tibet. Whom do you think they fear?*

A. Of course, the Chinese are always suspicious and distrustful of Tibetans. Wherever there is a Tibetan village, there is a larger contingent of Chinese military personnel.

My information is that though they are trying to show the world that Tibetans are happy during the 26th anniversary celebrations, yet they are taking every precautionary measure to restrict the movement of Tibetans.

There is an obvious concentration of both military and secret service personnel in and around Lhasa. There are also large numbers of Chinese soldiers and civilians inducted into Tibet, in the name of construction workers for the 26th anniversary of the so-called Autonomous Region of Tibet celebrations next month. Our information is that about 80,000 to 90,000 Chinese technicians and labourers have been brought into central Tibet.

Q. *So far, each delegation which you have sent to China has met with deadlock. If the Chinese were to release political prisoners, reduce the garrison and concede a genuine internal autonomy to Tibet, would you consider it then to be one country?*

A. The Tibetan issue is very complicated. The basic question is the complete satisfaction of the Tibetan people.

"One country, two systems" might be an interesting concept if the entire world became a sort of one country. Within it those people who believe in certain ideals, certain ideologies, would live together as their own community and adopt their own system. And the neighbour next door would function under a different system. That I believe is possible and good.

Q. *What this question means is that Tibet would still be linked to China. In general, would you be prepared to accept this as one country?*

A. In general, no.

Q. *Lenin maintained that to shift colonisation there had to be strong movement from within a country, and for the oppressor to lose the will to continue the fight. Have you any knowledge of such a movement within Tibet?*

A. Actually there are many indications that feelings of bitterness are everywhere in Tibet. So I think sooner or later these inner feelings will come out. For example, the Chinese always move about in strength. No military truck moves alone, which is an indication that they need to take precautions. There is also evidence of fires and some kind of small-scale sabotage.

Q. *You have mentioned in some recent statements that conditions in Tibet are somewhat improved. Does this mean that the internal situation causes you no specific anxieties at present?*

A. No, I am not very satisfied. As you know, it is now more than 30 years since communist China forcibly occupied Tibet. During this period the religion and culture of Tibet have been destroyed and the people have undergone tremendous economic deprivation.

The greatest loss, however, has been their freedom. According to information that we have gathered so far, 1.2 million Tibetans have died as a direct result of the brutal occupation by the Chinese. Now, however, there is an even greater danger of the Tibetans being completely assimilated into the vast sea of the Chinese population.

For instance, at the beginning of this century, the Manchus were a people of a distinct race with their own culture and traditions. Today in Manchuria there are only two to three million Manchus among 75 million Chinese. In Eastern Turkistan, called Sinkiang by the Chinese, the Chinese population in 1949 was 200,000 and today there are about seven million of them in a total population of 13 million. Another example: there are 8.5 million Chinese in Inner Mongolia and only 2.5 million Mongols.

Now in the Kokonor area of northeastern Tibet—where I was born—according to a recent Chinese newspaper report there are 70,000 Tibetans and 2.5 million Chinese.

The Chinese are widely publicising the special care and attention they give to the so-called, "Tibet Autonomous Region", which comprises the western and central parts of Tibet, yet they are sending large numbers of young Chinese into the eastern and northeastern parts of Tibet.

It is impossible to estimate accurately the immense material loss that the Tibetans have suffered under Chinese colonisation. Yet the Chinese have the audacity to publicise widely that 7.2 billion yuans have been spent on developing Tibet over the past three decades.

This amount is actually their expenses in maintaining about 300,000 military and 1.7 million civilian personnel in the region. It is only a fraction compared to the cost of what they have destroyed and removed.

South China Morning Post, 26-8-1985

5

MESSAGE FOR BEIJING

I am encouraged to note that the Chinese leaders are more open-minded and moderate compared to those in the past.

I hope that they will try to understand better the real situation in Tibet and, based on that understanding, adopt a policy that is pragmatic and morally principled.

It is my belief that in human society it is not sufficient just to satisfy the basic needs such as food shelter and clothing .... freedom is essential and basic. For the Tibetan people, freedom is an inalienable right.

It is good that the Chinese have recently been taking some interest in the history of Tibet. The history of a nation is naturally based on historical records and nowhere is there a single record that states that Tibet has at any time been a part of China.

There have been periods when the Mongols and Manchus had some influence over Tibet but then, where is there a nation which has not experienced such influences be it military, religious, cultural or through the marital relationship of its rulers?

Such influences and acts of aggression have been used in the past, as well as in the present, by stronger powers to claim sovereignty over weaker nations. But the Tibetan people have never voluntarily agreed to become part of China.

I call on unbiased and impartial scholars of international law to give their opinion on this aspect of the Sino-Tibetan relationship. China has the right to its own happiness and prosperity but not at the expense of another nation or people.

6

INTERVIEW TO TV NETWORK[5]

Q. *Our first knowledge about Tibet came from a book by Heinrich Harrer (Seven Years in Tibet). Then, for the past days we have been in touch with the Tibetan people. It doesn't look to us that the Tibetan people deserve this bad Karma of exile and persecution as well as invasion of their country by the Chinese.*

A. Buddhists believe in beginningless rebirth. So certain bad *Karmas* which may not have been committed in a certain life time may have been committed in some other life time. It is not necessary to have accumulated the bad *karmas* at one time and at one place. Different beings at different time and place may have accumulated the same amount of *karma*. They then are born at one time and at one place. The suffering that they undergo is the result of their common karmic effect.

Today, we are having this beautiful weather; we are enjoying this together at one place and at the same time. But the *karma* which gave us this opportunity may have been accumulated by us at different places. Yet the result is that we are experiencing this together at this moment and at this place. It is not necessary that on account of our having the same experience now we should have created the cause of this particular moment at one place jointly.

Q. *In the case of Tibet .... even after the invasion of your country, killing thousands of your people, prohibiting your culture, your religion and all facets of your life, you still manage to keep Tibet alive in exile. Not only that, the Chinese finally had to relent and to open Tibet a bit more. Now they are telling that we should look at facts and are*

[5] This interview to the Spanish TV Network and Euskal TV Network given at Dharamsala on April 30, 1986 appeared under the title "Tibetan Determination Difficult to Destroy".

inviting Your Holiness to visit Tibet. What is the strength of Tibet to make the Chinese recognise that Tibet is something strong which cannot be destroyed so easily, instead of proceeding in the same method as before?

A. I think, one, the Chinese themselves. They are facing many difficulties in their own land, in China. So they have to change their overall policy. Then regarding Tibet, I think it is the peoples' will, their determination which mattered. The Chinese, for the last more than three decades, tried through every means to suppress our people but completely failed. So they are trying to adopt a different method, a different way like sugar-coated pill. Then of course, truth is on our side.

There are many reasons why Tibetan people's determination is still strong. Firstly, historically, geographically, culturally, and racially it is obvious that Tibet and Tibetans are quite different from China and Chinese. In every field there is a clear distinction. So although relations between China and Tibet are almost 2,000 years old that never diminished Tibetan identity. It always remained there.

Another factor is, although all Tibetans may not be politically minded yet the faith in Buddhism is very strong. Whenever they pass through tragedy, Buddhism gives them inspiration and encouragement. Thus it is very difficult to destroy the Tibetans' determination.

Lastly, the behaviour of the Chinese contributes to this. Their extreme rudeness and atrocities have become counter-productive. Therefore we have to be grateful to the Chinese.

Q. *Your Holiness meant this when you said Chinese were also your best teacher?*

A. Yes.

Q. *We observe that Tibetan Buddhism is spreading all over the world. More and more people seem to be getting interested in it. Would this interest of the world have occurred had not the Tibetans been forced into exile by the Chinese?*

A. If you mean this situation may not have occurred if we were still in Tibet, then my answer is yes. In the past, Tibet remained in extreme isolation. So although some changes might have taken place the general situation may have remained unchanged. Talking from this point of view, although our present situation is tragic yet it has also given us the opportunity of establishing contacts with the outside world and specially with various religious groups.

Q. *In what way do you think could Tibet—its religion, its people contribute to the Western world?*

A. I think in different religious and spiritual fields. A Christian could learn certain methods from Buddhism. There are already some Westerners who adopt certain Buddhist methods for their own practices; certain techniques to improve their mental alertness. Then there are Westerners who remain in Western society but at the same time practise Buddhism, specially Tibetan Buddhism. I think we will eventually know from their experiences, the contribution of Tibetan Buddhism to Western society.

I try to make a distinction between the essence of Buddhism and the cultural part of Tibetan Buddhism. The essential part is more or less the same everywhere while the cultural part may change from country to country. So I think it may not succeed if a Westerner adopts Tibetan Buddhism in its complete form, as practised by Tibetans, in a Western society. It will help if we take the essence and adopt it to the existing conditions.

Q. *The symbol of Christianity, which Jesus said is religion of love, is a bleeding man hanging from a cross with a thorn crown. It is amazing that this is understood as a religion of love. When reading about Buddhism we found several things which we would like you to explain. For instance, we have seen forms of Buddhas directly related to sex, to anger, in ways like demons, etc. How do these match with the Buddha of Compassion?*

A. In Buddhism there are three categories: the so-called Hinayana or lesser vehicle, Mahayana or greater vehicle and Tantrayana. The followers of Hinayana aim for the Salvation of oneself while those of Mahayana aim for the liberation or salvation for entire sentient beings. In these two the difference is only in the motivation. Naturally, as soon as one thinks about others then the most important thing is compassion.

In Tantrayana comes sex and wrathful manifestation. The basic practice is love and compassion. In order to develop these, certain human weaknesses like desire, attachment, sexual feeling, hatred, anger, etc., have to be overcome. Tantrayana uses some human weaknesses in a particular way. For instance, sex is utilised to subdue the grosser consciousness. Once this is done you automatically increase your deeper consciousness. Having achieved this it is turned into wisdom.

Q. *For more than 3,000 years, probably much more, mankind have been indulging in mutual killing, assassination, kidnapping, raping, torturing and committing all sorts of crimes. But when we look at other creatures we never see a bird or a tiger kill other animals except to subsist. So for how long are human beings going to think that we are the king of the creation instead of thinking that we are a sort of sick diseased monkeys with not very active intelligence?*

A. As Buddhists we believe human form or human brain is most sophisticated. So being more sophisticated naturally if we use it in a proper way it is much more constructive than the brains of other species. But if used wrongly then it is much more destructive. Whereas in other beings the potential is limited. Even if used in a negative way, it does not cause much destruction. This not being the case with human beings, it is worthwhile to develop the mind in a positive way.

Q. *In the 19th century one man (Charles Darwin) said that man came from apes. At first everybody thought he was a genius. Later they thought he went against religion; that he was mad, that it was a crime to say that human beings came from monkeys. It looks like this man could have been a Tibetan because long back, much earlier than the 19th century, the Tibetans were saying that man came from the apes. We would like to know what you have to say about it?*

A. I think a section of Tibetan ancestors came from monkeys while some immigrated from India. That kind of a story is there; the father is considered a monkey, the mother a demon. So it united the spiritual story and the scientific story.

Q. *Continuing the same question why is it, according to Your Holiness, that women always take the worst part in all the stories? For Christians it was a woman who led the man to commit the first universal sin while in Tibet it was a woman who was the demon. Why do you think it is always women who have the negative aspect? Is it that women always bring trouble to men?*

A. As far as intellectual side is concerned, I think our ancestor mother may be greater than our father. So this is not so negative.

Q. *Some books by Lobsang Rampa and Alexander David-Neel, who introduced Tibet for the first time to the West, mention caves in Tibet in which are hidden secrets of supreme importance for humanity. How much credit should we give to this? Do you think any secret is hidden in caves in Tibet?*

A. I don't know. I have no information. However, we can take it in another sense. Today our knowledge has expanded greatly with the help of science and technology. But knowledge regarding our own mind, our deep nature, is still limited in Western world. This is because consciousness is formless and cannot be touched, and so cannot be measured with instruments. It can only be known through meditation and other methods.

   Regarding the expansion of human knowledge about human brain, mind, etc., I think Tibetans can contribute. So that is something like hidden caves in Tibetan brain. In that sense some credence can be given to the stories.

Q. *The Inquisition Movement in Europe led the youths in the West not to be religious and to understand religion as something that you have to do rather than a feeling of religion. In Dharamsala we talked to many Tibetan youths. We observed that all of them have a deep religious feeling. They consider religion an important part of their existence and important part of being Tibetan. We have been struck by this. Do you think it will be possible to maintain this religious feeling among Tibetan youths in this modern world: now that Tibetan youths are going to all parts of the world?*

A. That depends on one's knowledge. If some one has a deep knowledge about Buddhism, I think it will be difficult to lose it. But if one's knowledge is superficial then it will be easier to lose it. With superficial knowledge one can't realise the value. If there is no value, then there is no need to keep it.

Q. *Tibet has some institutions, some personalities who are very peculiar: the man who predicts the weather, the astrologer, the oracle and probably many others. Do you think these institutions can be, and should be maintained in the future modern Tibet? Will they be able to play some role in the state politics or state decisions?*

A. That I don't know. But these mysterious experiences are there and will remain, although what involvement they will have in the Government I can't say.

Q. *They have played important role in giving advice about some particular situations. In the future ....*

A. Yes. For instance, the State Oracles, these deities have special relationship with the Dalai Lama as an individual. The Dalai Lama is serving in the Government, so in that way there is some involvement.

Q. *India, despite having helped the Tibetans very much, does not officially recognise the existence of a Tibetan Government-in-Exile, nor does any other country in the world. But at the same time all countries agree that Your Holiness is spiritual and temporal leader of the Tibetans. What is the reason for the world in recognising you and not recognising the Tibetan Government or Tibet when it is so evident historically? What interpretation do you give to this absurd fact?*

A. That is modern politics. Power politics. The independence of Tibet is something true, but we are weak while the liar is quite powerful. So that is politics.

7

MACLEAN'S[6]

Q. *Do you feel any progress is being made in your negotiations with the Peking government?*

A. In some aspects there has been progress. For example, our sense of communication has improved. On the other hand. concrete progress has proved to be elusive. In the present age, when most countries are decolonizing, China persists in her policy of colonization of Tibet.

Q. *Why do you continue to demand nothing less than total independence for Tibet?*

A. The main problem is that there is not much respect for truth on the Chinese side. For many years they have simply respected the power of violence and intimidation. But we hope their attitude will improve. We hope that they will realistically consider their colonial attitudes. By taking over Tibet they have opened up a large land border touching on several countries with whom they traditionally do not have friendly relations. This has created numerous security problems for everyone concerned, problems that cost China millions of dollars. For many centuries Tibet has served as a buffer zone. We feel that it is in everyone's interest, not least of all China's, for it to regain this status.

Q. *But after nearly three decades, have Tibetans tired of opposing the Chinese?*

A. What is striking here is that the most nationalistic (among them) are those youths who were taken away for education in China. While in China they were given the official party line, but when they returned to Tibet they saw the difference between Communist ideology and the

[6] *McLean's* correspondent Glenn Mullin interviewed His Holiness the Dalai Lama at Dharamsala

actual practice. This has created a deeply resented disillusionment and a renewed determination for Tibetan independence. On the other hand, many of them seem to have psychological problems resulting from the Chinese oppression. Alcoholism has become widespread.

Q. *What do you think of recent Chinese policy changes towards Tibet, including opening it to foreign tourists and encouraging economic reforms?*

A. The bulk of the benefits are earmarked for the Chinese. But there are side benefits for the Tibetans, mostly of a political nature. The opening of Tibet to foreign travel does help in increasing outside awareness of the situation there. Everyone can now see the nature of Chinese colonial rule in Tibet.

Q. *How do you evaluate Chinese claims that they are allowing greater freedom of religious expression?*

A. This is being done only on a superficial level. They have permitted the Tibetans to open a few monasteries and temples, but only as showcases for tourists. A handful of new Tibetan youths are permitted to enter these monasteries, but even then the study period allowed to them is far too inadequate to allow for real learning. This makes a problem for Buddhism, which relies heavily upon study and learning for the transmission of spiritual knowledge.

Q. *How do you feel about Peking's policy of relocating ethnic Chinese to Tibet?*

A. The number of 'imported' Chinese is alarming. Much of the fertile land has been taken over by Chinese immigrants, while the native Tibetans are being pushed back into remote, desolate places. The Tibetans have become a minority in their own land. If this policy is allowed to continue, Tibet will no longer be a Tibetan area. It will be another land populated by Han Chinese and dominated by Han culture. Already, the Chinese have cut down and carried away most of our forests and have destroyed much of our natural wildlife.

Q. *In recent decades interest in Buddhism has spread throughout the West. How do you react to this?*

A. Buddhism is very sophisticated philosophically and strongly stresses rationality. In this sense it is very modern in its sensitivity and outlook. There is a basis here for co-operation and dialogue with Western sciences. Every religion has its own character and atmosphere. I truly respect Christianity and the contribution it has made and continues to make to world civilization. But no one religion is appropriate for all types of people. Just as Buddhism is not best for everyone, Christianity is not appropriate to all types of dispositions. For people who want to follow a path of skeptical inquiry and reason rather than a path of faith, Buddhism may prove useful.

Q. *What future do you see for Tibet?*
A. We Tibetans complain over the fact that China invaded our country and now colonizes it. But this isn't because we hate the Chinese. They provided us with a supreme test of courage. Now it is time for them to leave. They should go home and tend to the problems of their own country. This would be better for them as well as for the Tibetans. We have a right to follow our own destiny, to live according to our own culture and identity. Nobody has the right to colonize others. I feel that the Buddhist emphasis on love, compassion and patience has aided us considerably in coming through this difficult period of our history. It has helped us to maintain a sense of clarity, strength and humour. The Tibetan people can still smile and laugh. They can still look to the future with hope. We call it *sem-zangpo*, 'the good heart'. As a people, we still possess 'the good heart'. I'm very proud of my people—they have done well.

*Maclean's,*Canada: 29-9-1986

8

THE TELEGRAPH

Q. *Your Holiness, at Thursday's press conference you had expressed your willingness to mediate to solve the Sri Lanka, Gorkhaland and Punjab problems. But what about the continuing problem of the six million Tibetans, which surely is your primary concern? Does it indicate that you are getting tired and frustrated in dealing with the Tibetan problem, especially with no solution in sight?*

A. No, no certainly not. My main responsibility is towards solving the Tibetan problem. I am always, thinking on different lines, on different levels. As the Dalai Lama my main concern is Tibet and six million of the country's people. As a Buddhist monk, I have to try to be concerned with means to contribute to the welfare of all beings—even insects and animals—and particularly, humanity. Thirdly, as a human being, I always feel that today we need the realisation of oneness of all human beings. And with that you should have some kind of moral responsibility. I express this to other people and practice that myself. So this (willingness to mediate) is an effort in that direction.

Q. *What is the present state of your relations with China? In 1984, there was a marked improvement but your scheduled visit to that country the next year was cancelled. In this context, does a status quo prevail or have there been some fresh happenings?*

A. I think the situation remains the same as it was last year. There has been no improvement so far.

Q. *Have there been any fresh set backs in your relations with China?*

A. We had some problems with one of my proposed delegations to Tibet.

Q. *When did this happen?*

A. At the beginning of this year. We were planning to send a delegation to Tibet. It was supposed to be a fact-finding delegation. But then there were some problems with their travel documents. So the delegation could not go.

Q. *Has there been any subsequent proposal to send a delegation to China?*

A. No.

Q. *Have you spelt out the basic requirements for a settlement with China?*

A. At this moment it is very difficult to say. This is also not the proper time (for the settlement). Tibet, you know, is occupied by the Chinese. So the Chinese policy regarding Tibet will depend on the internal situation of China. Although Deng Xiao Ping[7] is carefully preparing for a smooth transition, you never know what will happen.

Q. *Do you mean to say that the political situation in China is very uncertain?*

A. Yes. Some of my friends share the same view. Some of them say there is every danger of a military takeover in China. The situation in China is also very chaotic, they say. Another school of opinion says that things will now improve. So there are different kinds of views on the Chinese situation. It is quite safe to say that things are not settled in that country. Therefore as far as the Tibetan problem is concerned, this is not the proper time to take a decision. We want to continue a dialogue with the Chinese government. We also want their government to do that. This is good. In the last few years, we have sent a number of fact-finding delegations to China.

Meanwhile, inside Tibet, there have been improvements in certain fields. The economic condition is improving and also the general education of the people. There is also some kind of respect for and a recognition of the Tibetan culture. There has been some kind of positive change.

Q. *So is China loosening its grip on Tibet?*

A. No, not that really. In China, there is more freedom of religion today. In one way the Chinese authorities are following a more moderate policy with some more freedom, but in the political field they are tightening their grip. Often, on the pretext of striking against criminals, they arrest or strike against political minded people. And one very serious thing is that China is following a policy of demographic

[7]Chinese Premier

aggression. More and more Chinese are coming to Tibet. In some parts of Tibet, the Chinese are becoming a majority and the Tibetans a minority in their land. A local Chinese newspaper said that in my birthplace in Tibet, the Tibetan population was little over seven hundred thousand, while the Chinese population with well over 2.5 million in 1982. In the autonomous region of Tibet, such a situation has not arisen so far. But, more and more Chinese are coming. This is very serious.

Q. *What do you think of the current state of the Indo-Chinese relations?*

A. This is a complicated question. Actually the demarcation of the border is not accepted by the Chinese. If you look at the long history of the Chinese civilisation you will see that, they always expand. So, the problem of Tibet is also connected with Sino-Indian relations. So unless Tibet becomes a land of peace, India will have some problems.

Q. *But the Indian government does not recognise Tibet as a separate country. At the same time you have your Government-in-Exile at Dharamsala in Himachal Pradesh. Do you not feel that there is an inherent contradiction in India's stand on Tibet?*

A. There are Indian politicians and intellectuals who believe that this is a wrong policy. I also feel that this policy is not correct. But at the same time, the government has to be realistic. So in the Indian political atmosphere, there is very little value of truth and justice. Influence of power is very strong.

Q. *Coming back to the political situation in India, how do you view the Punjab problem?*

A. The problem can be analysed in two ways. Some people are politically motivated. This motivation is very difficult to resolve through reason or dialogue.

Q. *The crisis in Punjab is again connected strongly with religion?*

A. I am coming to that. One category of people are using religion and trying to discriminate between Sikhs and Hindus. Through patience and understanding, it can be solved. I see my role as a neutral mediator in solving the problem.

Q. *Did you send feelers to the Centre expressing your desire to mediate in Punjab?*

A. On a few occasions I mentioned this to some concerned people in the Central government. They are prominent people.

Q. *You have shown a keen interest in the possibility of synthesising Marxism with Buddhism. How do you intend to go about this?*

A. I have had an interest in Marxism for many years now ..... There is a kind of internationalism in Marxist theory. All the working class people of the world have the same status, according to this theory. There is a feeling of solidarity among the workers.

Q. *Do you think that an ideology combining the tenets of Marxism and Buddhism would be feasible?*

A. Yes, I have that kind of a feeling. The Marxists have their plus and minus points. They endured a great deal of suffering for the benefit of the people. Their energies come through hatred as I said earlier. (The Dalai Lama told newsmen on Thursday that the Marxian philosophy had an element of 'hatred' as it was concerned with class struggle and elimination of class enemies). Their love or kindness is not adequate. The Chinese mental training is not sufficient. Eventually, this brings about self ruin. Like Chairman Mao. He was not like Rajendra Prasad or Mahatma Gandhi. They had a kind of spiritual stand apart from their political views. So, in spite of getting power, they remained good human beings. They were well balanced.

Today many socialist countries have achieved their good goals. But they are worried, they may lose their goals eventually. There should be balance and self discipline. I feel in some countries Buddhism and Marxism can be complementary.

The Telegraph, 23-11-1986

9

SUNDAY

Q. *Your Holiness do you approve of continuing violence in an essentially Buddhist country, Sri Lanka?*

A. I must admit, this is very unfortunate. But then history is replete with instances of human beings, due to their weaknesses, using religion for purposes other than those it is meant to be. So often religion by its misuse becomes another instrument to divide human beings and bring problems or sufferings to them. That is what is now happening in Sri Lanka. It is a rather unfortunate thing.

Q. *Is there any justification for this kind of violence?*

A. No, absolutely not.

Q. *As a practising Buddhist and a foremost leader of the Buddhist religion don't you ever feel that you have some role in defusing the tension and prevent insensate killings that are going on in Sri Lanka?*

A. Yes, I very much want them to stop. I have already made quite a few attempts from behind the scenes. I am eager and willing to offer my good offices and make any contribution that can ease the situation there.

Q. *Can you be a little more specific in this regard? For instance, what has been the nature of your behind-the-scene attempts? Did you send any message or messages to India or Sri Lanka expressing your distress over the situation? Did you contact Buddhist preachers in Sri Lanka?*

A. Well, on two occasions I have made public statements recording my distress. I have also asked my friends and acquaintances in Sri Lanka to keep me informed about the situation there and if in any way I can be of use.

Q. *What are their reports like?*

A. It is a very difficult and complicated situation. And as a Tibetan refugee living in exile, sometimes it is difficult for Tibetans even to go to Sri Lanka for a first-hand understanding of the situation.

Q. *Why is it so? Your Holiness can certainly visit Sri Lanka?*

A. I don't know.

Q. *But given the opportunity would you go to Sri Lanka?*

A. Sometime back I did want to visit Sri Lanka but the Sri Lanka government has postponed it indefinitely.

Q. *Does it mean that they do not want to give a visa to you?*

A. I don't think so. I presume, they have some difficulties.

Q. *We have been hearing for quite some time that you would like to visit Tibet. Will you be going to Tibet soon?*

A. It was in early 1983 that I thought of going to Tibet to find out what my people want me to do. Since then the situation has deteriorated and unless the situation improves I do not plan to go to Tibet now. Things are certainly better in Tibet today than they were before 1979. The Tibetans do not starve any more. They can now have better education. There is also certain amount of freedom regarding religious practices. Even then I think a visit to Tibet at this time will not serve any useful purpose.

Q. *Why do you think so?*

A. Unfortunately, Tibet is under Chinese occupation. So, whatever happens in China has inevitable repercussions on Tibet. I feel that the situation in China is not as stable as it appears. Some of my friends who have a good knowledge of Chinese affairs even tell me that the situation there is so uncertain that I should not be surprised if the army takes over power. The radical supporters of the 'Gang of Four', I am told, are yet to be subdued completely. In such a fluid situation, even if I strike a deal with the present Chinese government, there is no guarantee that the next government will honour it. That is why, I say, no useful purpose will be served by my going to Tibet. I am not in a hurry to take a decision. May be, after a few years when things are clearer I will decide what to do.

Q. *Are you under any pressure from the government of India to return now that India and China are trying to be friends again?*

A. No, I am not under any pressure from the Indian government.

Q. *To what extent, did your presence in India lead to the Sino-Indian border war in 1962?*

A. I do not think it was the major cause. Even if I had not come to India, the border clash would have taken place. Because, China never accepted the demarcation agreed upon by the Tibetan government and India regarding Tibet's common border with India.

Q. *Do you then think that India has harmed her own interests by accepting China's sovereign rights to Tibet?*

A. I think, India did not do the correct thing. Here, I would like to point out that Tibet is very much related to India's northern border and its security. Before the Chinese came to Tibet its border with India was among the safest in the world. There was not a single Indian soldier on the border as there was no threat to India's security from Tibet. Now you have to keep thousands of soldiers to secure the border.

Q. *You are strongly incensed by, what you call, the Chinese occupation of Tibet. What do you have to say about the Russian troops moving into Afghanistan or the Vietnamese to Kampuchea?*

A. Very unfortunate. But the situation is different from what it is in Tibet. Both in Afghanistan and Kampuchea at least a section of the people of those countries invited external forces. But in Tibet, not a single Tibetan, even today wants the Chinese to be there.

Q. *At one time the USA was the foremost advocate of your cause. What is the US attitude towards the Tibet question now?*

A. Before replying to this question, I want to make it clear that the American people still sympathise with us. The American administration, however, is not as sympathetic as we would like it to be. We are only six million people and the Chinese, over 1000 million. Obviously, the American administration is following a practical policy, a policy which gives them immediate benefits. But the Tibetans are certainly hurt.

Q. *Do you feel that you have been let down by the USA?*

A. Yes, to a certain extent. In the early Sixties and late Fifties, the Americans were deeply involved in Tibet. That was also not a good thing.

Q. *Could you please elaborate?*

A. Yes, the CIA was involved in Tibetan guerrilla insurgency in Tibet. I came to know of it much later. Another thing I want to make clear: neither the CIA nor any outsider had anything to do either in the Tibetan uprising or my subsequent escape to India. I say this because many people say that my escape was planned by the CIA.

Q. *What are the chances of Tibet becoming an independent country?*

A. We are always optimistic and we know for sure dharma will prevail in the end.

Q. *Tibet has been opened up to the foreign visitors. What do you think of it?*

A. I welcome this. The world can now know more about Tibet and of the conditions there. The Chinese say that Buddhism has no place in the modern world. It is something foolish, a superstition. But visitors will find that Buddhism still survives even in a communist society and despite many barriers set up against it.

Q. *While living in exile what do you miss most?*

A. For one, the climate. The climate in Lhasa is much more congenial than what you have in Dharamsala. In summer, Dharamsala is too hot, in winter too cold and in monsoon too much rain. The climate in Lhasa is temperate.

Q. *What else?*

A. The milk that we got from *djomo*, which is cross between the Yak and the cow. It's so delicious. And, of course, the *tsampa*, a kind of barley wheat. We get some of these from Ladakh and other places but they are much inferior. Not first class. But then here we get plenty of fruits. When in Tibet we used to get fruits from India and it took between two to three weeks for those fruits to reach Tibet via Kalimpong, Gangtok and the Nathu La pass.

Q. *Will there be another Dalai Lama after you?*

A. That depends on the circumstances. But I believe in reincarnations and in my daily prayers I recite a verse from an Indian reincarnation of the Bodhisattva which says: "As long as the sentient beings remain, I will remain in order to serve them." So, whether my successor is named Dalai Lama or not the institution will certainly survive.

Q. *If communist rule benefits your people would you embrace Marxism?*

A. I don't think there is any conflict between Marxism and my kind of Buddhism, Mahayana Buddhism. In fact, for quite some years, I have been deeply engaged in trying to secure a synthesis between Marxism and Buddhism. Buddhism can lend spiritual content to materialistic Marxism and is hence the best spiritual ideology for a socialist society.

Sunday, 7/13-12-1986

IV

Human Rights and Universal Responsibility

Chapter IV
HUMAN RIGHTS AND UNIVERSAL RESPONSIBILITY

My suggestion or advice is very simple, that is: to have a sincere heart. I believe that this is something basic and that anyone can approach any problem in this way, irrespective of the ideology he may belong to or even if he is an unbeliever. Real, true brotherhood, a good heart towards one's fellow men, this is the basic thing. I believe that if you have a true feeling of brotherhood whether you are a scientist, an economist, or a politician, whatever profession you may follow, you will always have this concern for your fellow beings. I also believe that if you have this concern for others then whatever the effects that might result from the profession you follow, you will always be concerned as to whether it is going to benefit or harm your fellow beings. I personally feel that this concern for others is lacking today. Many people emphasise on thinking only of themselves and have a selfish motive. I feel that basically the cause of many problems is due to this lack of concern for others and that if we really develop this kind of a sincere feeling and a sense of universal responsibility, many of the problems we face today like pollution, the energy crisis and the population crisis, can be solved. If we have such a sincere feeling we need not worry about the self-sufficiency of the world. What I am referring to is that today in certain parts of the world we have poverty and starvation and in other parts of the world abundance of wealth. This is an example. So if you have a genuine concern for others, I feel all this suffering is needless and avoidable, because the world has sufficient resources to overcome these problems. The main thing is whether you have the real sense of universal responsibility. Basically then the most important thing is a heart.

—Dalai Lama

1

UNIVERSAL RESPONSIBILITY AND THE GOOD HEART

When I first landed in the West, I noticed rather superficially a number of things which seem to differentiate the West from the East, and particularly from my own country, Tibet. It was, however, easy enough to understand these superficial differences in terms of the different cultural, historical and geographical backgrounds which have shaped a particular way of life and behaviour pattern. But in my mind I always feel that you are a human being, just as I am and that we are all basically the same: we are all human beings. The differences are really minor; the essential thing is that we are all human beings and in that respect we are all the same. I want happiness but not suffering, just as you do. And just as I have a right to achieve happiness, you too have an equal right.

Therefore, there is no fundamental difference between the East and the West or between you and me. Such differences as seem to exist are superficial and superimposed in many ways which cannot and should not separate man from man. Whenever I meet "foreigners", I feel there is no barrier between us; to me such meetings are man-to-man relationships, heart-to-heart contacts.

The need for a man-to-man relationship is becoming increasingly urgent. Today the world is becoming smaller and smaller, more and more interdependent. We all depend very much on each other. In ancient times problems were mostly family-size and were therefore tackled at family level, but now the situation is no longer the same. Today we have become so interdependent and so closely connected with each other that without a sense of universal responsibility our very existence or survival would be difficult. For example, one nation's problems can no longer be solved by itself entirely or satisfactorily, because much depends on the attitude and cooperation of other nations. Therefore I believe that for human happiness, human action based on concern for others is necessary. Throughout the ages a number of teachers belonging to different faiths have tried to teach the same kind of idea and I think that today we need it perhaps more than ever before.

Unless we have a sense of universal responsibility, the feeling for other people's suffering just as we would feel our own suffering, in other words a good heart, it is difficult to achieve human happiness and world peace. I feel a natural heart-to-heart human relationship, transcending all artificial barriers like colour and creed, can solve many of the problems that plague us today. In this way we can know each other's way of thinking and achieve a better understanding, a real understanding, unfettered by inhuman considerations.

If we are able to develop a better understanding among ourselves, then on the basis of that understanding we can share and try to overcome the suffering of others and achieve happiness for others. Happiness for yourself comes automatically as a result of this concern for others. I feel the few should be willing to sacrifice for the many. Let us compare ourselves, you and I: you are clearly in the majority while I am a single individual. Therefore I consider you (audience) are much more important than myself, because you are in the majority.

Compassion for others (as opposed to self) is one of the central teachings of Mahayana Buddhism. In this connection I would like to quote a verse which conveys the message:

If you are unable to exchange your happiness
For the suffering of other beings,
You have no hope of attaining Buddhahood,
Nor even of happiness in this present life.

This means that if you are able to do the opposite of what the verse says, you will not only be able to achieve the ultimate goal, Buddhahood, but you will also be able to overcome your everyday problems and attain peace of mind through this practise. The essence of the Mahayana School, which we try to practise, is compassion. In Mahayana Buddhism you sacrifice yourself in order to attain salvation for the sake of other beings.

Avalokitesvara is conceived as the 'Lord of Mercy' but the real Avalokitesvara is compassion itself. In other words, Avalokitesvara symbolises an ideal quality most valued by the Tibetans. It is this quality which we must strive to cultivate in ourselves from a limited quantum to the limitless. This indiscriminating, unmotivated and unlimited compassion for all is obviously not the usual love that you have for your friends, relatives or family. The love which is limited to your near and dear ones is alloyed with ignorance, with attachment. The kind of love we advocate is the love you can have even for someone who has done harm to you. This kind of love is to be extended to all living beings and it can be extended to all living beings.

The development of a kind heart, or feeling of closeness for all human beings, does not involve any kind of the religiosity we normally associate with it. It is not just for people who believe in religion; it is for everyone, irrespective of race, religion or of any political affiliation. It is for anybody who considers himself first and foremost a member of the human family and who sees things in larger terms. In any case, are we not brought up in love by our parents right from the time of our birth? Do we not agree that love plays an important part in human life? It consoles when one is helpless and distressed, and it consoles when one is old and lonely. It is a dynamic force that we should develop and use, but often tend to neglect, particularly in our prime years when we experience a false sense of security. The rationale for loving others is the recognition of the simple fact that every living being has the same right to have the same desire for happiness and to avoid suffering, and the consideration that you as one individual are one life-unit as compared with the multitude of others in their ceaseless quest for happiness.

Viewed thus, individual happiness ceases to be a conscious self-seeking effort; it automatically becomes a by-product, but by no means inferior in quality or quantity, of the whole process of loving and serving others. According to the Mahayana School of Buddhism you must not only think in terms of human beings in this regard but of all sentient beings. And ultimately all sentient beings have the potentiality of attaining Buddha-hood.

Therefore, taking into account the three points we have been discussing, namely, the desire, the right and the possibility of achieving happiness and avoiding suffering, and always keeping in mind one's relative insignificance in relation to others, we can conclude that it is worthwhile to sacrifice one's own benefit for the benefit of others. When you are trained in this kind of outlook, a true sense of compassion, a true sense of love and respect for others becomes possible and in due course a reality.

An enlightened outlook is not moralistic or religious in the conventional sense; it is not only good for those to whom such an approach is compassionately applied, but is beneficial to the individual himself as well. Our everyday experience confirms that a self-centred approach to problems can be destructive not only to society but to the individual himself. It does not solve problems, it multiplies them. For instance, when you encounter some problems, if you point your finger at yourself and not at others, this gives control over yourself and calmness in a situation where otherwise self-control becomes problematic. If, on the other hand, when something bad happens you point at others and blame them, then your anger, hatred or jealousy, all these bad thoughts increase, and as a result you no longer feel happy. For example, when you are agitated you will not even have proper sleep, so you will ultimately suffer. For others also, when you develop or increase bad thoughts and feelings, your neighbours and friends will also feel disturbed. Instead, do just the opposite; put the blame on yourself for all the bad things, respect others and love others. If you do this it leaves others as well as yourself at peace. This is the essence of Mahayana Buddhism.

I shall illustrate what I have been trying to say by quoting some verses. The fist verse says:

I consider all living beings
More precious than 'wish-fulfilling gems'—
A motivation to achieve the greatest goal:
So may I at all times care for them all.

The second verse is also extremely beneficial in our daily life:

May I consider anyone I come to associate with
Always more virtuous than myself.

Therefore, even if someone harms or hurts you badly, you should think of his good qualities and thus develop humility towards others.

The most important verse is the one which follows:

If one whom I've helped my best
And from whom I've expected much—
Harms me in a way I can't imagine:
May I regard such a person my best teacher!

This person is your greatest teacher for, when you are in a good mood and when your close friends are not criticising you, there is nothing to make you aware of the bad qualities you have. But when a person criticises you and exposes your faults, only then are you able to discover your faults and make amends. So your enemy is your greatest friend because he is the person who gives you the test you need for your inner strength, your tolerance and your respect for others. He is therefore a true teacher from this point of view. Instead of feeling angry with or hatred towards such a person, one should respect him and be grateful to him.

Although I have drawn examples from the Mahayana School of Buddhism, the aim of developing true friendship, brotherhood, love and respect for others is something which in essence is found in all religions. Religions contribute towards achieving peace of mind and serenity, but it is not necessary for a person to be a follower of a particular religion in order to achieve it. He could employ Buddhist techniques of achieving peace of mind by cultivating certain qualities without becoming a Buddhist. It seems to me that these inner qualities are really human qualities. If you have these—compassion, love and respect for others, honesty and humility—then you can call yourself a real human being. Anger, attachment, hatred, jealousy and pride, all these bad qualities are our common enemies. If we want to be really good human beings we must cultivate the good qualities and then we will have less trouble, less problems.

Today we face a number of problems. Some are natural calamities, which we must accept and face as best as we can. But some others are man-made problems created by our own misbehaviour, bad thoughts, which can be avoided. One such problem arises from ideological or even religious conflicts when men fight each other for means or methods, losing sight of human ends or goals. All different faiths and different systems are only methods to achieve a goal which for the average person is happiness in this life. Therefore at no time should we place means above ends: the supremacy of man over matter and all that it entails must be maintained at all times. The different ideologies, systems and religions of the world are meant for mankind to achieve human happiness.

I have learnt a great deal from other peoples during my tour. Tibet was materially backward in the sense that Tibetans in the past never enjoyed the comfort and luxury you have as a result of scientific discoveries and technological advancement. But, spiritually, Tibet was very rich. Apart from Buddhism which took deep roots in the country, many great ancient sciences, arts and ideas from her neighbouring countries found their way into Tibet, which gradually became a melting pot of great Asian civilisations. Before this tour, we took, Tibet's spiritual greatness for granted and almost ignored our material backwardness.

What amazed me during my tour is that many of you in the West seem to be very much worried about the material progress that you have made. I have heard a great deal of complaint against the material progress that has been made and yet paradoxically it has been the very pride of the Western world. I see nothing wrong with material progress provided man takes precedence over progress. In fact it has been my firm belief that in order to solve human problems in all their dimensions we must be able to combine and harmonise external material progress with inner mental development.

In my opinion material progress is certainly highly necessary and is a good thing, as it is of benefit to mankind. What is essential and would be more beneficial is that we should be able to balance material progress with mental development. But the various talks that I have had during the last few days with people from different walks of life, I am convinced that man must be placed above materialism, and that we must realise the true value of human beings. Materialism should serve man and not man serve material progress. And as long as we keep our goals and methods in their proper perspective, material progress will continue to benefit mankind.

I have liked science and technology since my childhood and I realise now more than ever before that material progress is highly necessary to mankind but at the same time I believe material things provide us mainly with physical comfort, not with mental peace. As I have already mentioned, good human qualities—honesty, sincerity, a good heart—cannot be bought with money, nor can they be produced by machines, but only by the mind itself. We can call this the inner light or God's blessing or human quality. This is the essence of mankind.

To this human end different religions have a very important role to play. Despite different conceptions of the universe, life after death, etc., all religions are essentially the same in their goal of developing a good human heart so that we may become better human beings. Of course, if you are out to find differences among religions, you will find plenty. This is only obvious. But the essence of religion is the development of a good heart, a true sense of brotherhood, love and respect for others.

Those of you who have taken an interest in Buddhism or have even become Buddhist, have done so because you have found it suitable to you, it is not good to change one's religion for the sake of it or because of one's dislike for some other religion. Religion is at best a tool to help you to train your mind in some desirable direction. Religion exists in order that you may practice something that will help you to control your mind;

the aim is to transform the bad self-destructive thoughts like anger, avarice, pride, jealousy, hatred—into their direct opposites. On recognising the destructive nature of bad thoughts, you practice religion in order to overcome them and in Mahayana Buddhism you do so not for yourself only but for the sake of all other beings.

In religion there are no national or man-made boundaries. Religion can and should be used by any people or person who find it beneficial. What is important for each seeker is to choose the religion which is most suitable to himself. However, I believe that the embracing of a particular religion like Buddhism does not mean the rejection of another religion or one's own community. In fact it is important that those of you who have embraced Buddhism should not cut yourself off from your own society; you should continue to live within your own community and with its members. This is not only for your sake but for others also, because by rejecting your community you obviously cannot benefit others, which actually is the basic aim of religion.

In Tibet there used to be a few Tibetan Christians. They followed the Christian faith but remained very much Tibetan. There is a verse by an ancient Tibetan teacher which says that you must change your mind but your external behaviour should remain as it is. You should also respect other religions. As I said earlier, the essence of all religions is basically the same: to achieve a true sense of brotherhood, a good heart, respect for others. If we can develop these qualities from within our heart, then I think we can actually achieve true peace.

Above all, we must put others before us and keep others in our mind constantly: the self must be placed last. All our doings and thinking must be motivated by compassion for others. The way to acquire this kind of outlook is that we must accept the simple fact that whatever we desire is also desired by others. Every being wants happiness, not suffering. If we adopt a self-centred approach to life by which we attempt to use others for our own self-interest, we might be able to gain temporary benefit but in the long run we will not succeed in achieving even our personal happiness, and hope for next life is out of the question.

Questions and Answers

Q. *What do you aim at in your present travels around the world?*

A. To be able to meet various people, to meet thinkers of the West.

Q. *What may come out of those meetings, do you hope?*

A. I have certain ideas which I want to exchange with those people. Today we have many problems: Certain problems are mainly due to our own attitude and how we look at things, and because of this I feel that if you can change the mental attitude or outlook towards these things, much can be accomplished. In this respect it is extremely important to take into consideration right now how we are going to educate the younger generation. The present overall world situation itself is in such a condition that despite the fact that many know what is right and what is wrong, very often they are compelled by situations and circumstances to indulge in wrong actions. Similarly I had talks with His Holiness the Pope on these points.

Q. *Your Holiness, you have been in several European countries in the last few weeks. Have you detected any one or more common factors and features about the life in those countries?*

A. Most of them are very similar. In this respect my attitude towards other people is that I always feel they are human beings. From this viewpoint, wherever I go, wherever I am, I feel just the same. Now I come from the East, particularly Tibet which has been isolated for many years, but in the deeper sense there is no difference. On the surface there are many differences but these are minor ones. I always feel this, therefore among the European countries I have found less differences.

Q. *What is the impression of Your Holiness during your first trip, of the people in the Western world of, the ordinary man?*

A. The impression I have is to a large extent also influenced by my own attitude towards others. As I mentioned earlier, I always look at everyone as a human being, I don't emphasise on the differences but emphasise the similarity, as a human being. For example we are meeting here; I am looking at you as a human being, not as an extraordinary human being, or a Westerner or German or anything like that, but just as a human being. So I always feel there is no barrier if I adopt such an attitude—this is a human being just like me. This is very helpful for me personally in easily accepting any situation. Of course the West is highly developed, has a high living standard, which is very important and for life it is necessary, so material progress is very good. Now the question is to balance or combine human values and material progress. If you concentrate everything on material progress and lose all the human values, then that would be dangerous, that is not correct. Material progress itself is meant for human beings. Now if you have lost human values then it is of course wrong, but I feel there are many people who are interested in a combination of material progress and inner development.

Q. *Your Holiness, may we ask you to tell us about your impression on your trip to Europe until now?*

A. The high living standard, which is very good and very important. But at the same time other problems are also being created because of this material progress. People complain about the noise, pollution, overcrowding, less mental peace—these kinds of things. Our very life is a paradox, contradictory in many senses; whenever you have too much of one thing then you have problems created by that. You always have extremes and therefore it is very important to try and find the middle way, to balance the two.

Q. *May I raise the old Kipling question: can East and West meet? I am not thinking in a political sense, but in a spiritual one.*

A. I feel that it is possible and in fact it is necessary also, because there is a need to create a universal responsibility; this is very important. Whether Easterner or Westerner everybody is basically a human being. Superficial differences are there, but deep down we are all the same, we have the same feelings. Whatever is good and comfortable every one of us wants, whatever is uncomfortable like suffering we try to avoid and every one of us has the same right to this. On the basis of such a thinking it is possible to build the whole world into one family, a family which doesn't have internal frictions. That is the only solution, the only answer.

Q. *Would you like to say a little more about what seems to you the main human problems at the moment? What do you see as the part of the human problem with which we should be most concerned? Is it attachment to material things in the West, is it our lack of any religious sense?*

A. We are all human beings, we are all the same; everybody wants a happy life and does not want suffering and everybody has the right to try and achieve happiness and avoid suffering. But in some parts of the world you have quite high living standards and facilities and in other parts there is poverty, hunger and disease and these sorts of things. Now if you accept that these are all the same human beings with the same equal rights, it is a sad thing, the situation is quite unfortunate. Secondly, today in the society of human beings everybody is talking about peace and justice but when we are facing certain problems it is difficult to put these concepts into practice because of the overall circumstances or pressures. So, in the society of human beings if there is no justice, no truth, if everything is done through money or power, then it would be extremely unfortunate, very sad.

Q. *Materialism is a philosophy which sees material things as all-important. How can we help people who do not believe in spiritual things to develop spiritual values?*

A. The best is to set a good example yourself.

Q. *You believe that both material and mental progress are good and can exist side by side. How does Your Holiness think the two of them, often contradictory, can develop at the same time and in harmony—the mental and the material progress?*

A. This is my aim; in fact, the object of my visit to Europe is also mainly based on this. It is quite obvious that without material progress we will lack many comforts, so we must have material progress. At the same time without inner peace material things alone are not sufficient. There are many signs which indicate that material progress alone is not sufficient for man, that there is something lacking. Therefore the only way is to combine these two. As to how it should be combined, here again I think it is very complicated and many factors will have to be taken into consideration. I firmly believe that if we take a liberal outlook, a broad outlook, and if you plan properly, this combination can be achieved not only by a few individuals or a few nations, but worldwide. Of course it is very difficult.

Q. *You have particularly spoken about the universal feeling that should be created among men. How does Your Holiness feel that this universal feeling can be achieved and in what way can religion, for example Buddhism, contribute to this universal feeling?*

A. I am fully convinced that there is a great need for this development of universal responsibility. I also feel there are many ways and methods of trying to develop this kind of a feeling and as yet I am still trying to find which method would be the most suitable. My impressions are: I feel that one way is by developing a liberal outlook and having a wider perspective; like for example when you are faced with a problem, by looking at it not from a close distance but from a wider perspective. If you are able to do this then you are able to have better foresight. I feel that today we are trying to solve many problems temporarily, we don't investigate the real cause of the problems, for example it is like treating a sore by just trying to cure it without investigating what the basic cause of the sore is.

Another way, which I basically think is the most important, is this feeling for others, a feeling of closeness, trying to share the suffering of others. In my opinion these are the two ways of achieving this universal responsibility. But the most important responsibility lies on the younger generation; in the educational system where there is bad influence it should be avoided as far as possible. For example when you see too much violence on television or other mass media, I feel that it has a great influence on the person.

Q. *But how can the individual develop this feeling of universal respon-sibility?*

A. We have to emphasise the importance of this and also try to put it into practice. Even today we have individuals as well as organisations who stress the importance of these points and I feel these need more emphasis; it is necessary to expand the influence of these organisa-tions. But it is very difficult and it also takes time. That is why I place more hope on future generations rather than on the present. The present generation is living in this world under great pressure, under a very complicated system, amidst confusion. Everybody talks and speaks about peace, justice, equality but it is very difficult to put it into practice. This is not because the individual person is bad but because the overall environment, the pressure, the circumstances are so strong and overwhelming, I have a feeling that the younger generation has a very heavy responsibility to achieve something in this direction.

Q. *Where does religion enter in this context? Is it possible to develop this feeling of universal responsibility without religion?*

A. Yes.

Q. *Would you say that religion should be the servant of man rather than man the servant of religion?*

A. Yes. Religion does help to develop the right attitude of mind, it is important.

Q. *What basic values should this universal responsibility be based on? What is right and what is wrong?*

A. I feel the basis is that every one of us does not want suffering and every one of us wants something comfortable or a happy life. There is a verse which says that just as your physical body would not like the slightest pain, so you have to realise that the other being also has a similar feeling. For example, when you talk about rights, like the human rights, the question is what do these rights finally boil down to. Ultimately it boils down to the feeling of "I" and on the basis of that feeling you want happiness and bliss and you do not want suffering. And just as you have these desires, your fellow-being has similar desires; therefore if you have a right, it is not correct to say that others do not have that right. On the basis of these rights that you have and the rights that others have, if you believe these are similar, then others too have those rights. Now if you compare which is the more important, you are just one single person whereas the others are limitless. There are thousands of millions of people, therefore, the others are much more important, because you are just one individual. I feel that this way of thinking is a democratic way of religion.

Q. *Would His Holiness please tell us how it is practical to observe and practise this love of humanity in a world such as ours today?*

A. This is really a difficult point, yet we have no alternative but to make an attempt towards solving this. In order to do so I think there are many ways, many methods of doing this. It is my hope that some special study or research on this point could be carried out in order to make a thorough investigation of this important matter. I am not saying this in connection with religion but in connection with human happiness. To put it in other words, it is a question of the survival of mankind and it would be difficult to explain in detail how it should be done because it would be very lengthy explanation.

Q. *Does Your Holiness think that the very special kind of Buddhism practised in Tibet in its original form could benefit European people?*

A. Yes, for some people it would be of benefit, because for religion there is no national boundary. Even among Tibetans we have Christians as well as Muslims. We are all the same. What is important is which faith or religion is more suitable to you.

Q. *Does the Dalai Lama think that the values of Buddhism in Tibet will spread or be useful in the Western countries?*

A. Perhaps there are some things that can be picked out from it. In any case religion is something for all men, it is a common property, there are no man-made boundaries for that. It should be used for any people or for any person for whom it may be found beneficial. I believe that each religion has its own qualities, its own values. Also for these past many centuries the various different kinds of religions have benefited, in their own way, the many different kinds of peace on this earth.

Q. *In your opinion what is the essence of religion?*

A. Compassion.

Q. *Would His Holiness like to say more about this purpose of religion, as he understands it?*

A. I feel that the purpose of religion is basically to attain peace and happiness for mankind. Christians say love for God, love for neighbour, love for fellow beings. This is my personal interpretation of Christianity. And just as you have love for God, love for your neighbours, so the purpose of having love for God is to be able to make yourself close to God. If you are close to God you have a motive to listen to His voice, and His voice or teaching is that we should love one another. Basically the most important thing is this love for others. In Buddhism also every emphasis is on love for others.

Q. *We started with responsibility and spirituality; now we are on to love God and love your brother. What we are looking for is the moment when spirituality and responsibility become the same thing and when the love of God and the brother become the same experience. Can you help us to see how that is so?*

A. Among all those who accept religion, each follower has his own sort of system, his own method in order to achieve that goal. I want to stress that it is not necessary for everyone to follow one path, nor is there only one way. Without faith, without belief, I am quite sure we can achieve this.

Q. *Without faith?*

A. Yes.

Q. *Each person holds certain beliefs which he thinks are true and these are different from the beliefs held by other people, they are disagreeing. Can they all be right?*

A. You cannot say that there is only one religion and that one religion is the best, or that a particular religion is the best. Now for example I am a Buddhist but I cannot say Buddhism is the best, although for me Buddhism is the best. Generally we cannot say Buddhism is the best. For certain people Christianity is much more important than Buddhism, so for them Christianity is best.

Q. *Can you tell us something about the influence of modernization in Western countries on your religion?*

A. I feel that there should be no contradiction. I think the essence of Buddhism is kindness, compassion. This is the essence of every religion, but particularly in Mahayana Buddhism, I think this is very important and everybody can practise it without deeper faith. Simply you are a human being; everybody appreciates kindness. In fact when we grow up, we grow up in the kindness of our parents and without that sort of kindness we cannot exist. This is very clear because today you find that children who are not brought up with the loving care of their parents, or where there is a disruption in the family, are later on psychologically affected. For a human being kindness, a warm heart, is very important. I always feel this is a very precious thing because you cannot buy this kindness or warmth of heart with money. In Europe there are very good shops but there's no shop which sells kindness; you must build it within. You can transplant heart but you cannot transplant a warm heart. May be in the future some scientists might be able to transplant certain cells of the heart, which ensure kindness or something like that, it would be excellent.

Q. *Could you give a description of the character of the good person, the good man which we should all be like?*

A. I think it is generally a person with a good heart, or say, kindness. If you have this basic quality of kindness or good heart, then all other things, education, ability will go in the right direction. If you have a bad heart, then knowledge or ability are used in the wrong direction; instead of helping others it creates more trouble.

Q. *You spoke of the importance of the good heart. Do you think all men have inherently the potential for a good heart, or that some may not possess it?*

A. Every man has the basis of goodness. Not only human beings, you can find it among animals or insects, for instance when we treat a dog or horse lovingly.

Q. *We would all feel, I expect, that one of the roles of religion as such is to protect the good heart from being spoilt by that which will make it evil.*

A. Yes, if you take religion in the right way. If you use religion the wrong way, then there is a holy war, or something like that may happen in the name of religion; but it only creates more hatred. That is using religion in the wrong way.

Q. *Why then does everyone not have a good heart now? What is that makes people bad?*

A. There are more chances of developing the bad qualities, if one were to accept the theory of rebirth, then there are many reasons in the past and previous lives. If you consider the present situation, may be to a large extent environment would also play an important part. If the feeling or attitude of most of your neighbours is just a competitive and selfish motive, or some such consideration, then you will always feel isolated and also that there is no one you can trust. This is very bad. Ultimately compassion and respect for others diminish, because you may be put in a position where you find there is no alternative but to defend yourself; then one naturally holds a selfish motive.

Q. *Are there not some things so evil that you should hate them?*

A. Your own bad thoughts. The real enemy is not outside but inside. Now here, you see, it is necessary to make a distinction between external enemies and internal ones. External enemies are not permanent: if you respect him the enemy will become your friend. But there is one enemy who is always an enemy, with whom you should never compromise, that is the enemy inside your heart. You cannot change all these bad thoughts into your friend, but you have to confront and control them.

Q. *Your Holiness wrote in your book "My Land and My people" about unity of religions. Practically spoken, how or by what means could this unity ever be achieved?*

A. As I explained before, just as each religion has its own respective philosophy and there are similarities as well as differences among the various religions, so we must go according to what is suitable to each individual. Just as in the world you have many different kinds of food—for example on my present tour of the ten European countries I have had quite a variety—so there are many different kinds of dishes. You cannot tell all the people that they must take one particular kind of food. What is important is what is suitable for a particular person. For example in the different food habits of different people we don't have any disputes, because each one takes what is suitable for him. Similarly religion is a food for the mind and as we all have different tastes we must take that which is most suitable for us. The important thing is that we must have peace of mind. Just as in Buddhism we have love of all beings, love for others, similarly in Christianity you have love for God, love for your fellow beings. In these the emphasis is similar, so the important thing is these similarities. As I said earlier, if we look from a wider perspective, I feel there are no problems, we can go together. It is impossible to have one religion and it would even be needless and unnecessary. In fact if this would happen it would be a great loss, because each respective religion has its own qualities and merits all of which would be lost.

Q. *Is there not a resemblance between the two religions (Christianity and Buddhism)?*

A. Yes, I agree with you; this is very true. If you look at different religions as an instrument to develop a good heart, love for others, respect for others, a true sense of brotherhood, in this respect all religions are the same, because basically in all religions the purpose is to make man a better human being. All these different complicated philosophies were not meant to make man more confused, they were meant to help man transform himself into a better human being. Therefore the most important thing is to look at the purpose of religion, the main aim, not at the secondary things that are involved, and if we go in the right direction of looking at the main aim, then all religions can go together.

What I was most interested in discussing is that all the major religions of the world can contribute towards the peace of mankind, can act for the benefit of mankind, and what I wanted to know or discuss was how these different religions can best be used so that this goal can be achieved. In this 20th century we must make proper use of religion, but how to use it in the best way, the most effective way? We will have to leave aside the different philosophies because that is the business of each religion. It would be impossible to have one religion, one philosophy, it is foolish. In fact we would be destroying many of the good characteristics of each respective religion.

Q. *Is there any connection between peace of mind and world peace?*

A. Oh certainly. Without proper mental peace it is difficult to achieve proper world peace; therefore there is a connection. Many of the problems that we face today are because of our hatred. As human beings we have good qualities as well as bad ones. Now anger, attachment, jealousy, hatred are the bad traits; these are the real enemies. From a certain point of view our real enemy, the true troublemaker, is inside. So these bad thoughts remain active and as long as you have these it is difficult to attain mental peace.

Q. *What would the first steps be to teach the young and also others to have peace of mind, as I understand this is the essential concern of His Holiness?*

A. My approach to this is not purely from the Buddhist point of view. In fact in order to achieve this peace of mind it is not necessary that a person must be religious. There are many people among non-believers who sacrifice their own life for the benefit of the masses or the majority which means less selfishness, more respect for others. It is extremely important to realise that what you feel, what you want is exactly what others also want and feel. You are asking about the first step but I have just begun the search in this direction. It is difficult to initiate action because although this kind of thing is very simple to talk about, when you have to put it into practice it is extremely difficult.

Q. *In the Occident, in Europe, we have quite a problem of generation; the relations between young and old people are somewhat strained, the veneration of old age is lost. Do you have similar problems nowadays in Tibet, with Tibetan young people?*

A. Yes, it is natural that there are some problems, but generally speaking in the Asian countries the relationship between children and parents is very good. There is a generation gap, but because the family relationship is usually harmonious, they respect each other, particularly the children respect their parents and elders.

Q. *Can I say something about the mental unrest among young people? A lot of my friends, and myself included, really feel this unrest and that we are searching for something. But our predicament is that we don't know how to understand what we are really looking for, so we get* caught up in creeds, in the various things that are going around, and these stop people from thinking about what it is they are really missing. I was wondering if you had any ideas about how to make people really understand what it is they are searching for? I think they don't know what it is.

A. It is difficult to say what in particular you should follow, because for each individual it would differ; it may require a different method which is suitable for that person. But generally—of course I am a Buddhist and so according to the Buddhist viewpoint—the main thing is realisation of human beings. A human being is not just a part of matter but more than that. We are something else, we have emotions; although it is very bad, it is the basis of all bad thoughts. But in any case we have these qualities, this nature, so a human being is above matter. Now on this basis comes the realisation of respect for others' rights, for other people also have the same feelings; therefore realise this and respect their rights. In other words, love for God is very important, but for me love for others is much more important. In this respect all religions say the same thing: love for others, respect for others. Christ sacrificing himself for man is a good example. If you have this feeling towards others, I think you yourself will feel happy and your neighbours or your friends will also feel much more comfortable. And as for you, patience is also important. It is difficult to achieve this in one moment; sometimes it takes time, so have patience. But of course I don't know, this is just my own feeling.

Q. *I had reached the borders of your country once but found the same trouble with institutions and the problems in trying to get anywhere. I wonder what you think about the problem of institutions in a wide sense being the greatest barrier that people have to some extent in communicating and spreading this happiness that you talk about? Because we have it and I don't think anyone in the West would deny that this is a huge problem. Is it the same for you and is it something you consider has to be fought? Power structures, institutions for the sake of institutions? Young people at least see this as a very difficult problem, only they don't go the right way about dealing with it. They try and confront power instead of trying to understand what makes people do certain things. Young people are very anti-authoritarian. They don't like anybody who gets up and says. "I know", or "You come to me for advice, I know". This arouses great resistance amongst young people and I just wonder what your feelings are on this problem of power and authority?*

A.   First of all we will have to consider whether the authority is just or not. If it is just, it is right and helpful to comply with it. But if it is unjust and unreasonable, I feel you have the right to rebel against it. This is just a straight answer to your question. Of course you have to take into consideration many factors that might be involved in taking a particular course of action. If you are talking with reference to certain social systems, traditional systems, then I agree with you 100 per cent. I hate formality and these sort of things. You make yourself a prisoner, you pretend to be something else, you try to hide your real feelings and then make yourself a different person. Now if we want to change these traditional systems or institutions made by man we have the right to do so. The systems were not created to bind people but in order to help them. They were made in order to create some sense of discipline or authority.

Q.   *I think what I am trying to ask you is about the method. Would you object violently if things become intolerable and totalitarianism is institutionalised, or does one go on hoping and trying to change things from within? This sounds very general, but I think you understand what I mean.*

A.   Yes. Of course I just mentioned these things. It is very difficult to generalise, but basically I am a firm believer in non-violence. Now here violence is a method, not the aim or goal, and it depends on the motive and the result. If the motive is good, not selfish, but for the good of the masses or a large number of people, that amounts to compassion, then it would result in benefit for many. Here comes the method. In such circumstances if there is no alternative to violence, then of course it may be all right—the motive being good, the result will be good, and since there is no other means available except violence, then it is good.

Q.   *My question is a very simple one. For many young people, certainly in the West, life seems to be difficult. Old authorities have ceased to exist. In this kind of world, from our own experience we know life has been very varied and we know also about the intense spiritual aspiration, what advice would you give to a young person whether he is a Jew, a Christian, a Tibetan, or a Hindu? What would be your advice to them how best to live and make their contribution to a better and happier world?*

A. This is a difficult question. I really don't know, but my suggestion or advice is very simple, that is: to have a sincere heart. I believe that this is something basic and that anyone can approach any problem in this way, irrespective of the ideology he may belong to or even if he is an unbeliever. Real, true brotherhood, a good heart towards one's fellow men, this is the basic thing. I believe that if you have a true feeling of brotherhood whether you are a scientist, an economist, or a politician, whatever profession you may follow, you will always have this concern for your fellow beings. I also believe that if you have this concern for others then whatever the effects that might result from the profession you follow, you will always be concerned as to whether it is going to benefit or harm your fellow beings. I personally feel that this concern for others is lacking today. Many people emphasise on thinking only of themselves and have a selfish motive. I feel that basically the cause of many problems is due to this lack of concern for others and that if we really develop this kind of a sincere feeling and a sense of universal responsibility, many of the problems we face today like pollution, the energy crisis and the population crisis, can be solved. If we have such a sincere feeling we need not worry about the self-sufficiency of the world. What I am referring to is that today in certain parts of the world we have poverty and starvation and in other parts of the world abundance of wealth. This is an example. So if you have a genuine concern for others, I feel all this suffering is needless and avoidable, because the world has sufficient resources to overcome these problems. The main thing is whether you have the real sense of universal responsibility. Basically then the most important thing is a heart.

Q. *In the Occident, in Europe, we have an increasing problem with drugs, especially with young people. I would like to know whether drugs have ever been used, or are being used, in meditative practice in Vajrayana and are drugs at all a suitable means to deepen or broaden our consciousness?*

A. Drugs are not used. Although I do not personally have any experience, from talking to people who have taken drugs I have the impression that by taking drugs you lose your discriminative power, the power to concentrate, and I feel that this would not be helpful for higher meditation.

Q. *What do you think about drugs? Can they be beneficial or are they harmful?*

A. Generally speaking drugs are not good. The mental development should be carried out by internal means, not through external means.

Q. *People who take drugs claim they have enlightenment within a moment, the time it takes to snap your fingers. On what level or rather in what layer or sheath of the personality does this so-called enlightenment take place? Please explain also the danger of drugs.*

A. I have no experience. Some people say it helps very much, but in any case my view is this: Enlightenment or improvement or internal progress should be through mental practice, mental training, not by external means like drugs or injections or operations.

Q. *Can you give us any picture of how you see the future, what it means to you?*

A. It seems to me that this present atmosphere of the world is not very happy. Generally you know what is right and what is wrong, yet despite this knowledge, you almost always take the opposite direction; because of the pressure of the atmosphere, you cannot act in the right way. So from my viewpoint at least this is certainly not beneficial, but we can change this. Therefore I have much more hope in the future, for the younger generation. As I mentioned before the goal or aim is happiness for everyone. All mankind desires a happy life. In order to achieve that goal different people adopt different methods. Some people try to achieve it through science and technology, some through religious practices and some through different government system, different ideologies. If we look at the main goal, then all the others are different methods to reach that goal.

Q. *And you see the goal as happiness?*

A. Yes. There are various kinds of happiness. Certain happiness like bliss is something much more deep, but the deeper or higher happiness or inner bliss cannot be achieved by the masses. A few individuals can achieve this, mainly through the Christian belief in God—as a Buddhist there are certain methods to achieve this higher bliss or happiness. But I am talking of general happiness, the real peace and worldly progress. In this respect I always feel it is very important to develop universal responsibilities, irrespective of different ideologies or faiths. Now the world is becoming smaller and smaller, we are dependent on each other. In such an atmosphere you must have universal responsibility. If we have this feeling, I am quite sure we can solve many problems the right way, through peaceful means. This is my main topic for discussion. I realise it is rather difficult to make a good human being, but despite that it is worthwhile to try. It may take 50, 80, or 100 years, but as I am a religious person I feel it is reasonable to think this way and to try. In this field I want to know other people's views, especially in Western countries: the views of people who are born here, live here—this is my main reason for this visit.

Q. *You look to the future with hope but what do you see in the present day life that makes you optimistic for the future and if so in which case, which particular things give you optimistism?*

A. I believe that this solution, combination of inner development and material progress, is actually connected with the very survival of man himself. And you see, a good heart towards your neighbour, your fellow men, is something very important for life. If in the society of mankind, there is really no justice, no truth, if everything is done by money and power, then it would be difficult to live. Sometimes this atmosphere does have great influence. There are many good systems, for example democracy, and in each system there are many good points. Of course there are bad points also, mostly caused by money and power. As a human being we must live on this earth not for our generation but for the next one, so if there is really no justice and no truth then it would be very sad and very unfortunate. This is my main concern. Also as an Easterner we have many problems like poverty and disease, lack of education. In the West you are highly developed in the material sense, the living standard is remarkably high, which is very important, very good. Yet despite these facilities you have mental unrest, that is, among the youth and among politicians. This is not a healthy sign; it is a clear indication that there is something wrong, something lacking. So this is my theme and because of it I am a little optimistic.

2

ON UNIVERSAL RESPONSIBILITY

As the twentieth century draws to a close, we find that the world has grown smaller and the world's people have become almost one community. Political and military alliances have created large multinational groups, industry and international trade have produced a global economy, and worldwide communications are eliminating ancient barriers of distance, language and race. We are also being drawn together by the grave problems we face: overpopulation, dwindling natural resources, and an environmental crisis that threatens our air, water, and trees, along with the vast number of beautiful life forms that are the very foundation of existence on this small planet we share.

I believe that to meet the challenge of our times, human beings will have to develop a greater sense of universal responsibility. Each of us must learn to work not just for his or her own self, family or nation, but for the benefit of all mankind. Universal responsibility is the real key to human survival. It is the best foundation for world peace, the equitable use of natural resources, and through concern for future generations, the proper care of the environment.

For some time, I have been thinking about how to increase our sense of mutual responsibility and the altruistic motive from which it is derived. Briefly, I would like to offer my thoughts.

One human family

Whether we like it or not, we have all been born on this earth as part of one great human family. Rich or poor, educated or uneducated, belonging to one nation or another, to one religion or another, adhering to this ideology or that, ultimately each of us is just a human being like everyone else: we all desire happiness and do not want suffering. Furthermore, each of us has an equal right to pursue these goals.

Today's world requires that we accept the oneness of humanity. In the past, isolated communities could afford to think of one another as fundamentally separate and even existed in total isolation. Nowadays, however, events in one part of the world eventually affect the entire planet. Therefore we have to treat each major local problem as a global concern from the moment it begins. We can no longer invoke the national, racial or ideological barriers that separate us without destructive repercussion. In the context of our new interdependence, considering the interests of others is clearly the best form of self-interest.

I view this fact as a source of hope. The necessity for cooperation can only strengthen mankind, because it helps us recognize that the most secure foundation for the new world order is not simply broader political and economic alliances, but rather each individual's genuine practice of love and compassion. For a better, happier, more stable and civilized future, each of us must develop a sincere, warm-hearted feeling of brother- and sisterhood.

The medicine of altruism

In Tibet we say that many illnesses can be cured by the one medicine of love and compassion. These qualities are the ultimate source of human happiness, and our need for them lies at the very core of our being. Unfortunately, love and compassion have been omitted from too many spheres of social interaction for too long. Usually confined to family and home, their practice in public life is considered impractical, even naive. This is tragic. In my view, the practice of compassion is not just a symptom of unrealistic idealism but the most effective way to pursue the best interests of others as well as our own. The more we—as a nation, a group or as individuals—depend upon others, the more it is in our own best interests to ensure their well-being.

Practising altruism is the real source of compromise and cooperation; merely recognizing our need for harmony is not enough. A mind committed to compassion is like an overflowing reservoir—a constant source of energy, determination and kindness. This mind is like a seed; when cultivated, it gives rise to many other good qualities, such as forgiveness, tolerance, inner strength and the confidence to overcome fear and insecurity. The compassionate mind is like an elixir; it is capable of transforming bad situations into beneficial ones. Therefore, we should not limit our expressions of love and compassion to our family and friends. Nor is compassion only the responsibility of clergy, health care and social workers. It is the necessary business of every part of the human community.

Whether a conflict lies in the field of politics, business or religion, an altruistic approach is frequently the sole means of resolving it. Sometimes the very concepts we use to mediate a dispute are themselves the cause of the problem. At such times, when a resolution seems impossible, both sides should recall the basic human nature that unites them. This will help break the impasse and, in the long run, make it easier for everyone to attain their goal. Although neither side may be fully satisfied, if both make concessions, at the very least, the danger of further conflict will be averted. We all know that this form of compromise is the most effective way of solving problems—why, then, do we not use it more often?

When I consider the lack of cooperation in human society, I can only conclude that it stems from ignorance of our interdependent nature. I am often moved by the example of small insects, such as bees. The laws of nature dictate that bees work together in order to survive. As a result, they possess an instinctive sense of social responsibility. They have no constitution, laws, police, religion or moral training, but because of their nature they labour faithfully together. Occasionally they may fight, but in general the whole colony survives on the basis of cooperation. Human beings, on the other hand, have constitutions, vast legal systems and police forces; we have religion, remarkable intelligence and a heart with a great capacity to love. But despite our many extraordinary qualities, in actual practice we lag behind those small insects; in some ways, I feel we are poorer than the bees.

For instance, millions of people live together in large cities all over the world, but despite this proximity, many are lonely. Some do not have even one human being with whom to share their deepest feelings, and live in a state of perpetual agitation. This is very sad. We are not solitary animals that associate only in order to mate. If we were, why would we build large cities and towns? But even though we are social animals compelled to live together, unfortunately, we lack a sense of responsibility towards our fellow humans. Does the fault lie in our social architecture— the basic structures of family and community that support our society? Is it in our external facilities—our machines, science and technology? I do not think so.

I believe that despite the rapid advances made by civilization in this century, the most immediate cause of our present dilemma is our undue emphasis on material development alone. We have become so en-grossed in its pursuit that, without even knowing it, we have neglected to foster the most basic human needs of love, kindness, cooperation and caring. If we do not know someone or find another reason for not feeling connected with a particular individual or group, we simply ignore them. But the development of human society is based entirely on people helping each other. Once we have lost the essential humanity that is our foundation, what is the point of pursuing only material improvement?

To me, it is clear: a genuine sense of responsibility can result only if we develop compassion. Only a spontaneous feeling of empathy for others can really motivate us to act on their behalf. I have explained how to cultivate compassion elsewhere. For the remainder of this short piece, I would like to discuss how our present global situation can be improved by greater reliance on universal responsibility.

Universal responsibility

First, I should mention that I do not believe in creating movements or espousing ideologies. Nor do I like the practice of establishing an organization to promote a particular idea, which implies that one group of people alone is responsible for the attainment of that goal, while everybody else is exempted. In our present circumstances, none of us can afford to assume that somebody else will solve our problems; each of us must take his or her own share of universal responsibility. In this way, as the number of concerned, responsible individuals grows, tens, hundreds, thousands or even hundreds of thousands of such people will greatly improve the general atmosphere. Positive change does not come quickly and demands ongoing effort. If we become discouraged we may not attain even the simplest goals. With constant, determined application, we can accomplish even the most difficult objectives.

Adopting an attitude of universal responsibility is essentially a personal matter. The real test of compassion is not what we say in abstract discussions but how we conduct ourselves in daily life. Still, certain fundamental views are basic to the practice of altruism.

Though no system of government is perfect, democracy is that which is closest to humanity's essential nature. Hence those of us who enjoy it must continue to fight for all people's right to do so. Furthermore, democracy is the only stable foundation upon which a global political structure can be built. To work as one, we must respect the right of all peoples and nations to maintain their own distinctive character and values.

In particular, a tremendous effort will be required to bring compassion into the realm of international business. Economic inequality, especially that between developed and developing nations, remains the greatest source of suffering on this planet. Even though they will lose money in the short term, large multi national corporations must curtail their exploitation of poor nations. Tapping the few precious resources such countries possess simply to fuel consumerism in the developed world is disastrous; if it continues unchecked, eventually we shall all suffer. Strengthening weak, undiversified economies is a far wiser policy for promoting both political and economic stability. As idealistic as it may sound, altruism, not just competition and the desire for wealth, should be a driving force in business.

We also need to renew our commitment to human values in the field of modern science. Though the main purpose of science is to learn more about reality, another of its goals is to improve the quality of life. Without altruistic motivation, scientists cannot distinguish between beneficial technologies and the merely expedient. The environmental damage surrounding us is the most obvious example of the result of this confusion, but proper motivation may be even more relevant in governing how we handle the extraordinary new array of biological techniques with which we can now manipulate the subtle structures of life itself. If we do not base our every action on an ethical foundation, we run the risk of inflicting terrible harm on the delicate matrix of life.

Nor are the religions of the world exempt from this responsibility. The purpose of religion is not to build beautiful churches or temples, but to cultivate positive human qualities such as tolerance, generosity and love. Every world religion, no matter what its philosophical view, is founded first and foremost on the precept that we must reduce our selfishness and serve others. Unfortunately, sometimes religion itself causes more quarrels than it solves. Practitioners of different faiths should realize that each religious tradition has immense intrinsic value and the means for providing mental and spiritual health. One religion, like a single type of food, cannot satisfy everybody. According to their varying mental dispositions, some people benefit from one kind of teaching, others from another. Each faith has the ability to produce fine, warm-hearted people and despite their espousal of often contradictory philosophies, all religions have succeeded in doing so. Thus there is no reason to engage in divisive religious bigotry and intolerance and every reason to cherish and respect all forms of spiritual practice.

Certainly, the most important field in which to sow the seeds of greater altruism is international relations. In the past few years the world has changed dramatically. I think we would all agree that the end of the Cold War and the collapse of communism in Eastern Europe and the former Soviet Union have ushered in a new historical era. As we move through the 1990s it would seem that human experience in the twentieth century has come full circle.

This has been the most painful period in human history, a time when, because of the vast increase in the destructive power of weapons, more people have suffered from and died by violence than ever before. Furthermore, we have also witnessed an almost terminal competition between the fundamental ideologies that have always torn the human community: force and raw power on the one hand, and freedom, pluralism, individual rights and democracy on the other. I believe that the results of this great competition are now clear. Though the good human spirit of peace, freedom and democracy still faces many forms of tyranny and evil, it is nevertheless an unmistakable fact that the vast majority of people everywhere want it to triumph. Thus the tragedies of our time have not been entirely without benefit, and have in many cases been the very means by which the human mind has been opened. The collapse of communism demonstrates this.

Although communism espoused many noble ideals, including altruism, the attempt by its governing elites to dictate their views has proved disastrous. These governments went to tremendous lengths to control the entire flow of information through their societies and to structure their education systems so that their citizens would work for the common good. Although rigid organization may have been necessary in the beginning to destroy previous oppressive regimes, once that goal was fulfilled, the organization had very little to contribute towards building a useful human community. Communalism failed utterly because it relied on force to promote its beliefs. Ultimately, human nature was unable to sustain the suffering it produced.

Brute force, no matter how strongly applied, can never subdue the basic human desire for freedom. The hundreds of thousands of people who marched in the cities of Eastern Europe proved this. They simply expressed the human need for freedom and democracy. It was very moving. Their demands had nothing whatsoever to do with some new ideology; these people simply spoke from their hearts, sharing their desire for freedom, demonstrating that it stems from the core of human nature. Freedom, in fact, is the very source of creativity for both individuals and society. It is not enough, as communist systems have assumed, merely to provide people with food, shelter and clothing. If we have all these things but lack the precious air of liberty to sustain our deeper nature, we are only half human; we are like animals who are content just to satisfy their physical needs.

I feel that the peaceful revolutions in the former Soviet Union and Eastern Europe have taught us many great lessons. One is the value of truth. People do not like to be bullied, cheated or lied to by either an individual or a system. Such acts are contrary to the essential human spirit. Therefore, even though those who practice deception and use force may achieve considerable short-term success, eventually they will be overthrown.

On the other hand, everyone appreciates truth, and respect for it is really in our blood. Truth is the best guarantor and the real foundation of freedom and democracy. It does not matter whether you are weak or strong or whether your cause has many or few adherents, truth will still prevail. The fact that the successful freedom movements of 1989 and after have been based on the true expression of people's most basic feelings is a valuable reminder that truth itself is still seriously lacking in much of our political life. Especially in the conduct of international relations we pay very little respect to truth. Inevitably, weaker nations are manipulated and oppressed by stronger ones, just as the weaker sections of most societies suffer at the hands of the more affluent and powerful. Though in the past, the simple expression of truth has usually been dismissed as unrealistic, these last few years have proved that it is an immense force in the human mind and, as a result, in the shaping of history.

A second great lesson from Eastern Europe has been that of peaceful change. In the past, enslaved peoples often resorted to violence in their struggle to be free. Now, following in the footsteps of Mahatma Gandhi and Martin Luther King, Jr., these peaceful revolutions offer future generations a wonderful example of successful, non-violent change. When in the future major changes in society again become necessary, our descendants will be able to look back on the present time as a paradigm of peaceful struggle, a real success story of unprecedented scale, involving more than a dozen nations and hundreds of millions of people. Moreover, recent events have shown that the desire for both peace and freedom lies at the most fundamental level of human nature and that violence is its complete antithesis.

Before considering what kind of global order would serve us best in the post-Cold War period, I think it is vital to address the question of violence, whose elimination at every level is the necessary foundation for world peace and the ultimate goal of any international order.

Non-violence and international order

Every day the media reports incidents of terrorism, crime and aggression. I have never been to a country where tragic stories of death and bloodshed did not fill the newspapers and airwaves. Such reporting has become almost an addiction for journalists and their audiences alike. But the overwhelming majority of the human race does not behave destructively; very few of the five billion people on this planet actually commit acts of violence. Most of us prefer to be as peaceful as possible.

Basically, we all cherish tranquillity, even those of us given to violence. For instance, when spring comes, the days grow longer, there is more sunshine, the grass and trees come alive and everything is very fresh. People feel happy. In autumn, one leaf falls, then another, then all the beautiful flowers die until we are surrounded by bare, naked plants. We do not feel so joyful. Why is this? Because deep-down, we desire constructive, fruitful growth and dislike things collapsing, dying or being destroyed. Every destructive action goes against our basic nature; building, being constructive, is the human way.

I am sure everybody agrees that we need to overcome violence, but if we are to eliminate it completely, we should first analyse whether or not it has any value.

If we address this question from a strictly practical perspective, we find that on certain occasions violence indeed appears useful. One can solve a problem quickly with force. At the same time, however, such success is often at the expense of the rights and welfare of others. As a result, even though one problem has been solved, the seed of another has been planted.

On the other hand, if one's cause is supported by sound reasoning, there is no point in using violence. It is those who have no motive other than selfish desire and who cannot achieve their goal through logical reasoning who rely on force. Even when family and friends disagree, those with valid reasons can cite them one after the other and argue their case point by point, whereas those with little rational support soon fall prey to anger. Thus anger is not a sign of strength but one of weakness.

Ultimately, it is important to examine one's own motivation and that of one's opponent. There are many kinds of violence and non-violence, but one cannot distinguish them from external factors alone. If one's motivation is negative, the action it produces is, in the deepest sense, violent, even though it may appear to be smooth and gentle. Conversely, if one's motivation is sincere and positive but the circumstances require harsh behaviour, essentially one is practising non-violence. No matter what the case may be, I feel that a compassionate concern for the benefit of others—not simply for oneself—is the sole justification for the use of force.

The genuine practice of non-violence is still somewhat experimental on our planet, but its pursuit, based on love and understanding, is sacred. If this experiment succeeds, it can open the way to a far more peaceful world in the next century.

I have heard the occasional Westerner maintain that long-term Gandhian struggles employing non-violent passive resistance do not suit everybody and that such courses of action are more natural in the East. Because Westerners are active, they tend to seek immediate results in all situations, even at the cost of their lives. This approach, I believe, is not always beneficial. But surely the practice of non-violence suits us all. It simply calls for determination. Even though the freedom movements of Eastern Europe reached their goals quickly, non-violent protest by its very nature usually requires patience.

In this regard, I pray that despite the brutality of their suppression and the difficulty of the struggle they face, those involved in China's democracy movement will always remain peaceful. I am confident they will. Although the majority of the young Chinese students involved were born and raised under an especially harsh form of communism, during the spring of 1989 they spontaneously practised Mahatma Gandhi's strategy of passive resistance. This is remarkable and clearly shows that ultimately all human beings want to pursue the path of peace, no matter how much they have been indoctrinated.

The reality of war

Of course, war and the large military establishments are the greatest sources of violence in the world. Whether their purpose is defensive or offensive, these vast powerful organizations exist solely to kill human beings. We should think carefully about the reality of war. Most of us have been conditioned to regard military combat as exciting and glamorous— an opportunity for men to prove their competence and courage. Since armies are legal, we feel that war is acceptable; in general, nobody feels that war is criminal or that accepting it is a criminal attitude. In fact, we have been brainwashed. War is neither glamorous nor attractive. It is monstrous. Its very nature is one of tragedy and suffering.

War is like a fire in the human community, one whose fuel is living beings. I find this analogy especially appropriate and useful. Modern warfare is waged primarily with different forms of fire, but we are so conditioned to see it as thrilling that we talk about this or that marvellous weapon as a remarkable piece of technology without remembering that, if it is actually used, it will burn living people. War also strongly resembles a fire in the way it spreads. If one area gets weak, the commanding officer sends in reinforcements. This is like throwing live people into a fire. But because we have been brainwashed to think this way, we do not consider the suffering of individual soldiers. No soldier wants to be wounded or die; none of his loved ones wants any harm to come to him. If one soldier is killed, or maimed for life, at least another five or ten people—his relatives and friends—suffer as well. We should all be horrified by the extent of this tragedy, but we are too confused.

Frankly, as a child, I too was attracted to the military. Their uniforms looked so smart and beautiful. But that is exactly how the seduction begins. Children start playing games that one day lead them into trouble. There are plenty of exciting games to play and costumes to wear other than those based on the killing of human beings. Again, if we as adults were not so fascinated by war, we would clearly see that to allow our children to become habituated to war games is extremely unfortunate. Some former soldiers have told me that when they shot their first person they felt uncomfortable but as they continued to kill it began to feel quite normal. In time, we can get used to anything.

It is not only during times of war that military establishments are destructive. By their very design, they are the single greatest violators of human rights, and it is the soldiers themselves who suffer most consistently from their abuse. After the officers in charge have given beautiful explanations about the importance of the army, its discipline and the need to conquer the enemy, the rights of the great mass of soldiers are almost entirely taken away. They are then compelled to forfeit their individual will, and in the end, to sacrifice their lives. Moreover, once an army has become a powerful force, there is every risk that it will destroy the happiness of its own country.

There are people with destructive intentions in every society, and the temptation to gain command over an organization capable of fulfilling their desires can become overwhelming. But no matter how malevolent or evil are the many murderous dictators who currently oppress their nations and cause international problems, it is obvious that they cannot harm others or destroy countless human lives if they don't have a military organization accepted and condoned by society. As long as there are powerful armies there will always be the danger of dictatorship. If we really believe dictatorship to be a despicable and destructive form of government, then we must recognize that the existence of a powerful military establishment is one of its main causes.

Militarism is also very expensive. Pursuing peace through military strength places a tremendously wasteful burden on society. Governments spend vast sums on increasingly intricate weapons when, in fact, nobody really wants to use them. Not only money but also valuable energy and human intelligence are squandered, while all that increases is fear.

I want to make it clear, however, that although I am deeply opposed to war, I am not advocating appeasement. It is often necessary to take a strong stand to counter unjust aggression. For instance, it is plain to all of us that the Second World War was entirely justified. It "saved civilization" from the tyranny of Nazi Germany, as Winston Churchill so aptly put it. In my view, the Korean War was also just, since it gave South Korea the chance of gradually developing democracy. But we can only judge whether or not a conflict was vindicated on moral grounds with hindsight. For example, we can now see that during the Cold War, the principle of nuclear deterrence had a certain value. Nevertheless, it is very difficult to assess all such matters with any degree of accuracy. War is violence and violence is unpredictable. Therefore, it is far better to avoid it if possible, and never to presume that we know beforehand whether the outcome of a particular war will be beneficial or not.

For instance, in the case of the Cold War, though deterrence may have helped promote stability, it did not create genuine peace. The last forty years in Europe have seen merely the absence of war, which has not been real peace but a facsimile founded on fear. At best, building arms to maintain peace serves only as a temporary measure. As long as adversaries do not trust each other, any number of factors can upset the balance of power. Lasting peace can be secured only on the basis of genuine trust.

Disarmament for world peace

Throughout history, mankind has pursued peace one way or another. Is it too optimistic to imagine that world peace may finally be within our grasp? I do not believe that there has been an increase in the amount of people's hatred, only in their ability to manifest it in vastly destructive weapons. On the other hand, bearing witness to the tragic evidence of the mass slaughter caused by such weapons in our century has given us the opportunity to control war. To do so, it is clear we must disarm.

Disarmament can occur only within the context of new political and economic relationships. Before we consider this issue in detail, it is worth imagining the kind of peace process from which we would benefit most. This is fairly self-evident. First we should work on eliminating nuclear weapons, next, biological and chemical ones, then offensive arms, and finally, defensive ones. At the same time, to safeguard the peace, we should start developing in one or more global regions an international police force made up of an equal number of members from each nation under a collective command. Eventually this force would cover the whole world.

Because the dual process of disarmament and development of a joint force would be both multilateral and democratic, the right of the majority to criticize or even intervene in the event of one nation violating the basic rules would be ensured. Moreover, with all large armies eliminated and all conflicts such as border disputes subject to the control of the joint international force, large and small nations would be truly equal. Such reforms would result in a stable international environment.

Of course, the immense financial dividend reaped from the cessation of arms production would also provide a fantastic windfall for global development. Today, the nations of the world spend trillions of dollars annually on upkeep of the military. Can you imagine how many hospital beds, schools and homes this money could fund? In addition, as I mentioned above, the awesome proportion of scarce resources squandered on military development not only prevents the elimination of poverty, illiteracy and disease, but also requires the sacrifice of precious human intelligence. Our scientists are extremely bright. Why should their brilliance be wasted on such dreadful endeavours when it could be used for positive global development?

The great deserts of the world such as the Sahara and the Gobi could be cultivated to increase food production and ease overcrowding. Many countries now face years of severe drought. New, less expensive methods of desalinization could be developed to render sea water suitable for human consumption and other uses. There are many pressing issues in the fields of energy and health to which our scientists could more usefully address themselves. Since the world economy would grow more rapidly as a result of their efforts, they could even be paid more!

Our planet is blessed with vast natural treasures. If we use them properly, beginning with the elimination of militarism and war, truly, every human being will be able to live a wealthy, well-cared-for life.

Naturally, global peace cannot occur all at once. Since conditions around the world are so varied, its spread will have to be incremental. But there is no reason why it cannot begin in one region and then spread gradually from one continent to another.

I would like to propose that regional communities like the European Community be established as an integral part of the more peaceful world we are trying to create. Looking at the post-Cold War environment objectively, such communities are plainly the most natural and desirable components of a new world order. As we can see, the almost gravitational pull of our growing interdependence necessitates new, more cooperative structures. The European Community is pioneering the way in this endeavour, negotiating the delicate balance between economic, military and political collectivity on the one hand and the sovereign rights of member states on the other. I am greatly inspired by this work. I also believe that the new Commonwealth of Independent States is grappling with similar issues and that the seeds of such a community are already present in the minds of many of its constituent republics. In this context, I would briefly like to talk about the future of both my own country, Tibet, and China.

Like the former Soviet Union, Communist China is a multinational state, artificially constructed under the impetus of an expansionist ideology and up to now administered by force in colonial fashion. A peaceful, prosperous and above all politically stable future for China lies in its successfully fulfilling not only its own people's wishes for a more open, democratic system, but also those of its eighty million so-called "national minorities", who want to regain their freedom. For real happiness to return to the heart of Asia—home to one-fifth of the human race—a pluralistic, democratic, mutually cooperative community of sovereign states must replace what is currently called the People's Republic of China.

Of course, such a community need not be limited to those presently under Chinese Communist domination, such as Tibetans, Mongols and Uighurs. The people of Hong Kong, those seeking an independent Taiwan, and even those suffering under other communist governments in North Korea, Vietnam, Laos and Cambodia might also be interested in building an Asian Community. However, it is especially urgent that those ruled by the Chinese Communists consider doing so. Properly pursued, it could help save China from violent dissolution, regionalism and a return to the chaotic turmoil that has so afflicted this great nation throughout the twentieth century. Currently China's political life is so polarized that there is every reason to fear an early recurrence of bloodshed and tragedy. Each of us—every member of the world community—has a moral responsibility to help avert the immense suffering that civil strife would bring to China's vast population.

I believe that the very process of dialogue, moderation and compromise involved in building of community of Asian states would itself give real hope of peaceful evolution to a new order in China. From the very start, the member states of such a community might agree to decide its defence and international relations policies together. There would be many opportunities for cooperation. The critical point is that we find a peaceful, non-violent way for the forces of freedom, democracy and moderation to emerge successfully from the current atmosphere of unjust repression.

Zones of peace

I see Tibet's role in such an Asian Community as what I have previously called a "Zone of Peace": a neutral, demilitarized sanctuary where weapons are forbidden and the people live in harmony with nature. This is not merely a dream—it is precisely the way Tibetans tried to live for over a thousand years before our country was invaded. As everybody knows, in Tibet all forms of wildlife were strictly protected in accordance with Buddhist principles. Also, for at least the last three hundred years, we had no proper army. Tibet gave up the waging of war as an instrument of national policy in the sixth and seventh centuries, after the reign of our three great religious kings.

Returning to the relationship between developing regional communities and the task of disarmament, I would like to suggest that the "heart" of each community could be one or more nations that have decided to become zones of peace, areas from which military forces are prohibited. This, again, is not just a dream. Four decades ago, in December 1948, Costa Rica disbanded its army. Recently, 37 per cent of the Swiss population voted to disband their military. The new government of Czechoslovakia has decided to stop the manufacture and export of all weapons. If its people so choose, a nation can take radical steps to change its very nature.

Zones of peace within regional communities would serve as oases of stability. While paying their fair share of the costs of any collective force created by the community as a whole, these zones of peace would be the forerunners and beacons of an entirely peaceful world and would be exempt from engaging in any conflict. If regional communities do develop in Asia, South America and Africa and disarmament progresses so that an international force from all regions is created, these zones of peace will be able to expand, spreading tranquillity as they grow.

We do not need to think that we are planning for the far distant future when we consider this or any other proposal for a new, more politically, economically and militarily cooperative world. For instance, the newly invigorated forty-eight member Conference on Security and Cooperation in Europe has already laid the foundation for an alliance between not only the nations of Eastern and Western Europe but also between the nations of the Commonwealth of Independent States and the United States. These remarkable events have virtually eliminated the danger of a major war between these two superpowers.

I have not included the United Nations in this discussion of the present era because both its critical role in helping create a better world and its great potential for doing so are so well known. By definition, the United Nations must be in the very middle of whatever major changes occur. However, it may need to amend its structure for the future. I have always had the greatest hopes from the United Nations, and with no criticism intended, I would like simply to point out that the post-World War II climate under which its charter was conceived has changed. With that change has come the opportunity to further democratize the UN, especially the somewhat exclusive Security Council with its five permanent members, which should be made more representative.

In conclusion

I would like to conclude by stating that, in general, I feel optimistic about the future. Some recent trends portend our great potential for a better world. As late as the fifties and sixties, people believed that war was an inevitable condition of mankind. The Cold War, in particular, reinforced the notion that opposing political systems could only clash, not compete or even collaborate. Few now hold this view. Today, people all over the planet are genuinely concerned about world peace. They are far less interested in propounding ideology and far more committed to coexistence. These are very positive developments.

Also, for thousands of years people believed that only an authoritarian organization employing rigid disciplinary methods could govern human society. However, people have an innate desire for freedom and democracy, and these two forces have been in conflict. Today, it is clear which has won. The emergence of non-violent "people's power" movements have shown indisputably that the human race can neither tolerate nor function properly under the rule of tyranny. This recognition represents remarkable progress.

Another hopeful development is the growing compatibility between science and religion. Throughout the nineteenth century and for much of our own, people have been profoundly confused by the conflict between these apparently contradictory world views. Today, physics, biology and psychology have reached such sophisticated levels that many researchers are starting to ask the most profound questions about the ultimate nature of the universe and life, the same questions that are of prime interest to religions. Thus there is real potential for a more unified view. In particular, it seems that a new concept of mind and matter is emerging. The East has been more concerned with understanding the mind, the West with understanding matter. Now that the two have met, these spiritual and material views of life may become more harmonized.

The rapid changes in our attitude towards the earth are also a source of hope. As recently as ten or fifteen years ago, we thoughtlessly consumed its resources, as if there was no end to them. Now, not only individuals but governments as well are seeking a new ecological order. I often joke that the moon and stars look beautiful, but if any of us tried to live on them, we would be miserable. This blue planet of ours is the most delightful habitat we know. Its life is our life; its future, our future. And though I do not believe that the Earth itself is a sentient being, it does indeed act as our mother, and like children, we are dependent upon her. Now mother nature is telling us to cooperate. In the face of such global problems as the greenhouse effect and the deterioration of the ozone layer, individual organizations and single nations are helpless. Unless we all work together, no solution will be found. Our mother is teaching us a lesson in universal responsibility.

I think we can say that, because of the lessons we have begun to learn, the next century will be friendlier, more harmonious, and less harmful. Compassion, the seed of peace, will be able to flourish. I am very hopeful. At the same time, I believe that every individual has a responsibility to help guide our global family in the right direction. Good wishes alone are not enough; we have to assume responsibility. Large human movements spring from individual human initiatives. If you feel that you cannot have much of an effect, the next person may also become discouraged and a great opportunity will have been lost. On the other hand, each of us can inspire others simply by working to develop our own altruistic motivation.

I am sure that many honest, sincere people all over the world already hold the views that I have mentioned here. Unfortunately, nobody listens to them. Although my voice may go unheeded as well, I thought that I should try to speak on their behalf. Of course, some people may feel that it is very presumptuous for the Dalai Lama to write in this way. But, since I received the Nobel Peace Prize, I feel I have a responsibility to do so. If I just took the Nobel money and spent it however I liked, it would look as if the only reason I had spoken all those nice words in the past was to get this prize! However, now that I have received it, I must repay the honour by continuing to advocate the views that I have always expressed.

I, for one, truly believe that individuals can make a difference in society. Since periods of great change such as the present one come so rarely in human history, it is up to each of us to make the best use of our time to help create a happier world.

3

ON HUMANITY[1]

December 24, 1993

I am extremely happy to be here again in Auroville to meet with all you people who are working in Auroville and are dedicated to your work and to achieving the goals of Auroville. I would like to thank you for asking me to come here and visit Auroville again, and I take this opportunity to especially thank the organizer.[2]

Now, I will try to speak through my broken English.

Since my last visit, I have seen much progress and many developments have taken place and I'm extremely happy about it. You have done many, many things.

I had the impression from my last visit that in spite of a few trees and bushes, it was basically a barren land. Now, today, it has become almost like a forest, a jungle.

This has happened because of your dedication and your full involvement. You dedicated all your time and energy to certain principles and also you worked as a team with, I think, a very good sense of community. This is extremely important and very good, and therefore I would like to express my deep, deep appreciation to all of you, as a person who admired your late Founder.

I'm a person who does not believe in national boundaries. For me, all human beings are the same. If you look at the earth from outer space, national boundaries have no significance. Today, I think because of the increase in population, and also because of the modern economy and technology, the world has truly become just like one human family. Therefore we need some kind of sense of universal responsibility.

I am a person who believes in these principles and so I'm really impressed by Auroville and would like to express my deep appreciation.

---

[1] H.H. the Dalai Lama addressed the gathering at the Aurobindo Ashram at Auroville.
[2] This was spoken through the Secretary.

I also noticed that there is a very good harmony, a good relationship with the local people, and many of the local Indians seem to be fully participating and enjoying working with Westerners. This is very good. You have the spirit of community, irrespective of different religions, cultures, races. We really need that. Then, now, what else to say?

When you have some clear idea and certain objectives and these objectives are sustained by reason, by logic, then naturally there comes some kind of will or determination to aim for that goal. With that will, you can work even harder and your enthusiasm becomes stronger. All the difficulties and obstacles—and there are difficulties, there are obstacles—will be overcome by that! You gain even more courage. Therefore, ultimately, motivation is very important, it is of supreme importance.

I believe that today we human beings, in spite of many achievements and material development through science and technology, are still facing many problems. Generally speaking many people in the rich nations, in spite of a beautiful surface and comfort, have often some kind of mental unrest deep down, underneath. In the developed nations also, some kind of moral crisis is brewing.

At the same time, although East and West used to be two separate blocs, both of them having nuclear weapons and each of them mainly based on an ideology or a system, now these blocs have disappeared. It is of course very good but then, lately, chaotic situations have developed, like in Bosnia or in some former Soviet Republics: there is some unrest, some killing and bloodshed, and this of course is very sad.

Still on the subject of humanity, there is the gap between the Southerners and the Northerners. One part of the world has a high living standard: in education and health, in everything the standard is quite high. They have more than they need, a lot of surplus. Then in another part of the same world, you have the same human beings with the same human flesh, the same mind, living in similar situations, with an innate desire for a happy life, with every right to be happy people, to have a happy family.

So on one side you have millions of people enjoying a high standard of living, and on the other side, millions of people whose basic human necessities are not met, who face even starvation. Now this situation, this gap is not only morally wrong, but practically also it is a source of problems!

So long as that gap remains, humanity will face problems. For example, today developed nations are facing the problem of new immigrants, of job seekers coming from poor countries. In the long run, if this gap remains, naturally it will give rise to a very unhealthy situation. Distances today are hardly of much significance. Everyone depends on everyone else, and therefore we have to find ways and means to change this situation.

And another problem is the environment although, being a Tibetan, I only became aware of the environmental problem very recently. When we were in Tibet, we had a small population and the climate was dry, we did not face many problems with the environment. In fact we had hardly any problem. We could drink water from any river. So, when I first understood or heard of polluted water, that "this water can be drunk and this water is polluted and cannot be drunk", in the beginning I was a little bit surprised and I said "wait". Then I learned the importance of environment, and it really became very serious.

War, bloodshed, etc., are things which strike us immediately. But pollution, environmental problems are not immediately visible, they are not so striking, but invisibly they spread. And once we realize what is happening, the problem has already become very serious, and then may be it is too late. The environmental problem is now a very important, a serious matter.

Also when we think about humanity, when we think about the rights of every human individual, then we should not forget about the coming generations. Not only the next generation, but the ones after that, they are also human beings. These people are our own descendants, our own children and our children's children, so as their forefathers, we have the responsibility to think of their rights, their lives!

When we think in these terms, then it is clear that not one or two individual nations can solve these problems. The entire humanity has to work as one team. When we talk about these things, of course they sound understandable, but when we want to put them into practice, to implement them, it becomes very difficult.

For that reason, I believe in these small individual institutions or organizations like Auroville which are actually working in that direction and taking practical initiatives.

So, you can see that your work, your dedication, in the long run is extremely beneficial for humanity. You should think on these lines. Then, you will develop the inner force which moves you forward without a feeling of fatigue.

One more thing. It is important for a person to perform compassionate work. With some work you will immediately get a big salary, a big profit, so because of that, you may sometimes find it easier to work hard. But with compassionate work, which is of a more spiritual nature, you really need the inner force and full dedication, and in the end you will get more satisfaction.

Another factor which is very important according to my own personal experience and the first-hand experience of some of my friends, is calmness of mind. When your mind is calm, then it automatically brings patience and your health is also improved. Then you can engage in harder work.

I believe the basic factor in peace of mind is compassion, or human affection. If you think about your own experience, then the reason is quite clear: when your mind, your heart, is more of a compassionate nature, then automatically it opens up what I call a kind of "inner door". Then through that door you can communicate with your fellow human beings, without any difficulties, whether you have known them before or not. Immediately when you see a fellow human being at once you feel: "Oh! Another human being, just like my brother or my sister." You can communicate easily, you can communicate heart to heart. That immediately expels fear and doubt.

Take another case: if you feel here (*pointing to his heart*): hatred, jealousy, then it automatically closes your inner door. As a result, you find it difficult to communicate with your fellow human beings because of your own negative feelings here (*again pointing to his heart*). You also get the impression that other people also have some similar feelings. So, automatically you develop suspicion or doubt, and that suspicion or doubt brings fear, and then the fear fuels more frustration. Within your circle, you become more hesitant, and eventually your health will also suffer.

So peace of mind, human love and compassion, loving kindness to all and human affection are key factors. When we think about peace of mind, when we think about a happy life, we should not forget about the value of human compassion. It is important to remember that the major religions also teach us the importance of compassion, love and forgiveness.

But, essentially, there can be two separate things—religion and basic human values or the good qualities that you can call "secular moral ethics". Without being a religious believer, you can be a compassionate person. Therefore, if a person feels that in different religious traditions there is something effective or something useful, of course it is very good. But even if those people do not feel that religion is very relevant to their daily lives, it doesn't matter, they can remain non-believers, but at the same time they shouldn't neglect the basic human qualities such as human affection.

Obviously, I believe that the basis of human nature is gentleness. Many people feel that the basis of human nature is aggression. Let us think about it, let us examine it. Yes, certainly anger, hatred, greed and aggression together with human intelligence are part of human nature.

If you look at human history, the aggressive human nature has played an important role, it has caused much wrong in human history. But, certainly, the dominant force in our mind is affection or gentleness. The dominant human force is human compassion and affection.

Now, let us reason, think about our lives. Our life begins with our mother, nourishing us with her milk, it can be our mother or someone else. If we look at the child at birth, one sees that he naturally feels through his body, he has a very close physical feeling towards his mother or whoever is feeding him. It is a very intimate feeling! Without that feeling, the child would not suck the breast. It is a law of nature. And that is the most important period for the child. It is the beginning of his life. There is no room for anger at that time, only affection.

Now take education. When we are getting a lesson from a teacher, that person shows us compassion, love, and a sense of concern. The lesson that comes from the mouth of that person has real value! You can feel that it has value! And the lesson goes deep, not only in our brain, but also in our heart!

Take another case: if a very important lesson comes from a person who never shows affection or concern towards you as his student, then that lesson can of course go up here (*pointing to his head*), but not down here (*pointing to his heart*).

Now, when we get sick, we call for one doctor or another. But, according to my own experience, when I meet a really qualified doctor with sophisticated machines, but without a smile, a doctor who acts like a robot without much human feeling, then sometimes I have a little doubt about this doctor! But if the doctor (even if he has less sophisticated equipment) is full of smiles and has a lot of human feeling, then I am much more comfortable (*laughing*). I start to think: "Oh! This doctor will do his best!" Here also human affection is very much involved.

Now, on to our last day, the day of our death. When a person is dying, even an ordinary doctor will usually advise people to keep a peaceful atmosphere around the person, not to disturb him. "Quiet!" The person, whether he is disturbed or not, will die! In any case he is dying. You may think: "It does not matter much!" But if in your state of mind there is more compassion, and the dying person is surrounded by silence or by close friends, then the dying person will feel happier.

It is the law of nature and the nature of our life.

Regarding your health: for every part of your body, it is very relevant to have a peaceful mind, rather than an agitated mind. When your mind remains calm and more compassionate, your blood circulation is always normal. When your mind becomes more agitated, then it will eventually worsen. Everybody is very much healthier with a compassionate mind than with an angry mind. That is human nature, basic human nature.

Thinking along these lines my conclusion is that basic human nature is gentleness or compassion. It is therefore much more logical if we act according to our basic nature, i.e., gentleness. Unfortunately we often act in a contradictory manner. There is potential, if we make efforts to remain aware, we can change. We can transform ourselves, just like in Auroville the barren land has been transformed and is full of life. Similarly, each individual human being, using his intelligence and determination, can change! According to my own experience, with effort I can change, and to a certain extent I have changed my mental attitude. And it has brought me much, much benefit. Therefore, to develop peace of mind, compassion and human affection are very, very important factors. There is no point in neglecting these basic and good human qualities.

Each individual human being has in himself the potential or seed of these good qualities. The only question is whether we want to make the effort or not, that is the question. Otherwise, we can change. We can change our minds through mental training, just like we can train our physical bodies.

Therefore, for individuals who really seek peace of mind, the method is there, the potential is there. They do not necessarily need to go to the market, or to some sophisticated hospital, and pay a lot of money, and try to get peace of mind or some kind of compassionate mind. Without paying anything, you can develop it! Even in the supermarket, you cannot buy peace of mind. You cannot buy a happy mind, a compassionate mind.

For the compassionate mind, the seed of these good things is in you from your birth, it is already there. I feel that it is very important to realize this and to think about it.

Now concerning religion: when we talk about religion or religious traditions, we immediately get a picture of a temple or different customs or rituals. This is not truly speaking the real sense of religion: these are not necessarily religious things. Generally speaking, the real sense of religion has to do with a positive mind. A positive mind means that which ultimately brings us benefit or happiness, and the method by which these things are generated: this is the essence of religion.

The reason is quite clear: the external features of religion can be utilized in a negative way. They are therefore not essential, and not necessarily religious either. The essence of religion, like compassion, cannot be negative! For example, the recitation by mouth (*Mantras*), is of course part of religious practice, but while you are reciting some mantras, you can be thinking of hatred, of profit or how to cheat this gentleman or that one. You can think about these things while you are reciting your mantra, but that is not a true religious action.

Then, meditate on compassion. That is true religion! Because while you meditate on compassion, you cannot think about hatred. These two thoughts cannot go together. These two thoughts which oppose each other cannot go together. So, therefore, meditation on compassion is the essential religion.

If we can realize the essentials of the major religious traditions, then that is what is relevant to our modern daily lives. If we look at the superficial or the ritualistic level, these may not be relevant in our daily lives. If we think about the deeper level, all the major religious traditions carry the same message, although the presentation about love and compassion may differ because of different philosophies, but the general concept of compassion is the same. Once we realize the importance of this and we appreciate the deeper value of the human mind, then it automatically brings genuine respect towards all other religions. So, that also acts as a foundation for the development of harmony between different religious traditions. This is also very crucial.

Now, sometimes, religions also become yet one more instrument to divide humanity. So compassion, a compassionate mind has many, many important roles.

And according to my own little experience, we can change. We can transform ourselves. Therefore, those people who feel OK about what I just said, can try to experiment with it in their daily lives. At least, spend a few minutes every day, analyse these things and try to develop compassion, and eventually compassion will become a part of your life. Then you'll be a truly happy person.

If you find that my talk has not much relevance to your daily life, then just forget it. (*Laughter*) There is not much problem.

So, thank you very much. That's all.[3]

Thank you very much.

I would like to express my deep appreciation for these gifts. I specially very much appreciate that you mentioned about Tibet and particularly Claude my old friend who had always shown deep concern about Tibet.

We, Tibetans are in this country [India] for more than 34 years. We are refugees. But not refugees from a natural disaster, but because of the political situation.

Tibet, even according to the Chinese, has a civilization as old as the Chinese civilization and it had a unique environment. Later due to the introduction of Buddhism in Tibet, Tibet developed its own unique cultural heritage, its own culture with its own written language and it produced its own history. So, Tibet is a separate country from China, there is no doubt about it!

Since the Chinese invasion, a lot of destruction and suffering has taken place, even the late Panchen Lama who often spoke on behalf of the Chinese—obviously his inner person was very strongly Tibetan, but because of the circumstances, he was compelled to speak only according to the Chinese policy—even he, just two days before his sudden death—he said that "since the Chinese have occupied Tibet" (*laughing*), (no, no he did not use the word "occupation" of course), he said "since the Chinese came to Tibet, there are many developments, but these developments cannot match with the destruction".

I truly believe if the invaders had brought something good—they themselves claim to be the liberators—if the liberators had brought good things, history is history, the past is the past, and things would have been

---

[3]Some children then gave a few presents to the Dalai Lama.

different today. But in reality, the liberators have brought us only misery and fear. Therefore after more than 40 years of Chinese invasion, the gap between the Chinese and the Tibetans is still wide, it is even widening.

Now when we were in Tibet (until early 1959), the crisis was not a racial crisis, the crisis was only due to the invasion, but since then, the crisis has worsened due to the Chinese behaviour. It now involves many different aspects and factors: one aspect is the environment, another is racial discrimination; there is also cultural genocide and human rights violations and all this besides the invasion. Therefore, the Tibetan issue is something important.

To take the example of the environment, the major rivers which flow in the Asian continent have their source in Tibet: once Tibet is polluted or eroded or nuclear waste is dumped there, if something happens, it will affect major areas in Asia. That is why it is an important issue.

For all these reasons, I appreciate your concern, your understanding and your sympathy. I really appreciate it.

Today we are passing through a difficult period, so we really need your help.

Thank you very much!

V

Glimpses of A Great Life

V

Glimpses of A Great Life

Devotees in waiting (*Courtsey* : Yog Joy)

His Holiness (*Courtsey* : Yog Joy)

His Holiness (*Courtsey* : Yog Joy)

(*Courtsey*: Yog Joy)

(*Courtsey* : Yog Joy)

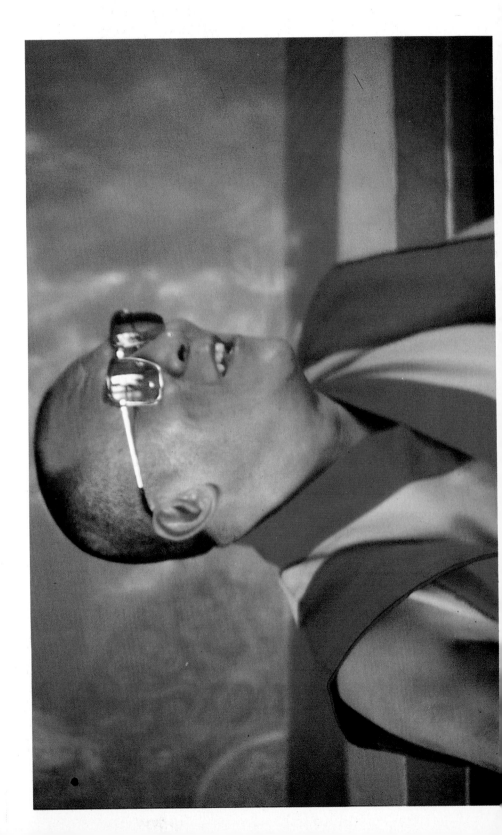

Chapter V
GLIMPSES OF A GREAT LIFE

I often told my mother that I was going to go to Lhasa. I used to straddle a window sill in our house pretending that I was riding a horse to Lhasa. I was a very small child at the time, but I remember this clearly. I had a strong desire to go there. Another thing I didn't mention in my autobiography is that after my birth, a pair of crows came to roost on the roof of our house. They would arrive each morning, stay for a while and then leave. This is of particular interest as similar incidents occurred at the birth of the First, Seventh, Eighth and Twelfth Dalai Lamas. After their births, a pair of crows came and remained. In my own case, in the beginning, nobody paid attention to this. Recently, however, perhaps three years ago, I was talking with my mother, and she recalled it. She had noticed them come in the morning, depart after a time, and then the next morning they came again. Now, the evening after the birth of the First Dalai Lama, bandits broke into the family's house. The parents ran away and left the child. The next day when they returned and wondered what had happened to their son, they found the baby in a corner of the house. A crow stood before him, protecting him. Later on, when the First Dalai Lama grew up and developed in his spiritual practice, he made direct contact during meditation with the protective deity, Mahakala. At this time, Mahakala said to him, "Somebody like you who is upholding the Buddhist teaching needs a protector like me. Right on the day of your birth, I helped you." So we can see, there is definitely a connection between Mahakala, the crows, and the Dalai Lamas.

—Dalai Lama

1

A DAY IN HIS LIFE[1]

When I wake up at four o'clock, I automatically start reciting the *Ngagjhinlab* mantra. It's a prayer that dedicates everything I do, my speech, my thoughts, my deeds, my whole day, as an offering, a positive way to help others. Like all monks, I obey a vow of poverty, so there are no personal possessions. My bedroom has just a bed and the first thing I see when I am awake is the face of the Buddha on a holy seventeenth-century statue from Kyirong, one of the very few that escaped the Chinese desecration. It's cold when I wake up, as we are at 7000 feet, so I do some exercises, wash and dress quickly.

I wear the same maroon robe as all the monks do. It's not of good quality, and it's patched. If it was of good material and in one piece, you could sell it and gain something. In this condition you can't. This reinforces our philosophy of becoming detached from worldly goods. I meditate until five-thirty and make prostrations. We have a special practice to remind ourselves of our misdeeds and I make my confession and recite prayers for the well being of all sentient beings.

Then at daybreak, if the weather is fine, I go into the garden. This time of day is very special to me. I look at the sky. It's very clear and I see the stars and have this special feeling—of my insignificance in the cosmos. The realization of what we Buddhists call impermanence. It's very relaxing. Sometimes I don't think at all and just enjoy the dawn and listen to the birds.

Then Penjor or Loga, monks from Namgyal monastery who have been with me for 28 years, bring my breakfast. It's half-Tibetan, half Western mixture. *Tsampa*—roasted barley flour—and porridge. While I have breakfast, my ears are busy listening to the news on the BBC World Service.

[1] As told to Vanya Kewley

Then at about six, I move into another room and meditate until nine. Through meditation, all Buddhists try and develop the right kind of motivation—compassion, forgiveness and tolerance. I meditate six or seven times a day.

From nine until lunch I read and study our scriptures. Buddhism is a very profound religion and, although I have been studying it all my life, there is still so much to learn.

Unfortunately nearly all our ancient books and manuscripts have been destroyed by the Chinese. It's as though all the Gutenberg bibles and Domesday books in the world had been destroyed. No record. No memory. Before the Chinese invasion, we had over six thousand functioning monasteries and temples. Now there are only thirty-seven.

I also try and read Western masters. I want to learn more about Western philosophy and science. Especially nuclear physics, astronomy and neurobiology. Often Western scientists come and discuss the relationship between our philosophy and theirs, or compare their work on the brain function and Buddhism experience of different levels of consciousness. It is an absorbing exchange, for all of us!

I often get up and go and fiddle with things. Charge batteries for the radio, repair something. From childhood I have been fascinated with mechanical things—toys, small cars, aeroplanes—things I could explore with my hands. We had an old movie projector in Lhasa that belonged to the Thirteenth Dalai Lama. It was looked after by an ancient Chinese monk. But when he died, no one else knew how to make it work. So I learnt how to make it go, but it was trial and error, as I couldn't read the instructions. I only spoke Tibetan. So now sometimes I work in my workshop repairing things like watches or clocks. Or planting things in the greenhouse. I love plants, especially delphiniums and tulips, and love to see them grow.

At twelve-thirty I have lunch, usually non-vegetarian, though I prefer vegetarian. I eat what I'm given. Sometimes thupa—soup with noodles, occasionally momo—steamed dumplings with meat—and skabakleb— deep-fried bread with meat inside.

The afternoon is taken up with official meetings with the *Bka'zhag* (Tibetan cabinet in exile), or deputies from the Assembly of Tibetan People's Deputies. But there are always people who come from Tibet, with or without the permission of the Chinese, mostly without—brave people who escape over 17,000 - foot Himalayan passes.

It is very painful for me. They all have sad stories and cry. Practically everyone tells me the names of relatives who have been killed by the Chinese, or died in Chinese prisons or labour camps. I try to give them encouragement and see how I can help them practically, as they arrive here destitute and in very bad health.

Very often they bring along their children here. They tell me it is the only way they can learn our language, faith and culture. We put the younger ones in the Tibetan Children's Village here or in Mussoorie. Older ones who want to be monks we send them for training in our monasteries in South India.

Although Tibetans want me to return [to Tibet]. I get messages from *inside* not to return under the present circumstances. They don't want me to be a Chinese puppet like the Panchen Lama. Here, in the free world, I am more useful to my people as a spokesman. I can serve them better from outside.

Sometimes Pema, my youngest sister, who runs the Tibetan Children's Village for orphans here, comes and discusses problems. Like all monks, I don't see much of my family; my parents are dead. My elder brother, Norbu, is Professor of Tibetan studies in Bloomington, Indiana. Thondup, a businessman, lives in Hong Kong.

Unfortunately my middle brother, Lobsang Samden, died two years ago. We were very close. He lived and studied with me in the Potala where we used to indulge in all sorts of mischief. Before his death, he worked here at the medical centre. I miss him very much.

At six I have tea. As a monk, I have no dinner. At seven it is television time, but unfortunately they transmit discussion programmes. And as one is from Amritsar and the other from Pakistan, and I don't know Punjabi or Urdu, it's all talk to me. But occasionally there is a film in English. I like the BBC series on Western civilization, and those wonderful nature programmes.

Then it's time for bed and more meditation and prayers and by eight-thirty or nine I fall asleep. But if there is a moon, I think that it is also looking down on my people imprisoned in Tibet. I give thanks that, even though I am a refugee, I am free here, free to speak for my people. I pray especially to the patron deity of Tibet, Avalokitesvara, for them. There is not one waking hour when I don't think of the plight of my people, locked away in their mountain fastness.

2

THE LIFE OF A MONK

Q. *What were your first feelings on being recognized as the Dalai Lama? What did you think had happened to you?*

A. I was very happy. I liked it a lot. Even before I was recognized, I often told my mother that I was going to go to Lhasa. I used to straddle a window sill in our house pretending that I was riding a horse to Lhasa. I was a very small child at the time, but I remember this clearly. I had a strong desire to go there. Another thing I didn't mention in my autobiography is that after my birth, a pair of crows came to roost on the roof of our house. They would arrive each morning, stay for a while and then leave. This is of particular interest as similar incidents occurred at the birth of the First, Seventh, Eighth and Twelfth Dalai Lamas. After their births, a pair of crows came and remained. In my own case, in the beginning, nobody paid attention to this. Recently, however, perhaps three years ago, I was talking with my mother, and she recalled it. She had noticed them come in the morning, depart after a time, and then the next morning they came again. Now, the evening after the birth of the First Dalai Lama, bandits broke into the family's house. The parents ran away and left the child. The next day when they returned and wondered what had happened to their son, they found the baby in a corner of the house. A crow stood before him, protecting him. Later on, when the First Dalai Lama grew up and developed in his spiritual practice, he made direct contact during meditation with the protective deity, Mahakala. At this time, Mahakala said to him, "Somebody like you who is upholding the Buddhist teaching needs a protector like me. Right on the day of your birth, I helped you." So we can see, there is definitely a connection between Mahakala, the crows, and the Dalai Lamas.

[1] An interview by John Avedon

Another thing that happened, which my mother rememberd very clearly, is that soon after I arrived in Lhasa, I said that my teeth were in a box in a certain house in the Norbulignka. When they opened the box, they found a set of dentures which had belonged to the Thirteenth Dalai Lama. I pointed to the box, and said that my teeth were in there, but right now I don't recall this at all. The new memories associated with this body are stronger. The past has become faint, more vague. Unless I make a specific attempt to develop such a memory, I don't recall it.

Q. *Do you remember your birth or the womb state before?*

A. At this moment, I don't remember. Also, I can't recall if at that time when I was a small child, I could remember it. However, there was one slight external sign perhaps. Children are usually born with their eyes closed. I was born with my eyes open. This may be some slight indication of a clear state of mind in the womb.

Q. *When you were a little boy, how did you feel on being treated by adults as an important person? Were you apprehensive or even frightened at being so revered?*

A. Tibetans are very practical people. Older Tibetans would never treat me that way. Also, I was very self-confident. When I first approached Lhasa on the Debuthang plain, the Nechung Oracle came to further verify that I was the correct choice. With him came an old, very respected, and highly realized *geshay* from Loseling College of Drepung Monastery. He was deeply concerned whether or not I was the correct choice. To have made a mistake in finding the Dalai Lama would be very dangerous. Now he was a religious man—not someone in the government. He came into the tent where I was in a group audience, and determined that unquestionably I was the right choice. So you see, though there were certain very experienced old people who wanted to be sure, I apparently put on a good performance and convinced them. I was never uneasy in my position. Charles Bell has mentioned that I was taking it all quite casually. To do with fear, there's one thing I remember clearly. One night I wanted to visit my mother, who had come with the rest of my family to Lhasa. I was in the tent of the regent. A very large bodyguard was standing by the entrance. It was evening, sunset, and this man had a bad, damaged eye. I remember being scared, frightened then, to go out of the tent.

Q. *Between the ages of sixteen and eighteen, after you assumed temporal power, did you change?*

A. Yes, I changed .... a little bit. I underwent a lot of happiness and pain. While putting up with that and from growing, gaining more experience, from the problems that arose and the suffering, I changed. The ultimate result is the man you see now.

Q. *How about when you just entered adolescence? Many people have a difficult time defining themselves as an adult. Did this happen to you?*

A. No. My life was very much in a routine. Two times a day I studied. Each time I studied for an hour, and then spent the rest of the time playing. Then at the age of 13, I began studying philosophy, definitions, debate. My studies increased, and I also studied calligraphy. It was all in a routine though, and I got used to it. Sometimes, there were vacations. These were very comfortable, happy days. Losang Samten, my immediate elder brother, was usually at school, but during these times he would come to visit. Also, occasionally my mother would bring special bread from our province of Amdo. Very thick and delicious. She made this herself.

Q. *Did you have an opportunity to have a relationship with your father when you were growing up?*

A. My father died when I was 13.

Q. *Are there any of your predecessors in whom you have a special interest or with whom you have a particular affinity?*

A. The Thirteenth Dalai Lama. He brought a lot of improvement to the standards of study in the monastic colleges. He gave great encouragement to the real scholars. He made it impossible for people to go up in the religious hierarchy, becoming an abbot and so forth, without being totally qualified. He was very strict in this respect. He also gave tens of thousands of monks ordinations. These were his two main religious achievements. He didn't give many initiations, or many lectures. Now, with respect to the country, he had great thought and consideration for statecraft—the outlying districts in particular—how they should be governed and so forth. He cared very much about how to run the government more efficiently. He had great concern about our borders and things of that type.

Q. *During the course of your own life, what have been your greatest personal lessons or internal challenges? Which realizations and experiences have had the most effect on your growth as an individual?*

A. Regarding religious experience, some understanding of *shunya* [emptiness: lack of independent self-nature]—some feeling, some experience—and mostly *bodhichitta*, altruism. It has helped a lot. In some ways, you could say that it has made me into a new person, a new man. I'm still progressing. Trying. It gives you inner strength, courage, and it is easier to accept situations. That's one of the greatest experiences.

Q. *On the bodhichitta side, are you speaking about a progressive deepening of realization or a certain moment associated with external experience?*

A. Mainly internal practice. There could also be external causes or circumstances. External factors could have played a part in the development of some feeling for bodhichitta. But mainly, it has to come from internal practice.

Q. *Can you cite a specific moment from your practice when you crossed a threshold?*

A. Regarding shunya theory, first shunya theory, then bodhichitta feeling ..... Around '65, '66, in that period. This is really a personal matter. For a true religious practitioner, these things must be kept private.

Q. *OK. Not asking you about your own deepest experience, but in terms of the course of your life—the events of your life—how have these affected you as a man? How have you grown through experiencing them?*

A. Being a refugee has been very useful. You are much closer to reality. When I was in Tibet as the Dalai Lama, I was trying to be realistic, but somehow because of circumstances, there was some distance, I think. I was a bit isolated from the reality. I became a refugee. Very good. So there was a good opportunity to gain experience and also determination or inner strength.

Q. *When you became a refugee, what helped you gain this strength? Was it the loss of your position and country, the fact of everyone suffering around you? Were you called on to lead your people in a different way than you had been accustomed to?*

A. Being a refugee is a really desperate, dangerous situation. At that time, everyone deals with reality. It is not the time to pretend things are beautiful. That's something quite different. You feel involved with reality. In peace time, everything goes smoothly. Even if there is a problem, people pretend that things are all right. During a dangerous period, when there's a dramatic change, then there's no scope to pretend that everything is fine. You must accept that bad is bad. Now when I left the Norbulingka, there was danger. We were passing very near the Chinese military barracks. It was just on the other side of the river, where the Chinese check post was. You see, we had definite information two or three weeks before I left, that the Chinese were fully prepared to attack us. It was only a question of the day and hour.

Q. *At that moment, when you crossed the Kyichu River and met the party of Khampa guerillas waiting for you, did you assume a direct leadership capacity? Who, for instance, made the decisions on your flight?*

A. As soon as we left Lhasa, we set up an inner group, a committee to discuss each point. Myself and eight other people.

Q. *Was it your idea to make it unanimous?*

A. Yes. Those who were left behind in Lhasa also established a People's Committee. Something like a revolutionary council. Of course, from the Chinese viewpoint, this was a counter revolutionary committee. Chosen by the people, you see, within a few days .... They set up that committee and all major decisions were made by it. I also sent a letter to that committee, certifying it. In our small committee, those who were escaping with me, we discussed the practical points each night. Originally, our plan was to establish our headquarters in southern Tibet, as you know. Also, I mentioned to Pandit Nehru—I think on the 24th of April, 1959—that we had established a temporary Tibetan government, shifted from Lhasa to southern Tibet. I mentioned this casually to the Prime Minister. He was slightly agitated. "We are not going to recognize your government", he said. Although this government had been formed while still inside Tibet, and I was already in India.

Q. *I'd like to ask you about being the incarnation of the Bodhisattva of infinite compassion, Avalokitesvara [Tibetan: Chenrezi]. How do you personally feel about this? Is it something you have an unequivocal view of one way or another?*

A. It is difficult for me to say definitely. Unless I engaged myself in a meditative effort, such as following my life back breath by breath, I couldn't say exactly. We believe that there are four types of rebirths. One is the common type, wherein a being is helpless to determine his or her rebirth, but only incarnates in dependence on the nature of past actions. The opposite is that of an entirely enlightened Buddha, who simply manifests a physical form to help others. In this case, it is clear that the person is a Buddha. A third is one who, due to past spiritual attainment, can choose, or at least influence, the place and situation of rebirth. The fourth is called a blessed manifestation. In this the person is blessed beyond his normal capacity to perform helpful functions, such as teaching religion. For this last type of birth, the person's wishes in previous lives to help others must have been very strong. They then obtain such empowerment. Though some seem more likely than others, I cannot definitely say which I am.

Q. *From the viewpoint then of the realistic role you play as Chenrezi, how do you feel about it? Only a few people have been considered, in one way or another, divine. Is the role a burden or a delight?*

A. It is very helpful. Through this role I can be of great benefit to people. For this reason I like it: I'm at home with it. It's clear that it is very helpful to people, and that I have the karmic relationship to be in this role. Also, it is clear that there is a karmic relationship with the Tibetan people in particular. Now you see, you may consider that under the circumstances, I am very lucky. However, behind the word luck, there are actual causes or reasons. There is the karmic force of my ability to assume this role as well as the force of my wish to do so. In regard to this, there is a statement in the great Shantideva's *Engaging in the Bodhisattva Deeds* which says, "As long as space exists, and as long as there are migrators in cyclic existence, may I remain—removing their suffering." I have that wish in this lifetime, and I know I had that wish in past lifetimes.

Q. *With such a vast goal as your motivation, how do you deal with your personal limitations, your limits as a man?*

A. Again, as it says in Shantideva, "If the blessed Buddha cannot please all sentient beings, then how could I?" Even an enlightened being, with limitless knowledge and power and the wish to save all others from suffering, cannot eliminate the individual karma of each being.

Q. *Is this what keeps you from being overwhelmed when you see the suffering of the six million Tibetans, who on one level, you are responsible for?*

A. My motivation is directed towards all sentient beings. There is no question, though, that on a second level, I am directed towards helping Tibetans. If a problem is fixable, if a situation is such that you can do something about it, then there is no need to worry. If it's not fixable, then there is no help in worrying. There is no benefit in worrying whatsoever.

Q. *A lot of people say this, but few really live by it. Did you always feel this way, or did you have to learn it?*

A. It is developed from inner practice. From a broader perspective, there will always be suffering. On one level, you are bound to meet with the effects of the unfavourable actions you yourself have previously committed in either body, speech or mind. Then also, your very own nature is that of suffering. There's not just one factor figuring into my attitude, but many different ones. From the point of view of the actual entity producing the suffering, as I have said, if it is fixable, then there is no need to worry. If not, there is no benefit in worrying. From the point of view of the cause, suffering is based on past unfavourable actions accumulated by oneself and no other. These karmas are not wasted. They will bear their fruit. One will not meet with the effects of actions that one has not done oneself. Finally, from the viewpoint of the nature of suffering itself, the aggregates of the mind and body have as their actual nature, suffering. They serve as a basis for suffering. As long as you have them you are susceptible to suffering. From a deeper point of view, while we don't have our independence and are living in someone else's country, we have a certain type of suffering, but when we return to Tibet and gain our independence, then there will be other types of suffering. So, this is just the way it is. You might think that I'm pessimistic, but I am not. This is the Buddhist realism. This is how, through Buddhist teaching and advice, we handle situations. When fifty thousand people in the Shakya clan were killed one day, Shakyamuni Buddha, their clansman, didn't suffer at all. He was leaning against a tree, and he was saying, "I am a little sad today because fifty thousand of my clansmen were killed." But he, himself, remained unaffected. Like that, you see. This was the cause and effect of their own karma. There was nothing he could do about it. These sorts of thoughts make me stronger; more active. It is not at all a case of losing one's strength of mind or will in the face of the pervasive nature of suffering.

Q. *I'm interested in what you do to relax: gardening and experimenting with electronics.*

A. Oh, my hobbies. Passing time. When I can repair something, it gives me real satisfaction. I began dismantling things when I was young because I was curious about how certain machines functioned. I wanted to know what was inside the motor, but these days I only try to fix something when it breaks.

Q. *And gardening?*

A. Gardening in Dharamsala is almost a hopeless thing. No matter how hard you work, the monsoon comes and destroys everything. You know, a monk's life is very gratifying; very happy. You can see this from those who have given up the robes. They definitely know the value of monkhood. Many have told me how complicated and difficult life is without it. With a pretty wife and children you may be happy for sometime. In the long run, though, many problems naturally come about. Half of your independence—your freedom—is lost. If there is some benefit or meaning in experiencing the trouble which arises on giving up your independence, then it is worthwhile. If it is a situation which helps people effectively, then it is good. The trouble becomes worthwhile. But if it isn't, it is not worthwhile.

Q. *But none of us would even be here talking about this unless we had mothers and fathers!*

A. I'm not saying that having children is bad, or that everyone should be a monk. Impossible.

   I think that if one's life is simple, contentment has to come. Simplicity is extremely important for happiness. Having few desires, feeling satisfied with what you have is very vital. There are four causes which help produce a superior being. Satisfaction with whatever food you get. Satisfaction with rags for clothing, or acceptance of any covering—not wishing for fancy or colourful attire. Satisfaction with just enough shelter to protect yourself from the elements. And finally, an intense delight in abandoning faulty states of mind and in cultivating helpful ones in meditation.

VI
Kindness and Compassion

Chapter VI
KINDNESS AND COMPASSION

I am a religious person, and from my viewpoint all things first originate in the mind. Things and events depend heavily on motivation. A real sense of appreciation of humanity, compassion and love, are the key points. If we develop a good heart, then whether the field is science, agriculture, or politics, since motivation is so very important, these will all improve. A good heart is both important and effective in daily life. If in a small family, even without children, the members have a warm heart to each other, a peaceful atmosphere will be created. However, if one of the person feels angry, immediately the atmosphere in the house becomes tense. Despite good food or a nice television set, you will lose peace and calm. Thus, things depend more on the mind than on matter. Matter is important, we must have it, we must use it properly, but this century must combine a good brain—intelligence—with a good heart.

The human essence of good sense finds no room with anger. Anger, jealousy, impatience, and hatred are the real trouble makers; with them problems cannot be solved. Though one may have temporary success, ultimately one's hatred or anger will create further difficulties. With anger, all actions are swift. When we face problems with compassion, sincerely and with good motivation, it may take longer, but ultimately the solution is better, for there is far less chance of creating a new problem.

Sometimes we look down on politics, criticizing it as dirty. However, if you look at it properly, politics in itself is not wrong. It is an instrument to serve human society. With good motivation—sincerity and honesty—politics becomes an instrument in the service of society. But when motivated by selfishness with hatred, anger, or jealousy, it becomes dirty.

—Dalai Lama

1

COMPASSION AND THE INDIVIDUAL

One great question underlies our experience, whether we think about it consciously or not: What is the purpose of life? I have considered this question and would like to share my thoughts in the hope that they may be of direct, practical benefit to those who read them.

I believe that the purpose of life is to be happy. From the moment of birth, every human being wants happiness and does not want suffering. Neither social conditioning nor education nor ideology affect this. From the very core of our being, we simply desire contentment. I don't know whether the universe, with its countless galaxies, stars and planets, has a deeper meaning or not, but at the very least, it is clear that we humans who live on this earth face the task of making a happy life for ourselves. Therefore, it is important to discover what will bring about the greatest degree of happiness.

How to achieve happiness

For a start, it is possible to divide every kind of happiness and suffering into two main categories: mental and physical. Of the two, it is the mind that exerts the greatest influence on most of us. Unless we are either gravely ill or deprived of basic necessities, our physical condition plays a secondary role in life. If the body is content, we virtually ignore it. The mind, however, registers every event, no matter how small. Hence we should devote our most serious efforts to bringing about mental peace.

From my own limited experience I have found that the greatest degree of inner tranquillity comes from the development of love and compassion.

The more we care for the happiness of others, the greater our own sense of well-being becomes. Cultivating a close, warm-hearted feeling for others automatically puts the mind at ease. This helps remove whatever fears or insecurities we may have and gives us the strength to cope with any obstacles we encounter. It is the ultimate source of success in life.

As long as we live in this world we are bound to encounter problems. If, at such times, we lose hope and become discouraged, we diminish our ability to face difficulties. If, on the other hand, we remember that it is not just ourselves but everyone who has to undergo suffering, this more realistic perspective will increase our determination and capacity to overcome troubles. Indeed, with this attitude, each new obstacle can be seen as yet another valuable opportunity to improve our mind!

Thus we can strive gradually to become more compassionate, that is , we can develop both genuine sympathy for others' suffering and the will to help remove their pain. As a result, our own serenity and inner strength will increase.

Our need for love

Ultimately, the reason why love and compassion bring the greatest happiness is simply that our nature cherishes them above all else. The need for love lies at the very foundation of human existence. It results from the profound interdependence we all share with one another. However capable and skillful an individual may be, left alone, he or she will not survive. However vigorous and independent one may feel during the most prosperous periods of life, when one is sick or very young or very old, one must depend on the support of others.

Interdependence, of course, is a fundamental law of nature. Not only higher forms of life but also many of the smallest insects are social beings who, without any religion, law or education, survive by mutual cooperation based on an innate recognition of their interconnectedness. The most subtle level of material phenomena is also governed by interdependence. All phenomena, from the planet we inhabit to the oceans, clouds, forests and flowers that surround us, arise in dependence upon subtle patterns of energy. Without their proper interaction, they dissolve and decay.

It is because our own human existence is so dependent on the help of others that our need for love lies at the very foundation of our existence. Therefore we need a genuine sense of responsibility and a sincere concern for the welfare of others.

We have to consider what we human beings really are. We are not like machine-made objects. If we were merely mechanical entities, then machines themselves could alleviate all of our sufferings and fulfil our needs. However, since we are not solely material creatures, it is a mistake to place all our hopes for happiness on external development alone. Instead, we should consider our origins and nature to discover what we require.

Leaving aside the complex question of the creation and evolution of our universe, we can at least agree that each of us is the product of our own parents. In general, our conception took place not just in the context of sexual desire but from our parents' decision to have a child. Such decisions are founded on responsibility and altruism—the parents' compassionate commitment to care for their child until it is able to take care of itself. Thus, from the very moment of our conception, our parents' love is directly involved in our creation.

Moreover, we are completely dependent upon our mother's care from the earliest stages of our growth. According to some scientists, a pregnant woman's mental state, be it calm or agitated, has a direct physical effect on her unborn child.

The expression of love is also very important at the time of birth. Since the very first thing we do is suck milk from our mother's breast, we naturally feel close to her, and she must feel love for us in order to feed us properly; if she feels anger or resentment her milk may not flow freely.

Then there is the critical period of brain development from the time of birth up to at least the age of three or four, during which time loving physical contact is the single most important factor for the normal growth of the child. If the child is not held, hugged, cuddled or loved, its development will be impaired and its brain will not mature properly.

Since a child cannot survive without the care of others, love is its most important nourishment. The happiness of childhood, the allaying of the child's many fears and the healthy development of its self-confidence all depend directly upon love.

Nowadays, many children grow up in unhappy homes. If they do not receive proper affection, in later life they will rarely love their parents and, not infrequently, will find it hard to love others. This is very sad.

As children grow older and enter school, their need for support must be met by their teachers. If a teacher not only imparts academic education but also assumes responsibility for preparing students for life, his or her pupils will feel trust and respect and what has been taught will leave an indelible impression on their minds. On the other hand, subjects taught by a teacher who does not show true concern for his or her students' overall well-being will be regarded as temporary and not retained for long.

Similarly, if one is sick and being treated in hospital by a doctor who evinces a warm human feeling, one feels at ease and the doctor's desire to give the best possible care is itself curative, irrespective of the degree of his or her technical skill. On the other hand, if one's doctor lacks human feeling and displays an unfriendly expression, impatience or casual disregard, one will feel anxious, even if he or she is the most highly qualified doctor and the disease has been correctly diagnosed and the right medication prescribed. Inevitably, patients' feelings make a difference to the quality and completeness of their recovery.

Even when we engage in ordinary conversation in everyday life, if someone speaks with human feeling we enjoy listening, and respond accordingly; the whole conversation becomes interesting, however unimportant the topic may be. On the other hand, if a person speaks coldly or harshly, we feel uneasy and wish for a quick end to the interaction. From the least to the most important event, the affection and respect of others are vital for our happiness.

Recently I met a group of scientists in America who said that the rate of mental illness in their country was quite high—around twelve per cent of the population. It became clear during our discussion that the main cause of depression was not a lack of material necessities but a deprivation of the affection of others.

So, as you can see from everything I have written so far, one thing seems clear to me: whether or not we are consciously aware of it, from the day we are born, the need for human affection is in our very blood. Even if the affection comes from an animal or someone we would normally consider an enemy, both children and adults will naturally gravitate towards it.

I believe that no one is born free from the need for love. And this demonstrates that, although some modern schools of thought seek to do so, human beings cannot be defined as solely physical. No material object, however beautiful or valuable, can make us feel loved, because our deeper identity and true character lie in the subjective nature of the mind.

Developing compassion

Some of my friends have told me that, while love and compassion are marvellous and good, they are not really very relevant. Our world, they say, is not a place where such beliefs have much influence or power. They claim that anger and hatred are so much a part of human nature that humanity will always be dominated by them. I do not agree.

We humans have existed in our present form for about a hundred thousand years. I believe that if during this time the human mind had been primarily controlled by anger and hatred, our overall population would have decreased. But today, despite all our wars, we find that the human population is greater than ever. This clearly indicates to me that love and compassion predominate in the world. And this is why unpleasant events are "news"; compassionate activities are so much a part of daily life that they are taken for granted and, therefore, largely ignored.

So far I have been discussing mainly the mental benefits of compassion, but it contributes to good physical health as well. According to my personal experience, mental stability and physical well-being are directly related. Without question, anger and agitation make us more susceptible to illness. On the other hand, if the mind is tranquil and occupied with positive thoughts, the body will not easily fall prey to disease.

But of course it is also true that we all have an innate self-centredness that inhibits our love for others. So, since we desire the true happiness that is brought about by only a calm mind, and since such peace of mind is brought about by only a compassionate attitude, how can we develop this? Obviously, it is not enough for us simply to think about how nice compassion is! We need to make a concerted effort to develop it; we must use all the events of our daily life to transform our thoughts and behaviour.

First of all, we must be clear about what we mean by compassion. Many forms of compassionate feeling are mixed with desire and attachment. For instance, the love parents feel for their child is often strongly associated with their own emotional needs, so it is not fully compassionate. Again, in marriage, the love between husband and wife—particularly at the beginning, when each partner still may not know the other's deeper character very well—depends more on attachment than genuine love. Our desire can be so strong that the person to whom we are attached appears to be good, when in fact he or she is very negative. In addition, we have a tendency to exaggerate small positive qualities. Thus when one partner's attitude changes, the other partner is often disappointed and his or her attitude changes too. This is an indication that love has been motivated more by personal need than by genuine care for the other individual.

True compassion is not just an emotional response but a firm commitment founded on reason. Therefore, a truly compassionate attitude towards others does not change even if they behave negatively.

Of course, developing this kind of compassion is not at all easy! As a start, let us consider the following facts:

Whether people are beautiful and friendly or unattractive and disruptive, ultimately they are human beings, just like oneself. Like oneself, they want happiness and do not want suffering. Furthermore, their right to overcome suffering and be happy is equal to one's own. Now, when you recognize that all beings are equal in both their desire for happiness and their right to obtain it, you automatically feel empathy and closeness for them. Through accustoming your mind to this sense of universal altruism, you develop a feeling of responsibility for others: the wish to help them actively overcome their problems. Nor is this wish selective; it applies equally to all. As long as they are human beings experiencing pleasure and pain just as you do, there is no logical basis to discriminate between them or to alter your concern for them if they behave negatively.

Let me emphasize that it is within our power, given patience and time, to develop this kind of compassion. Of course, our self-centredness, our distinctive attachment to the feeling of an independent, self-existent "I", works fundamentally to inhibit our compassion. Indeed, true compassion can be experienced only when this type of self-grasping is eliminated. But this does not mean that we cannot start and make progress now.

How we can start

We should begin by removing the greatest hindrances to compassion: anger and hatred. As we all know, these are extremely powerful emotions and they can overwhelm our entire mind. Nevertheless, they can be controlled. If, however, they are not, these negative emotions will plague us—with no extra effort on their part!—And impede our quest for the happiness of a loving mind.

So as a start, it is useful to investigate whether or not anger is of value. Sometimes, when we are discouraged by a difficult situation, anger does seem helpful, appearing to bring with it more energy, confidence and determination.

Here, though, we must examine our mental state carefully. While it is true that anger brings extra energy, if we explore the nature of this energy, we discover that it is blind: we cannot be sure whether its result will be positive or negative. This is because anger eclipses the best part of our brain: its rationality. So the energy of anger is almost always unreliable. It can cause an immense amount of destructive, unfortunate behaviour. Moreover, if anger increases to the extreme, one becomes like a mad person, acting in ways that are as damaging to oneself as they are to others.

It is possible, however, to develop an equally forceful but far more controlled energy with which to handle difficult situations.

This controlled energy comes not only from a compassionate attitude, but also from reason and patience. These are the most powerful antidotes to anger. Unfortunately, many people misjudge these qualities as signs of weakness. I believe the opposite to be true: that they are the true signs of inner strength. Compassion is by nature gentle, peaceful and soft, but it is also very powerful. It is those who easily lose their patience who are insecure and unstable. Thus, to me, the arousal of anger is a direct sign of weakness.

So, when a problem first arises, try to remain humble and maintain a sincere attitude and be concerned that the outcome is fair. Of course, others may try to take advantage of you, and if your remaining detached only encourages unjust aggression, adopt a strong stand. This, however, should be done with compassion, and if it is necessary to express your views and take strong countermeasures, do so without anger or ill-intent.

You should realize that even though your opponents appear to be harming you, in the end, their destructive activity will damage only themselves. In order to check your own selfish impulse to retaliate, you should recall your desire to practice compassion and assume responsibility for helping prevent the other person from suffering the consequences of his or her acts.

Thus, because the measures you employ have been calmly chosen, they will be more effective, more accurate and more forceful. Retaliation based on the blind energy of anger seldom hits the target.

Friends and enemies

I must emphasize again that merely thinking that compassion and reason and patience are good will not be enough to develop them. We must wait for difficulties to arise and then attempt to practice them.

And who creates such opportunities? Not our friends, of course, but our *enemies*. They are the ones who give us the most trouble. So if we truly wish to learn, we should consider enemies to be our best teachers!

For a person who cherishes compassion and love, the practice of tolerance is essential, and for that, an enemy is indispensable. So we should feel grateful to our enemies, for it is they who can best help us develop a tranquil mind! Also, it is often the case in both personal and public life, that with a change in circumstances, enemies become friends.

So anger and hatred are *always* harmful, and unless we train our minds and work to reduce their negative force, they will continue to disturb us and disrupt our attempts to develop a calm mind. Anger and hatred are our real enemies. These are the forces we most need to confront and defeat, not the temporary "enemies" who appear intermittently throughout life.

Of course, it is natural and right that we all want friends. I often joke that if you really want to be selfish, you should be very altruistic! You should take good care of others, be concerned for their welfare, help them, serve them, make more friends, respond with more smiles. The result? When you yourself need help, you find plenty of helpers! If, on the other hand, you neglect the happiness of others, in the long term you will be the loser. And is friendship produced through quarrels and anger, jealousy and intense competitiveness? I do not think so. Only affection brings us genuine close friends.

In today's materialistic society, if you have money and power, you seem to have many friends. But they are not friends of yours; they are the friends of your money and power. When you lose your wealth and influence, you will find it very difficult to track these people down.

The trouble is that when things in the world go well for us, we become confident that we can manage by ourselves and feel we do not need friends, but as our status and health decline, we quickly realize how wrong we were. That is the moment when we learn who is really helpful and who is completely useless. So to prepare for that moment, to make genuine friends who will help us when the need arises, we ourselves must cultivate altruism!

Though sometimes people laugh when I say it, I myself always want more friends. I love smiles. Because of this I have the problem of knowing how to make more friends and how to get more smiles, in particular, genuine smiles. For there are many kinds of smiles such as sarcastic, artificial or diplomatic smiles. Many smiles produce no feeling of satisfaction, and sometimes they can even create suspicion or fear, can't they? But a genuine smile really gives us a feeling of freshness and is, I believe, unique to human beings. If these are the smiles we want, then we ourselves must create the reasons for them to appear.

Compassion and the world

In conclusion, I would like briefly to expand my thoughts beyond the topic of this short piece and make a wider point: individual happiness can contribute in a profound and effective way to the overall improvement of our entire human community.

Because we all share an identical need for love, it is possible to feel that anybody we meet, in whatever circumstances, is a brother or sister. No matter how new the face or how different the dress and behaviour, there is no significant division between us and other people. It is foolish to dwell on external differences, because our basic natures are the same.

Ultimately, humanity is one and this small planet is our only home. If we are to protect this home of ours, each of us needs to experience a vivid sense of universal altruism. It is only this feeling that can remove the self-centred motives that cause people to deceive and misuse one another. If you have a sincere and open heart, you naturally feel self-worthy and confident, and there is no need to be fearful of others.

I believe that at every level of society—familial, tribal, national and international—the key to a happier and more successful world is the growth of compassion. We do not need to become religious, nor do we need to believe in an ideology. All that is necessary is for each of us to develop our good human qualities.

I try to treat whoever I meet as an old friend. This gives me a genuine feeling of happiness. It is the practice of compassion.

2

ADDRESS TO DIPLOMATS[1]

I don't know on what I should emphasise more but in any case I am really happy to be here with you and to see many old friends. We have known each other for a long time during a difficult period. Some of my old friends seem to have gained more weight, some seem thinner, in any case, their hair has become whiter. I myself, have more white hair here and there. There is increasingly less and less hair in the centre. I am becoming bald and getting more white hair. It seems there is a competition between the two; so I think afterwards the Dalai Lama's head will soon become either white or will become bald. I don't know. I think I prefer white.

So you see that is the nature of human life; changing. Our life, not only human life, but whole universe is momentary, changing all the time. Now one thing which always remains the same is wanting happiness and not suffering. That feeling, that desire is always there and that is the basis of human evolution. Now as a Buddhist, as a person who believes in spiritualism, that desire is something right. Of course there are, from the Buddhist point of view, different kinds of desires. One kind of desire is that which is based on reason. For example the desire to achieve happiness and the desire to overcome problems. That is right. Another kind of desire such as extreme greediness has no foundation of reason. This kind of desire, instead of solving problems and achieving something, becomes a problem in itself leading to more disastrous consequences. There is, however, nothing wrong in having the desire or the basic feeling of wanting happiness. After all sentient beings, including human beings, have that kind of feeling.

[1] His Holiness the Dalai Lama was given a reception by the Association of Indian Diplomats at New Delhi on January 29, 1985.

Now the question is how to achieve happiness: the genuine happiness and mental peace. As a Buddhist and also as a person who has passed through difficult periods, I find the most influential factor is one's own mental attitude. If one's own mental attitude is somehow wrong, somehow of an irritative type, what you call feelings of hatred or feelings of that kind then even the most peaceful and comfortable environment will not give you peace. On the other hand if our mental attitude is something peaceful, something gentle, then even a very hostile environment will have very little effect on one's inner peace. Since the basic source of happiness is one's own mental attitude, the training of mind to develop that attitude is something very useful and very effective. Like the physical body—if your physical body becomes weak then it is easily affected by other factors. If your basic physical body is fit and healthy then small things are less likely to cause illness. So similarly if your basic mind is sound something very stable and at peace then external factors can do very little to disturb it. If your mind is very weak and vulnerable it will easily become the cause of mental problem and suffering. Sometimes even your friends can irritate you despite their good motivation.

The basis for developing the correct mental attitude, as all the different religions emphasise, is love and kindness. If you develop love, kindness and compassion on the basis of genuine sense of brotherhood, sisterhood and consider all of humanity as your family it will give you tremendous mental strength and stability. And that in turn gives you mental peace. With mental peace you could utilise the best part of human brain because at the time when your mind is at peace your mind remains very sharp and clear. If your mind is full of hatred or irritation then its sharpness will diminish. At that moment there is every possibility of taking the wrong decision. So on international level, or national level or family level the stability of mind is something very important. The source of a stable mind is love and kindness. Anger and hatred will immediately destroy the stability of mind. I believe this is not only a part of religious practice but as human beings and as members of the human family we need to develop the right kind of mental quality. I think you know these things better. You are experienced diplomats. You have faced many, many problems and handled them with your skill. So it may not be proper for me to mention these things.

In any case this is my own experience. When you are passing

through a difficult period if your mind is clear and stable that difficult period is nothing but the best opportunity to gain more experience, more knowledge and greater inner strength. Future success depends entirely on present determination. Determination comes from hope. Without hope you can't have determination. Therefore, courage and hope are the very basis of future. For that mental stability is very important. These are my daily practices.

This also has relevance to the question of world peace. Peace can not be produced by nice documents or as mentioned earlier violence cannot be eliminated by violence. Comparative peace of the present day as a result of what you call nuclear deterrent may work for some time but definitely it is not the ultimate alternative. A genuine world peace can be achieved only through mental peace. This mental peace comes from a genuine sense of brotherhood and sisterhood based on love and kindness.

Today unlike in the past we very much depend on each other in the economic field. We may be politically enemies but in economic sphere we need each other. So, whether we like it or not, this is the reality. Since we have to remain together it is far better to live harmoniously than with suspicion, cheating or threatening each other. Even for atheists who do not believe in God or rebirth or karma, even these people so long as they remain as members of the human family, they need love and compassion. So I believe that the practice of love and compassion is a universal religion. Everybody needs these things. I think the reason is quite simple. If some one wants happiness then he must take care of the basic source of happiness. Money, wealth and power, the other sources of happiness, are not very reliable. It is very clear that even a rich millionaire can have mental trouble and anxiety despite his wealth and power. He has to live on drugs and tranquillisers. So wealth, money and power are of course one source of happiness but not definite. Usually I call it fifty-fifty. You may get mental peace through wealth or you may get mental trouble from wealth. Now the thing which is definitely hundred per cent reliable source of happiness is love and compassion. So it is very simple. If you want that result, that fruit, you must take care of the source of that fruit. That you don't need to buy, you don't need to go to a doctor for treatment. So long as human mental consciousness is there you could develop a warm heart.

As a human being, right from the beginning we grow up under our parents' love and care. Our main *gurus* are our parents and our main temple is our own home. Once we leave our parents and our home, if we lose the basic human quality, i.e., human warmth we can't find our own peace and we will become a trouble maker in the society. Isn't it? One may be very educated, and intelligent but when intelligence and knowledge are used in the wrong way in human society it will bring trouble.

Man in his very nature is a kind of social animal and we have to live together even if we may not like each other. Since this being the case altruism is one of the most important things. Even animals and insects could develop certain limited altruism. We human beings have such a good brain. So why can't we practice altruism? Even between parents and children, husband and wife peace comes from love, kindness, mutual respect and understanding. Once you lose these basic human qualities then trouble starts. In other words you could say that the entire future depends on warm heart of the present generation.

For this in earlier societies religion was a very important factor. Today I think the most important factor is our education system. It seems that in different countries people are expressing some critical views about present educational system but nobody has found a proper system. But I believe it is very important to think very seriously about the way the child is brought up right from the beginning. It is very, very important for the future and for world peace and for individual peace.

As I mentioned earlier from my little experience the best way to achieve mental peace and happiness is to practice love, kindness and tolerance. But in order to do this you need patience. If you remain an impatient person it is difficult to develop love and compassion. Patience is very important. Now in order to develop or practice patience and tolerance you need an enemy. If you think on these lines and think deeper you will appreciate the enemy's behaviour. This really teaches you patience and tolerance. In this way even your enemy becomes a true friend or a true teacher or a helper for the development of your inner strength. Now in my case it is the Chinese. We are only six million and the Chinese have a huge population. Despite sympathy we have few friends and they on the other hand may not have sympathy but more friends. Isn't it? From that viewpoint it is in a way discouraging sign. But I always believe that truth and justice will ultimately prevail. Right from the time when human civilization began the value of justice existed and the basic reason for this is the need for fulfilment of human satisfaction. Under

Chinese domination there is definitely no human satisfaction. So people express their negative attitude. So long as justice and truth are on one's side and so long as there is human determination things will change. When I think about the Chinese side and our own side then it gives me more strength, more courage, determination and of course patience and tolerance. So in a way the Chinese are my most gracious guru. That does not mean we accept the guru's word if there is no reason, if there is no proper justification. Then we have the right to argue and to challenge. The Buddha himself taught us that we should accept his teachings if we are convinced that they are based on reason and reality as a result of our own experimentation and investigation. So like that it is towards the Chinese guru also. If they act and say with reason and with understanding of human values of course we will accept. If they say or act differently without consideration of these things then we cannot accept. These are my present thoughts and my experiences. So now I would like to learn or to know and have suggestions or advice from my old experienced friends. Thank you.

Q. *His Holiness has very kindly agreed to answer any questions we put to him. May I start by asking you a question. Your Holiness, you had once said that if you put the leaders of the two super powers on a beautiful island they are bound to come to an understanding. You think that is valid today in the present conditions?*

A. Yes, I do believe so. Now although people are trying to achieve something about nuclear arms control and disarmament but right from the beginning as soon as they come together they see each other with mutual suspicion and distrust. In fact one of my old Indian friends who had some connection with these talks told me that as soon as officials come together they start negotiations with a great suspicion and that was the real obstacle. Because of this they cannot reach agreement on even certain easy things. If you think on the basic human level differences of ideology, government systems or economic systems would become secondary. I feel that in order to develop the necessary mutual trust it will be useful for the leaders simply to get together, as you mentioned, on a beautiful island on a vacation and get to know each other as human beings who do not want suffering and who very much care about their own children, children's children. So leaders from America and from Russia should come to one place with their families not as a president or chairman or like that but simply introduce themselves to each other on the basic human level. This would help to grow mutual trust which would eventually lead to discussing more complicated matters. This is my idea.

Q. *As you know right in front of Lhasa, right in front of the Potala palace there was and I hope there is still the huge column of stone with large inscriptions that in the year of Grace 762 Tibetans inflicted heavy defeat on China and as a result of their defeat China was obliged to give thousands of bales of silk per year as a tribute. The Chinese have always claimed, quite wrongly, and misled the whole world with the fiction that Tibet has been a part of China. Would you consider that scholars from Tibet—you have great scholars—not only of medicine and religion but in other spheres—and scholars from India and other parts of the world combined analyse and collect the evidence to disprove the Chinese claim of total sovereignty over Tibet. Would you consider such a proposal worthy of consideration because, more than anything else, the whole world realises that 22 years of suppression by China has not been able to subjugate the free spirit of the Tibetan people and that they have still the highest love and respect for you. And of nationalism, racially apart, historically, culturally, religiously and even geographically Tibet has always been a distinct region, separate from China. The Indian Government, I see quite ill advisedly, recognised Chinese sovereignty and for which they deservedly paid a very heavy price. It destroyed their entire claim. Would it be possible to collect all the evidence in this regard and to have it translated into various languages for world wide distribution so that Tibet will always have an independent, sovereign, distinct cultural personality of its own quite distinct from the Huns. I think this little suggestion from me based on some of studies done recently might be put forward for consideration.*

A. Thank you very much. I agree. I think time has come to do a thorough study about the relation, the nature of relation, between China and Tibet over the centuries. I think it is very important to do this kind of study since the Chinese themselves say that we should "seek truth from fact". This is very good. So if they really follow that slogan then I feel that now time has come for them to learn about the past history as well as present aspirations of the Tibetan people. We Tibetans have a version of the past as well as the present condition in Tibet. The

Chinese version we have already learnt under the Chinese whip. Now it is time for the Chinese to learn the Tibetan version with an open mind—on the basis of their new slogan "seeking truth from fact". In this way you may find the truth or reality.

It is very important for scholars, intellectuals to study and to investigate into the actual legal status of Tibet. I think this year one well documented and researched book will be published.

Such studies are also very important for this country. Through historical factors as well as geographical factors, India and Tibet are very, very close. Sometimes I joke with some Indian friends that Chinese aggression is only physical aggression so it could not control the Tibetan mind but Indian aggression, that is the spread of Buddhism and Indian culture, had really occupied the Tibetan mind. So you are the more effective aggressor. In fact just one month ago I met a Tibetan who recently visited his own home town in Tibet. He told me that when he arrived there his friends, his relatives as well as even those who he did not know him simply asked him whether he had brought some soil from Boddh Gaya or some leaf from the Boddh tree and that kind of thing. And they say that every Tibetan Buddhist scripture started with an introductory sentence in an Indian language followed by translation of it in Tibetan language and then remaining of the scripture in Tibetan. So one of his friends told him that every Tibetan religious book started with an introduction in Indian language and there isn't a single text which starts in Chinese language. So you see mentally Tibetans are very much close to this country. As I said on many occasions in that sense India is our real guru and Tibetans chelas—disciples. So when the disciple is facing some problem the guru has some special responsibility.

Q. *Your Holiness, you have rightly emphasised that love and compassion is the true basis of happiness. It takes patience to develop love and compassion. The World today is very impatient. It is in a hurry, wants to run. Doesn't want to sit and meditate. Now how do we reconcile the requirement of patience, development of patience in the present state with the world in a hurry. You must have given a lot of thought to this in your meditation. Please enlighten us. What can we do? The world indeed calls for patience, love and compassion. How can we reconcile the hurry of the world with the need for patience, love and compassion?*

A. My observation is that those communities which are materially highly developed, through their experience, started to realise the limitations of materialism. Some people are thinking whether materialism is the full answer for humanity or not. So I think that growing number of people are thinking that material development is not the full answer for humanity. Now on the other hand in the developing countries people are still very much concerned about the matters of stomach, poverty, illiteracy and so on. Here we have a different situation from that which exists in the developed countries. In India, I think, you need to lay more emphasis on the preservation of Indian tradition. India has very rich philosophy and spiritual traditions. While it is necessary to take ideas from Western science and technology in order to develop fully in the material field, you must preserve very seriously your own richness of tradition.

Q. *Can we do something to accelerate the process of the realisation of importance of spiritual humanism?*

A. I remember, few years back when I met some of the Professors—I think from university of Delhi — we discussed the students' mental attitude about different classes and subjects such as Indian philosophy or comparative religious studies and in other fields of studies. One Professor told me that there are some differences. This shows again, as I mentioned earlier, the importance of education. Now the suitability of education system in this country might be questionable after all this is based on English education system. During British rule they introduced the British system, i.e., English education system. I think the education system is very, very important.

   Also sometimes I get the impression that those who believe in Dharma and belong to spiritual communities are perhaps little bit too orthodox. This gives the impression that religion is something out of date. The younger generation may not take serious interest in religion not because of the religious teachings themselves but because of those who practice them. I am not criticising anyone. But don't you think that some are little too orthodox and too much old fashioned? So the basic thing is to take the very important essence: Not the ceremonial or the ritual things.

Q. *Your Holiness I would like guidance on three questions. You have opened so many questions, so many doors, it is impossible to settle all these in a half hour discussion. Three questions from me and I shall like to put them forward. First, in discussing human happiness you assume that this is something everybody wants. But this is something recently tested in America. A lady in great distress was teaching the need for being happy in the West Coast of America and she was asked this question by a young man standing up in the audience, "tell me Madame, could happiness bring me money". So this kind of people do exist. Secondly, you spoke, quite rightly, of the need for a peaceful mind. But throughout history it has also been found that many creative works of artists, singers, musicians, painters, sculptors although they are perfectly at peace as far as human relations are concerned they have to be of very feverish mind, very tense mind which makes them so disturbed that they have got to create various forms of art. Therefore, the question arises whether there are various kinds of peace in mind, some ways we need peace and others where we need fever, extreme passion in order to improve and create a response which is also equally important for human evolution. And the third point is that Your Holiness, emphasis has been on the individual but there is an ideology which does not accept individual as a unit at all. Now that ideology says there is no need for an individual in any form, colour, creed, anywhere. But the whole thing should be treated as a social group in which the individual is submerged. Now how do you view this?*

A. I don't know. Difficult to say. On your first question. I think if any one who is very much concerned about money, if you ask that person what is the purpose of money, buying something more, making more friends. Then ask what is the purpose of making more friends, of buying more things. The ultimate answer is for mental satisfaction. I think, you see, that a particular person may not realise what is the real mental satisfaction. Then of course in human community there are some people whose minds do not function with reason. Such people can ask very strange questions. I think you should question the very purpose of every action. The prime mover is the consciousness with desire, with motivation, whether religious person or an atheist or any other person, even animals move with motivation, desire to achieve something consciously or sub-consciously.

On the second question: Mental peace does not mean passivity that something does not matter. From Buddhist viewpoint altruism gives you mental peace. With altruism in action if circumstances demand you may even take life, purely on the basis of altruism. For example, one Jataka story mentions that in order to save the lives of 499 persons the Buddha's reincarnation killed one person. The motivation in altruism was both towards 499 persons and also the supposed killer who was thinking of killing 499 persons and taking their wealth. If the reincarnation of the Buddha allowed the killer to follow his plan ultimately that person would suffer as a result of taking 499 persons' lives. So it was altruism to stop and to save him from that sin. He himself sacrificed and took that action. So, you see, another definition of peace of mind may be such consciousness or mental stability that gives you complete satisfaction and ultimately causes no suffering. Is this something relevant to your question?

Q. *I am in love with a woman and because of my passion of love I am in total torment. I write the most beautiful poem in the world because of this love. Now if I do not have that creative instinct which is brought out by the disturbance of my mind, that if my mind is totally passive, I cannot write this poem. Your comment?*

A. I think then there is a difference. Peace of mind does not mean your mind remaining at rest and actionless. Not that kind. There are of course different kinds of love or desire as I mentioned earlier. One love is actually not based on reason but ignorance. That love, for example you had described for your girl friend, is without proper reason and simply emotional kind. So with a small disturbance it breaks. Another kind of love based on reason is that just as I, all sentient beings want happiness and don't want suffering and just as I have the right to be happy, to get rid of the suffering, all sentient beings have the equal right. If someone shows me kindness, human warm heart I will be happy. Therefore, I must show love, kindness and warm feeling to others. On this basis one could develop feeling of love and kindness and strengthen it further through investigation and meditation. The other kind of love is based on illusion.

On your third question: The question arises how does human society exist? The human society is made up of individuals joined together into a human community, human society. Human society becomes a nation and so on. If you want to change the way of thinking of human society you cannot impose it from above but it must come from individual human initiative. So ultimately it is related to the individual.

I think there are certain systems today which have no regard for individual rights. They simply think about the community or society and carry out mass movements such as brain washing, propaganda but it did not work properly. The society as a whole appears to have accepted and have become indoctrinated but deep down as individuals people hold different opinion. So in such societies I find many people with two faces. One might express something in a group but when we meet individually the same person will have a different point of view. This means that the indoctrination may appear to have worked in a society as a whole but in actual fact it has not succeeded. So individual still remains something different.[2]

[2]Shri C.S. Jha then thanked His Holiness the Dalai Lama.

3

COMPASSION IN GLOBAL POLITICS

This century is very sophisticated. Through various factors, mainly material, the world is becoming smaller and smaller, providing the peoples of the world with good opportunities to meet and talk with each other. Such contact provides a valuable chance to increase our understanding of each other's way of living, philosophy, and beliefs, and increased understanding will lead naturally to mutual respect. Because of the world's having become smaller, I have been able to come here today.

As we meet, I always keep in mind that we are the same in being human beings. If we emphasize the superficial differences, I am an Easterner and furthermore a Tibetan from beyond the Himalayas, with a different environment and a different culture. However, if we look deep down, I have a valid feeling of I, and with that feeling, I want happiness and do not want suffering. Everyone, no matter where they are from, has this valid feeling of I on the conventional level and in this sense we are all the same.

With this understanding as a basis, when I meet new people in new places, in my mind there is no barrier, no curtain. I can talk with you as I would to old friends even though this is the first time we meet. In my mind, as human beings you are my brothers and sisters; there is no difference in substance. I can express whatever I feel, without hesitation, just as to an old friend. With this feeling we can communicate without any difficulty and can contact heart to heart, not with just a few nice words, but really heart to heart.

Based on such genuine human relation—real feeling for each other, understanding each other—we can develop mutual trust and respect. From that, we can share other peoples' suffering and build harmony in human society. We can create a friendly human family.

This attitude is very useful. If we put too much emphasis on the superficial differences—culture, ideology, faith, race, colour, wealth, and education—if we make small rigid discriminations, we cannot avoid making additional suffering for human society. A troublesome atmosphere will be created from these exaggerated but very small differences.

Also, in world politics such small discriminations create uncontrollable problems. For instance, in Asia, the Middle East, Africa, or Latin America, strife comes sometimes from religious feelings, sometimes from race, sometimes from ideology. The same is true for my own country, Tibet, due to certain attitudes of our great neighbour, the People's Republic of China, that appeared during the Cultural Revolution. In this manner human ways of thinking create problems in addition to the basic ones that we must face.

For instance, although thousands upon thousands of refugees from Cambodia and Vietnam were dying, some people were talking about the politics of those refugees rather than handling the immediate problem properly. This is particularly saddening. That people in need are ignored for such reasons reveals what we are lacking—though we are intelligent and powerful, strong enough to exploit peoples or destroy the world, we lack real kindness and love. We need to realize right from the beginning that basically we are human beings who do not want to die and likewise these people are also human beings who do not want to die. They have the right to live as human beings; they need help.

First we must help; then, later we can talk about the causes, the politics that led to their tragedy, and so forth. There is an Indian saying: If you are struck by a poisonous arrow, it is important first to pull it out; there is no time to ask who shot it, what sort of poison it is, and so on. First handle the immediate problem, and later we can investigate. Similarly when we encounter human suffering, it is important to respond with compassion rather than to question the politics of those we help. Instead of asking whether their country is enemy or friend, we must think, "These are human beings, they are suffering, and they have a right to happiness equal to our own."

We are not lacking in terms of the development of science and technology; still, we lack something here in the heart—real inner warm feeling. A good heart is needed.

With the basic understanding of all humans as brothers and sisters, we can appreciate the usefulness of different systems and ideologies that can accommodate different individuals and groups which have different dispositions different tastes. For certain people under certain conditions a certain ideology or cultural heritage is more useful. Each person has the right to choose whatever is most suitable. This is the individual's business on the basis of deep understanding of all other persons as brothers and sisters.

Deep down we must have real affection for each other, clear realization or recognition of our shared human status. At the same time, we must openly accept all ideologies and systems as means of solving humanity's problems. One country, one nation, one ideology, one system is not sufficient. It is helpful to have a variety of different approaches on the basis of a deep feeling of the basic sameness of humanity. We can then make joint effort to solve the problems of the whole of humankind. The problems human society is facing in terms of economic development, the crisis of energy, the tension between the poor and rich nations, and many geopolitical problems can be solved if we understand each others' fundamental humanity, respect each others' rights share each others' problems and sufferings, and then made joint effort.

Even if we cannot solve certain problems, we should not regret it. We humans must face death, old age, and disease as well as natural disasters, such as hurricanes, that are beyond our control. We must face them; we cannot avoid them. But these sufferings are quite sufficient for us—why should we create other problems due to our own ideology, just differing ways of thinking? Useless! It is sad. Thousands upon thousands of people suffer from this. Such a situation is truly silly since we can avoid it by adopting a different attitude, appreciating the basic humanity which ideologies are supposed to serve.

Four or five hundred years ago in this country the native Indians lived in small communities, more or less independently; even family by family, they were mostly independent. However, now there is no question that even nation to nation, continent to continent, we are heavily dependent on each other. For instance, thousands upon thousands of new cars are moving in the streets of New York, Washington, or here in Los Angeles, but without oil they cannot move. Though at the moment human beings are carried by cars, if that fuel is finished, the humans will have to carry these big cars.

Prosperity depends on other factors in other places. Whether we like it or not, this shows that we are interdependent. We can no longer exist in complete isolation. Unless we have real cooperation, harmony, and common effort, difficulties will be created. Since we must live together, why not do so with a positive attitude, a good mind? Why is it that instead we feel hatred for each other and bring more trouble to the world?

I am a religious person, and from my viewpoint all things first originate in the mind. Things and events depend heavily on motivation. A real sense of appreciation of humanity, compassion and love, are the key points. If we develop a good heart, then whether the field is science, agriculture, or politics, since motivation is so very important, these will all improve. A good heart is both important and effective in daily life. If in a small family, even without children, the members have a warm heart to each other, a peaceful atmosphere will be created. However, if one of the person feels angry, immediately the atmosphere in the house becomes tense. Despite good food or a nice television set, you will lose peace and calm. Thus, things depend more on the mind than on matter. Matter is important, we must have it, we must use it properly, but this century must combine a good brain—intelligence—with a good heart.

Everybody loves to talk about calm and peace whether in a family, national, or international context, but without *inner* peace how can we make real peace? World peace through hatred and force is impossible. Even in the case of individuals there is no possibility to feel happiness through anger. If in a difficult situation one becomes disturbed internally overwhelmed by mental discomfort, then external things will not help at all. However, if despite external difficulties or problems, internally one's attitude is of love, warmth, and kind-heartedness, then problems can be faced and accepted easily.

The human essence of good sense finds no room with anger. Anger, jealousy, impatience, and hatred are the real trouble makers; with them problems cannot be solved. Though one may have temporary success, ultimately one's hatred or anger will create further difficulties. With anger, all actions are swift. When we face problems with compassion, sincerely and with good motivation, it may take longer, but ultimately the solution is better, for there is far less chance of creating a new problem.

Sometimes we look down on politics, criticizing it as dirty. However, if you look at it properly, politics in itself is not wrong. It is an instrument to serve human society. With good motivation—sincerity and honesty—politics becomes an instrument in the service of society. But when motivated by selfishness with hatred, anger, or jealousy, it becomes dirty.

This is true not only for politics but also for religion. If I speak about religion with selfish motives or with hatred, then though I am talking about religion, it is not useful because the feeling behind it is bad. Things depend on our own motivation. Through money or power you cannot solve all problems. The problem in the human heart must first be solved. Then, the other human-created problems will be solved naturally.

My opinion is that since everybody belongs to this world, we must try to adopt a good attitude worldwide, a good feeling for our fellow brothers and sisters. In my particular case, we Tibetans are carrying on a struggle for our rights. Some say that the Tibetan situation is only political, but I feel it is not. We Tibetans have a unique and distinct cultural heritage just as the Chinese have. We do not hate the Chinese; we deeply respect the riches of Chinese culture which spans so many centuries. Though we have deep respect and are not anti-Chinese, we six million Tibetans have an equal right to maintain our own distinctive culture as long as we do not harm others. Materially we are backward, but in spiritual matters—in terms of the development of the mind—we are quite rich. We Tibetans are Buddhists, and the Buddhism which we practice is a rather complete form of Buddhism. Also, we have kept it active, very much alive.

In the past century we remained a peaceful nation with our unique culture. Now, unfortunately, during the last few decades, this nation and culture are being deliberately destroyed. We like our own culture, our own land; we have the right to preserve it.

Also, the six million Tibetan people are human beings, no matter whether we are a materially backward country or not. We are six million human souls with the right to live as human beings. This is the problem.

I am serving our cause with the motivation of service to humankind, not for reasons of power, not out of hatred. Not just as a Tibetan but as a human being, I think it is worthwhile to preserve that culture, that nation, to contribute to world society. This is why I am persisting in our movement, and though some people see this as a purely political matter, I know it is not.

We hope very much that the over-all attitude of the People's Republic of China is changing, but we are cautious due to our past experience. I do not say this out of wish to criticize; rather, it is a fact. Upon investigation you can determine whether it is fact or not; time will tell.

I believe that human determination and will power are quite sufficient to challenge outside pressure and aggression. No matter how strong the evil force is, the flame of truth will not diminish. This is my belief.

As a friend, my request and wish is that individually and as an organization you try to promote a sense of brotherhood and sisterhood. We must promote compassion and love; this is our real duty. Government has too much business to have time for these things. As private persons we have more time to think along these lines—how to make a contribution to human society by promoting the development of compassion and a real sense of community.

In conclusion, no doubt you feel I am talking of an impractical dream. However, we human beings have a developed brain and limitless potential. Since even wild animals can gradually be trained with patience, the human mind also can gradually be trained, step by step. If you test these practices with patience, you can come to know this through your own experience. If someone who easily gets angry tries to control his or her anger, in time it can be controlled. The same is true for a very selfish person; first that person must realize the faults of a selfish motivation and the benefit in being less selfish. Having realized this, one trains in it, trying to control the bad side and develop the good. As time goes by, such practice can be very effective. This is the only alternative.

Without love, human society is in a very difficult state; without love, in the future we will face tremendous problems. Love is the centre of human life.

VII
Tibetan Buddhism

Chapter VII
TIBETAN BUDDHISM

The impact of Buddhism had transformed the fabric of Tibetan society with its fundamental concepts of non-violence and concern for the welfare of others. As an integral part of Tibetan identity, Buddhism influenced all the modes of artistic expression, such as literature, scripture, painting and architecture. Tragically, this precious legacy was largely destroyed in Tibet after the Chinese invasion in 1959 followed by the so called, "cultural revolution".

The Dalai Lama is not only keeping alive the spirit of the Tibetan people in exile, but also working for the preservation and promotion of Tibetan heritage, its traditional art, culture and religion. According to him "Buddhism is one of the many religions which teaches us to be less selfish and more compassionate. It teaches us to be humane, altruistic and to think of others in the way we think for ourselves. Our daily thoughts and actions should be directed towards the benefit of others. Mahayana emphasises self-sacrifice and the development of altruism while Hinayana teaches us the importance of not harming others. The practice of Buddhism in essence is, therefore not to harm others under any circumstances, and help others as much as possible." For this reason Buddha said: "A spiritually evolved mind itself is happiness; a deluded mind is suffering." Because of this attitude, Buddhism lays its greatest emphasis not upon belief in anything or anyone but upon the practical cultivation of a positive, wholesome, creative mind, and upon the elimination of emotional afflictions such as greed, anger, attachment, ignorance and so forth. This automatically leads to the increase of happiness and to the decrease of misery for both oneself and others.

"Buddha once said, 'You are your own saviour or you are your own enemy.' This applies to all of us. Take myself, for example. If I try to cultivate goodness and the positive mind within myself, I am my own saviour. On the other hand, if I permit negativity to overpower my stream of being, I become my own destroyer."

—Editor

1

THE BUDDHIST APPROACH TO KNOWLEDGE

Previously in Tibet on religious occasions all the people would go to the shrines and temples to make devotional offerings. Poor and rich alike, businessmen and farmers, learned monks and illiterate nomads: all would come together to engage in spiritual rites.

Now a different fate has overtaken the Tibetan people. Due to our own bad Karma, our country has fallen under foreign domination of a ruthless invader. Our mountainous land of peace and calm has become a land of terror and great suffering. In the place of the colourful dress that we Tibetans so much loved, the people are forced to wear alien uniforms signifying their position under an imposed Chinese communist scheme— officers, prisoners, labourers, exemplary volunteers, party members, reactionaries, and so on—and to live in a state of tension and fear. Their days and nights must pass in terror and insecurity. Few are the families who have not lost one or more members to the brutal Chinese oppression, or who do not have close relatives being held somewhere in the concentration camps. We here in voluntary exile may have difficulties as refugees, but at least we are free. We are not forced to attend indoctrination meetings every evening, nor told where we can and cannot go and what we can and cannot think, read or say. And what is most dear to every Tibetan heart, we are free to practise our religion.

There are many different religions in this world. Each of them has its own special qualities, its own unique way of presenting the spiritual path. We Tibetans chose Buddhism as our national religion. Buddhism is a unique and profound religion because it is not a path of faith but a path of reason and knowledge. Buddha himself stated that his doctrine should be accepted not on faith but only in the light of reason and logical inquiry. He also stated that many of his teachings were not literally true but required an interpretative approach, and therefore that his followers must personally weigh every point of doctrine to see if it is directly valid or only figuratively so: He advised that any teachings which are impractical or do not stand the test of logical security should not be accepted. Because he taught over a period of many years to many types and levels of beings— to peoples of great, average and meagre intelligence—his teachings require careful analysis.

Great Indian masters such as Nagarjuna and Asanga, both of whom were prophesied by Buddha himself, wrote many treatises on what teachings are literally true and what are merely figurative or for people of inferior understanding. Were all teachings literally true, there would have been no need for Buddha himself to have advised us to personally examine each teaching and to reject or reinterpret those which do not withstand logical investigation. Nor would there have been a need for him to have prophesied the coming of Nagarjuna and Asanga to elucidate his doctrines. Therefore Buddha did not ask us to accept everything he taught; he advised that we personally examine and re-examine each teaching and practise only those which meet our own standards of logic and reason. In this way we are enabled to put into practice those teachings which are in harmony with our own level of development and capacity, and to see the other teachings in the light of our experience. The different schools of Buddhism have largely arisen due to this facet of the teachings, with each school stressing a specific aspect of the doctrine as being fundamental and literal, and placing teachings other than this as peripheral and figurative. Thus Buddha presented an approach to his doctrine that is both vast and profound.

Had Buddha not relied upon truth in his teachings, were his teachings mere superstition, he would not have advised us to critically judge his words in this way. Instead, he would have given us a dogma like, "Believe what I say or else you will come to experience misery". The fact that he always advocated reason over blind acceptance indicated that his doctrine is founded on truth, not fiction. The more we analyse a superstition or a falsehood, the weaker becomes our belief in it, whereas the more we investigate truth, the stronger becomes our belief. This is the nature of truth and falsehood. In my last meeting with Mao Zse Dung, he told me, "Religion is poison. It harms mankind and gives no benefit. It has poisoned Tibet and Mongolia". When he said this, I could not believe him; and the more I thought it over, the stronger became my disbelief in his words. On the one hand he had not looked deeply enough into the general purpose and effects of religion, and in particular was ignorant of profound philosophical teachings of Buddhism. Therefore he thought that Buddhism was not relevant to present-day reality. He witnessed certain cases in which religion was used by some monks to extract an easy living from simple-minded people and concluded that all religion is merely a method whereby clever people seek to escape work and to live in comfort. Mao was not an evil or a bad man; he just misunderstood many things in life, religion being an important one of them.

As I said earlier, every religion has its own qualities and its own approach. The mark of Buddhism is that it is essentially humanistic rather than formally religious in its presentation. It attempts to define the problems confronting our lives and to set forth a number of remedies to these problems. Unlike most world religions, it does not hinge on the concept of God. It speaks of man and of how he can gain perfection. Many religions begin with the idea of a God and then use this idea to resolve all the problems confronting existence, such as creation and evolution. Although this is an easy answer, it is not logically proveable. Therefore Buddha avoided it and tried to present a doctrine that in every way could be established through reason.

By avoiding the use of the God-theory, Buddha also avoided the many problematic side-effects that come with it. For example, one danger of centring one's doctrine on the concept of God is that the people can come to feel themselves immensely humbled: they can worship God and perhaps one day even get to sit at his feet, but they can never equal Him. God is one entity and we humans, being merely His creations, are destined forever to be inferior to Him. We can blindly accept and practise what He says or we can suffer the consequences of defying our Creator and Sustainer. This has the positive effect of lessening one's ego: and the teachings to be practised, such as morality, love, devotion, etc., are always useful. But there is the danger that the people will not appreciate the full greatness of the human potential. Also, religions based on the God-theory usually do not permit rejection of the "Words of God", even if they contradict all reason. This can very easily stunt the growth of philosophical inquiry. Furthermore there are a number of philosophical problems immediately created by the presentation of the God-theory, for example, if God is all-powerful and if He created everything and is now sustaining it, then He also created all the suffering and injustice. Thus, we can conclude that He is extremely cruel and evil, like a mother who purposely gives birth to a child just to torture it and to summit it to great pain. In order to avoid these kinds of problems, Buddha tried to present a doctrine based purely on reason, and a path expressed solely in terms of human problems and human goals. He declared man himself to be responsible for his present existence, and provided a number of methods whereby this present state in which we find ourselves can be evolved and cultivated until perfection itself is attained. He pointed to man himself as being the maker of his own destiny, the agent responsible for his own evolution or degeneration. The Buddhas are not Creators; they are but teachers and guides for those who would listen to them. Whether or not a person chooses to take advantage of their guidance is up to the individual himself.

According to Buddhist scriptures, the creator of the world as we now know is nothing other than the ripening force of our own previous deeds and Karmas. Every action of ours establishes an imprint on the mind that contributes to our future evolution. In brief, happiness is always a product of creative activity and suffering of negative activity. Moreover, negative activity and action arise solely as a result of a deluded mind and positive actions as a result of a positive mind. Therefore, the aim of all religious practice is to cultivate and strengthen positive, creative states. A mind thus cultivated is both disciplined and calm and gives peace to the person who possesses it as well as to all with whom it comes in contact. We can easily witness its immediate effects upon both the individual and the society, and we can also clearly see the negative effects of a destructive mind. The far-reaching effects, which extend over years and lifetimes, are of course more subtle and require highly developed perception or logical reasoning to fathom. In the case of the Chinese invasion of Tibet we can see the immediate effects of the uncivilised and inconsiderate act of aggression in the number of the dead left on both sides and in the ill-feeling left in the wake of the invasion. It will of course breed only hatred and more violence. From the Chinese side, the cause is the previously collected negative karma which in turn was created by delusion. If one's mind is spiritually evolved, one no longer creates this type of problem for oneself or others. For this reason Buddha said: "A spiritually evolved mind itself is happiness; a deluded mind is suffering." Because of this attitude, Buddhism lays its greatest emphasis not upon belief in anything or anyone but upon the practical cultivation of a positive, wholesome, creative mind, and upon the elimination of emotional afflictions such as greed, anger, attachment, ignorance and so forth. This automatically leads to the increase of happiness and to the decrease of misery for both oneself and others.

Buddha once said, "You are your own saviour or you are your own enemy." This applies to all of us. Take myself, for example. If I try to cultivate goodness and the positive mind within myself, I am my own saviour. On the other hand, if I permit negativity to overpower my stream of being, I become my own destroyer. Had Mao seen religion in this light, I do not think that he could have called it poison.

These days many Asian scholars are talking about the similarities between Buddhist and communist social views. It is true that they have a lot in common, but there are a number of fundamental differences. For instance, communism places its emphasis upon materialism, upon the things of this life, whereas, although Buddhism recognises the importance of a stable material basis, it is essentially a spiritual view and sees the material world as a tool with which to develop more lasting, inner qualities. In other words, the Communist is primarily concerned with the body, which is lost at death, whereas the Buddhist is concerned primarily with the mind, which goes on into future existence. In terms of the two levels of truth—the deeper reality and the conventional, relative truth—communism concentrates upon a superficial level of the latter while Buddhism feels that in order for the latter to be really understood the former must be clearly known. In brief, communism thinks mainly about how people can fill their bellies, while Buddhism, although recognizing the importance of a full stomach, sees the mind as ultimately being at the basis of both happiness and sorrow and therefore, more like the modern psychologist, seeks to create a state of mental harmony within people and thus to enable them to cope with all life situations more effectively. It tries to generate a condition of spiritual enlightenment within them by exposing them to deeper levels of reality.

As I said earlier, Buddhism is a path of reason and logical inquiry. In Tibet, because we were born with it as our religion, we often took it for granted. Many people, therefore, embraced its practice not on a basis of profound understanding but purely out of faith as an unconscious development in their lives. Thus their practice was like a castle built on ice, and when they were forced out of their natural environment by the Chinese invasion, it degenerated and collapsed. For those with a firm basis, however, the change reinforced and deepened their faith. Their contact with different values and views, such as Western science and technology, deepened their understanding of and conviction in Buddhist practise. Thus the Chinese taught us an important lesson, and we should be grateful to them for it. We should learn from it, and in future should rely upon an understanding based upon our own reasoning rather than upon quotations from Buddha, Longchen or Tsong Khapa. Almost everyone in Tibet was Buddhist and therefore our beliefs were rarely challenged, whereas this is no longer the situation. We should follow the approach of the Indian master Dharmakirti, who questioned everything and thus gained an unshakeable understanding of every teaching. In his *Pramanavartika* he examines subjects like karma, past and future lives, the relationship between mind and body, the concept of a beginning and an end to cyclic existence, the possibility of liberation and Buddhahood, and so forth, in a very critical way. We should develop our understanding of these topics along the lines he indicated, and perhaps write a few commentaries updating his ideas.

The dividing line between a Buddhist and a non-Buddhist is that the former is someone who takes refuge in the Three Jewels: the Buddha, who is the teacher and the goal to be attained; the Dharma, or the teachings and the path to be realized; and the Sangha, or the holders of the robes and the advanced practitioners of the Dharma. Again, it is very important that this refuge is taken on the basis of a deep understanding of what these Three Jewels signify. Merely to call oneself a Buddhist is of little value; one must have the inner experience of dissatisfaction with mundane existence and the recognition that refuge in the Three Jewels, together with the spiritual practice that this refuge implies, will help one transcend this mundane state of being. Then one should gain a firm understanding of the Karmic laws of cause and effect and exert oneself at developing harmony with them. In brief, we should make every effort to purify our mindstreams of negative traits and to develop every positive quality, such as love, compassion, detachment, higher meditation, wisdom and so forth. We must take direct responsibility for our own spiritual lives and rely upon nobody or nothing, for even the Buddhas of the ten directions and three times are unable to help us if we do not help ourselves. If another being were able to save us, surely he would already have done so. It is time, therefore, that we help ourselves. At the moment we are blessed with human life and with all the possibilities that this implies. Unlike animals and lower life-forms, we are able to pluck the fruit of enlightenment, an act of ultimate goodness to both ourselves and others. However, death is pressing upon us from every side, threatening to rob us of this precious opportunity at any moment, and when we die nothing can be taken with us but the seeds of our life's work and our spiritual knowledge. A king loses his kingdom, and a crippled beggar leaves behind even his walking stick. We should quickly seize enlightenment while we still have the chance. In much less than a century all of us here will be dead. May be someone will say, "The Dalai Lama once gave a sermon here"; only this faint memory of today will remain. We cannot be sure that we will be alive even tomorrow. There is no time to procrastinate, I who am giving this teaching have no guarantee that I will live out this day. I hope that my life will be as long as fruitful as that of Gedun Drub, the First Dalai Lama (1391-1474), for at the moment many people are depending upon me but who knows? Therefore I practise as intensely as I can, and advise you to do the same. But do not practise blindly. Practise with a basis of wisdom and understanding. Then your spiritual strength will grow more vast and profound each day, and no matter what circumstances life throws upon you, your progress along the path will be undaunted. Our life here as refugees in India is not easy, but if we rely upon the practice of Buddha dharma it can be an excellent catalyst for spiritual development. And hopefully within a few years or decades we will be able to return to our country and to the loved ones we were forced to leave behind. Let's pray for this end, and make every effort that it may be realized.

Here I have just expressed a few thoughts that came to my mind. There is no stamp of authority behind what I say as the Dalai Lama, the Buddhist monk Lobsang Tenzin Gyatso. If there is anything you like in what I have said, fine. If not, no problem; all you have to do is to reject it. Do not accept anything merely because it was said by someone called "Dalai Lama". Accept it only if it seems reasonable to you and is of benefit to you and your spiritual life.

2

TRADITIONS OF TIBETAN BUDDHISM

From very ancient times, Tibet and India have maintained very close intercourse in the fields of culture, education, religion, literature and art. Thoughts and ideas of profound significance emanating from India and flowing freely into the fertile and receptive soil of Tibet brought about cultural and social changes of revolutionary magnitude. India was regarded not only as the fountain-head of many great philosophical ideas and systems but also as the source of spiritual inspiration and of initiatives leading to fruitful action. However, of all these influences, Buddhism stands out as the paramount cause of the splendid metamorphosis that changed the entire course of Tibet's history. The glorious light of wisdom, embodied in the noble doctrine of Buddhism, having spread throughout India, found its way into Tibet, and, in course of time, became a sovereign power of unexcelled brilliance. Historically, the culture of Tibet is firmly rooted in the Buddha Dharma. Generations of Tibetan intellectuals studied and developed a profound culture that closely accorded with the original principles and philosophy of the Dharma. Down through the centuries, their dedicated services brought about extraordinary developments which are unique among the literary and cultural achievements of the nations of the world. A galaxy of Indian scholars gave Tibet their perennial wisdom and opened the eyes of Tibetans to vastly expanded horizons. This helped to form the Tibetan mentality, which delights in penetrating analysis and examination and in exploring the virgin fields of the mind, thus opening up boundless vistas of intellectual development. As a result, Tibetan thought was greatly enriched and this is one of the primary reasons why Tibetans have always regarded India with a peculiarly fervent veneration as the guide who led their country into wisdom's realm.

Prior to the introduction of Buddhism, Bon, a native tradition, was the dominant faith of Tibet. Recorded history tells us that Tibet received its initial impact of Buddhism when the first Indian pundit, Buddharakshita, visited Tibet during the reign of Lhatho-thori, the 25th King of Tibet (who was later recognised as one of the earthly manifestations of the Samanatabhadra Bodhisattva). The way of Buddhism became pro nounced in the seventh century A.D. when Thonmi Sambhota, a brillian intellectual court minister, was sent to India by King Song-tsen-Gampo o Tibet for educational studies.

After studying for a number of years at the feet of numerous Indian pundits in the various branches of learning, Thonmi Sambhota returned to Tibet. He not only invented the letters of the Tibetan alphabet, the firs of its kind in Tibet, but also translated the Karandavushutra (mDo-sde-za ma-tog) and Sachhipurnamudra (dPan-skong-phyag-rgya-pa) into Ti betan. Besides, Thonmi Sambota in collaboration with various Indian scholars is reputed to have translated 21 Sutras from Sanskrit into Tibetan. These were the first Buddhist Sutras in Sanskrit to be translated into Tibetan. Thereafter, an extensive corpus of literature grew up. A host of Indian and Tibetan pandits and Lotsawas (scholar translators) set about translating into Tibetan the Sutras and Tantras brought from India and Nepal. The Kangyur, consisting of over one hundred bulky volumes, and the Tengyur, consisting of over two hundred volumes, were both trans lated in full during this period.

The Lord Buddha bestowed upon the world his unique teachings which are enshrined in the systems commonly known as Hinayana and Mahayana, of which the latter includes the body of teaching known as Tantrayana. The Hinayana doctrine was handed down through a lineage of seven hierarchies, and its progress through the avenues of time was unimpeded and unrestrained. Unlike Hinayana, Mahayana did not progress smoothly, but suffered persecution at the hands of heretical and pagan forces on three different occasions. It was, therefore, considerably weakened.

Guru Padma Sambhava, a famous Tantric teacher from India (who is believed to have hailed from Dhanakosha Island), visited Tibet in the eighth century A.D. and preached the esoteric Vajrayana Doctrine (the Adamantine Wheel of the Great Mystery) to a group of twenty-five followers including King Tritsong-De-Tsen. In the course of time, he founded the Nyingma School of Vajrayana in Tibet. In the eleventh century A.D., Dipankara Srijnana, an outstanding scholar from Vikramshila University in India, came to Tibet and taught Sutras and Tantras extensively. His disciples such as Khonton, Ngok and Drom founded the Kadampa School in Tibet.

Towards the end of the eleventh century A.D. Marton Chokyi Lodroe, a famous Tibetan translator, paid three visits to India, during which he studied at the feet of such stalwarts as Pandit Naropa, and after returning to Tibet, undertook an extensive translation and propagation of the knowledge gained from those far-famed Indian scholars. Later on, the doctrine which he propounded and handed down through Jetsun Milarepa and Nyam-may Dagpa Lharje came to be known as Kagyud.

In the twelfth century A.D. Khon Konchok Gyalpo inherited the Doctrine of Lam-Dres (the Path and the Enlightenment) from Drokme Lotsawa. This doctrine was preserved and fostered through five hierarchies of Sakya Lamas, and their followers came to be known as the Sakya Sect.

In the fourteen century A.D. there emerged a famous figure called Jamgon Je Tsongkhapa, who is reputed to have made a thorough study of the inner meanings of the entire corpus of Sutras and Tantras. The lineage established by his followers such as Gyaltshab Je and Khedrub Je is known as the Gandenpa or Gelug Sect.

Besides these, there are a number of subsidiary sects founded by learned individuals in Tibet.

Admittedly, there are a few differences between Mahayana and Hinayana in their way of expressing the teachings; but the ultimate goal of both schools is identical in that both aim at helping sentient beings to attain the supreme status of Buddhahood. The entire esoteric system (Vajrayana) of the Doctrine has been classified into two distinct groups—internal and external, between which there is a great difference. The people of Tibet regard the Sutras and Tantras which they preach and practise as being firmly rooted in the Lord Buddha's Teachings. Whenever further elucidation are required, they consult works containing the excellent conclusions arrived at by the learned Indian scholars of whom I have spoken. The commentaries of Nagarjuna, Aryadeva, Buddhapalita, Chandrakirti, Shantideva and so on are held in special esteem, and are frequently referred to. Indeed, it is traditionally held that the teachings and commentaries expounded by those learned Indian scholars are the sole source to which one can turn for clarification of the Sacred Doctrine.

In conclusion, I wish to observe that the sages and pundits of India and Tibet have bequeathed to us the wisdom and experience they had acquired by long years of diligent study, practice, meditation and reflection. Their noble efforts contributed to building up a bridge which has united the people of our two countries like children of the same family. This unique relationship will remain forever as a perfect example of international fraternity and understanding.

Happiness, Karma and the Mind

Many billions of years elapsed between the origin of this world and the first appearance of living beings upon its surface. Thereafter it took an immense time for living creatures to become mature in thought—in the development and perfection of their intellectual faculties; and even from the time men attained maturity up to the present, many thousands of years have passed. Through all these vast periods of time, the world has undergone constant changes, for it is in a continual state of flux. Even now, many comparatively recent occurrences which appeared for a little while to remain static are seen to have been undergoing changes from moment to moment. One may wonder what is it that remains immutable when every kind of material and mental phenomenon seems to be invariably subject to the process of change, of mutability. All of them are forever arising, developing and passing away. In the vortex of these changes, it is Truth alone which remains constant and unalterable—in other words, the truth of righteousness (Dharma) and accompanying beneficial results, and the truth of evil action and its accompanying harmful results. A good cause produces a good result, a bad cause a bad result. Good or bad, beneficial or harmful every result necessarily has a cause. This principle alone is abiding, immutable and constant. It was so before man entered the world, in the early period of his existence, and in the present age; and it will be so in all ages to come.

All of us desire happiness and the avoidance of suffering and of everything else that is unpleasant. Pleasure and pain arise from a cause, as we all know. Whether certain consequences are due to a single cause or to a group of causes is determined by the nature of those consequences. In some cases, even if the cause factors are neither powerful nor numerous, it is still possible for the effect factors to occur. Whatever the quality of the result factors, whether they are good or bad, their magnitude and intensity directly correspond to the quantity and strength of the cause factors. Therefore, for success in avoiding unwished-for pains and in acquiring desired pleasures, which is in itself no small matter, the relinquishment of a great number of collective cause factors is required.

In analysing the nature and state of happiness, it will be apparent that it has two aspects. One is immediate joy (temporary); the other is deeper joy (ultimate). Temporary pleasures comprise the comforts and enjoyments which people crave, such as good dwellings, lovely furniture, delicious food, good company, pleasant conversation, and so on. In other words, temporary pleasures are what man enjoys in this life. The question as to whether the enjoyment of these pleasures and satisfaction derived purely from external factors needs to be examined in the light of clear logic. If external factors were alone responsible for giving rise to such pleasures, a person would be happy when these were present and, conversely, unhappy in their absence. However, this is not so. For, even in the absence of external conditions leading to pleasure, a man can still be happy and at peace. This demonstrates that external factors are not alone responsible for stimulating man's happiness. Were it true that external factors were solely responsible for, or that they wholly conditioned the arising of, pleasure and happiness, a person possessing an abundance of these factors would have illimitable joy, which is by no means always so. It is true that these external factors do make partial contribution to the creation of pleasure in a man's lifetime. However, to state that the external factors are all that is needed and therefore the exclusive cause of happiness in a man's span of life is an absurd and illogical proposition. It is by no means sure that the presence of such external factors will beget joy. On the contrary, factual happenings such as the experiencing of inner beatitude and happiness despite the total absence of such pleasure-causing external factors, and the frequent absence of joy despite their presence, clearly show the cause of happiness to be dependent upon a different set of conditioning factors.

If one were to be misled by the argument that the above-mentioned conditioning factors constitute the sole cause of happiness, to the preclusion of any other conditioning causes, that would imply that (resulting) happiness is inseparably bound to external causal factors, its presence or absence being exclusively determined by them. The fact that this is obviously not so is a sufficient proof that external causal factors are not necessarily or wholly responsible for the phenomenon of happiness.

Now what is that other internal set of causes? How are they to be explained? As Buddhists, we all believe in the law of Karma, the natural law of cause and effect. Whatever external causal conditions someone comes across in subsequent lives result from the accumulation of that individual's action in previous lives. When the Karmic force of past deeds reaches maturity, a person experiences pleasurable and unpleasurable mental states. They are but a natural sequence of his own previous actions. The most important thing to understand is that, when suitable (Karmic) conditions resulting from the totality of past actions are there, one's external factors are bound to be favourable. The coming into contact of conditions due to (Karmic) action and external causal factors will produce a pleasurable mental state. If the requisite causal conditions for experiencing interior joy are lacking, there will be no opportunity for the occurrence of suitable external conditioning factors; or, even if these external conditioning factors are present, it will not be possible for the person to experience the joy that would otherwise be his. This shows that inner causal conditions are essential in that these are what principally determine the experience of happiness (and its opposite). Therefore, in order to achieve the desired results, it is imperative for us to accumulate both the cause-creating external factors and the cause-creating internal (karmic) conditioning factors at the same time.

To state the matter in simple terms, for the accrual of good inner (karmic) conditioning factors, what are principally needed are such qualities as having few wants, contentment, humility, simplicity and other noble qualities. Practice of these inner causal conditions will even facilitate changes in the aforementioned external conditioning factors that will convert them into characteristics conducive to the arising of happiness. The absence of suitable inner causal conditions, such as having few wants, contentment, patience, forgiveness, and so on, will prevent one from enjoying pleasure, even if all the right external conditioning factor are present. Besides this, one must have to one's credit the force of merits and virtues accumulated in past lives. Otherwise, the seeds of happiness will not bear fruit.

The matter can be put in another way. The pleasures and frustrations, the happiness and suffering experienced by each individual are the inevitable fruits of beneficial and evil action he had perpetrated, thus adding to his store. If, at a particular moment in this present life, the fruits of person's good actions ripen, he will recognize, if he is a wise man, that they are the fruits of (past) meritorious deeds. This will gratify him and encourage him to achieve more merits. Similarly, when a person happens to experience pain and dissatisfaction, he will be able to bear them calmly if he maintains an unshakeable conviction that, whether he wishes it or not, he must suffer and bear the consequences of his own (past) deeds, notwithstanding the fact that normally he will often find the intensity and extent of his frustration hard to bear. Besides, the realization that they are nothing but the fruits of unskilled action in the past will make him wise enough to desist from unskilled deeds henceforth. Likewise, the satisfying thought that, with the ripening of past (evil) karma, a certain part of the evil fruit accrued by former unskilled action has been worked off, will be a source of immense relief to him.

A proper appreciation of this wisdom will contribute to grasping the essentials for achieving peace of mind and body. For instance, suppose a person is suddenly afflicted with critical physical suffering due to certain external factors. If, by the force of sheer will-power (based on the conviction that he is himself responsible for his present misery and sufferings), he can neutralize the extent of his suffering then his mind will be much comforted and at peace.

Now let me explain this at a rather higher level. This concerns the strivings and efforts that can be made for the systematic destruction of dissatisfaction and its causes.

As stated before, pleasure and pain, happiness and dissatisfaction are the effects of one's own good and bad, skilled and unskilled actions. Skillful and unskillful (Karmic) actions are not external phenomena. They belong essentially to the realm of mind. Making strenuous efforts to build up every possible kind of skillful karma and to put every vestige of unskillful karma away from us is the path to creating happiness and avoiding the creation of pain and suffering. For it is inevitable that a happy result follows a skillful cause; and that the consequence of building up unskillful causes is suffering.

Therefore, it is of the utmost importance that we strive by every possible means to increase the quality and quantity of skilful actions and to make a corresponding paring down of our unskilful actions.

How is this to be accomplished? Meritorious and unmeritorious causes which result in pleasure and pain do not resemble external objects. For instance, in the human bodily system, different parts such as lungs, heart and other organs can be replaced with new ones. But this is not so in the case of Karmic actions, which are purely of the mind. The earning of fresh merits and the eradicating of bad causes are purely mental processes. They cannot be achieved with outside help of any kind.

The only way to accomplish them is by controlling and disciplining the hitherto untamed mind. For this, we require a fuller comprehension of the element called mind.

Through the gates of the five sense organs a being sees, hears, smells, tastes and comes into contact with a host of external forms, object and impressions. Let the form, sound, smell, taste, touch, and mental events which are the relations of the six senses be shut off. When this is done, the recollection of past events on which the mind tends to dwell will be completely discontinued and the flow of memory cut off. Similarly, plans for the future and contemplation of future action must not be allowed to arise. It is necessary to create a vacuum in place of all such processes of thought if one is to empty the mind of all such processes of thought. Freed from all these processes, there will remain a pure, clean, distinct, and quiescent mind. Now let us examine what sort of characteristics constitute the mind when it has attained this stage. We surely do possess something called mind, but how are we to recognize its existence? The real and essential mind is what is to be found when the entire load of gross obstructions and aberrations (i.e., sense impressions, memories, etc.) has been cleared away. Discerning this aspect of real mind, we shall discover that, unlike external objects, its true nature is devoid of form or colour; nor can we find any basis of truth for such false and deceptive notions as that the mind originated from this or that, or that it will move from here to there, or that it is located in such-and-such a place. When it comes into contact with no object, mind is like a vast, boundless void, or like a serene, limitless ocean. When it encounters an object, it at once has cognizance of it, like a mirror instantly reflecting a person who stands in front of it. The true nature of mind consists not only in taking clear cognizance of the object but also in communicating a concrete experience of that object to the one experiencing it. Normally, our forms of sense cognition, such as eye-consciousness, ear-consciousness, etc., perform their functions on external phenomena in a manner involving gross distortion. Knowledge from sense cognition, being based on gross external phenomena, is also of a gross nature. When this type of gross stimulation is shut out, and when this concrete experiences and clear cognizance arise from within, mind assumes the characteristics of infinite void similar to the infinitude of space. But this void is not to be taken as the true nature of mind. We have become so habituated to consciousness of the form and colour of gross objects that, when we make concentrated introspection into the nature of mind, it is, as I have said, found to be a vast, limitless void free from any gross obscurity or other hindrances. Nevertheless, this does not mean that we have discerned the subtle, true nature of the mind. What has been explained above concerns the state of mind in relation to the concrete experience and clear cognizance by the mind which are its functions, but it describes only the relative nature of mind.

There are in addition several other aspects and states of mind. In other words, taking mind as the supreme basis, there are many attributes related to it. Just as an onion consists of layer upon layer that can be peeled away, so does every sort of object have a number of layers; and this is no less true of the nature of mind as explained here; it, too has layer within layer, state within state.

All compounded things are subject to disintegration. Since experience and knowledge are impermanent and subject to disintegration, the mind of which they are functions (nature) is not something that remains constant and eternal. From moment to moment, it undergoes change and disintegration. This transience of mind is one aspect of its nature. However, its true nature, as we have observed, has many aspects, including consciousness of concrete experience and cognizance of objects. Now let us make a further examination in order to grasp the meaning of the subtle essence of such a mind. Mind came into existence because of its own cause. To deny that the origination of mind is dependent on a cause, or to say that it is a designation given as a means of recognizing the nature of mind aggregates, is not correct. To our superficial observance, mind, which has concrete experience and clear cognizance as its nature, appears to be a powerful, independent, subjective, complete, ruling entity. However, deeper analysis will reveal that this mind, possessing as it does the function of experience and cognizance, is not a self-created entity, but is dependent on other factors for its existence. Hence it depends on something other than itself. This non-independent quality of mind substance is its true nature which, in turn, is the ultimate reality of the self.

Of these two aspects, viz., the ultimate true nature of mind and a knowledge of that ultimate true nature the former is the base, the latter, an attribute. Mind (self) is the basis, and all its different states are attributes. However, the basis and its attributes have from the first pertained to the same single essence. The non-self-created (depending on a cause other than itself) mind (basis) and its essence, Shunyata, have

unceasingly exited as the one, same, inseparable essence from begin-
ning-less beginning. The nature of Shunyata pervades all elements.
However, as we are now, since we cannot grasp or comprehend the
indestructible, natural, ultimate reality (Shunyata) of our own minds, we
continue to commit errors and our defects persist.

Taking mind as the subject and mind's ultimate reality as its object
one will arrive at a proper comprehension of the true essence of mind, i.e.,
its ultimate reality. And when, after prolonged, patient meditation one
comes to perceive and grasp at the knowledge of mind's ultimate reality
which is devoid of dual characteristics, one will gradually be able to
exhaust the delusions and defects of the central and secondary mind such
as wrath, love of ostentation, jealousy, envy and so on.

Failure to identity the true nature of mind will be overcome through
acquisition of the power to comprehend its ultimate reality. This will, in
turn eradicate lust and hatred and all other secondary delusions emanating from the basic ones. Consequently, there will be no occasion for
accumulating de-meritorious karma. By this means the creation of (evil)
karma affecting further lives will be eliminated; one will be able to
increase the quality and quantity of meritorious casual conditioning and
to eradicate the creation of casual conditioning affecting future lives apart
from the bad karma accumulated earlier.

In the practice of gaining a perfect knowledge of the true nature of
mind, strenuous and concentrated mental efforts are required for comprehending the object. In our normal condition as it is at present, when our
mind comes into contact with something it is immediately drawn to it. This
makes comprehension impossible. Therefore, in order to acquire great
dynamic mental power, the very maximum exertion is the first imperative.
For example, a big river flowing over a wide expanse of shallows will
have very little force; but when it passes through a steep gorge, all the
water is concentrated in a narrow space and therefore flows with great
force. For a similar reason all the mental distractions which draw the mind
away from the object of contemplation are to be avoided and the mind
kept steadily fixed upon it. Unless this is done, the practice for gaining a
proper understanding of the true nature of mind will be a total failure.

To make the mind docile, it is essential for us to discipline and control
it well. Speech and bodily activities which accompany mental processes
must not be allowed to run on in an indiscreet, unbridled, random way.
Just as a trainer disciplines and calms a wild and willful steed by

subjecting it to skillful and prolonged training, so must the wild, wandering, random activities of body and speech be tamed to make them docile, righteous, and skillful. Therefore the Teachings of the Lord Buddha comprise three graded categories that is, viz. Shila (Training in Higher Conduct) Samadhi (Training in Higher Meditation), and Prajna (Training in higher Wisdom), all of them for disciplining the mind.

Studying, meditating on and practising the three grades of trisiksha in this way, one accomplishes progressive realization. A person so trained will be endowed with the wonderful qualities of being able to bear patiently the miseries and suffering which are the fruit of his past Karma. He will regard his misfortune as blessings in disguise, for they will enlighten him as to the meaning of nemesis (karma) and convince him of the need to concentrate on performing only meritorious deeds. If his past (evil) karma has not as yet borne fruit, it will still be possible for him to obliterate this unripe karma by utilizing the strength of the four powers, namely: 1. Determination to attain the status of Buddhahood; 2. Determination to eschew de-meritorious deeds, even at the cost of his life; 3. The performance of meritorious deeds, and 4. Repentance.

Such is the way to attain immediate happiness, to pave the way for attaining liberation in future, and to help avoid the accumulation of further demerits.

Combining The Three Vehicles

The method employed for the practice of the Buddha Dharma (the Teaching of the Buddha) are diverse, for they depend upon the capacity and inclination of the individual mind. This is because those who are to be trained are not endowed with a uniform standard of intelligence. Some people have a sharp intelligence while others are gifted only with limited understanding. Accordingly, the Lord Buddha delivered His Teaching to suit varying degrees of intelligence and receptivity. Notwithstanding these many levels of instruction, it is still possible to provide a description of the general method of practising the Buddha Dharma as a whole. From the doctrinal standpoint, the Buddha Dharma can be said to consist of four schools of thought. These are: (i) Vaibhasika, (ii) Sautrantika, (iii) Vijnanavada and (iv) Shunyavada. In term of practice, the Buddha Dharma is classified into three categories, also known as the three vehicles, viz. (i) Shravakayana or Hinayana, (ii) Pratyekabuddhayana and (iii) Bodhisattvayana or Mahayana. As Shravakayana and Pratyekabuddhayana are basically of the same form, they are commonly known as Hinayana. So we have the two main vehicles—Mahayana and Hinayana. Mahayana is further subdivided into the vehicles of Prajnaparamitayana or the 'Cause Vehicle of Perfection' and the Vajrayana or the 'Effect Vehicle of the Adamantine wheel' which is also known as the "Great Secret".

Whether one practises Mahayana or Hinayana, the 'Cause Vehicle', or the 'Effect Vehicle' of Mahayana, each of these is a valid form of the glorious Teaching of the Lord Buddha. Sometime it may happen that a person who has not made a proper study of, or not yet fully realized, all these doctrines of the Blessed One will find himself puzzled by what appear to be some elementary contradictions between the concepts of Mahayana and Hinayana, or of Sutra and Tantra. For indeed the Buddha Dharma does have different and contradictory aspects, namely permissive and prohibitive precepts, within the vast concourse of its philosophical system. This gives rise to different and varying forms of practice and conduct. Only by delving deeply into these seeming contradictions, after equipping oneself by a deep study and by clearly comprehending the body of Lord Buddha's Teaching in all its aspects, will one acquire a comprehensive knowledge of the methods and system of its procedure and practice.

When this knowledge has been attained, the realization will dawn upon the seeker that those permissive and prohibitive aspects of the Buddha's Teaching have both been designed to advance the practitioner gradually and progressively along the right path, according to his capabilities and his intellectual development. In other words, the aim of all the yanas is to discipline the defiled and untamed mind of the individual, and to strengthen and clarify the precepts in accordance with the progressive development of the mind.

Then in what way can the teaching be fully carried out by a person practising the Buddha Dharma? A Tibetan saying answers the question in the following ways:

"Outward conduct is practised in accordance with Vinaya (Hinayana).

Inwardly, mental activity is practised with bodhimind (Mahayana)

Practised in secrecy is Tantra (Vajrayana)."

The above may be exemplified as follows. A Shramanara or Bhikshu, having pledged himself to observe the vows, acts in accordance with the rules of the Vinaya. Such a person is then motivated with the thought of attaining the status of Buddhahood for the liberation of all sentient beings. He therefore strives to practise the 'six perfections' and the 'four attributes' of a Bodhisattva. (The six perfections are: generosity, morality, forbearance, perseverance, collectedness and wisdom. The four attributes are: charity according to the needs of the recipient, courtesy in speech, encouraging others to practise virtues, and guiding others in the practice of virtues. Apart from this, he also trains himself in the two principal ways of meditation according to the esoteric teaching. In this manner, he will be practising all the teachings of Mahayana, Hinayana, Sutra and Tantra. This process is similar to that found in all the writings of the great Indian teachers.

"Outward conduct is practised in accordance with Vinaya." This can be explained as follows. There are eight categories of moral rules concerning the outward conduct practised in accordance with Vinaya discipline. The most important among them are the ones meant for Bhikshus. Bhikshus have to observe 253 rules of Vinaya. There are other secondary rules, but the set of 253 is the most important. They mostly concern the speech and physical conduct of Bhikshus.

The second saying, i.e., "Inwardly, mental activity is practised with bodhimind" means that the Bhikshu or the person concerned is motivated with the thought of liberating all sentient beings and also of acquiring the wisdom which perceives the Shunyata (Void). Equipped with such motives, he seeks to acquire the attributes of Sublime Thought as set down in the Transcendental Wisdom of the Mahayana and to achieve the great qualities emanating from the Sublime Thought.

The explanation of the third saying, "Practised in secrecy is Tantra" is that, in order to fulfil the great and glorious task of liberating all sentient beings, for which the status of Buddhahood is to be attained within the shortest time possible, the method of Tantra (esoteric teaching) is practised in secret. Tantra is unlike the other methods, being a distinct and special method, unique in character. It prepares and conditions the body in a special way for treading the path to that goal.

In this way, a person finally completes the progressive practices involved in all the methods—Mahayana, Hinayana, Sutra and Tantra. Just as a doctor prescribes different kinds of diet in accordance with the progress in a patient's health, so does a person practise these different methods as his mind progressively develops during his journey towards Enlightenment. The aim of all of them is to train the mind of the individual.

Tantra is classified into four divisions:

1. Kriya Tantra: This stresses the importance of purifying external activities.
2. Charya Tantra: This stresses the parallel importance of both external and internal (mental) activities.
3. Yoga Tantra: This stresses the importance of internal (mental) activities, i.e., meditation .
4. Anutara Yoga Tantra: This stresses the supreme importance of inner activity, regardless of the purification of external activities, i.e., it involves a higher type of meditation.

No special methods have been enunciated in the Kirya Tantra. Charya Tantra and Yoga Tantra for the subtle meditative concentration on the various life centres of the physical body that regulate and control the breathing, the movement of seminal fluids and blood circulation, whereas methods for such purpose are found in abundance in Anuttara Yoga. Nonetheless, when anyone is practising any one of these four classes of Tantra, the first thing required of him is the preparation of his mind, technically known as the "ripening of the mind". For this he must receive the requisite formal initiation from a competent teacher into the secret form of spiritual knowledge. The next step is observance of the sacred vows and rules of conduct prescribed in the Tantric teachings. In the case of the first three classes of Tantra, the person proceeds to the practice of the mental activity of concentrating on the non-self-existing (Shunyata) nature of the deity. In the case of the fourth, one practises the path of the Utpanna Karma leading to maturity, and the path of the Sampanna Karma leading to freedom. At the stage of Utpanna Karma, the initiated person identifies himself with the person of the deity which he has taken as the object of meditation. Only when he has achieved the power of meditation in the Utpanna Karma, can he proceed to the next stage of Sampanna Karma. In Sampanna Karma the person concentrates on acquiring the power of controlling the system of his breathing, blood circulation and the procreative forces of semen. Through these processes one advances to the acquirement of the status of Buddhahood. This in other words means that the person will acquire the power resulting from the self-existing body (Svabhavakaya), truth body (Dharmakaya), beautific body (Sambhogakaya), and emanation body (Nirmanakaya), and the five kinds of divine wisdom.

The methods which will aid in the practise of the Buddha Dharma (as explained above) can be briefly summarised as follows. First and foremost, one has to gain a complete understanding of the meaning of the method to be practised. For this, one must listen to numerous sermons, lectures and explanations on the subject from adepts. The meaning of what they teach must be pondered again, whereafter comes the next step of performing a concentrative meditation on the meaning pondered. These three processes should be combined in equal proportions without neglecting any one of them. This will make one become the true possessor of three great qualities, namely, learning, nobility and virtue. A learned man will become noble only when he puts into real practice what he has learnt, and not by mere words. Similarly, a noble man who has gained complete control over his mind, but is lacking in extensive knowledge of discourses and precepts will fall short of the definition of being learned. He must become genuinely proficient in a wide variety of subjects that come under the purview of the Buddha Dharma. The achievement of these two requirements plus the acquirement of the motive to do good for others will make a person truly possessing the three qualities of being learned, noble and good.

Between Misery and Joy

The faculty of reasoning distinguishes man from animals and other living creatures. Human beings are capable of investigating many things which animals cannot. Because they are able to discover and perceive things lying beyond the direct perceptions of their sense-organs, most men, whether they are Buddhists, Hindus, Christians, or belong to any other denomination, offer prayers or devotional recitations of one kind or another. Are such prayers and recitations due merely to custom, are they mere rituals to embellish daily life? The answer is definitely negative, because controlling and disciplining the mind is or should be the primary purpose of all prayers and religious recitations.

Though there are various methods of disciplining the mind, to think primarily for the benefit of others is immensely important. Benevolent thought for others will bring happiness both to them and to oneself, whereas if one thinks only of one's own selfish comfort and happiness, nothing but suffering can result. As the great Indian Pundit Shantideva has said: "All suffering in this world is due to egoistic desire for selfish comfort and happiness. All happiness is the fruit of selfless desire for the comfort and happiness of others."

Happiness, whether it is transient or ultimate, is a direct or indirect result of a sincere desire for the welfare of others. The main cause of suffering is egoistic desire for one's own comfort and happiness or its indirect effects. In this strife-torn world of ours, this is always true, no matter whether the sufferings in question are on a large scale such as those resulting from disagreement between different nations or the perpetration of a wicked act which brings about the loss of many lives, or on a smaller scale such as the bickering between insects. In all such cases, egoism is the root cause.

When mutual co-operation between neighbours and nations is motivated by benevolent thoughts for each other, such motivation is of the highest value. It is fitting that we should attach greater importance to unselfish desire for the comfort and happiness of others than to egoistic desire for self-beatitude and happiness. Generally speaking, all beings possessing a mind feel discomforted when they come across something unpleasant which they cannot appreciate however trivial it may be. Knowing that others, too, suffer when they encounter things that discomfort them, one should make every effort to avoid doing anything that might be the cause of discomfort or suffering to another being. This principle can be the foundation of peace and of all means of bringing about or consolidating world peace, such as disarmament. When all thoughts likely to cause suffering, such as a desire to resort to violence are erased from the mind, then speech and action, which stem from thought, will be devoid of evil intent. Similarly, the success of disarmament and other peace movements stems from a determination to achieve peace which first takes form in the mind and is subsequently translated into speech and action. Speech and action unsupported by firm intention in the mind will achieve nothing, however one may try. Basically, the inability to control and discipline the mind is at the bottom of all the troubles and problems of the world. Therefore, in this life of ours, whether we believe in rebirth or not, if we generate and send our benevolent thoughts towards all beings from men down to the tiniest insects, the world will inevitably be a happier place to live in. Happiness is gained for oneself and others by concentrating chiefly on others. What the world needs today is compassion and love. It is, therefore, of the utmost importance that we cultivate kindly thoughts for others so that thinking fondly of their welfare becomes an ingrained habit of mind.

Sect and Sectarianism

What exactly do we mean when we use the word 'religion' as a term common to all our doctrinal systems? By referring to the Latin roots of the word, we can trace its origin to the prefix *re-*(again) and the verb *ligare* (to tie up); therefore the primitive meaning of 'religion' would seem to be "to bind again". Now how does the concept of binding up or tying up come to be applied as the common term for all our various teachings? The common enemy of all religious disciplines, the target of all moral precepts laid down by the great teachers of mankind, is selfishness of mind. For it is just this which causes ignorance, anger and passion which are at the root of all the troubles of the world. The great teachers wanted to lead their followers away from the path of negative deeds caused by ignorance and to introduce them to the path of righteousness. They all agreed that the prime necessity for this is to bind up and control the undisciplined mind which harbours selfishness; for, with their great wisdom, they saw it to be the origin of all ill. Therefore, we can find in the very word which embraces all our spiritual teachings the key to and foundation of unity and harmony. We can easily ascribe the superficial disparities of dogma and appellation to the differences of time, place, culture, language, etc., prevailing at the time each religion came into being. By concentrating on the actual practice of each individual devotee, we shall discover with absolute certainty that we share the same sublime aim. To cite the great mentor, the saint-scholar Tsong Khapa:

All precepts when realized are found free of contradiction.
Every teaching is a precept for actual practice.
This is the easy way to penetrate into our Teachers' meaning,
And to avoid the great ill of abandoning the path.

The spirit of non-contradiction expressed in this so-called 'Path of the Quadrangle' provides the key to a broad philosophical acceptance of the spirit and function of religion. For, by maintaining sharp awareness of the function as expressed in the actuality of all teachings, we can escape the ruinous error of sectarian discrimination and partisanship, and we can avoid the grave sin of casting aside any religious teaching. It gives me great pleasure to repeat these words which were spoken long ago in the Land of Snows; for I am sure they will make an outstanding contribution to the development of unity and of a spirit of co-operation which are vital to keeping alive the flame of the spirit and preserving discipline in these difficult times of strife and partisanship all over the world.

To make use of an analogy: a skilled physician ministers to his patients individually, giving each the appropriate medicine necessary to cure his particular disease. Furthermore, the method and materials of treatment will vary according to the particular combination of circumstances of time and country. Yet all the widely differing medicines and medical methods are similar in that each of them aims to deliver the suffering patient from his sickness. In the same way, all religious teachings and methods are similar in that they are intended to free living beings from misery and the cause of misery, and to provide them with happiness and the cause of happiness. To cite a very famous verse from ancient India:

By not committing any evil,
By accomplishing every goodness,
To subdue one's own mind absolutely—
That is the teaching of the Buddha.

Until recently, the people in my Land of Snowy Mountains were left in complete isolation from their religious fellows all over the world. Although in ancient times, Buddhism and Buddhist culture were largely brought from India by the great pundits of India's classical age and the great Tibetan scholars and translators who studied under them, and there was in general a close connection between the two countries, in more recent times we were regrettably cut off from developments in the modern world. Now that we have suffered the great national disaster of virtual genocide, as is universally known, we can no longer doubt the impracticability of isolationism in modern times.

Nowadays the world is becoming increasingly materialistic, and mankind is reaching towards the very zenith of external progress, driven by an insatiable desire for power and vast possessions. Yet by this vain striving for perfection in a world where everything is relative, they wander ever further away from inward peace and happiness of the mind. This we can all bear witness to, living as we do plagued by unremitting anxiety in this dreadful epoch of diabolical weapons. It becomes more and more imperative that the life of the spirit be avowed as the only firm basis upon which to establish happiness and peace.

Therefore I pray that the precious light of the spirit will reign in the world for a long time, dispelling the dark shadows of materialism. It is imperative for all of us to resolve upon making great efforts to hold its essence steadfastly in our hearts, and thence to disseminate it all over the world, opening the minds and hearts of all to its healing power. In so resolving, we eschew the path of mundane power, for the healing power of the spirit naturally follows the path of the spirit; it abides not in the stone of fine buildings nor in the gold of images, nor the silk from which robes are fashioned, nor even in the paper of holy writ, but in the ineffable substance of the mind and the heart of man. We are free to follow its dictates as laid down by the great teachers to sublimate our heart's instincts and purify our thoughts. Through actual practice in his daily life, man will fulfill the aim of all religion, whatever its denomination. And when the inner radiance generated by the practice of spirituality comes to light up the world again, as it has done in certain eras in the past, the masses who comprise the great nations of the world may take their inspiration from the bodhimind of love and mercy, may relinquish their obsession with the vain pursuit of power, and may take refuge in the discipline of religion, the inexhaustible source of blessing the universal panacea.

The Two Truths

Buddhism has flourished in Tibet for over a thousand years. During these centuries, it has been carefully preserved and has become the basis of our culture. Nevertheless, although our culture has been nourished by many things of worth from neighbouring countries, we have on the whole been very much on our own.

In Tibet we practised Buddhism in its entirety. In garb and conduct the monks practised according to the rules of the Vinaya Sutras; in the training of mind, we followed the Mahayana philosophy; and we also practised Tantric Buddhism. That is why I have used the phrase "in its entirety". Today, however, we are passing through a period of unimaginable difficulty and hardship.

The world today is engulfed in conflicts and sufferings to such an extent that everyone longs for peace and happiness; that longing has unfortunately led them to be carried away by the pursuit of ephemeral pleasure. But there are a few learned people who, dissatisfied by what is ordinarily seen or experienced, think more deeply and search for true happiness. I believe that the search will continue. As we make greater material progress and are able to satisfy our daily needs more fully, man will continue to search for Truth, not being satisfied with material progress alone. Indeed, I am convinced that the search for Truth still will grow even keener.

In past centuries, there have been many learned teachers who have laid down various paths to the realisation of truth. Among them, Lord Buddha is one, and my study of Buddhism has led me to form the opinion that, despite the difference in the names and forms used by the various religions, the ultimate truth to which they point is the same.

In Buddhism we have relative truth and absolute truth. From the viewpoint of absolute truth, what we feel and experience in our ordinary daily life is all delusion. Of the various delusions, the sense of discrimination between oneself and others is the worst form, as it creates nothing but unpleasantness for both sides. If we can realize and meditate on ultimate truth, it will cleanse our impurities of mind and thus eradicate the sense of discrimination. This will help in creating true love for one another. The search for ultimate truth is, therefore, vitally, important.

In the search for ultimate truth, if it fails to dawn on us it is we who have not found it. Ultimate truth exists. If we think deeply and reflect carefully, we shall realize that we ourselves have our existence in ultimate truth. For example, I am talking to you and you are listening to me. We are generally under the impression that there is a speaker and an audience and that there is the sound of words being spoken, but, in ultimate truth, if I search for myself I will not find it, and if you search for yourselves you will not find them. Neither speaker nor audience, neither words nor sound, can be found. They are all void like empty space. Yet they are not completely non-existent. They must exist, for we are able to feel them. What I am saying is being heard by you, and you are in turn thinking on the subject. My speech is producing some effect, yet if we search for them we cannot find them. This mystery relates to the dual nature of truth.

Anything whose existence is directly perceivable by us can be classified as pertaining to relative truth. But, in ultimate truth, neither the searcher nor the object being searched for exists. Ultimate truth is void like empty space, beyond every form of obstruction and complication. Once we understand this, we can achieve true mental peace. It is my hope that as the world becomes smaller and smaller owing to material progress and better communications, we shall, as a result, all be able to understand more about ultimate truth. When this happens, I have great hope that we shall achieve true world peace.

Love and Compassion

In our approach to life, be it pragmatic or otherwise, a basic fact that confronts us squarely and unmistakably is the desire for peace, security and happiness. Different forms of life at different levels of existence make up the teeming denizens of this earth of ours. And, no matter whether they belong to the higher groups such as human beings or to the lower groups such as animals, all beings primarily seek peace, comfort and security. Life is as dear to a mute creature as it is to a man. Even the lowliest insect strives for protection against dangers that threaten its life. Just as each one of us wants happiness and fears pain, just as each one of us wants to live and not to die, so do all other creatures.

The faculty of reasoning, the ability to think and the power of expression distinguish man as a being superior to his mute friends. In the quest for peace, comfort and security, the methods applied by man are diverse and, sometimes, radically opposed to one another. All too frequently, the means adopted are cruel and revolting. Behaving in a way that is utterly unbecoming to his human status, man indulges in inhuman cruelties, torturing his fellow men as well as members of the animal kingdom just for the sake of selfish gain; such behaviour has almost become the order of the day. Such unskilled actions bring suffering to oneself as well as to others. Having been born as human beings, it is vitally important for us to practise benevolence and perform meritorious deeds for ourselves and others in this life and in lives to come. To be born a human being is a rare experience, and it is wise to use this golden opportunity as effectively and skillfully as possible.

Buddhism, with its emphasis on universal love and compassion impregnated with ideas that are wholly non-violent and peaceful, offers a means, at once unique and eternal, for the successful attainment of that state of security and happiness where-from man and beast can derive common benefaction. It can rightly be asserted that loving-kindness and compassion are the two corner stones on which the whole edifice of Buddhism stands . Destruction or injury to life is strictly forbidden. Harming or destroying any being from the highest to the lowest, from a human to the tiniest insect, must at all cost be avoided. The Blessed One said: "Do not harm others. Just as you feel affection on seeing a dearly beloved person, so should you extend loving-kindness to all creatures." Those who follow the Mahayanist way are admonished not only to abstain from doing injury but also to cultivate a great spirit of compassion involving an eager longing to save all sentient beings from pain and misery.

The arising of mahakaruna in the mind will prepare the ground for the perfect fruition of the precious bodhimind, which is a necessary condition for attaining the supreme status of a Bodhisattva. One is called a Bodhisattva when one's mind is filled with the pure compassion and equanimity which proceed from bodhimind. As whatever we do in our everyday life results from the functioning of our minds, ultimate peace and Buddhahood are the results of bodhimind and compassion. The Lord Buddha has said: "Bodhimind is the seed of all Dharma. If you wish to acquire the supreme status of a Boddhisattva, you must cultivate the quality of bodhimind which should be as firm as a rocky mountain." Another Buddhist scholar, Acharya Chandrakirti, wrote: "In the beginning, mahakaruna (boundless compassion) is like a seed; it becomes as water and manure in the middle, and as ripe fruit at the end." All these sayings emphasize the matchless efficacy of bodhimind. The intention to do good to others, the persistent thought in one's heart of the welfare of others, will spontaneously create happiness among the people around us. To return good for evil, benevolence for injury, love for hate, and compassion for anger, are some of the characteristics of the quality of bodhimind. Deeds of benevolence and loving kindness, not responding to ill-will from the other side, will delight the hearts of all. Indulgence in resentment and vengeance will only further and increase miseries to oneself and others in this life and in lives to come.

Whatever method is adopted for the cultivation of the quality of bodhimind, the fact remains that the birth-cycles of all sentient beings are beginningless, and that numberless times in their previous lives they have each fulfilled the role of a mother. The feeling of a mother for her child is a classic example of love. For the safety, protection and welfare of her children, a mother is ready to sacrifice her very life. Recognising this, Children should be grateful to their mother and express their gratitude by performing virtuous deeds. In the same way, a person motivated by the thought of bodhimind strives with all his might for the welfare of every sentient being whether it be a human or a fowl of land or sea. At the same time, he will treat all the beings as he treats his mother. In repayment of her maternal love, it will be his constant endeavour to do only what is benevolent. In short, the cultivation of compassion and loving-kindness for all sentient beings will bring peace and happiness to oneself and others. Ill-will, malice and malevolent acts will only be a source of suffering to all.

The noble aspiration to Buddhahood, to cultivate bodhimind in thought and to practise charity, forbearance, morality, kindness and so on are all for the sake of living beings. It is for them that these ennobling and uplifting qualities are sought. The creatures that inhabit this earth—be they human beings or animals—are here to contribute, each in its own peculiar way, to the beauty and prosperity of the world. Many creatures have toiled singly or jointly to make our life comfortable. The food we eat, the clothes we wear, have not just dropped from the sky. Many creatures have laboured to produce them. That is why we should be grateful to all our fellow creatures. Compassion and loving kindness are the hallmarks of achievement and happiness. Let us practise them for the welfare of all.

The Bodhimind

All religions, in teaching moral precepts to mould the functions of mind, body and speech, have primarily the same noble goal. They all teach us not to lie or bear false witness, not to steal or take other's lives and so on. That there are so many different religions to bring happiness to mankind is analogous to the treatment of a particular disease by different methods. For, in the most general terms, all religions aim to help each living being to avoid misery and acquire happiness. Thus, although we can find causes for preferring individual interpretations of religious truth, there is much greater cause for unity stemming from the heart. In the present state of the world, the need to evolve a great measure of unity among the followers of the different religions has become especially important. Moreover, such unity is not an impossible ideal.

Bodhimind forms the central theme of Mahayana Buddhism in Tibet. We believe that the concept of the bodhimind will go a long way in helping to achieve basic unity and a spirit of co-operation among the followers of different creeds. We believe that striving in itself will effect great results. The Blessed One acquired bodhimind after making innumerable sacrifices and intensely concentrated efforts. For three immeasurable aeons, he practised the deeds of a Bodhisattva, making unstinting sacrifices and undergoing great hardships, thus gradually acquiring the dual accumulations of merit and wisdom. Finally, at Buddha Gaya, he attained to the supreme Enlightenment which is called Buddhahood. Emancipated from the misery that follows clinging to the extremes of the mundane and the sublime, he reached that perfect equanimity that flows from the ultimate ineffable peace called Nirvana, free from every fault. His intellect perfected beyond the minutest error or illusion, he proceeded to evolve the many forms of the Holy Dharma, turning the Threefold Wheel of the Dharma in accordance with the system of the Four Noble Truths and of Interdependent Origination, all in revelation of the dual truth (relative and absolute).

The inspiration to achieve this ineffable bodhimind can be expressed in this way: "I must attain the supreme state of omniscient Buddhahood, so that I can liberate all sentient beings from this ocean of misery, Samsara, and establish them in the ultimate happiness of Nirvana." This inspiration creates a longing to devote one's energy to both the profound and extensive stages of the path of Mahayana. It is the root of the practice for accomplishing the Bodhisattva deeds, which connotes generosity, morality, patience, perseverance, meditation and wisdom. To be more precise, from the first three, generosity, morality and patience, stems the accumulation of virtue. From the last two, meditation and wisdom, stem the accumulation of sublime wisdom. And the fourth one, perseverance, leads to both accumulations. In short, the key to the practice of Mahayana Buddhism in Tibet is dual co-ordination at every level, the co-ordination of virtue and wisdom, method and knowledge, Tantra and sutra, relative and absolute. Simultaneously, careful attention must be paid to the inherent moral implications of all the Buddha's teachings, i.e., desisting from harming others and cultivating the spirit of loving-kindness. Viewed from the perspective of the bodhimind, the goal is to maintain indiscriminating compassion towards all living beings without making any distinction of race, nationality, class or tenuous status of friend or enemy. In time, the great nations of the world, inspired by the bodhimind may cease to manipulate everything, both sacred and profane, in a vain pursuit of power, and instead try to create a peaceful world by regulating the mind's activities to accord with Dharma, the inexhaustible treasure.

Buddha Dharma and The Society

For many centuries man has been talking about justice, harmony and peace. In these modern days of material abundance and stupendous advancement in science and technology it seems that the more sophisticated our lives become, the less we seem to be conscious of these high ideals. And yet, there is no doubt about the need for these, for without them the very survival of human society is at stake. As followers of Buddha Dharma we must make our contributions towards the realisation of these.

The achievement of justice, harmony and peace depends on many factors. I would like to think about them in terms of human benefit—in the long run rather than for the short. I realise the difficulty of the task before us. But we have no alternative. The world has shrunk and has become more interdependent than ever before. Nations have no choice but to be concerned about the welfare of others, not only because of their belief in humanity, but because it is in their self-interest. Under the circumstances, there is definitely a growing need for human understanding, and a sense of universal responsibility. The key to the achievement of these high ideals lies in generating a good and kind heart. For, unless we develop a feeling of humanness, we can neither hope to achieve universal happiness nor lasting peace.

I believe in the need for human understanding and harmony for a wider reason, which is simply that we are all human beings. Geographical, cultural and physical differences are superficial. Even differences of faith and ideology are transcended when we begin to think of ourselves as human beings. We all want happiness and do not want suffering, and every human being has the right to pursue happiness. For in the final analysis, all of us basically have the same hopes and aspirations, and all of us belong to the same human family.

Buddhism is one of the many religions which teaches us to be less selfish and more compassionate. It teaches us to be humane, altruistic and to think of others in the way we think for ourselves. Our daily thoughts and actions should be directed towards the benefit of others. Mahayana emphasises self-sacrifice and the development of altruism while Hinayana teaches us the importance of not harming others. The practice of Buddhism in essences is, therefore not to harm others under any circumstances, and help others as much as possible.

By living in a society we should share the sufferings of our fellow beings and practise compassion and tolerance, not only towards our loved ones but also towards our enemies. This is the test of our strength and practice, and is what Mahayana stresses. Unless we can set an example by our own practice we cannot hope to convince others of the value of dharma by mere words. We should engage in the same high standards of integrity and sacrifice that we ask of others. The ultimate purpose of Buddhism, and for that matter all religions, is to serve and benefit man. That is why it is of the utmost importance for us to ensure that Buddhism is always employed to realise the happiness and peace of man and not to convert others or to derive benefit from them.

In this ever-changing world there are two important things that Buddhists should keep in mind. The first is self-examination. We should re-examine our own attitude towards others and constantly check ourselves to see whether we are acting properly. Before pointing our finger at others we should point it towards ourselves. Secondly, we must be prepared to admit our faults and stand corrected.

There is no doubt that Buddha Dharma is faultless; but over the centuries as it was practised in many parts of the world—including my country till about two decades ago—social and traditional influences have crept into it. We should after careful examination be prepared to correct and weed these out when they are no longer beneficial or relevant.

The Buddha's teachings consist of Hinayana and Mahayana, and of Tantrayana, which is an important part of Mahayana. Much incorrectly ascribed information, and a lack of appreciation and proper understanding of the deeper significances of these paths have led to many false impressions and misconceptions about them. I would, therefore, like to say something about the way these teachings were studied and practised in Tibet with the hope that it will help to create a better comprehension of them.

During his own lifetime, Sakyamuni Buddha gave many discourses and instructions, from which later arose the four Schools of Buddhist tenets namely, Vaibhasika, Sautrantika, Chittamatra and Madhyamaka, and the two systems of practice and experience, Sravaka Pratyekabudhayana and Bodhisattvayana. In Tibet all these teachings were studied and practised thoroughly and with great devotion. Though it was the Madhyamaka tenet that Tibetan Buddhists finally settled for, they in no way looked down upon the other schools, and in fact, studied their tenets with equal enthusiasm and interest, as the most effective means of understanding and realising the deeper significances of the upper schools. Even their conduct and discipline patterns were governed by the directions of the Vinaya, a Hinayana tradition, the teachings of which are regarded as the basis of all Buddhist practices. Hinayana consists of four major orders, Mahasamghika, Sarvastivada, Sthavira and Sammitiya which are subdivided into eighteen sects. Today only two of these four orders, Sarvastivada and Sthavira, exist.

Tibetans practice the Vinaya according to the Sarvastivadin tradition while a number of countries like Sri Lanka follow the Sthavira tradition. There are no major difference between the two and they only vary in terms of enumeration, and commission and omission of minor rules. For instance, according to the Sarvastivadin tradition, Bikshus are required to observe 253 vows, while according to the Sthavira tradition they are only required to keep 227 vows. Similarly, there is a slight difference in the number of Bikshu downfall vows (suddha-prayaschika) as the Sarvastivadins have ninety while the Sthaviras have ninety-two vows. However, there is no such variation regarding the major vows of defeats (para-jika), remainders (samaghavasesa) and forfeiters (naihsargika payattika).

As I have said before, Tibetan Buddhists not only have a deep respect for Hinayana but, in fact, in their practice they try to integrate Hinayana observances in their conduct and day to day life, while internally they strive to develop bodhimind and to practise Tantrayana in secrecy.

Mahayana primarily seeks the state of Buddhahood for the sake of others. In conjunction with this aspiration, sixteen aspects of the four truth such as impermanence and the thirty-seven practices to enlightenment (Bodhipaksika dharmas), Mahayanists practise the six or ten perfections (paramitas), and the four means of gathering disciples.

Vajrayana has four sets of Tantra: Kriya, Charya, Yoga and Anuttara-yoga, and is basically a path of practice where a practitioner tries to realise the subtle mind through the medium of developing a stabilised realisation of the unison of Samatha and Vipasyana by concentrating on the various channels and the currents of energy of the body. Nowadays it seems to be attracting much interest and also many people seem to be stressing the similarities that exist between non-Buddhist and Buddhist Tantras to an extent of saying that they are both the same. I think this is a gross misconception and feel that one would understand Buddhist Tantra clearer if one observes that mere similarities in certain practices do not justify the assertion that the two systems are the same. Otherwise, we would have to say that the Sutra teachings are the same as non-Buddhist teachings because both propound similar teachings with regards to certain practices and developments such as *dhyana* and arupysampttya. Moreover, if one analyses carefully, one will find that the very basis upon which Tantrayana is founded is vastly different from those of non-Buddhist Tantra teachings, for Buddhist Tantrayana is based upon the fundamental teachings and realisation of bodhimind and the theory of anatama (selflessness).

Efforts are also being made in various parts of the world for religious unity and for better understanding among the different faiths. It is indeed an important task, but we must remember that there is no quick and easy solution. We cannot hide the differences that exist among various faiths, and neither can we hope to replace the existing faiths by a universal belief. Each religion has its own distinctive qualities and contributions to make, and each in its own way is suitable to a particular group of people. For I believe that each of them basically aims at transforming man into a better and decent human being. The world needs them all. Therefore I feel that if we want to achieve harmony and good-will not only among followers of Buddhism but also among different religions, we must make every effort to create better understanding and more respect for one another's religions. Above all we must never use religion for selfish reasons such as to promote communal interests.

However difficult it may be for us to achieve these goals, I think we owe it to all mankind to make every effort. It is my hope that there would be a better understanding among Buddhists and, on a larger scale, a sense of universal responsibility and brotherhood between all spiritual traditions.

Questions and Answers

Q. *Your Holiness, here in Dharamsala, and also on your visit to the West you have had considerable contact with Western people, who at present are showing a deep interest in the Tibetan spiritual traditions. Whenever the Buddhadharma has been absorbed into a new society, it has always been modified so as to have the greatest impact on the minds of the people. What can and what cannot be modified, particularly in the context of Dharma in the West?*

A. The fundamentals of the principal practices of Dharma ought not to be changed. For example, the basis of bodhichitta (the altruistic attitude of striving for Buddhahood as a means of benefiting all beings) and shunyata (emptiness, the ultimate nature of mind and of all things) will always be required by practitioners. However, in order to get at the essence of these practices, their secondary details—such as the sequential order of the ways in which they are approached, the specifics of the visualization involved in them and so forth—might well be modified to accord with the differing mentalities of given people.

There were certain differences in the practices of ancient India and Tibet, yet the essential factors of bodhichitta, the core of the Mahayana, were identical. The differences were only in how bodhichitta was actualized. Even in India there were a number of approaches to it, such as "The Exchange of Self-cherishing for the Cherishing of Others", taught in Shantideva's "Venturing into the Deeds of a Bodhisattva" (Bidhisattvacaryavatara) and "The Method of Six Causes and One Effect", taught in Atisha's "Light on the Path" (Bodhipathapradipa). These different techniques were meant to suit different circumstances. Both aimed at developing the same bodhichitta and at outlining the practices of the Six Perfections.

Therefore, the details of various practices can differ to suit the Western mentality, and not only to suit the Western mentality in general but also to suit the individual practitioner's dispositions.

Q. *All the great masters have stressed the importance of having a spiritual teacher in order to avoid misunderstanding either the teachings or one's meditational experiences. Unfortunately, at present there are very few teachers and many who wish to learn. Is it advisable for such a person to just read a meditation manual and then practise from it?*

A. This is possible. Certain advanced meditations are dangerous if practised without the guidance of an experienced teacher, but simple meditations, such as those on impermanence, love, compassion or the development of samadhi, are good.

Without a teacher, it is best to limit oneself to small and simple meditations.

Q. *Many people wish to take up a spiritual practice but feel committed to devoting most of their time to job, family, etc. Is it possible to transform those concerned into sources of spirituality?*

A. The major attitudes one needs in order to do this are kindness and bodhichitta.

It is difficult to explain bodhichitta in brief and still be correct. Perhaps we can say that it is the motivation to help oneself so as to be able to help others. This profoundly kind attitude, bodhichitta, is the basis of all Mahayana teachings.

To make ordinary activities spiritual, this attitude of kindness must be incorporated within every action of daily life. Certain meditations cannot be practised while you are working, for example in a factory, but meditation upon kindness and compassion can be. If you sincerely try, Dharma can always be practised.

Q. *The Buddhadharma as practised by Tibetans involves meditation upon a vast array of symbols and deities. Does Your Holiness see this as presenting any problems to the Western mind, with its monotheistic background?*

A. This depends on the individual's character. Some people like these deities very much. Each person must think about what suits him best.

Q. *Some say that these symbols and deities should be altered so as to correspond with those of our own culture.*

A. This cannot be, if you follow Buddhadharma, the deities meditated upon should have a sound reference in the teachings of Buddha Vajradhara. They cannot be arbitrarily created nor can they be blended with those of other methods. It is best to follow with diligence the path most suited to you. If you choose Buddhadharma, practise it purely. Then, if you achieve its results, fine, if you mix practices and achieve nothing, you shouldn't blame Dharma.

Of the various Buddhist meditational deities, the best is Buddha. If you like others, practise on them; if you don't simply take Buddha.

Q. *Is this 'liking' due to one's karmic dispositions?*

A. It has to do with karmic dispositions. Buddhism speaks of idiosyncrasies, talent admiration and underlying tendencies, which together with one's intellect, circumstances and so forth constitute one's karmic dispositions. These are major factors determining which path one should follow.

Q. *Many occidental translators of Tibetan texts lay great emphasis upon the external rather than the inner aspects of spiritual magic. How was this problem avoided in Tibet when the tantric texts were translated from Sanskrit into Tibetan?*

A. This does not seem to have been an excessively great problem in Tibet. However, there undoubtedly have been certain people who did not incorporate Dharma into their mental attitudes. In actuality, anyone who practises tantric methods for such purposes as to destroy an enemy is not really a spiritual person. Whether or not a person is actually a spiritual practitioner is determined by the long-term benefits that his practice brings, not by the methods he uses.

Buddha Vajradhara taught Tantra to help beings attain enlightenment, not to give them an instrument for harming others. He always emphasised that Tantra is a secret doctrine, for in the hands of someone without the background of bodhichitta and other qualifications it can be dangerous and not at all beneficial.

The commentary to the "Root Text of Manjushri" (Manjushri Mula Tantra) tells a story of a Brahmin by the name of Kanaka, who was a practitioner of the Yamantaka Tantra. Although he was an extremely strong meditator with tremendous concentration and power, he fell into hell. His practice, meant to bring him enlightenment, only harmed him. In a commentary to the "Root Text of Guhyasamaja" (Guhyasamaja Mula Tantra) the same point is stressed.

Anything that has happened in Tibet along these lines is not good and any such interest elsewhere is the same.

The true tantric practitioner has taken a commitment not to show whatever magical powers he may possess. According to the Vinaya rules, even if you are an Arhant you should not openly reveal your attainments to others. It is the same in Tantra; if with little reason you expose your powers, even though you have certain qualifications the basis of your practice will degenerate.

Q. *Of all Buddhist practices, those of the Tantrayana have attracted the most attention among Westerners and not the preliminary practices but the very advanced Completion Stage practices which involve meditation on chakras, nadis, consorts and so forth. What are the advantages and disadvantages of this interest and what are the preliminaries of tantric practice?*

A. It is very good that Westerners have this interest in the Completion Stage. However, it is of little value to perform these without first becoming proficient in the practices of the Development Stage, where samadhi is developed and one's attitude towards Tantra matured by means of meditation upon the mystic mandala. Furthermore, this interest should be based on the motivation to benefit all beings; a difficult prerequisite. Interest motivated by mere idle curiosity lacks the proper foundation.

Meditation upon the Completion Stage of Tantra can be

extremely dangerous, perhaps bringing many types of sickness and even death to the unqualified practitioner. Medicines cannot cure a sickness arising from performing these practices incorrectly; the only antidote is the proper application of a specific meditation.

Q. *In brief, what is the difference between Hindu and Buddhist Tantra?*

A. To fully understand their differences is extremely difficult. However, in brief, there are differences in both action and philosophy. In terms of action, the Buddhist Tantra is based on the bodhichitta motivation, which the Hindu Tantra lacks. In terms of philosophy, Buddhist Tantra is based on the theory of anatma, or selflessness, whereas the Hindu is based on the theory of a truly-existent self. Other yogas, such as breathing exercises, chakra and nadi practices, etc., have many similarities but subtle differences.

Q. *As self-cherishing and ego-holding are forces which have been active since beginningless time, is it possible to set out upon a spiritual path without developing a negative egoism towards it, leading to sectarianism?*

A. To avoid that, it is necessary to take care that your Dharma practice is really a Dharma practice. This way, although the power of familiarity with ego is great, its effects are not overwhelming. If you study Dharma but do not actually apply it, your so-called spiritual activities can easily become directed at material gain, fame and so forth. In which case only egoism and such negativities as anger, attachment, sectarianism, etc., are developed. However, if each word of Dharma that you hear is used to cultivate your mind then every single word brings only benefit, and no matter how much Dharma learning you amass, your learning will never go to the development of egoism.

The most important point is to be very careful in the beginning with your motivation in receiving a teaching or starting a practice. If this is done well, there is little danger.

Q. *Buddha Sakyamuni once said in a Sutra that sectarianism has a karmic consequence more severe than killing a thousand Buddhas. Why is this so?*

A. The essential purpose of the Buddhas giving teachings is to eliminate both mistaken states of mind and the experience of suffering. This is also the reason that they have worked to achieve enlightenment. The Buddhas' only motivation is to benefit others, which they fulfil by teaching; so despising any of their teachings is worse than despising the Buddhas. This is the implication of following one Dharma tradition while disparaging other traditions.

Furthermore, the Buddhas themselves respect all the traditions of the teachings, so for us not to do so is to despise all the Buddhas.

There are many ways to look at this Sutra quotation. What is the duty, so to speak, of a Buddha? Only to teach Dharma. And it is Dharma which has brought that Buddha to his state of attainment. Now, in Buddhadharma we do not accept the theory of a Creator; everything depends on oneself. The Buddha cannot directly fulfil their wish to help beings, they can only do so through the media of their teachings. We might say that they are handicapped. Therefore, the teachings that they give are more precious and important than are they themselves. Because of the varying capacities and inclinations of being, the Buddhas have taught various methods of practice and philosophy. If we follow one of these and yet belittle others, we abandon the Dharma and consequently the Buddhas as well.

Q. *Does Your Holiness think that the various world religions were founded by emanations of the Buddhas manifesting in accordance with mentalities of specific societies?*

A. This is highly possible. The founder of any religion could be an emanation of a particular Buddha. It is for this very reason that we should treat all religions with deep respect.

Q. *Then why do these different religions so often fight with one another?*

A. This is a different matter. For a truly religious person there is never any basis for quarrel or dispute. Yet it is a fact that there have been so-called religious wars. However, the people involved in these were not practising religion but were merely using religion as an instrument of power. The actual motivation was selfish, not spiritual. Religious wars are not a question of contradictions between religions at all.

Leaving aside the disparities between the doctrines of different religions, there are many ostensible contradictions within the teachings of Buddha. For example, for certain reasons to some people he taught that there is no truly-existent self, whereas to others he taught that there is. So what is a Buddha's purpose in teaching? It is neither to boast nor to demonstrate how much he knows, but to benefit others. Also, he is not concerned with those of his generation alone but with many generations and different kinds of people. Therefore, his teachings must have many different levels of meaning, some often seemingly contradictory. Knowing this, there is never a valid reason for religious quarrels and disputes.

Q. *How does Tibetan Buddhism interpret the value of religion?*

A. The real objective of religion (Dharma) is to serve the functions of a protector—a source of refuge. A system which provides security makes for a utilitarian, functional religion. And yet, whatever and howsoever might be the external activities, behaviours and form provided for by the system, it cannot be viewed as falling within the perspective of a functional religion if it fails to provide, even elementarily, a means of refuge or protection. A religion involves practice of methods and modes conducive to the realization of serenity, discipline, joyous detachment, and self-control. It should be observed that normally it is through the inattentive body, speech, and mind that all harmful and unethical factor-conditions are created. Therefore, it naturally presupposes that the pacification, training, and taming of the physical, mental, and verbal activities are of fundamental importance. To sum up, it is essential, first of all, to rectify, nullify, and put a stop to all physical misconduct (pertaining to body), followed by that of the speech. Rectification of the unwholesome physical and verbal actions is in itself a method for controlling the mind. As to the method to be adopted for taming the mind, the entire ramifications of the present mental strains and faults, beginning from the most serious and ending in the subtlest, are to be fully eradicated. Regarding the manner of eradication, the objective can be achieved in two ways; one, energetic suppression of some of the more pronounced and evident defilements, and two, progressive elimination of all mental defilements, gross or subtle; and ultimately by eradicating their very sources (seed or first cause) in such a way that these are rendered impotent even when coming in contact with their ripening conditions. Such a process of eradication is total and complete.

Q. *What meaning is given to the concept of Karma in Tibet?*

A. Karma and its fruit can roughly be described as volitional action and its fruits, or moral psychological cause and effect. Methods of explaining the true nature of karma and its fruits are diverse and many. A generalized description would be that all phenomena and objects are the results of causes. An effect is produced by a cause. Whether the result is good or bad depends upon the individual mind. A negative cause and effect is indestructible and irrevocable. Take the example of a plant sapling. The effect, plant sapling, comes into being because of its previous cause, i.e., the seed. The quality of its effect is dependent upon the quality of its corresponding cause. Similarly, pleasure and pain, or happiness and suffering, which are the lot of sentient beings, come from the individual's past causes—good or bad. It is all because of the operation of the inexorable law of cause and effect. The discovery that Karma exists and is a fact and reality, that it increases, that there is no fruit unless conditioned by karma, and that nothing can hide from karma, is a truth of great significance.

Q. *The traditional scriptures speak of the Three Vehicles. Why did the Buddha teach three paths?*

A. Although the scriptures do speak of three Vehicle—the Hearer's Vehicle, the Solitary Realizer's Vehicle and the Bodhisattva Vehicle—the first two of these are counted as one, the Hinayana. The Bodhisattva Vehicle, or Mahayana, is subdivided into the "casual Vehicle of the Practice of the Perfections" and the "Resultant Vehicle of the Practice of Tantra". Thus in Tibet we usually speak of the two vehicles, the Hinayana and the Mahayana.

There are many different ways to look at these two. First we'll consider them from the point of view of practice.

It is very important to have as an external basis the observance of the Vinaya, i.e., maintaining one of the four ordination of a monk or nun, or either of the two traditions of a lay person.

For a monk, the three foundations of practice should be followed: Rainy Season Retreat, Bi-monthly Purification and the Ceremony Ending Rainy Season Retreat. These are all Hinayana practices.

In addition to the above, one should take up the practice of compassion, bodhichitta and the conducts of the Six Perfections, which are Casual Mahayana.

One person can perform all these practices for the attainment of enlightenment: they do not obstruct one another nor cause any constrictions within the practitioner. Therefore, one person can practice all of them without contradiction. With this approach there can be no basis for Hinayana disparaging Mahayana, Mahayana disparaging Hinayana, Sutrayana disparaging Tantra and so forth. Such is the relationship of the vehicles from the point of view of action.

From the point of view of philosophy, Buddhadharma can be divided into the Four Schools (Vaibashika, Sautrantika, Yogacara, and Madhyamika) which all come from India. In one way these seem to be mutually exclusive. However, the purpose of seemingly conflicting teachings within the framework of Buddhist philosophy is to provide a graduated approach to the higher philosophies, leading to an ever greater, and eventually ultimate understanding. Therefore, none of the four schools of philosophy is to be abandoned.

In Tibet there are four major traditions: Nyingma, Sakya, Kagyu and Gelug. From the point of view of practice, they are all Mahayanists following the unity of Sutrayana and Tantrayana, as described above, on the basis of Hinayana. From the point of view of philosophy, they are all Madhyamikas (who train in accordance with the graduated philosophical stages explained above). They do not differ from the points of view of action or philosophy. Their differences are due to the time of their coming to Tibet, the different lineages of Lamas who have introduced them, the different emphasis on the various aspects of practice and the terminologies by which their teachings are transmitted. All four lead to Buddhahood. Therefore, it is absolutely wrong to say one is better than another, or to disparage any of them.

Q. *What is the exact meaning of Nirvana? There is considerable confusion about this in the West, the general idea being that it means annihilation.*

A. Literally, liberation or salvation (Tibetan: Tharpa) means freedom from bondage. Beings are ensnared and bound by karma and delusion. When the unsatisfactoriness or *dukkha* resulting from the bondage of (volitional actions) karma and delusion, or the state of unsatisfactoriness experienced owing to related influences of karma and delusion, is eradicated and tranquillized, one dwells in the state known as liberation. It is true that the various schools of Buddhist thought differ in expounding the true nature and import of the term 'liberation'. However, broadly speaking, it can be interpreted as the destruction of or freedom from unsatisfactoriness and its causes, given rise to by one's karma and delusion, and their resulting dominant influences. Destruction of or freedom from unsatisfactoriness and its causes is achieved and effected by the strength of one's inner efforts, i.e., exercise of counteracting forces; or by virtue of the attainment of the supreme wisdom that comprehends shunyata (emptiness).

The theory of shunyata or emptiness is common ground for all the four main schools of Buddhist thought. However, the most perfect and excellent description of the meaning of shunyata, profound and vast as it, can be found only in the Madhyamika school of Buddhist thought, which is regarded as the principal school among the four. The term shunyata or voidness does not mean that there is nothing, that nothing exists, like describing that a flower called sky-flower does not exist at all. Shunyata is attributeless, but implies that whatever is born of a cause exists; yet exists only in relation to or dependent upon something other than itself. Its origination is not origination in fact: that is Shunya. Things are simply mental designations and nothing else. They are non-self-existing. All objects are shunya by nature. They are void. They are empty of permanent substance or self because they are non-self-existing, being dependent upon causes other than themselves. But this does not mean that objects do not exist at all.

The "I" (self) is a denomination named in relation to the aggregates (groups of physical and mental properties dependent on grasping). It is generally believed that the "I" (self) and aggregates each have their own separate existences. However, Buddhists recognize and identify the nature of the self ("I") and the aggregates as being related. The "I" depends upon the aggregates for existence. For instance, a chariot is the name given to its different parts collectively. Similarly, it is possible for us to speak of the self or "I" only in relation to the aggregates. To quote the words of the Master: "A chariot is named as such in relation to the cohesive whole of its different parts. Likewise, a relative living being is just a name designated in relation to the collectiveness (cohesive whole) of the aggregates." All the four main schools of Buddhist thought freely subscribe to this point of view, in spite of the fact that the approach adopted by each school in explaining the nature of the conditioned "I" is quite different. Of the four schools, Madhyamika is reckoned to be the most important. Madyamika is again divided into two sub-schools: Prasangika and Sautantika. According to the Prasangika sub-school, the self or "I" is a mere name as construed by comprehension. Just as the self is a mere name as construed by comprehension, all objects are mere names as construed by comprehension. All objects are non-self-existent, i.e., they do not have an existence of their own.

Q. *What special relevance does Tibetan Buddhism have to the problems of the modern age?*

A. The Buddha's teachings comprise methods for securing a continuous process of mind-development by translating the teachings into actual practice in accordance with the needs and realities of life. For this, a proper understanding of the realities or facts of life, i.e., the nature of phenomena and objects as they really are, is necessary. Again, there are two aspects: first, knowledge of things and events which are beyond a man's comprehension (man's limited mind): second, knowledge of objects and phenomena which are within the grasp of the mind's comprehension. But, first of all, we must ask and find answers to the most relevant question as to what exactly is mind, what is its nature, how it works, and so on. Once this is known, the mind acquires the power to cognize the nature and working of phenomena and of objects as they really are. The mind becomes broad and free, increases in the bounds of patience and forgiveness, with a parallel progress in the deepening and broadening of the thinking faculties. Realization of mental prowess such as I have outlined here will be of the greatest service and benefit to humanity in the present century.

Q. *Tibetans consider the Tantrayana to be the most powerful teaching of Buddha. Why is tantric practice so effective?*

A. Casually speaking, we people of this world already have a similitude capable of being developed into the three bodies of a Buddha. Our five senses or present physical form is the basis of the physically appearing Emanation Body of a Buddha. The subtle dream body which is also the intermediate state Body between life and death, is like the Enjoyment body. In turn, the root to both of these is the Clear Light itself, which is capable of being developed into the actual Enlightenment of the Buddha, his Truth Body. The uncommon feature

of Tantra is to transform these three ordinary bodies into the bodies
of a Buddha.

Now I will explain how this is actually done. The human body
as a configuration of energy is made up of 72,000 channels, TK
currents of energy which travel through them and TK essential drops
or units of consciousness and energy conjoined which reside in the
channels. By manipulating the essential drops within the channels by
way of the currents we undergo different levels or states of consciousness. The type of consciousness we now have based on our present
configuration is one type, dream another, deep sleep another.
Fainting, heavy fainting or coma or when the breath stops are all
others. The final level of consciousness, Clear Light, is made manifest
at the time of death. This is the strongest and subtlest. Unused, it serves
as the basis for revolving the round of birth, old age, sickness and
death. Once one understands the nature of cyclic existence thoroughly one can be free of it. The best of all preparations for this is an
understanding now of the different types of consciousness through
making use of the channels, drops and inner airs or energies.

Tantra is extremely dangerous. Without proper guidance it
cannot be accomplished. Thus practised it will often lead to insanity
or death.

Q. *In Conclusion, does your Holiness have any general advice for
practitioners in the West?*

A. It is important to think very well before entering a particular spiritual
tradition. Once you have entered one you should stick to it. Do not be
like the man who tastes food in all the different restaurants but never
actually gets down to eating a meal. Think carefully before adopting
a practice; then follow it through. This way you will get some results
from dedicating even a little time each day. Alternatively, if you try
to follow all the various paths you will not get anywhere.

Also, patience in practice is required. In this age of machines
everything seems to be automatic. You may think that it is the same
with Dharma—that by merely turning on a switch you will gain
realization. Be patient. The development of mind takes time.

You should try to maintain a steady effort in practice. It is useless
to try very hard for a few months, then give up this kind of application
and then try very hard again. It is best to exert yourself in a constant

and steady way. This is extremely important.

If you have adopted Buddhism you should not consider yourself a 'great Buddhist' and immediately start to do everything differently. A Tibetan proverb states, 'Change your mind but leave your appearance as usual.'

In all of Buddhism and especially in the Mahayana, the benefiting of others is heavily stressed. In this context Shantideva says in "Venturing into the Deeds of a Bodhisattva, first investigate what is acceptable and what is unacceptable to the people (of the society in which you live); then avoid what is unacceptable." Of course, you must first consider whether or not what is acceptable and unacceptable is in contradiction with the Dharma. If the social norm does not contradict Dharma you should try to live in accordance with it. In this way people will respect you. This is not done out of vanity but in order to bring the maximum benefit to all.

In Dharma practice it is necessary always to keep an attitude of love towards others, for this is the basis of bodhichitta. Love is a simple practice yet it is very beneficial for the individual who practices it as well as for the community in which he lives, for the nation and for the whole world. Love and kindness are always appropriate. Whether or not you believe in rebirth, you will need love in this life. If we have love, there is hope to have real families, real brotherhood, real equanimity, real peace. If the mind of love is lost, if you continue to see other beings as enemies, then no matter how much knowledge or education you have, no matter how much material progress is made, only suffering and confusion will ensue. Beings will continue to deceive and overpower one another. Basically, everyone exists in the very nature of suffering, so to abuse or mistreat each other is futile. The foundation of all spiritual practice is love. That you practice this well is my only request. Of course, to be able to do so in all situations will take time, but you should not lose courage. If we wish happiness for mankind, love is the only way.

VIII
Meditation

Chapter VIII
MEDITATION

It is possible that unaided the reader may some times find it difficult to fully understand the import of the profound philosophy enunciated in Tibetan Buddhism. It may require careful concentration in understanding the theory and practice propounded in it. At times the inadequacy of the language as the vehicle to convey the exact meaning may present problems, for the philosophical terms in different languages do not always connote the same concepts. It is therefore necessary to comprehend and delve deep into their philosophical content. This will have to be followed by careful contemplation of what has been understood. Realisation will come only after constant meditation (*sadhana*) to be followed ultimately by enlightenment after prolonged practice. The condition precedent to the whole process is that it should be infused by an undercurrent of altruistic motive which is also its driving force, without which there can be no enlightenment. Both the primary as well as the ultimate objective of Tibetan Buddhism is to be good and to do good to others—to all sentient beings and humanity as a whole. In the absence of this altruistic motive it may be harmful even if one has some how attained enlightenment, for it is not to be practised for one's own selfish motive or benefit.

It has therefore been suggested that one should be extremely careful in selecting one's guide or *guru*. The qualifications and scholarship of one's guide must be examined with utmost care. Sometimes the selection may take as much as twelve years but the trouble is worth taking if one is keen to understand and practise Tibetan Buddhism. This can be achieved only after going through the different stages of consistent and intensive meditation.

—Editor

MEDITATION[1]

I am very happy to have come to your centre. I know something about the activities here and admire your views and aims of close understanding of many systems. My thought is to explain something briefly and roughly at first, and then we can have an informal discussion.

If you ask, "Do humans have rights?", yes, there are human rights. How is it that humans have rights? It is on the basis of the valid innate appearance of an I to our consciousness that we naturally want happiness and do not want suffering, and that wanting of happiness and not wanting of suffering itself, with this appearance as its basis, is the very reason for there being human rights.

There are many levels of the happiness which is to be accomplished and the suffering which is to be relieved. Millions and millions of people in this world are seeking a path to gain happiness and remove suffering, considering their own to be the best method. All the big schemes for worldly development—the five year plans and ten year plans—arise in dependence on the wish for happiness. We who are gathered here today are seeking a means different from the usual to achieve happiness and remove suffering. We are mainly concerned with techniques based not on money but on the internal transformation of thought.

Many wise persons in the past set forth techniques for changing, training, and transforming the mind, and it is most important for us to have respect for all of these systems as being altruistically oriented and having a common aim. Respecting these various systems, one studies them to discover their unique techniques and to discover which are the most helpful and appropriate for oneself in order to practice them. We must implement them; these teachings are of little value unless they are put into practice in our daily lives.

[1]This talk was delivered at Wisdom's Goldenrod, Ithaca, New York.

The tenets of philosophical systems are to be practised on the basis of a disciplined mental continuum; therefore, meditation is most important both in general and especially in the beginning. Perhaps today as I explain this topic, we could engage in an experiment. Would you like to participate? First, look to your posture: arrange the legs in the most comfortable position; set the backbone as straight as an arrow. Place your hands in the position of meditative equipoise four finger widths below the navel, with the left hand on the bottom, right hand on top, and your thumbs touching to form a triangle. This placement of the hands has connection with the place inside the body where inner heat is generated.

Bending the neck down slightly, allow the mouth and teeth to be as usual, with the top of the tongue touching the roof of the mouth near the top teeth. Let the eyes gaze downwards loosely—it is not necessary that they be directed to the end of the nose; they can be pointed toward the floor in front of you if this seems more natural. Do not open the eyes too wide nor forcefully close them; leave them open a little. Sometimes they will close of their own accord; that is all right. Even if your eyes are open, when your mental consciousness becomes steady upon its object, these appearances to the eye consciousness will not disturb you.

For those of you who wear eye glasses, have you noticed that when you take off your glasses, because of the unclarity there is less danger from the generation of excitement and more danger of laxity? Do you find that there is a difference between facing and not facing the wall? When you face the wall, you may find that there is less danger of excitement or scattering. These kinds of things can be determined through your own experience.

Within meditations that have an object of observation, there can be two types of objects: external or internal. Now, instead of meditating on the mind itself, let us meditate on an external object of observation. For instance, the body of a Buddha for those who like to look at a Buddha or a cross for those who like that, or whatever symbol is suitable for you. Mentally visualize that the object is about four feet in front of you, at the same height as the eyebrows. The object should be approximately two inches high and emanating light. Try to conceive of it as being heavy, for this will prevent excitement. Its brilliance will prevent laxity. As you concentrate, you must strive for two factors: first, to make the object of observation clear and, second, to make it steady.

Has something appeared to your mind? Are the sense objects in front of your eyes bothering you? If that is the case, it is all right to close them, but with the eyes closed, do you see a reddish appearance? If you see red with the eyes closed or if you are bothered by what you see when your eyes are open, you are too involved with the eye consciousness and thus should try to withdraw attention from the eye consciousness and put it with the mental consciousness.

That which interferes with the steadiness of the object of observation and causes it to fluctuate is excitement or, in a more general way, scattering. To stop that, withdraw your mind more strongly inside so that the intensity of the mode of apprehension begins to lower. To withdraw the mind, it helps to think about something that makes you more sober, a little bit sad. These thoughts can cause your heightened mode of apprehension of the object, the mind's being too tight, to lower or loosen somewhat whereby you are better able to stay on the object of observation.

It is not sufficient just to have stability. It is necessary also to have clarity. That which prevents clarity is laxity, and what causes laxity is an over-withdrawal, excessive declination, of the mind. First of all, the mind becomes lax; this can lead to lethargy in which, losing the object of observation, you have as if fallen into darkness. This can lead even to sleep. When this occurs, it is necessary to raise or heighten the mode of apprehension. As a technique for that, think on something that you like, something that makes you joyous, or go to a high place or where there is a vast view. This technique causes the deflated mind to heighten in its mode of apprehension.

It is necessary within your own experience to recognize when the mode of apprehension has become too excited or too lax and determine the best practice for lowering or heightening it.

The object of observation that you are visualizing has to be held with mindfulness. Then, along with this, you inspect, as if from a corner, to see whether the object is clear and stable; the faculty that engages in this inspection is called introspection. When powerful steady mindfulness is achieved, introspection is generated, but the uncommon function of introspection is to inspect from time to time to see whether the mind has come under the influence of excitement or laxity. When you develop mindfulness and introspection well, you are able to catch laxity and excitement just before they arise and prevent their arising.

Briefly, that is how to sustain meditation with an external object of observation. Another type of meditation involves looking at the mind itself. Try to leave your mind vividly in a natural state, without thinking of what happened in the past or of what you are planning for the future, without generating any conceptuality. Where does it seem that your consciousness is? Is it with the eyes or where is it? Most likely you have a sense that it is associated with the eyes since we derive most of our awareness of the world through vision. This is due to having relied too much on our sense consciousness. However, the existence of a separate mental consciousness can be ascertained; for example, when attention is diverted by sound, that which appears to the eye consciousness is not noticed. This indicates that a separate mental consciousness is paying more attention to sound heard by the ear consciousness than to the perceptions of the eye consciousness.

With persistent practice, consciousness may eventually be perceived or felt as an entity of mere luminosity and knowing, to which anything is capable of appearing and which, when appropriate conditions arise, can be generated in the image of whatsoever object. As long as the mind does not encounter the external circumstance of conceptuality, it will abide empty without anything appearing in it, like clear water. Its very entity is that of mere experience. In realizing this nature of the mind, we have for the first time located the object of observation of this internal type of meditation. The best time for practising this form of meditation is in the morning, in a quiet place, when the mind is very clear and alert.

There is yet another method of meditation which enables one to discern the ultimate nature of phenomena. Generally, phenomena are divided into two types: the mental and physical aggregates—or phenomena that are used by the I—and the I that uses them. To determine the nature of this I, let us use an example. When we say John is coming, there is some person who is the one designated by the name John. Is this name designated to his body? It is not. Is it designated to his mind? If it were designated to his mind, we could not speak of John's mind. Mind and body are things used by the person. It almost seems that there is an I separate from mind and body. For instance, when we think, "Oh, my lousy body!" or "My lousy mind!", to our own innate mode of appearance the mind itself is not the I, right? Now, what John is there who is not his mind or body? You also should apply this to yourself, to your own sense of I—where is this I in terms of mind and body?

When my body is sick, though my body is not I, due to the body's being sick it can be posited that I am sick. In fact, for the sake of the well-being and pleasure of the I, it sometimes even becomes necessary to cut off part of the body. Although the body is not the I, there is a relationship between the two; the pain of the body can serve as the pain of the I. Similarly, when the eye consciousness sees something, it appears to the mind that the I perceives it.

What is the nature of the I? How does it appear to you? When you do not fabricate or create any artificial concept in your mind, does it seem that your I has an identity separate from your mind and body? But if you search for it, can you find it? For instance, someone accuses you, "You stole this", or "You ruined such and such", and you feel, "I didn't do that!". At that time, how does the I appear? Does it appear as if solid? Does some solid, steady, and strong thing appear to your mind when you think or say, "I didn't do that!"

This seemingly solid, concrete, independent, self-instituting I under its own power that appears at such a time actually does not exist at all, and this specific non-existence is what is meant by selflessness. In the absence of analysis and investigation, a mere I as in, "I want such and such", or "I am going to do such and such", is asserted as valid, but the non-existence of an independent or self-powered I constitutes the selfless-ness of the person. This selflessness is what is found when one searches analytically to try to find the I.

Such non-inherent existence of the I is an ultimate truth, a final truth The I that appears to a non-analytical conventional awareness is the dependently arisen I that serves as the basis of the conventions of action, agent, and so forth; it is a conventional truth. In analysing the mode o subsistence or the status of the I, it is clear that although it appears to exis inherently, it does not, much like an illusion.

That is how the ultimate nature of the I—emptiness—is analysed. Jus as the I has this nature, so all other phenomena that are used by the I are empty of inherent existence. When analysed, they cannot be found at all but without analysis and investigation, they do exist. Their nature is the same as the I.

The conventional existence of the I as well as of pleasure and pair make it necessary to generate compassion and altruism, and because the ultimate nature of all phenomena is this emptiness of inherent existence it is also necessary to cultivate wisdom. When these two aspects—compassion and wisdom—are practised in union, wisdom grows more profound, and the sense of duality diminishes. Due to the mind's dwelling in the meaning of emptiness, dualistic appearance becomes lighter, and at the same time the mind itself becomes more subtle. As the mind grows even more subtle, reaching the subtlest level, it is eventually transformed into the most basic mind, the fundamental innate mind of clear light, which at once realizes and is of one taste with emptiness in meditative equipoise without any dualistic appearance at all, mixed with emptiness. Within all having this one taste, anything and everything can appear; this is known as "All in one taste, one taste in all".

Now perhaps we could have a discussion. Do you have any questions?

Q. *Why is it better to meditate in the morning?*

A. There are two main reasons. Physically, in the early morning—once you are used to it—all nerve centres are fresh, and this is beneficial. Also, there is a difference just in terms of the mind. Further, if you have slept well, you are more fresh and alert in the morning; this we can see in our own experience. At night I reach a point where I cannot think properly; however, after sleeping and then waking in the early morning, that thing, which yesterday I could not properly think through, automatically appears more clearly. This shows that mental power is much sharper in the morning.

Q. *Can you say something about meditation upon mantra as sound?*

A. With regard to mantras that one can observe in meditation, there are external sounds of oral repetition and internal sounds of mental repetition. There are also natural self-arisen sounds, such as the appearance of the inhalation and exhalation of breath as the tones of mantra.

One can set the form of the letters standing on the edge of a flat moon-disc or within light at the heart. If it is comfortable for you to do so, imagine that you are in the middle of this, like in the house of your body. If you have a sense of the main part of consciousness being around the eyes, it is possible to imagine light behind the eyes and then, strongly identifying yourself as being there in the middle of that light, move the light and consciousness down to the centre of the mantra circle which is at the heart. If you do this many times, you will gradually have the sense that you are right here in the heart. Then, with you in the centre of the mantra, it can be as if you are reading the letters of the mantra around you, not orally but mentally—reciting mantra but not with the mouth. There are many different techniques.

Q. *What is the most expedient means for overcoming resistance to meditation?*

A. Five faults are explained as obstacles to meditation. The first is laziness; second is to forget the advice on the object, that is, to forget the object; next are laxity and excitement; then failure to apply an antidote when laxity or excitement are present, and the last is to continue applying the antidotes when laxity or excitement have already been overcome. These are called the five faults. Eight antidotes are explained for them. The antidotes to laziness are, first of all, the *faith* that intelligently sees the value of meditative stabilisation, the prime value being that without it the higher paths cannot be generated. In dependence upon ascertaining the good qualities of meditative stabilisation, the *aspiration* which seeks to attain those qualities is induced. By means of that, *exertion* comes whereby you eventually attain *pliancy* causing body and mind to be free from unfavourable states and to be serviceable in a virtuous direction such that whatever virtue is done is powerful. These four are the antidotes to the first fault, laziness.

It is helpful not to practice too long in the beginning; do not over-extend yourself; the maximum period is around fifteen minutes. The important thing is not the length of the session but the quality of it. If you meditate too long, you can become sleepy, and then your meditation will become a matter of becoming accustomed to that state. This is not only a waste of time but also a habit that is difficult to eliminate in the future. In the beginning, start with many short sessions—even eight or sixteen sessions in a day—and then as you get used to the processes of meditation, the quality will improve, and the session will naturally become longer.

A sign that your meditative stabilisation is progressing well is that even though your meditative session may be long, it will feel as though only a short time has passed. If it seems that you have spent a long time in meditation even though you have spent only a little, this is a sign that you should shorten the length of the session. This can be very important at the beginning.

Q. *Within the Buddhist system, they speak of different levels of cognition* for which there are appropriate objects. On each level, who is the knower of these different modes of cognition?

A. There are many levels of consciousness, having different modes of perceiving objects, but they are all the same in being of a continuum of luminosity and knowing and in the fact that the mere I which is designated in dependence upon the continuum of consciousness is what knows them. Does that answer your question?

Among the various Buddhist systems, some posit *types of consciousness is the I itself. However, in the highest, most profound system, the Middle Way Consequence School (*Prasangika-Madhyamika*), that which is posited as the I is the mere I which is designated in dependence upon the continuum of consciousness.

Q. *What is the distinction between consciousness and the I?*

A. There are many different ways in which the I appears. One is for the I to appear to be factually different from the aggregates of mind and body and to be permanent, unitary, and under its own power. Another is for the I, within not appearing to be factually other than the aggregates, to appear to be the bearer of the burden of the aggregates or the master of them—a substantially existent or self-sufficient I. Then, another way is for the I to appear to be not posited through appearing to an awareness but to be established from the side of its own uncommon mode of subsistence. Then, another is for the I to appear to be inherently existent or existent in its own right, not seeming to exist through the force of nominality. Then, there is another in which, even though the I *appears* to exist in its own right, a mere I is all that is conceived. The conception of this last one is the only valid cognition among these.

What is the I? When it is sought analytically, it cannot be found. Nothing from among the mental and physical aggregates, nor the continuum of them, nor their collection can be posited as something that is the I. When a speckled coil of rope in the dark appears to you to be a snake due to the darkness of its location, the parts of the rope individually, the parts of the rope together, the continuum of those parts over time, none of these can be posited as a snake. The snake exists only through the force of the mind of the fearful person; from the side of the rope there is nothing that is established as a snake.

As in that example, nothing among the mental and physical

aggregates which are the basis of designation of the I, either separately or together or as their continuum over time, can be posited as something that is the I. Also, it is completely impossible to find the I as a factuality separate from the mind and body which are the basis of designation of I. Now, if you began to think that therefore the I does not exist at all, this would be damaged by conventional valid cognition. The fact that the I exists is obvious.

The existence of the I is certified by experience, by valid cognition, but it is unfindable among its bases of designation. Thus, the I only designatedly exists through the force of nominality or conceptuality, through a subjective force. On what does it nominally depend? Its mere nominal existence is posited in dependence upon its basis of designation.

With regard to the mental and physical aggregates which are its basis of designation and among which there are many grosser and subtler levels, the subtlest is the beginningless consciousness that goes throughout all lifetimes. Therefore, it is said that the I is designated through the power of nominality in dependence upon the beginningless and endless continuum of consciousness which is the main basis of designation. The I merely exists nominally, designated in dependence upon this continuum of consciousness. The conclusion is that except for a self that exists through the power of nominality, there is no self, no self that is established from its own side. This lack of establishment in the object's own right is the meaning of selflessness.

You might ask, "If the I and so forth exist through the power of conceptuality, through whose conceptuality are these designated— mine, yours, one in the past, present, or whatever?" This again is a case of analysing to try to find the object designated, and you will not find such. Therefore, existence through the force of conceptuality itself exists only through the force of conceptuality. Buddha said that all phenomena are only nominal and that mere nominality itself is only nominal. Emptiness itself is empty. Even Buddha is empty of inherent existence. Through emptiness the extreme of the reification of existence is avoided, but through the fact that things are not utterly nonexistent and instead are dependent-arising the extreme of utter nonexistence is avoided.

Q. *From where does consciousness arise?*

In meditation (*Courtsey* : S. N. Sinha)

In prayer (*Courtsey* : S. N. Sinha)

(*Courtsey* : Ms. Francoise Guerin)

On the way to Rajghat (*Courtsey* : S. N. Sinha)

Paying homage at Rajghat (*Courtsey* : Ms. Francoise Guerin)

In prayer (*Courtsey* : S. N. Sinha)

A. We say that consciousness is produced from consciousness. Consciousness must be produced from consciousness because it cannot be produced with matter as its substantial cause. Particles cannot create an entity of luminosity and knowing. Matter cannot be the substantial cause of consciousness, and consciousness cannot be the substantial cause of matter. Although in the Mind Only School matter is asserted as of the same entity as consciousness—almost as if there is nothing except consciousness, this is not asserted in the Middle Way Consequence School because such is damaged by reasoning. In this school, consciousness and matter are posited separately.

There is no way to posit consciousness except as being a continuation of former moments of consciousness; in this way consciousness can have no beginning, in which case rebirth can have no beginning. The mind in general has no beginning; the continuation of it has no beginning or end, but there are specific minds that have a beginning but no end and others that have no beginning but an end.

Q. *My question is in regard to the two truths. Conventional truths presuppose the inherent existence of subject and object, and ultimate truth means the non-inherent existence of subject and object. This seems clear, but when it is asserted that a conventional truth is not different from ultimate truth, I find this very difficult to understand.*

A. The Consequence School does not accept that subject and object inherently exist even conventionally. Due to misinterpretation of the view of the Consequence School, the lower systems say that therefore the Consequentialists have fallen into the extreme of nihilism; this indicates that even in their sight the Consequence School does not assert inherent existence even conventionally.

We do not say that the two truths are one, but that they are of one entity. They are, in fact, mutually exclusive. For instance, the back and front of the hand are of one hand, but the front and back of one hand are mutually exclusive. Similarly, when the conventionally existent I is asserted as the basis or substratum and its emptiness of inherent existence is posited as its mode of subsistence, this emptiness of inherent existence is the nature, basic disposition, or an attribute of the I, and the I is its substratum or basis. There is one entity of the mere I and its emptiness, but the I is found by conventional valid cognition, whereas its emptiness is found by ultimate valid cognition, and thus the I and its emptiness are mutually exclusive—the one is not the other. Therefore, the two truths are one entity within being, technically speaking, different isolates.

The main reason why the I or any other phenomenon is empty is because it is a dependent-arising. Dependent and independent are a dichotomy; when one is eliminated, the other is established. For instance, consider human and non-human: when something is established as one of these, it is eliminated that it is the other, and vice versa. When it is determined with respect to a specific phenomenon whether it is dependent or independent, in deciding that it is dependent, there is also an emptiness of independence with it, and that is what we call "emptiness of inherent existence". Also, when something is proved to be empty by the fact that it is a dependent arising, then it is within being existent that it is dependent. The non-existent cannot be dependent.

When you have become familiar with the reasoning of dependent-arising, the mere fact that something exists is sufficient reason for its being empty of inherent existence. However, since in most systems the fact that something exists is taken to indicate that it exists from its own side and is not empty of inherent existence, we use the reasoning of dependent-arising, reflecting on its implications.

Q. *Could you please say something about the Five Buddhas?*

A. These are the Buddhas of the five lineages. They are explained in terms of the five constituents, five aggregates, the five afflictive emotions, and the five wisdoms of the ordinary state. Let us consider the five constituents that are included within a person's continuum: earth, water, fire, wind, and space. These five constituents are the bases of purification to be purified into the five Buddha lineages. With respect to the form aggregate, when we die, this coarse body does not continue with us, but there is a subtler form aggregate that continues in the intermediate state through to the next life. Thus, if we consider the form aggregate without making a distinction between coarse and subtle, we can speak of a beginningless and endless continuum of the form aggregate. The purified aspect of this form aggregate is called Vairochana.

Consciousness is divided into minds and mental factors. There are six minds and fifty-one mental factors. One group of mental factors is comprised of the five omnipresent factors, among which one is feeling. This is the feeling aggregate. The purified form of the feeling aggregate is Ratnasambhava.

The purified aspect of the aggregate of discriminations is Amitabha; the aggregate of compositional factors, in its purified form, is Amoghasiddhi. Finally, the purified aspect of the aggregate of main consciousness is Akshobhya.

Whereas the five aggregates can be divided into gross and subtle forms, the five Buddha lineages apply to the subtler aggregates which have existed beginninglessly.

Q. *Are the subtler aggregates equivalent to the Buddhas of the five lineages?*

A. The five subtler aggregates will eventually be transformed into the Buddhas of the five lineages. They are now as if accompanied by mental defilements. When the defilements are removed, these factors do not become any coarser or subtler; their nature remains, but due to having become separated from the faults of mental pollution, they have become the Buddhas of the five lineages. So if you ask whether the Buddhas of the five lineages are present now in our continuums, these factors are currently bound by faults and since there cannot be a Buddha who has a fault, they are not Buddhas. One is not yet fully enlightened, but that which is going to become a Buddha is present; therefore, these factors presently existent in our continuums are Buddha seeds and are called the Buddha nature or the essence of the One Gone Thus (*Tathagatagarbha*).

More specifically, if you consider just the subtlest mind and the wind or energy that serves as its mount, the mere factor of luminosity and knowing of the subtlest mind itself as well as the energy associated with it are what will be transformed into the mind and body of a Buddha. This is the mind that will turn into an omniscient consciousness—a Buddha's mind; it is this mind which will be transformed, not some other mind coming from the outside. In other words, the Buddha nature is inherent; it is not imported from somewhere else.

This is true because the very entity of the mind, its nature of mere luminosity and knowing, is not polluted by defilements; they do not abide in the entity of the mind. Even when we generate afflictive emotions, the very entity or nature of the mind is *still* mere luminosity and knowing, and because of this we are able to remove the afflictive emotions.

It is suitable to think that the Buddhas of the five lineages *of the ordinary state* exist in us now, just as we speak of the three Buddha bodies of the ordinary state as being within us now. But it is not appropriate to speak of Buddhas, stainless and enlightened, rid of all faults and possessing all good qualities, as being in us now. If you agitate the water in a pond, it becomes cloudy with mud; yet the very nature of the water itself is not dirty. When you allow it to become still again, the mud will settle, leaving the water pure.

How are the defilements removed? They are not removed by outside action nor by leaving them as they are; they are removed by the power of antidotes, meditative antidotes. To understand this, take the example of anger. All anger is impelled and polluted by improper conceptuality. When we are angry at someone, what is that person like? How does he or she appear to your mind? How are you apprehending the person? That person appears to be self-instituted under his or her own power, and we apprehend the person as something really solid and forceful. And at the same time our own feelings appear equally substantial.

Both the object of our anger and subject, oneself, appear to exist concretely, as if established by way of their own character. Both seem forcefully to exist in their own right. But as I was saying earlier, things do not actually exist in this concrete way. As much as we are able to see an absence of inherent existence, that much will our conception of inherent existence and its assistance to anger be lessened.

The sign that our perceptions are superimposing a goodness or badness beyond what is actually present is that while desirous or angry we feel that the object is terrifically good or bad but afterwards when we think about the experience, it is laughable that we viewed the object that way; we understand that our perception was not true. These afflicted consciousness do not have any valid support. The mind which analytically searches for the inherent existence of an object finds ascertainment of its non-inherent existence through valid reasoning, and thus this kind of consciousness does have a valid foundation. Like a debate in court, one perception is based on reason and truth, while the other one is not. When the evidence is sufficient, in such a debate the true view eventually overpowers the other because it can withstand analysis.

It is impossible for the mind simultaneously to apprehend one object in contradictory ways. With respect to one object, therefore, as you get used to understanding its non-inherent existence, not only is it impossible at that time to generate a conception of inherent existence but also as strong as the correct realization becomes, so much, in general, does conception of its opposite weaken in force.

To generate such wisdom we engage in meditation because our minds, as they are now, are not very powerful. Our mind is presently scattered; its energies need to be channelled like the way water in a hydroelectric plant is channelled to create great force. We achieve this with the mind through meditation, channelling it such that it becomes very forceful, at which point it can be utilized in the direction of wisdom. Since all the substances for enlightenment exist within ourselves, we should not look for Buddhahood somewhere else.

With respect to purifying the afflictive emotions, it is in terms of this basic entity of an angry consciousness—mere luminosity and knowing—that it is purified into *Akshobhya*. As I said earlier, even when we generate an afflictive emotion, it does not pollute the nature of the mind, and it itself is pervaded by the factor of luminosity and knowing. Hatred is itself a consciousness, because of which it has a nature of mere luminosity and knowing, even though it conceives its object in an incorrect manner.

Thus, the substances that can turn into Buddhahood are with us now, but not actual Buddhahood. If you felt that Buddhahood must be here now just because its causes are, you would incur the fault that Dharmakirti demonstrated to such an asserting—that on the top of a single blade of grass where a small worm is staying there are the hundred elephants as which that worm will take rebirth in the future due to karma that is already in its continuum. There is the difference, however, that the seeds for being reborn as an elephant are newly accumulated through one's actions whereas the seeds of the Buddhas of the five lineages subsist within us naturally.

Q. *Do you associate the sun, or a solar deity, with any of the Buddhas of the five lineages?*

A. Though your question is brief, it requires a detailed answer. The sun and moon deities in Buddhism are, so to speak, ordinary deities. To understand the levels, it is necessary to make a division of the three realms: the Desire, Form, and Formless Realms. In each of these realms there are different societies of gods. There are four main groups in the Formless Realm and seventeen in the Form Realm. Within the Desire Realm, there are two types: societies of gods and societies of beings who are not gods, such as humans. Of the gods in the Desire Realm, there are six types: the gods of the Four Great Royal Lineages, the Heaven of the Thirty-Three, Those Free Combat, the Joyous, Those Enjoying Emanations, and Those Having Control Over Others' Emanations. The deities of the sun and moon probably are included within the gods in the Heaven of the Thirty-Three. All of these are still bound within cyclic existence.

Q. *Could you please say something about the nature of mandalas?*

A. Mandala, in general, means that which extracts the essence. There are many usages of the term mandala according to context. One type of mandala is the offering of the entire world system with the major and minor continents mentally made to high beings. Also, there are painted mandalas, mandalas of concentration, those made out of coloured sand, mandalas of the conventional mind of enlightenment, mandalas of the ultimate mind of enlightenment, and so forth. Because one can extract a meaning from each of these through practising them, they are all called mandalas.

Although we might call these pictures and constructed depictions mandalas, the main meaning is for oneself to enter into the mandala and extract an essence in the sense of receiving blessing. It is a place of gaining magnificence. Because one is gaining a blessing and thereupon developing realizations, it is called an extraction or assumption of something essential.

Q. *How does one choose a teacher or know a teacher to be reliable?*

A. This should be done in accordance with your interest and disposition, but you should analyse well. You must investigate before accepting a lama or guru to see whether that person is really qualified or not. It is said in a scripture of the Discipline (*Vinaya*) that just as fish that are hidden under the water can be seen through the movement of the ripples from above, so also a teacher's inner qualities can, over time, be seen a little through that person's behaviour.

We need to look into the person's scholarship—the ability to explain topics—and whether the person implements those teachings in his conduct and experience. A tantra says that you must investigate very carefully even if it takes twelve years. This is the way to choose a teacher.

I very much like the fact that you think seriously about these matters and put forward serious questions. We can now have silence and meditation.

We need to look into the person's scholarship—the ability to explain topics—and whether the person implements those teachings in his conduct and experience. A tantra says that you must invest quite very carefully, even if it takes five years. This is the way to choose a teacher.

I very much like the fact that you think seriously about these matters and put forward serious questions. We can now have silence and meditation.

IX
The Path To Enlightenment

Chapter IX
THE PATH TO ENLIGHTENMENT

Since Bodhisattvas are seeking to help all sentient beings, they take as their main object of abandonment the obstructions to omniscience and work at the antidote to these obstructions. For, without knowing all, it is possible to help a small number of beings but impossible fully and effectively to help a vast number. This is why it is necessary to achieve Buddhahood in order to be of effective service to sentient beings.

Unable to bear the suffering of sentient beings without doing something about it, you generate strong compassion and love, wishing beings to be rid of suffering and to possess happiness. Then, seeing that to accomplish this purpose there is no way but to achieve Buddhahood, you generate the altruistic intention to achieve enlightenment. This intention to yourself attain the omniscience of a Buddha in order to be of service to others is called the altruistic mind of enlightenment (*bodhichitta*). It involves two aspirations—seeking the welfare of others through seeking your own enlightenment.

It is important to realize that our personalities are not suddenly and completely transformed as we try to develop such thoughts. Our natures, our characteristic dispositions, change only gradually. Differences are not seen at once, but over time. If we cultivate the altruistic intention to become enlightened slowly and steadily and, after five or ten years have passed, consider the changes that have occurred in our way of thinking and actions, the results of our efforts—the improvement—will be clearly discernible.

—Dalai Lama

THE PATH TO ENLIGHTENMENT[1]

I am very happy to have the opportunity to give a lecture here in Toronto, Canada, to this assembly of Buddhists and persons interested in Buddhism. I would like to thank the Zen masters of this temple and the many Tibetans who have helped with the preparations. Today I will talk about the stages of the path to enlightenment, using Dzong-ka-ba's *Three Principal Aspects of the Path to Supreme Enlightenment* as a basis.

In order to be freed from cyclic existence, it is necessary to generate the intention to leave cyclic existence; this intention is the first of the three principal aspects of the path to enlightenment. It is also necessary to have the correct view of emptiness. In addition, if one wishes to achieve the highest liberation, the state of omniscience of the Great Vehicle, it is necessary to cultivate an altruistic intention to become enlightened, called the mind of enlightenment. These three the determination to be freed from cyclic existence, the correct view of emptiness, and the altruistic mind of enlightenment are the three principal aspects of the path.

Prior to giving a lecture, it is customary first to clear away obstacles. In Japan and Tibet, this is usually done by reciting the *Heart Sutra*, which is concerned with the teachings on the emptiness of inherent existence. Then, in order to tame harmful beings and remove obstacles, it is helpful to recite the mantra of a fierce manifestation in female form of the perfection of wisdom. Usually, when we recite mantra, we count the mantras on a rosary, moving the beads inward as a symbol of the entry of the blessings from the recitation; however, when the purpose of the recitation is to remove obstacles, the beads are turned in the opposite direction, outward, symbolizing the removal of those obstacles.

Next, we perform the offering of mandala. The meaning of this derives from the actions of the Buddha, who, in former lifetimes while

[1] This talk was delivered at the gathering of Buddhist community at Toronto.

training on the path, underwent a great many hardships without concern for his body, family, or resources, in order to hear and practice the teachings. As a symbol of this dedication and unselfishness, we make, prior to listening to Buddha's teachings, a mental offering of our body, resources, and roots of virtue. The entire world system which has been formed by our collective karma is offered, visualized in a glorified aspect, full of marvels and wonders.

Whether lecturing on the doctrine or listening to it, our attitude must be conjoined with a mind of refuge and a mind of altruism that is seeking to help others. To achieve this, a verse of refuge and mind generation is recited three times in conjunction with mental reflection and meditation:

> Until enlightenment I go for refuge to the Buddha,
> The doctrine, and the supreme of communities.
> Through the merit of listening to the doctrine
> May I achieve Buddhahood in order to help transmigrating beings.

In that good or bad effects arise in dependence upon good or bad motivation, cultivation of an altruistic motivation is very important. Thus, as the stanza is recited, its meaning should be cultivated in meditation.

Finally, at the beginning of a lecture on the doctrine there is a custom of repeating a stanza of praise to Buddha within being mindful of his kindness. This verse is taken from Nagarjuna's *Treatise on the Middle Way*, and the custom of reciting it was initiated by one of my teachers, Ku-nu Lama Den-dzin-gyel-tsen:

> I pay homage to Gautama
> Who, motivated by compassion,
> Taught the excellent doctrine
> In order to eliminate all [wrong] views.

Generally speaking, we have come together here because we share an interest in the Buddhist doctrine; we hope by our efforts to attain greater peace in our lives and to eliminate suffering as much as possible. Since we have bodies, we need food, clothing, shelter, and so forth, but these alone are not sufficient, for satisfying just these needs cannot fulfill the wishes of human beings. No matter how good our physical surroundings are, if there is no happiness in our minds, then unrest, depression, and so forth make it impossible for us to be at ease. We need to be able to seek out and achieve *mental* happiness, and knowing how to do this will enable us to overpower physical sufferings as well. Therefore, it is essential to combine effort for gaining external improvement with that focused on internal concerns.

Western civilization has made and continues to make great progress in material development, but if techniques can also be created for achieving internal happiness, modern society will become far more advanced. Without such internal growth, we become enslaved to external things, and even though called humans, we become like parts of a machine. Thus our discussion today will be concerned with how to achieve mental happiness and advancement.

Throughout history, many teachers have appeared, drawing on their own experience, to advise and guide others towards more fruitful ways of living. From among these many systems of advice, I will be speaking about that offered to humanity by the kind teacher, Shakyamuni Buddha. Within his teachings, levels of practice were delineated in accordance with the capacities of his followers. These fall into two major divisions, or vehicles: the Low Vehicle (*Hinayana, Theg dman*) and the Great Vehicle (*Mahayana, Theg chen*). Within the Great Vehicle, Buddha set forth a sutra system and a mantra system, distinguished by differing elements in the general corpus of the path for achieving the Buddha Bodies.

In addition, Buddha further defined four separate schools of tenets: Great Exposition School, Sutra School, Mind Only School and Middle Way School. These teachings of the two vehicles and of the four schools of tenets, as well as the sutra and tantra systems, are contained in approximately one hundred volumes of texts translated mainly from Sanskrit into Tibetan. Nearly two hundred volumes of commentary on these scriptures were written by Indian scholars and subsequently translated into Tibetan as well.

The scriptures are divided into four main groups: texts on discipline, which are mainly concerned with practices common to the Low Vehicle, a section on the Perfection of Wisdom, a collection of various sutras, and a section on tantra. According to the Vajrapanjara Tantra, an explanatory tantra, there are, within the tantra system, four sets of tantras: Action, Performance, Yoga, and Highest Yoga Tantra.[2]

---

[2] The *Vajrapanjara Tantra* says:
  Action Tantras are for the inferior. Yoga without actions is for those above them.
  The supreme Yoga is for supreme beings. The Highest Yoga is for those above them.

The systems of sutra, tantra, the Low Vehicle, and the Great Vehicle were spread throughout Tibet. Over time, based on various methods of transmission from particular teachers and distinctive usage of certain philosophical terms, there came to be slight differences in their interpretation and use. Many different schools evolved in Tibet, and these, in brief, can be condensed into four major schools which carry on the lineage of Buddha's teaching to the present time: Nying-ma, Sa-gya, Ga-gyu, and Ge-luk. Despite their superficial differences, these schools all come down to the same basic thought.

Today's text, the *Three Principal Aspects of the Path*, is a rendition of the many stages of the path into three principal paths, as set forth by Dzong-ka-ba (1357-1419). Although this text is concerned with the entire body of scripture, its main source is the Perfection of Wisdom Sutras.

In what way do these teachings derive from the Perfection of Wisdom Sutras? Contained within those sutras is the explicit teaching of emptiness and the hidden teaching of the stages of the path. From among the three principal aspects of the path, that aspect concerned with the correct view of reality stems from the explicit teachings of emptiness. Presentations of the correct view in the Great Vehicle are done in accordance with the Mind Only and Middle Way Schools. Dzong-ka-ba's text is based solely on the Middle Way system and, within the subdivisions of that school, is explicitly concerned with the Consequence School rather than the Autonomy School. It presents just the view of the Consequence School on emptiness. The remaining aspects of the path— the determination to become free from cyclic existence and the altruistic mind of enlightenment—derive from the hidden teachings in the Perfection of Wisdom Sutras on the paths and stages for achieving clear realization.

Two types of commentaries on the Perfection of Wisdom Sutras have developed: the system of interpretation transmitted from Manjushri through Nagarjuna that has to do with the explicit teachings on emptiness and one transmitted from Maitreya through Asanga on the hidden teachings on the stages of the path. Maitreya's *Ornament for Clear Realization* is the root text setting forth the hidden teachings of the stages on the path. It contains eight chapters: the first three set out the three exalted knowledges; the next four describe the practices of the four trainings; and the eighth chapter describes the Effect Truth Body. A comparison of Maitreya's text with the Perfection of Wisdom Sutras shows that those sutras are indeed the source for the teaching in the *Ornament for Clear Realization* of the hidden teachings on the stages of the path.

The motivation for listening to this teaching on the three principal aspects of the path should not be to gain personal benefit but rather to bring about health and happiness for all sentient beings throughout space since each and every one of them wants happiness and does not want suffering.

Now, to begin the text itself: At the beginning of composing a text it is customary for the author to pay homage to a high object, and this can be any of a number of objects of reverence. Here, Dzong-ka-ba pays homage to the "foremost holy lamas", for it is in dependence upon a qualified lama that the three principal aspects of the path are realized.

The high title "lama" alone does not qualify someone as a lama; the good qualities associated with the title must also be present. The three words—foremost (*rje*), holy (*btsun*), and lama (*bla ma*)—set forth the three qualities of a lama. "Foremost" describes a person who has diminished emphasis on this lifetime and is primarily concerned with future lifetimes and deeper topics. Such a person has a longer perspective than the short-sighted one of those who mainly look to the affairs of this life and thus, in relation to common beings whose emphasis is mainly on this life, is the foremost, or a leader. "Holy" refers to one who, as a result of developing renunciation for all forms of cyclic existence, is not attached to any of its marvels and is seeking liberation. A holy person has turned his or her mind away from attachment outside to the better things of cyclic existence and focussed it within. In the word "lama", "la" means high, and "ma" is a negative, which indicates that there is none higher; this is a person who has turned away from self-cherishing to cherishing others, has turned away from the lower concern for personal benefit in order to achieve the higher purpose of attaining benefit for others.

In applying these three words to the teachings in Dzong-ka-ba's *Great Exposition of the Stages of the Path*, the word "foremost" is connected with the paths of a being of small capacity, the word "holy" is connected with the paths of a being of middling capacity, and the word "lama" is connected with the paths of a being of great capacity. One who possesses all three levels is a "foremost holy lama". An earlier lama in Tibet made the connection between these three words here and the three levels of the path as the qualifications of a lama, but it is by no means necessary to use these three words strictly in this manner on all occasions. It is very important to distinguish the context of terms used in Buddhist texts; to apply a single meaning of a term in all different contexts can lead to confusion in understanding the meaning of a text.

Dzong-ka-ba pays homage to the foremost holy lamas who possess these qualifications in order to express his respect for them. A respectful attitude is maintained toward one's lamas for the sake of generating these three realizations within our own continuum. The meaning of the Tibetan word for homage, when broken down into its component syllables, is to want an unchangeable or undivertable state. In paying homage, Dzong-ka-ba is expressing a wish for unchangeable, undivertable understanding of these three topics.

Dzong-ka-ba met and studied with many lamas of the Nying-ma, Sa-gya, and Ga-gyu orders and, in particular, met personally with Manjushri and in dependence upon his kindness generated the non-erroneous view realizing the profound emptiness. In addition, it was the quintessential instruction of Manjushri to condense all the teachings of the path into these three principal aspects. Thus, it is to these holy lamas that Dzong-ka-ba pays homage at the beginning of the text.

Homage to the foremost holy lamas.

The promise to compose the text is contained in the first stanza:

I will explain as well as I can
The essential meaning of all the Conqueror's scriptures,
The path praised by the excellent Conqueror Children,
The port for the fortunate wishing liberation.

It is suitable to interpret the last three lines of this stanza as referring to one thing, in which case they would read: "... the essential meaning of all the Conqueror's scriptures, *which is* the path praised by the excellent Conqueror Children *and is* the port for the fortunate wishing liberation." However, these lines can also be taken as referring individually to the three principal aspects of the path. The first, "the essential meaning of all the Conqueror's scriptures", represents the determination to be freed from cyclic existence. "The path praised by the excellent Conqueror Children" refers to the altruistic intention to become enlightened, and "the port for the fortunate wishing liberation" indicates the correct view of emptiness.

How does the "the essential meaning of all the Conqueror's scriptures" refer to the determination to be freed from cyclic existence? As Dzong-ka-ba says in his *praise of Dependent-Arising*:

All of your various teachings
Are solely based on dependent-arising
And are for sake of [our] passing from sorrow.
You have nothing that does not tend toward peace.

All of Buddha's teachings are for the purpose of trainees' attaining freedom from cyclic existence; Buddha taught nothing that is not for the sake of peace. Since the determination to be freed from cyclic existence forms the root of the path which is the unmistaken means of achieving liberation, it is the essential meaning of all the Conqueror's scriptures.

In the next line, "the path praised by the excellent Conqueror Children", the term "Conqueror Children" refers to Bodhisattvas, beings who are born from the speech of the Conqueror Buddha. The path praised by them refers to the altruistic intention to become enlightened. Through generating the altruistic mind of enlightenment, one becomes a Bodhisattva, and by means of it one is able to help others.

"The port for the fortunate wishing liberation" refers to the correct view of emptiness. For, it is through this view that we can be freed from cyclic existence. As Aryadeva's *Four Hundred* says, "... the door of peace of which there is no second". Liberation is achieved only after the afflictive emotions and so forth are removed, and this must be accomplished by means of generating in our continuum their actual antidote, the correct view realizing the emptiness of inherent existence, and familiarizing with it again and again. Lacking the correct view of emptiness, we can never be liberated from cyclic existence, regardless of the other good qualities we may possess.

In the first verse, Dzong-ka-ba says that he will explain these three topics *as well as he can*. The meaning of this is either that he is assuming an humble attitude prior to composing the text or that he will do his best to explain these three topics in *brief* terms. In fact, at the time Dzong-ka-ba wrote the *Three Principal Aspects of the Path*, he had already, much earlier in his life, generated the determination to become free from cyclic existence and the altruistic intention to become enlightened as well as the view of emptiness according to its uncommon interpretation in the Consequence School. He had also arrived at the stage of completion of Highest Yoga Tantra, having attained either the first level, verbal isolation, or the second level, mental isolation, from among the five levels of the stage of completion in Highest Yoga Tantra according to the *Guhyasamaja Tantra*.

In the next stanza Dzonga-ka-ba makes an exhortation to those who are fit vessels for the doctrine to listen to this teaching:

Whoever are not attached to the pleasures of mundane existence,
Whoever strive in order to make leisure and fortune worthwhile,
Whoever are inclined to the path pleasing the Conqueror Buddha,
Those fortunate ones should listen with a clear mind.

The three topics mentioned in this stanza can also be applied to the three principal aspects of the path. Non-attachment to the pleasures of mundane existence refers to having the determination to be freed from cyclic existence. Making leisure and fortune worthwhile suggests that if the altruistic intention to become enlightened is generated, then the leisure and fortune which we humans have is being used in a meaningful and worthwhile manner. Being inclined to the path that pleases the Conqueror Buddha refers to an interested and faithful person's generating the correct view of emptiness in meditation; making use of an unmistaken path proceeding to liberation, one thereby fulfils Buddha's purpose in teaching the path. A person who is an appropriate listener to this text should possess a profound interest from the depths of the heart in the three principal aspects of the path to enlightenment, and thus Dzong-ka-ba states: "Those fortunate ones should listen."

Dzong-ka-ba speaks of the purpose for generating the determination to become free from cyclic existence:

Without a complete thought definitely to leave cyclic existence
There is no way to stop seeking pleasurable effects in the ocean of
existence.
Also, craving cyclic existence thoroughly binds the embodied.
Therefore, in the beginning determination to leave cyclic existence
should be sought.

Without this complete determination, there is no way to stop seeking pleasurable experience in the ocean of existence, and it is this craving for cyclic existence that thoroughly binds beings, illustrated here by those who have bodies. Therefore, in setting out on the path to enlightenment, it is important to develop a strong determination definitely to get out of cyclic existence. As Aryadeva says:

How could whoever is not discouraged about this
Be intent on pacification?

A person who cannot generate a sense of discouragement when looking at the artifacts of cyclic existence is incapable of generating the attitude of seeking liberation, peace.

To generate such a thought it is first necessary to understand the advantages of liberation and the faults of cyclic existence. Dharmakirti describes cyclic existence as the burden of mental and physical aggregates which are assumed under the influence of contaminated actions and afflictions. Hence, cyclic existence is not a place or an area but is to be identified within ourselves. Because our aggregates—our minds and bodies—are a consequence of former contaminated actions and afflictive emotions, they are not under our own control. This means that even though we want happiness and wish to avoid suffering, because our minds and bodies are controlled by former actions and afflictions, we are beset by many unwanted sufferings and lack the happiness we want. Once we have acquired such contaminated aggregates, they serve as the basis of the suffering we experience in the present and also induce sufferings in the future.

We very much value what we perceive to be our own; we say "my body" or "my mental and physical aggregates", cherishing them greatly. Yet, that which we cherish has actually a nature of suffering. Though we do not want birth, aging, sickness, or death, these unwanted sufferings arise in dependence upon the contaminated mental and physical aggregates we so much value. In order to alleviate this suffering we must question whether there is a technique for removing the contaminated mental and physical aggregates. Are these aggregates produced in dependence on causes, or are they produced causelessly? If they did not depend on causes, they could not change, but we know that they do change, and this indicates their dependence on causes; the mental and physical aggregates each have their respective substantial causes and co-operative conditions. Our minds having come under the influence of afflictive emotions, we engage in actions that establish in the mind predispositions impelling future cyclic existences. This is the contaminated process that forms our mental and physical aggregates into having a nature of suffering.

We possess mental and physical aggregates now, and we will still possess them when we attain Buddhahood, but the causation of the mental and physical aggregates *of cyclic existence* is rooted in the contaminated process that results from an uncontrolled mind and the actions that come from it. Therefore, it is possible to separate the mental and physical aggregates from the process of contaminated causation and thus from having a nature of suffering and yet their continuum remain in a pure form.

To remove the aggregates which are under the influence of contaminated actions and afflictions and thereby have a nature of suffering, it is necessary to stop the new accumulation of contaminated actions (karma, las) as well as to stop nourishing contaminated karmas which were previously accumulated. For this, it is necessary to remove the afflictive emotions.

There are many different types of afflictive emotions. As Vasubandhu's *Treasury of Knowledge* says, "The roots of cyclic existence are the six subtle increasers [of contamination]". That text speaks of five views and five non-views; the five views are then condensed into one and, combined with the five non-view afflictions, comprise the six basic root afflictions; desire, anger, pride, doubt, afflictive view, and obscuration. The root of all these afflictions is ignorance.

Ignorance can be identified in many different ways. From the viewpoint of the highest system, the Middle Way Consequence School, it is described as the conception of objects as having inherent existence whereas in fact they do not. Through the force of such ignorance, the other afflictive emotions are then generated. When we analyse whether this ignorance is intrinsic to the nature of the mind itself, we will find that, as Dharmakirti says, "The nature of the mind is clear light; the defilements are adventitious." Once the defilements do not subsist in the nature of the mind, it is possible to remove them through generating an antidote to them.

We are thoroughly habituated to the mistaken conception that objects truly exist, but this conception has no valid foundation. The opposite of it is the realization that phenomena do not inherently exist, and although we are not accustomed to this view, there are reasons which establish the non-inherent existence of phenomena; hence it has valid foundation, and through becoming familiar with the reasons establishing it, it is possible to generate the wisdom that is the opposite of ignorance.

Whereas ignorance and the wisdom that realizes non-inherent existence both have the same object of observation—any phenomenon—their mode of apprehension of that object is exactly opposite. Wisdom has a valid foundation and is well reasoned whereas ignorance has no valid foundation and is mistaken with respect to what it is conceiving. Thus, we can understand from our own experience that by increasing the strength of wisdom, ignorance will weaken. Qualities of mind are stable in that as long as their functioning has not deteriorated, it is not necessary to rely on new exertion for them to continue to exist. Therefore, it can be established that the wisdom which realizes selflessness can be generated and, as one familiarizes with it more and more, can eventually be increased limitlessly. When it is produced to its full extent, wisdom will cause ignorance—the mind that apprehends the opposite, inherent existence—gradually to decrease and finally to disappear entirely.

Afflictions and defilements are thus extinguished in the sphere of reality. Upon the extinction of the adventitious defilements through the power of their antidote, this purified sphere of reality is called liberation. The fact that the mind has a nature of luminosity and knowing is the basis for establishing that liberation can be achieved.

From another point of view, liberation is attained by knowing the final nature of the mind itself; it is not received from an outside source; it is not bestowed on us by someone else. By achieving liberation, the afflictive emotions are all removed, and due to this, regardless of the nature of the external conditions we encounter, we will no longer generate any afflictive emotions nor accumulate any new karma. The process of liberation depends upon the removal of the afflictive emotions, the chief of which is ignorance, and this in turn depends upon the generation of its antidote, wisdom. Since wisdom depends upon the determination to be freed from cyclic existence, without such determination liberation is impossible. Therefore, initially it is very important to develop the intention to leave cyclic existence. If you see the disadvantages of cyclic existence, you will lose attraction to it, generating an aspiration toward liberation from it. Through developing that wish, you will make effort at the techniques for getting out of cyclic existence.

The next stanza describes how to train in this attitude:

Leisure and fortune are difficult to find
And life has no duration,
Through familiarity with this,
Emphasis on the appearances of this life is reversed.

Through familiarity with the fact that "leisure and fortune are difficult to find and life has no duration", our usual emphasis on the appearances of this life is reversed. In this text, the determination to leave cyclic existence is generated through reflection in two stages: first, to remove the emphasis on appearances in this life and, then, to remove emphasis on appearances in future lifetimes. In Dzong-ka-ba's *Great Exposition of the Stages of the Path*, practices for being of small and middling capacity as well as the temporary fruits to be gained from these practices are described separately. Here in the *Three Principal Aspects*, however, these practices are merged within the one thought of developing the intention to leave cyclic existence.

There is no sense in being attached to this lifetime. No matter how long we live, which can be at most around one hundred years, eventually we must die, losing this valuable human life; further, it is indefinite when that will be—it could be any time. This life will disintegrate, and no matter how much prosperity we have, it will not help. No amount of wealth can buy an extension on life, and no matter how much money we have accumulated and have in the bank, even if we are millionaires, on the day of our death none of it can help; we have to leave it all. In this respect, the death of a millionaire and the death of a wild animal are alike. Though resources are necessary to life, they are certainly not a final object of attainment. Also, in spite of material wealth and progress, many types of suffering persist just by the fact that we have a human life, bringing unhappiness in many different ways, back to back.

Is it the very nature of human life that it be miserable? Is it unalterably so? Under the present circumstances, influenced by the process of conditioning we now experience, the very nature of life is indeed miserable. However, by means of the reasoning just set forth which establishes the possibility of attaining liberation, we can see that the causes that produce misery can be overcome through separating the mind from the afflictive emotions. Thus, it is clear that misery is not necessarily inherent to human existence. If we are able to make appropriate use of human thought, we can achieve something that is very valuable, whereas if we are concerned only with the affairs of this lifetime, we will waste this opportunity to use the powerful human brain we have already attained. Like investing a fortune to obtain something insignificant, the use of the human brain to achieve something of little importance is very sad. Realizing the weakness of such action, we need to generate the view that an emphasis solely on the affairs of this lifetime is silly, foolish. By cultivating this attitude, the determination to leave cyclic existence such emphasis will gradually weaken.

In renouncing this life, we do not simply ignore essential needs, such as hunger, but strive to reduce our attachment to affairs limited to this lifetime. Moreover, not just this lifetime but all of the marvellous prosperity and boundless resources of cyclic existence also have a nature of suffering, for ultimately they will deteriorate. Though one might attain a good lifetime in the future, there will be another after it, and another and another with no certainty that they will all be good. Thus, it is necessary not only to reduce our emphasis on the appearances of this lifetime but to remove attachment to future lives as well. We need to generate the thought that any lifetime under the influence of contaminated actions and afflictions is without essence, pithless.

Dzong-ka-ba says:

If You think again and again
About deeds and their inevitable effects
And the sufferings of cyclic existence
The emphasis on the appearances
Of future lives will be reversed.

Countless rebirths lie ahead, both good and bad. The effects of karma (actions) are inevitable, and in previous lifetimes we have accumulated negative karma which will inevitably have its fruition in this or future lives. Just as someone witnessed by police in a criminal act will eventually be caught and punished, so we too must inevitably face the consequences of faulty actions we have committed in the past even if we are not yet in prison. Once we have accumulated predispositions for suffering from non-virtuous actions in the past, there is no way to be at ease; those actions are irreversible; we must eventually undergo their effects.

If we are unable to remove the negative karma accumulated from past faulty actions, which is already present in seed form in our own minds, there is not much hope of gaining rebirths that are wholly good or in escaping the inevitable suffering of cyclic existence. Not only that, but also when we examine the better side of cyclic existence, we find that it does not pass beyond having a nature of suffering, eventually deteriorating. Life is afflicted with three types of suffering: the suffering of pain itself, the suffering of change, and the pervasive suffering of conditioning.

By analysing the inevitable consequences of previous faulty actions as well as the nature of suffering of even the marvels of cyclic existence we can lessen attachment to this and future lifetimes, developing the sense that liberation must be achieved. By combining these two thoughts—to overcome emphasis on the appearances of this life as well as emphasis on the marvels of cyclic existence in general—the determination to be freed from cyclic existence is generated.

What draws us into suffering—an untamed mind—is not external but within our own mental continuums. For it is through the appearance of afflictive emotions in our minds that we are drawn into various faulty actions. From the naturally pure sphere of the true nature of the mind these conceptions dawn, and through their force we engage in faulty actions leading to suffering. We need, with great awareness and care, to cause these conceptions to be extinguished back into the sphere of the nature of the mind, like clouds that gather in the sky and then dissolve back into the sphere of the sky. Thereby the faulty actions that arise from them will also cease. Mi-la-re-ba says, "... whether arising, arising within space itself, or dissolving, dissolving back into space." We need to know the status of things well, understanding what is erroneous and what is not and becoming able to dissolve these conceptions back into the sphere of reality.

Happiness comes through taming the mind; without taming the mind there is no way to be happy. The basis of this is a reasoned determination to be freed from cyclic existence. In the Buddhist scriptures it is explained that there is no beginning to the mind and hence no beginning to one's rebirths. In terms of reasoning, there is no way that consciousness can serve as a substantial cause of matter and no way that matter can serve as a substantial cause of consciousness. The only thing that can serve as a substantial cause of consciousness is a former consciousness. Through this reasoning, former and future lives are established.

Once there are future lifetimes, it can be decided that no matter how much prosperity and so forth you have in this lifetime—even if you are a billionaire—on the last day when you are dying you cannot take even one penny with you. No matter how many good friends you have, in the end you cannot take even one friend with you. What goes with you that is helpful is the strength of your own merit, your good deeds. Therefore, it is very dangerous to be one hundred per cent involved in affairs limited in perspective just to this lifetime. Although it would be impractical to put all of your time into deep matters that will help future lifetimes, it would be a good idea to put fifty per cent of your energy into concerns for this lifetime and fifty per cent into deeper topics. We have to live, we have a stomach which must be filled, but at maximum this life can be only around one hundred years and thus is very short compared to future lifetimes. It is worthwhile to think of your future lives too and worthwhile to prepare for them, reducing a little the involvement of the mind just in the affairs of this lifetime.

Is it not the case that when we examine the marvels of cyclic existence, we find that they actually have the nature of suffering? They are not such that no matter how much we use them, they are always pleasurable. For example, if you have many houses, since you are only one person, when you use a particular house, the other houses remain empty. Then, when you go to another of the houses, this house is not of much use. Similarly, even if you have a lot of money and stock up huge quantities of food, you have only one mouth and one stomach. You cannot eat more than one person's amount; if you ate enough for two, you would die. It is better right from the beginning to set limits and be content.

If you are not content but greedy, wanting this and wanting that, there is no way that all desires could be fulfilled. Even if you had control over all the world, it still would not be enough. Desire cannot be fulfilled. Moreover, when you are desiring, desiring, desiring, you face many obstacles, disappointments, unhappiness, and difficulties. Great desire not only knows no end but also itself creates trouble.

Pleasure and pain are effects. That pleasure and pain change indicates that they depend upon causes. Once they are caused, the happiness which you want is obtained through generating its causes, and the suffering which you do not want is removed through getting rid of its causes. If you have in your continuum a cause of suffering, even if you do not want that suffering, you will undergo it.

Since pleasure and pain are in a process of cause and effect, we can know what will come in the future in that future appearances depend upon the activities and thoughts we are engaged in now. Looked at this way, we can see that we are accumulating in every minute many karmas—actions—which will influence our rebirths in the future. Thus, it can be decided that if we do not utilize a method to bring about the end of the *causes* that impel the process of cyclic existence, there is no way to end suffering.

When we investigate it, our mental and physical aggregates which are under the influence of contaminated actions and afflictions are phenomena which have a nature of suffering. The *past* causes of our aggregates are impure; in terms of their *present* entities, mind and body serve as bases of suffering; and in terms of the *future* they induce suffering to be experienced later.

In the beginning we experience suffering during birth and then during childhood. At the end of life, there is old age—becoming physically decrepit, unable to move, see, and hear well, with many discomforts and many pains—and finally the suffering of death. Between the sufferings of birth and death we are held by various types of suffering—such as sickness, not getting what we want, getting what we do not want. In this way, these aggregates of mind and body serve as a basis for suffering.

Is this teaching pessimistic? Not at all. As much as you recognize suffering so much do you make effort toward victory over suffering. For instance, you work hard five days in the week to get more pay for the sake of more comfort and so forth; also, you make great effort early in your life so that later you can live happily. For greater comfort you make a sacrifice.

As much as you can increase recognition of suffering, so much closer do you approach the state of liberation from that suffering. Therefore, you should not take delight in the possibility of assuming in future lifetimes this type of body and mind which are under the influence of contaminated actions and afflictive emotions. Rather, you should seek a state in which the aggregates that serve as the basis of suffering are completely extinguished. The expanse of reality into which the defilements that induce suffering have been extinguished is called liberation.

We should turn away not only from attraction to the appearances of this lifetime but also from attraction to the marvels of cyclic existence in future lifetimes since as long as we have these contaminated aggregates, there is no hope for real peace. Thinking thus on the disadvantages of cyclic existence, it is possible to develop a wish to get out of cyclic existence to a state of liberation.

When investigating this way, it is necessary to proceed by way of a union of analytical meditation and stabilizing meditation. First, analytically investigate the reasons behind the determination to leave cyclic existence, and then when some conviction develops, stabilize—without analysing—on what you have understood. When your understanding begins to weaken, return to analytical meditation, then back to stabilizing meditation, and so forth.

What is the measure of having generated a fully qualified determination to leave cyclic existence after training in this way?

If, having meditated thus, you do not generate admiration
Even for an instant for the prosperity of cyclic existence
And if an attitude seeking liberation arises day and night,
Then the thought definitely to leave cyclic existence has been
    generated.

If, having overcome both the emphasis on the appearances of this life and attraction to the marvels of cyclic existence in general through repeated familiarization with these thoughts, you spontaneously and continuously seek to be freed from cyclic existence, without for a moment being distracted by attachment thinking from the depths, "This is wonderful", "I must have this", "Oh, if I only could have this", and so forth, you have then generated a fully qualified determination to be freed from cyclic existence.

This attitude, to be truly effective, must actually be implemented and not just verbalized. As Shantideva says:

Would a sick person be helped
Merely by reading a medical text?

It is not sufficient just to read about medicine, it must be taken internally in order to bring about a cure.

It is easy to lecture on the doctrine, or to hear it spoken, but very hard to put it into practice. Without actually practising the teachings, however, there is no way for good results to be produced. If the cause is only a verbal explanation, the effect cannot be anything more. When hungry, we need actual food; mere descriptions of tasty French or Chinese food cannot nourish us. As Buddha said, "I indicate the path of liberation to you; know that liberation itself depends upon you."

It may seem on first hearing them that these Buddhist ideas we have been discussing are very unusual and perhaps impossible to achieve. However, as Shantideva says:

There is nothing whatsoever that does not
Become easier when one is accustomed to it.

There is nothing which cannot eventually be achieved once he has grown accustomed to it. All these states gradually can be generated, by growing familiar with them. The test of these teachings is to make effort at them over a long period of time. As Buddha says in a tantra [in paraphrase], "If you put into practice what I have said and it cannot be achieved, then what I have said is a lie." Therefore, at first it is necessary to practice and gain experience; in this way you will come to understand the truth of Buddha's teachings.

This completes the section on the generation of determination to be freed from cyclic existence; its causes, the methods for generating this determination, and the measure of its having been generated. The second of the three principal aspects of the path is the altruistic intention to become enlightened. As Dzong-ka-ba says, the determination to leave cyclic existence must be conjoined with the altruistic intention to become enlightened. Without the conjunction of these two aspects, their practice will not serve as a cause of becoming a Buddha; thus, the next stanza sets forth the reason for cultivating the altruistic attitude:

> Also, if this thought definitely to leave cyclic existence
>> Is not conjoined with generation of a complete aspiration to highest enlightenment,
> It does not become a cause of the marvellous bliss of unsurpassed enlightenment.
> Thus, the intelligent should generate the supreme altruistic intention to become enlightened.

The altruistic intention to become enlightened, or mind of enlightenment, is a special attitude of seeking your own full enlightenment as a Buddha for the sake of sentient beings—the welfare of sentient beings being your main object of intent. In order to generate such an attitude, it is necessary to develop the great compassion which observes sentient beings and wishes them to be free from suffering and its causes. In order to generate that, it is necessary to reflect on the ways in which sentient beings suffer. This is done through extending to others the type of realization of suffering that you develop with respect to yourself when cultivating the determination to be freed from cyclic existence.

The next two stanzas describe the means for cultivating the altruistic intention to become enlightened, first outlining the sufferings that are characteristic of cyclic existence:

> [All ordinary beings] are carried by the continuum of the four powerful currents.
> Are tied with the tight bonds of actions difficult to oppose,
> Have entered into the iron cage of apprehending self [inherent existence],
> Are completely beclouded with the thick darkness of ignorance,

Are born into cyclic existence limitlessly, and in their births
Are tortured ceaselessly by the three sufferings.
Thinking thus of the condition of mothers who have come to such a
    state,
Generate the supreme altruistic intention to become enlightened.

These thoughts are very powerful and, if correctly applied to our own condition, can enhance the wish to leave cyclic existence. Then, by applying these realizations to the experiences of other sentient beings, compassion can be generated.

What is the meaning of being carried by the continuum of the four powerful currents? There are various interpretations, but here the essential meaning is that all beings are overwhelmed by the four powerful currents of birth, aging, sickness, and death. Though we do not want these sufferings, we nevertheless undergo them; like being carried away by the currents of a great river, we are under their force. Our being powerlessly carried away by these four powerful river currents is the result of being tied with the tight bonds of our own previous actions and their predispositions that are difficult to oppose, and we are tied with these tight bonds because of being under the influence of afflictive emotions such as desire and hatred. Those are generated due to our having entered into the very hard, obstructive, and difficult to penetrate cage of the innate apprehension of an inherently existent I and mine.

Observing our own I, or self, we misconceive it to be inherently existent and through this misconception are drawn into afflictive emotions that motivate actions which tie us in tight bonds and cause us to be swept away by the four powerful river currents of suffering. We are led into this faulty view of an inherently existent I by the force of the thick darkness of the misconception that other phenomena, primarily the mental and physical aggregates which are the basis of designation of the I, inherently exist. Based on that, we generate the misconception that the I and mine inherently exist, whereupon the afflictive emotions of desire, hatred, and so forth are generated, causing us to engage in contaminated actions, thereby accumulating the karmas that bind us tightly.

Through such a causal process, beings come to be fettered with these mental and physical aggregates that have a nature of the sufferings of birth, aging, sickness, and death. Because of this causal sequence we undergo the three types of suffering: physical and mental pain, the suffering of change, and the pervasive suffering of conditioning which is merely to be under the influence of a contaminated process of causation. Analysis of this situation of suffering and the sources of suffering in relation to yourself helps to generate the determination to be freed from cyclic existence, whereas reflection on the countless others who were your mothers in former lifetimes and are endlessly tortured by such suffering evokes the generation of love, compassion, and the altruistic intention to become a Buddha in order to be of service to them. We ourselves want happiness and want to avoid suffering, and the same is true for all other sentient beings oppressed by the misery of cyclic existence. Those who suffer in this way lack the knowledge of what to adopt and what to discard in order to achieve happiness and avoid suffering. As Shantideva says in his *Engaging in the Bodhisattva Deeds*:

Although [sentient beings] want to get rid of suffering,
They manifestly run to suffering itself.
Though they want happiness, out of confusion
They destroy their own happiness like an enemy.

Though people do not want suffering, they rush toward it; though they want happiness, out of confusion they achieve the opposite.

To help sentient beings achieve liberation, we need to help them to understand the techniques for achieving happiness and removing suffering through identifying without error what to adopt and what to discard. Dharmakirti's *Commentary on (Dignaga's) "Compendium of Valid Cognition"* says:

In order to overcome suffering [in others]
The merciful engage in methods.
When the causes of what arise from those methods are obscure [to oneself],
It is difficult to explain them [to others].

If you yourself do not know the topics that are needed in order to help others, there is nothing you can do. In order fully to bring about the welfare of other sentient beings it is necessary to know from a subtle level those things that will help others, the essential points of what to adopt and what to discard. Beyond this, you also need to know the dispositions, interests, and so forth of the sentient beings you seek to help. Thus, it is necessary to remove the obstructions to knowing all objects of knowledge. For, when all these obstructions have been removed, one has achieved the omniscience of a Buddha, the exalted wisdom knowing all aspects of objects of knowledge.

Since Bodhisattvas are seeking to help all sentient beings, they take as their main object of abandonment the obstructions to omniscience and work at the antidote to these obstructions. For, without knowing all, it is possible to help a small number of beings but impossible fully and effectively to help a vast number. This is why it is necessary to achieve Buddhahood in order to be of effective service to sentient beings.

Unable to bear the suffering of sentient beings without doing something about it, you generate strong compassion and love, wishing beings to be rid of suffering and to possess happiness. Then, seeing that to accomplish this purpose there is no way but to achieve Buddhahood, you generate the altruistic intention to achieve enlightenment. This intention to yourself attain the omniscience of a Buddha in order to be of service to others is called the altruistic mind of enlightenment (*bodhichitta*). It involves two aspirations—seeking the welfare of others through seeking your own enlightenment.

Based on the earlier description of the measure of having generated the determination to be freed from cyclic existence, we can understand the measure of having attained the altruistic mind of enlightenment; therefore, Dzong-ka-ba did not explicitly mention it. If, no matter what you are doing, in some portion of the mind there remains a constant intense wish for the welfare of sentient beings and a seeking of enlightenment for their sake, you have generated a fully qualified altruistic mind of enlightenment.

It is important to realize that our personalities are not suddenly and completely transformed as we try to develop such thoughts. Our natures, our characteristic dispositions, change only gradually. Differences are not seen at once, but over time. If we cultivate the altruistic intention to become enlightened slowly and steadily and, after five or ten years have passed, consider the changes that have occurred in our way of thinking and actions, the results of our efforts—the improvement—will be clearly discernible.

According to common sight, Shakyamuni Buddha spent six years practising austerities and leading an ascetic life. He made this display of renouncing the pleasures of his household, becoming a monk, renouncing worldly facilities, going into ascetic retreat, and so forth in order to indicate the difficulties of the path his followers should pursue. How could it be that Buddha would have had to expend such tremendous effort to achieve realization and yet we could achieve the same realization quickly and without much effort? We cannot.

Having reached the point where a portion of the mind is continuously involved with the wish to achieve Buddhahood for the sake of all beings, you should conjoin this with the rite of aspirational mind generation for the sake of making it more stable. Also, it is necessary to train in the causes that will prevent deterioration of the aspirational mind in this or future lifetimes.

Then, it is not sufficient merely to generate the aspirational form of the mind of enlightenment; the practical mind of enlightenment must also be generated, for intention alone is not enough. You must come to understand that further training is necessary—the practice of the six perfections: giving, ethics, patience, effort, concentration, and wisdom. Having trained in the wish to engage in these practices, you take the Bodhisattva vows actually to do so.

If these vows are taken and the practice of the six perfections has gone well, it is then possible to receive initiation and engage in the practice of mantra [tantra]. This is the fully qualified mode of procedure that is set forth in the great books, undertaken when there is time and opportunity to progress in this way. Otherwise, as is now the widespread custom, when you have some understanding of the three principal aspects of the path—the determination to be freed from cyclic existence, the altruistic intention to become enlightened, and the correct view of emptiness—and are making great effort at developing these attitudes, it becomes possible to enter the practice of mantra. However, if you do not have understanding of the three principal aspects of the path, do not have faith from the depths of the heart in the Three Jewels [Buddha, his doctrine, and the spiritual community], and so forth, it would be extremely difficult to say that you have actually attained mantric initiation even if you have attended a ceremony.

The foundation of the altruistic mind of enlightenment is a good heart, a good mind, at all times. All of us can benefit from cultivating this; we should not get angry, fight, backbite, and so forth. When people engage in such activities, they do so for the sake of personal concerns but actually are only harming themselves. Therefore, all of us need to do whatever we can to cultivate a good mind, a good heart. I am not just explaining this; I, too am doing as much as I can to practice it. Everyone needs to do whatever is possible, for as much as we can practice this, so much will it help.

If you engage in such practices and gain experience of them, your attitudes and way of viewing other people will change; then when a problem—which you have encountered before—arises, you will not respond with the same excitement as previously, will not generate the same negative attitudes. This change is not from something external, is not a matter of getting a new nose or a new hairstyle, but takes place within the mind. Some people can withstand problems whereas others cannot; the difference is one of internal attitude.

The change from putting these teachings into practice comes slowly. After some time, we may encounter those who tell us we have changed; this is a good sign that the practices have been effective. Such response is welcome, for it indicates that we are no longer bringing trouble to other people but are, instead, acting as a good citizen of the world. You may not be able to levitate, fly, or display similar feats, but such abilities are secondary and in fact counterproductive if you are making trouble in the world. What is important is to tame the mind, to learn to be a good person. If we practice this teaching, nirvana will gradually come, but if we act with bitterness and hatred, nirvana will only become more distant.

The emphasis in Buddhism is on oneself, on the *use* we make of this doctrine. Though Buddhist teachings offer the refuges of Buddha, the doctrine, and the spiritual community, these are to help us generate the power of our own practice. Among the three refuges, the main refuge is the doctrine, not the doctrine within someone else's continuum but that which we ourselves must generate in our own continuum. Without individual effort and practice, the Three Jewels of Buddha, the doctrine, and the spiritual community cannot provide any refuge.

This concludes the section of the altruistic intention to become enlightened; we have now reached the point of the last of the three principal aspects of the path, the correct view of emptiness. Why is it important to generate the wisdom realizing emptiness? Dzong-ka-ba says:

> If you do not have the wisdom realizing the way things are,
> Even though you have developed the thought definitely to leave
>   cyclic existence and the altruistic intention,
> The root of cyclic existence cannot be cut.
> Therefore work at the means of realizing dependent-arising.

"The way things are" refers to the mode of subsistence of phenomena, of which there are many levels. Here Dzong-ka-ba means the most subtle level, the final reality. Of the two truths, this is the ultimate truth. There are many conventional modes of subsistence, ways that phenomena abide, but the correct view of emptiness apprehends the final mode of subsistence, the ultimate truth.

Without the wisdom that realizes the final mode of subsistence of phenomena, even though you have made great effort in meditation and have generated both the determination to be freed from cyclic existence and the altruistic intention to gain enlightenment, the root of cyclic existence still cannot be severed. For, the root of cyclic existence meets back to ignorance of the mode of subsistence of phenomena, misconception of the nature of persons and other phenomena. It is necessary to generate a wisdom consciousness which, within observing the same objects, has a mode of apprehension directly contradictory with that of this ignorant misconception. Even though the mere wish to leave cyclic existence or the mere altruistic intention to become enlightened indirectly help, they cannot serve as direct antidotes overcoming the misconception that is the root of cyclic existence. This is why the view realizing emptiness is needed.

Notice that Dzong-ka-ba exhorts us to "work at the means of realizing dependent-arising", not "work at the means of realizing emptiness". This is because the meaning of dependent-arising resides in the meaning of emptiness, and conversely, the meaning of emptiness resides in the meaning of dependent-arising. Therefore, in order to indicate that emptiness should be understood as the meaning of dependent-arising, and vice versa, thereby freeing one from the two extremes, he says that effort should be made at the means of realizing dependent-arising.

Emptiness should be understood not as a mere negation of everything but as a negation of inherent existence—the absence of which is compatible with dependent-arising. If the understanding of emptiness and the understanding of dependent-arising become unrelated and emptiness is misinterpreted as nihilism, not only would emptiness not be understood correctly but also such conception would, rather than being advantageous, have the very great fault of falling to an extreme of annihilation. Therefore, Dzong-ka-ba explicitly speaks of understanding dependent-arising.

Then:
Whoever, seeing the cause and effect of all phenomena

Of cyclic existence and nirvana as infallible,
Thoroughly destroys the mode of misapprehension of
those objects [as inherently existent]
Has entered on a path that is pleasing to Buddha.

When, through investigating this final mode of subsistence of
phenomena, we come to understand the non-existence of the referent
object of the conception of self, or inherent existence, in persons or
phenomena—that is, when we realize the absence of inherent existence—within still being able to posit, without error, the cause and effect
of all the phenomena included within cyclic existence and nirvana, at that
time we have entered on the path that pleases Buddha. Emptiness is to be
understood within not overriding your understanding of the cause and
effect of mundane and supramundane phenomena which obviously bring
help and harm and cannot be denied. When emptiness is realized within
understanding the non-mistakenness, non-confusion, and non-disorder-
ing of the process of cause and effect, that is to say, dependent-arising,
this realization is capable of destroying all misapprehension of objects
as inherently existent.

As long as the two, realization of appearances—the infallibility of
dependent-arising—
And the realization of emptiness—the non-assertion [of inherent
existence]—
Seem to be separate, there is still no realization
Of the thought of Shakyamuni Buddha.

If the understanding of appearances as unconfused dependent-
arising and the understanding of the emptiness of inherent existence of
those appearances seem mutually exclusive, unrelated—if the understanding of the one does not facilitate understanding of the other or makes
the other seem impossible—then you have not understood the thought of
Shakyamuni Buddha. If it is the case that your realization of emptiness
causes realization of dependent-arising to lessen or that your realization
of dependent-arising causes realization of emptiness to lessen and these
two realizations alternate as if separate and contradictory, you do not
have the proper view.

Rather:

When [the two realizations exist] simultaneously without alternation
And when from only seeing dependent-arising as infallible,
Definite knowledge entirely destroys the mode of apprehension [of

the conception of inherent existence],
Then the analysis of the view [of reality] is complete.

The wisdom realizing the lack of inherent existence, the absence of a self-instituting entity, is induced through searching for and not finding an object designated, for instance, one's own body, using a method of analysis such as the sevenfold reasoning.[3] Finally, through the reason of the subject's being a dependent-arising, the practitioner induces ascertainment that it is devoid of inherent existence. For, once it is under the influence of other factors, it depends upon them, and it is through its dependence on something else that the subject is shown to be empty of existing under its own power. In that we establish, through the reason of dependence on something else, or dependent-arising, that a subject is empty of existing under its own power, a dependently arisen phenomenon is left as positable after the refutation.

If we investigate a human who appears in a dream and an actual human of the waking state by way of the sevenfold reasoning, to an equal extent no self-instituting entity can be found in either case. However, although the dream human and the actual human, when investigated with the sevenfold reasoning, are equally unfindable, this does not mean that a dream human is to be posited as a human. Such would contradict valid cognition which experiences conventional objects; a subsequent conventional valid cognition refutes that a dream human is a human whereas positing an actual human as a human is not damaged by conventional valid cognition.

Even though a human cannot be found when sought through the sevenfold reasoning, it is unsuitable to conclude that humans do not exist, because that assertion would be refuted by conventional valid cognition. Conventional valid cognition establishes actual human beings, and therefore, humans must be posited as existing. In that they are not findable under analysis such as the sevenfold reasoning but do exist, it can be decided that humans exist not by way of their own power but only under the influence of or in dependence upon other factors. In this way, the

[3] This is an analysis of whether the person and the mind-body complex are inherently the same entity or different entities, whether the person inherently depends on mind and body, whether mind and body inherently depend on the person, whether the person inherently possesses mind and body, whether the person is the shape of the body, and whether the person is the composite of mind and body.

meaning of being empty of being under its own power comes to mean depending on others.

When Nagarjuna and his students cite reasons proving the emptiness of phenomena, they often use the reason of dependent-arising, that phenomena are produced in dependence upon causes and conditions, etc. As Nagarjuna says in his *Treatise on the Middle Way*:

Because there are no phenomena
That are not dependent-arising,
There are no phenomena that are not
Empty [of inherent existence].

Once there is no phenomenon that is not a dependent-arising, there is no phenomenon that is not empty of inherent existence. Aryadeva's *Four Hundred* says:

All these [phenomena] are not self-powered;
Thus, there is no self [inherent existence].

No phenomenon exists under its own power; therefore, all phenomena are devoid of being established by way of their own character. As the reason why phenomena are empty, they did not say that objects are not seen, not touched, or not felt. Thus, when phenomena are said to be empty, this does not mean that they are empty of the capacity to perform functions but that they are empty of their own inherent existence.

Moreover, the meaning of dependent-arising is not that phenomena *inherently* arise in dependence upon causes and conditions, but that they arise in dependence upon causes and conditions like a magician's illusions. If you understand the meaning of emptiness and dependent-arising well, you can, with respect to one object, understand its inevitable unmistaken appearance as well as its emptiness of inherent existence; these two are not at all contradictory. Otherwise, you would think that it would be impossible to realize these two factors, the unfabricated reality of emptiness and the fabricated fact of dependent-arising, with respect to one object. However, once you have established the emptiness of inherent existence by the very reason of dependent-arising, it is impossible for the understanding of appearance and the understanding of emptiness to become separated.

An emptiness of inherent existence appears to the mind through the route of eliminating an object of negation which in this case is inherent existence. At that time, a mere vacuity which is the negative of that inherent existence appears to the mind; this is an absence which does not imply another positive phenomenon in its place. To understand emptiness it is necessary to eliminate an object of negation just as, for example, to understand the absence of flowers here in front of me it is necessary to eliminate the presence of flowers. When we speak of this vacuity which is a mere negation or negative of inherent existence, we are talking about the way in which emptiness appears to the mind—as a mere vacuity devoid of the object of negation. We are *not* saying that at that time there is no consciousness or person realizing emptiness, for in fact we are describing *how* this appears in meditation to the mind of the meditator.

In brief, by reason of the fact that phenomena are dependent-arisings, that they arise dependently, we establish that they are empty of inherent existence. Once dependent arising is used as the reason for the emptiness of inherent existence, then with respect to one basis [or object] the practitioner conveniently avoids the two extremes of inherent existence and utter non-existence.

When emptiness is understood from the very perception of appearances themselves—from the very perception of dependent-arising itself—this understanding of appearance assists in understanding emptiness. When an understanding of emptiness is achieved through the reason of perceiving just dependent-arising without depending on any other type of reasoning such that the understanding of the one does not harm the understanding of the other but instead they mutually help each other and there is no need to alternate understanding of appearances and understanding of emptiness as if they were unrelated and separate, the analysis of the view is complete.

As Chandrakirti says in his *Supplement to (Nagarjuna's) "Treatise on the Middle Way"*:

[When] a yogi does not find the existence of this [chariot],
How could it be said that what does not exist in the seven ways
     [inherently] exists?
Through that, he easily enters also into suchness.
Therefore, here the establishment of this [chariot] is to be asserted
     in that way.

When sought for in the seven ways, phenomena cannot be found; yet, they are posited as being existent. This existence derives not from the object's own power but from the other-power of conceptuality. Hence, a thorough understanding of how phenomena are posited conventionally helps in gaining an understanding of their ultimate nature.

Prior to this deep level of realization, when you gain a little understanding of emptiness, you might wonder whether the activities of cause and effect, agent, activity, and object are possible within emptiness. At that time, consider an image in a mirror which, while being a mere reflection, is produced when certain conditions are met and disappears when those conditions cease—this being an example of the feasibility of functionality within non-inherent existence. Or, contemplate your own experience of the obvious help and harm that come from the presence and absence of certain phenomena, thereby strengthening conviction in dependent-arising. If you start moving to the extreme of the reification of existence, reflect on emptiness. In other words, when you are tending toward the extreme of nihilism, reflect more on dependent-arising; then, when you begin to move toward the extreme of inherent existence, reflect more on emptiness. With such skilful alternation of reflecting on emptiness and on dependent-arising by means of a union of stabilizing and analytical meditation, your understanding of both dependent-arising and the emptiness of inherent existence will become deeper and deeper, and at a certain point your understanding of appearances and emptiness will become equal.

The text continues:

Further, the extreme of [inherent] existence is excluded
[by knowledge of the nature] of appearances
[existing only as nominal designations],
And the extreme of [total] non-existence is excluded [by
knowledge of the nature] of emptiness [as the absence
of inherent existence and not the absence of
nominal existence].

Among all four Buddhist schools of tenets as well as, for instance, the Samkhya and even the Nihilist schools, it is held to be true that the extreme of non-existence—misidentification of what exists as not existing—is cleared away by appearance and the extreme of existence—misidentifying what does not exist as existing—is cleared away by emptiness. However, according to the uncommon view of the Middle Way Consequence School, the opposite also holds true: by way of appearance, the extreme of existence is avoided, and by way of emptiness, the extreme of non-existence is avoided. This doctrine derives from the pivotal point that the meaning of dependent-arising is the meaning of emptiness and the meaning of emptiness is the meaning of dependent-arising.

The understanding of dependent-arising differs among the Mind Only School, Middle Way Autonomy School, and the Middle Way Consequence School. The Mind Only School posits the meaning of dependent-arising only in terms of compounded phenomena, those that arise from and are dependent upon causes and conditions. In the Middle Way Autonomy School, the meaning of dependent-arising is applied to all phenomena, permanent and impermanent, in that all phenomena depend on their parts. In the Middle Way Consequence School, dependent-arising is, in addition, interpreted as the arising or establishment of all phenomena in dependence on imputation or designation by conceptuality. The mutual compatibility of such dependent-arising and emptiness is to be understood.

In this vein, the text says:
If within emptiness the appearance of cause and effect
  is known,
You will not be captivated by extreme views.

When, from within the sphere of emptiness, cause and effect appear in dependence upon emptiness in the sense that dependent-arisings are feasible because of emptiness, it is as if the dependent-arisings of causes and effects appear from or are produced from emptiness. When in dependence upon emptiness you understand the feasibility of dependent-arising, you are released from the two extremes.

Thus, the understanding of emptiness itself helps you to avoid the extreme of non-existence. Also, when you understand that dependence upon causes and conditions, parts, or a designating consciousness contradicts inherent existence, that very understanding of dependent-arising will help you to avoid the extreme of over-reification of existence. Once the meaning of emptiness appears as dependent-arising such that what is just empty of inherent existence appears as cause and effect, it is impossible for the mind to be captivated by an extreme view reifying what does not exist or deprecating what does exist.

If this view of emptiness is practised in conjunction with just the determination to be freed from cyclic existence, it will act as a cause of liberation from cyclic existence. If it is cultivated also in conjunction with the altruistic intention to become enlightened, it serves as a cause of full enlightenment as a Buddha. Since the view realizing emptiness is a common cause of the enlightenment of all three vehicles—the vehicles of

Hearers, Solitary Realisers, and Bodhisattvas—it is compared to a mother.

The special practitioners of mantra for whom the mantra system was intentionally spoken must have as their view of reality the view of the Middle Way Consequence system. However, in general, it is not necessary to hold this view to be a practitioner of mantra; the philosophical view can be either Mind Only or Middle Way. However, mantra cannot be practised within a view lower than these; the coarse view of realizing only the selflessness of persons, as is set forth in the Great Exposition and Sutra Schools, is not sufficient.

This completes the discussion of the three principal aspects of the path to enlightenment: the determination to be freed from cyclic existence, the altruistic intention to become enlightened, and the correct view of emptiness. It is primarily through the perfections of concentration and wisdom that the distinctive profundity of the great power of mantra is found, with practice centred on these same three aspects.

The actual basis of practice is the altruistic intention to become enlightened, the determination to leave cyclic existence being a preparation for that. The six perfections are the topics of training of Bodhisattvas, and among them, the distinguishing features of mantra are concerned with the perfections of concentration and wisdom. Hence, all practices of all vehicles—small, great, and within the Great Vehicle, the Sutra and tantra systems—can be included within (1) the preparations, (2) the actual central part of the practices of Bodhisattvas, and (3) supplements to it.

Concluding the explanation of the three principal aspects of the path, Dzong-ka-ba gives advice that, once we have understood the important points of the three aspects, these paths and their fruits must be generated within our own continuum:

> When you have realized thus just as they are
> The essentials of the three principal aspects of the path,
> Resort to solitude and generate the power of effort.
> Accomplish quickly your final aim, my child.

This is initially accomplished through hearing the teaching, then by way of the thinking which removes false super impositions with respect to those topics and induces definite knowledge, and finally by meditation in which all distractions are removed and the mind is concentrated single-pointedly. In this way you should achieve the three principal aspects of the path and the fruit which they bring about, the omniscience of Buddhahood.

This concludes an explanatory transmission on the three principal aspects of the path, which are a great composite of practices, an excellent guide. In receiving such a transmission you also receive a blessing. If you train in these practices continuously, you will come to realize them.

It is very important to generate a good attitude, a good heart, as much as possible. From this, happiness in both the short term and the long term for both yourself and others will come.

X
Vision for Human Liberation

Chapter X
VISION FOR HUMAN LIBERATION

A lasting effort to protect human rights in a global democratic future also entails world wide demilitarization. Although this may sound idealistic, it is important to re-evaluate the concept of the military establishments for it is not only during times of war that military establishments are destructive. By design, military establishments are the single greatest violators of human rights and the most regular opponents of democracy. The existence of a powerful army increases the chance of military dictatorship. If we truly believe that a dictatorship is the most despicable and destructive form of government, and the very antithesis of democracy, then we must recognise that in the contemporary world, powerful military establishments can only contribute to the formation of tyranny. Many dictators in the developing world have only retained power because they controlled the weapons and armaments supplied by countries of the developed world. Tremendous amounts of money have been used to purchase guns rather than to feed people and meet basic human and environmental needs. It is tragic that in many countries there are no shortages of guns and bullets, but there are frequently severe shortages of food for people. Compared to its neighbouring countries in which the military plays a dominant role, Costa Rica (a country which was demilitarized) had done very well in areas such as education and health.

It becomes incumbent upon us to support universal human rights once we accept three fundamental notions: all people have an equal right to live in peace and happiness; people can only be happy when able to realize their inherent human affinities for freedom, equality and dignity; and protection of human rights is a precondition for the expression of natural affinities. Moreover, since those deprived of their rights are often also those least able to speak up for themselves, the responsibility for the protection of universal human rights rests with those who already enjoy these freedoms.

—Dalai Lama

1

THE PATH WITHOUT VIOLENCE

Mahatma Gandhi was a great human being with a deep understanding of human nature. He made every effort to encourage the full development of the positive aspects of the human potential and to reduce or restrain the negative. I consider myself to be one of the followers of Mahatma Gandhi.

Even as violence seems to be growing around us, we remember that the epitome of non-violence, Mahatma Gandhi, was himself assassinated. That act of violence revealed one aspect of the human personality, but we must remember that all of us have a most remarkable potential, the ability to develop infinite altruism and compassion and a brain capable of unlimited knowledge and understanding. This needs to be used in the right way for it is also capable of unlimited destruction.

Compassion as Daily Practice

I consider the cultivation of non-violence and compassion as part of my daily practice. I do not consider this as something that is holy or sacred but of practical benefit to myself. The practice gives me satisfaction, it gives me a peace that is very helpful to have sincere, genuine relationships with other people.

As a human being I love friends, I love their smiles. We must realise that human happiness is interdependent. One's own successful or happy future is related to that of others. Therefore, helping others or having consideration of their rights and needs is actually not only one's own responsibility but a matter of one's own happiness. So I often tell people if we have to be really selfish, then let us be wisely selfish. If we are warm-hearted we automatically receive more smiles and make more genuine friends. We human beings are social animals. No matter how powerful or how intelligent we are, it is virtually impossible to survive without another human being. We need others for our very existence. The practice of compassion and non-violence is in one's own self-interest.

Genuine non-violence is related to one's mental attitude. When we talk of peace we must mean genuine peace, not merely the absence of war. For example, in the last few decades there was relative peace on the European continent, but I do not think it was genuine peace. It was peace that came out of fear as a result of the Cold War.

Relevance of Non-Violence

What is the relevance of non-violence and compassion in today's world? Ahimsa or non-violence is an ancient Indian concept which Mahatma Gandhi revived and implemented in modern times not only in political but also in day-to-day life. That was his great achievement. The nature of non-violence should be something that is not passive but active in helping others you must do that. If you cannot, you must at least restrain yourself from harming others.

The 20th century, I think, is the most important century in human history. It has seen many outstanding scientific achievements and yet more human suffering than ever before. The human being in this century is basically the same, as 1,000 or 10,000 years ago. He has had the same negative feelings of anger and hatred but this century has seen an enormous increase in his destructive power. This has produced a desperate situation of fear. With the possibility of nuclear holocaust the picture seemed hopeless and unbearable. The future looked so bleak that it forced and helped the human mind to think of alternatives. This gives great hope.

During the fifties and sixties many people felt that the ultimate decision in any disagreement or conflict could only come through war or weapons that were believed to deter war. Today more and more people are realising that the proper way of resolving differences is through dialogue, compromise, negotiations, through human understanding and humility. It is a very great sign.

The events and developments of our century have encouraged the human being to become wiser, more mature. In many countries, I think the attraction to Gandhian philosophy is growing. Because the capacity for human destruction is so immense, because the threat to the environment is so great, people are developing a greater understanding of the meaning of non-violence and of compassion.

Sometimes people feel that human beings are not all that gentle;

after all there is so much violence, so many killings, so much tragedy. But if looked closely, of the more than five billion human beings the number who are engaging in negative activities or have negative thoughts is very small. If human nature was so bad I think we would not have had to worry about the population problem.

Compassion and love are not matters of religion, though many religions teach these things. When we are born, we do not have any religion but we are not free from human love and affection. This is not a matter of religion. I believe it is a separate thing. What religions do is to try to strengthen these qualities which are already there in human nature from birth.

Why is it necessary to make a distinction between religion and human nature? This is essential because of the five billion or so people on our planet no more than about one billion are "believers" or actively follow any organised religion. We are all members of the same human family. We must find ways of cultivating a deeper awareness of love and compassion, with or without religion. At the same time, we need to understand the negative expressions of the human mind such as anger, hatred and attachment.

Anger

What is anger? It is true that sometimes due to some tragedy in our lives or due to frustrated desires we feel negative feelings which express themselves more openly in anger. Anger brings forth extra energy, boldness and determination. It is possible to use this energy to take certain drastic actions. Usually decisions taken when your mind is dominated by anger are wrong decisions which bring unhappiness or regret.

When we face some external problem, it is often possible to escape it and find a solution, but when the anger or the hatred is within, you cannot do so easily. Once you have an understanding or realisation of the nature of your mind, then gradually it will change. As time goes on your attitude, even to the external enemy, will change. With understanding there will be forgiveness and an increase of your inner strength. As a result there will be less fear, less doubt and more self confidence, tolerance and patience. This is why I consider compassion to be the key.

That is my belief, my daily practice. This Buddhist monk, 57 years old now, finds that through my own little experience, through training, through analytical meditation I have changed. If we make the attempt we can change. We can improve ourselves.

We are human beings, our basic nature is that of love and compassion. When we see a tree with some branches dying we are sad. When we see greenery and buds growing into flowers we feel positive and happy. In human nature, there is a natural feeling for living things. I think the time has come to think about the basic cause of our suffering.

2
INTERVIEW TO SUNDAY[1]

Sunday: *You had predicted in 1990 that Tibet would be free in the next five to ten years. Do you see any indications which point towards such a possibility?*

The Dalai Lama: I believe in a few years time things may change, especially because the Soviet Union, which was the first communist country, has collapsed. In fact, the authoritarian systems throughout the world have collapsed except in China. But even in that country, the people's desire for democracy and freedom is increasing. I think the democratic movement is gaining strength both inside and outside China. I only pray that the democratic movement should be conducted through non-violence. If the movement turns violent, the common people will suffer.

As for the Tibetans, most of them are against Chinese rule, including those in high positions. And indications are that the Chinese, despite their reluctance, are having to follow a more liberal economic policy. This will have political effects as well.

Q. *But do you see any indications that Tibet will be freed of Chinese rule through your spiritual insight?*

A. Personally I claim no such quality. But some of my friends say there are some indications at the mysterious level.

Q. *Do you think your prolonged absence from Tibet has affected the morale of your people?*

A. I don't think so—not at all. There's no demoralisation. Perhaps, some very old people feel very worried that before they die, they may not see the Dalai Lama. But that's demoralisation at a personal level. But for the nation as a whole, nothing like that is happening.

[1] In the second week of August, 1992 the Dalai Lama conducted the Kalachakra initiation at Rekong Peo in Kinnaur, Himachal Pradesh. The ceremony, which had a special significance for world peace, was attended not only by those living in India, but by people from all over the world. This interview was given to Avirook Sen.

Q. *Have you contemplated returning to Tibet in the near future?*

A. In fact, two years ago, I expressed my desire to visit Tibet. I'm still very keen to make a short visit. This will create some positive atmosphere. This is my feeling.

Q. *Your path to freedom is, by your own admission, very similar to Mahatma Gandhi's. But he was operating from inside his country, so there's a difference in your approach ...*

A. That's true. But the aggressor was different. In the case of the British imperialists, there was at least the independence of the judiciary. And also, India is much bigger than Britain.

   In our case, under the communists, there's no independent judiciary. Neither is there a special court where you can get justice. In fact, in 1950, when the Chinese aggression reached Lhasa, I left the country for some time and returned after a few months in the hope that work could be done within Tibet.

   In 1956, when I was in India, I spent some time with Jawaharlal Nehru. On two occasions we had long discussions. I also received a lot of advice from the old Gandhian freedom fighters. They all said that I should return to Tibet and carry on the freedom struggle from there. I did exactly that. But there were no results. So, finally in 1959, when there were no alternatives, I went into exile.

Q. *What do you feel about India's stand on Tibet? New Delhi seems to be willing to extend humanitarian support, but keeps mum politically. Do you agree?*

A. Yes, India seemed to be scared of a Chinese backlash. But you see, in India, a policy was framed in the early fifties and now it is difficult to change that policy. That is a reality. I feel that India's stand regarding China, and particularly Tibet, is a little over-cautious.

Q. *The beating up of Tibetan demonstrators during Li Peng's visit to Delhi ...*

A. Yes, during Li Peng's visit to India, a lot of Tibetan refugees were beaten up by the police and the Tibetan people were upset at the high-handedness with which they were dealt with. I personally also felt sorry.

   But we must put such incidents on a broader perspective and not get upset by them. The relations between Tibet and India should not get strained. This is what I told the Tibetans in the camps in Delhi. If the Tibetans start feeling negatively towards India and Indian people, then they will only be helping the Chinese.

Q. *You are not just the religious head of Tibet, you are its temporal leader as well. This means you must be a politician. How do you mix religion and politics?*

A. No problems. I consider the national struggle, which is political, a spiritual task as well. So as a Buddhist monk, I do not find any contradiction in this kind of work. And in this case, our struggle also signifies a lot on the spiritual level. Also, I consider all my activities as part of my religious practice. If your motivation is sincere and compassionate, then all your activities become spiritual. This is my belief.

However, after we get independence, I have already decided that I will not take up any kind of leadership. I will live as an ordinary Tibetan citizen or just as a simple Buddhist monk.

Q. *Have you mobilised enough international opinion for your cause? Do you think the West is becoming more aware of Tibet?*

A. Oh Yes! Many countries have even passed parliamentary resolutions in our favour. However, we need more support. And the most important thing is that historically and culturally, Tibet and India are inseparable. Tibet's interest is India's interest and vice-versa.

I am very much aware of this, so wherever there's change of government in India, I write a letter to the new Prime Minister. When Morarji Desai become P.M., in his reply to my letter, he said Tibet and India are two branches of one Bodhi tree. His description is meaningful. After all, you see, the Tibetan civilisation began since Buddhism flourished in Tibet. We almost became followers of Indian spiritualism. Among all the Buddhist countries in the region—Thailand, Burma and Sri Lanka—I think Tibet adopted the Indian religious tradition most closely. The whole Tibetan civilisation, the way of life, is based on the Indian tradition.

Q. *How would you like to be remembered?*

A. Just as a human being. Perhaps as a human being who often smiled.

3

NEW YEAR MESSAGE, 1995

My ideas about universal responsibility have evolved from the ancient traditions of India. As a Buddhist monk my entire training has its roots in the culture of this great country. In a letter he once wrote to me, Mr. Morarji Desai expressed the situation very beautifully, "One Bodhi tree has two branches, that is India and Tibet." From a cultural and spiritual point of view we are like one people. Emotionally too I feel very close to this country. In ancient times India produced many great thinkers, whose insights contributed much to humanity's spiritual evolution. Even today, India is an inspiration, for in the face of great odds, democracy thrives.

Ahimsa or non-violence is a powerful idea that Mahatma Gandhi made familiar throughout the world. Non-violence does not mean the mere absence of violence. It is something more positive, more meaningful than that. The true expression of non-violence is compassion. Some people seem to think that compassion is just a passive emotional response instead of a rational stimulus to action. To experience genuine compassion is to develop a feeling of closeness to others combined with a sense of responsibility for their welfare. True compassion develops when we accept that other people are just like ourselves in wanting happiness and not wanting suffering, and that they have every right to pursue these.

Compassion compels us to reach out to all living beings, including our so-called enemies, those people who upset or hurt us. Irrespective of what they do to you, if you remember that all beings like you are only trying to be happy, you will find it much easier to develop compassion towards them. Usually your sense of compassion is limited and biased. We extend such feelings only towards our family and friends or those who are helpful to us. People we perceive as enemies and others to whom we are indifferent are excluded from our concern. That is not genuine compassion. True compassion is universal in scope. It is accompanied by a feeling of responsibility. To act altruistically, concerned only for the welfare of others, with no selfish or ulterior motives, is to affirm a sense of universal responsibility.

As a Buddhist monk, the cultivation of compassion is an important part of my daily practice. One aspect involves merely sitting quietly in my room, meditating. That can be very good and very comfortable, but the true aim of cultivating compassion is to develop the courage to think of others and to do something for them. For example, as the Dalai Lama, I have a responsibility to my people, some of whom are living as refugees and some of whom have remained in Tibet under Chinese occupation. This responsibility means that I have to confront and deal with many problems.

Certainly, it is easier to meditate than to actually do something for others. Sometimes I feel that to merely meditate on compassion is to take the passive option. Our meditation should form the basis for action, for seizing the opportunity to do something. The meditator's motivation, his sense of universal responsibility, should be expressed in deeds.

Whether we are rich or poor, educated or uneducated, whatever our nationality, colour, social status or ideology may be, the purpose of our lives is to be happy. For this, material development plays an important role. But at the same time it is more important to cultivate a corresponding inner development. Unless our minds are stable and calm, no matter how comfortable our physical condition may be, they will give us no pleasure. Therefore, the key to a happy life, now and in the future, is to develop a happy mind.

One of the most powerful emotions disturbing our mental tranquillity is hatred. The antidote is compassion. We should not think of compassion as being only the preserve of the sacred and religious. It is one of our basic human qualities. Human nature is essentially loving and gentle. I do not agree with people who assert that human beings are innately aggressive, despite the apparent prevalence of anger and hatred in the world. From the moment of our birth we require love and affection. This is true of us all, right up to the day we die. Without love we could not survive. Human beings are social creatures and a concern for each other is the very basis of our life together. If we stop to think, compared to the numerous acts of kindness on which we depend and which we take so much for granted, acts of hostility are relatively few. To see the truth of this we only need to observe the love and affection parents shower on their children and the many other acts of loving and caring that we take for granted.

Anger may seem to offer an energetic way of getting things done, but such a perception of the world is misguided. The only certainty about anger and hatred is that they are destructive; no good ever comes of them.

If we live our lives continually motivated by anger and hatred, even our physical health deteriorates. On the other hand, people who remain calm and open-minded, motivated by compassion are mentally free of anxiety and physically healthy.

At a time when people are so conscious of maintaining their physical health by controlling their diets, exercising and so forth, it makes sense to try to cultivate the corresponding positive mental attitudes too.

So far I have mentioned how a positive outlook can affect an individual. It is also true that the more compassionate a society, the happier its members will be.

The development of human society is based entirely on people helping each other. Every individual has a responsibility to help guide the community in the right direction and we must each assume that responsibility.

If we lose this essential humanity that is our foundation, society as a whole will collapse. What point will there then be in pursuing material improvement and from whom can we demand our rights? Action motivated by compassion and responsibility will ultimately bring good results. Anger and jealousy may be effective in the short term, but will ultimately bring us only trouble.

Fear is another major obstacle to our inner development. Fear arises when we view everyone else with suspicion. It is compassion that creates the sense of trust that allows us to open up to others and reveal our problems, doubts and uncertainties. Without it we cannot communicate with each other honestly and openly. Therefore, developing compassion is one of the most effective ways of reducing fear.

Compassion is fundamentally a human quality; so its development is not restricted to those who practice religion. Nevertheless, religious traditions have a special role to play in encouraging its development.

The common factor among all religions is that, whatever the philosophical differences between them, they are primarily concerned with helping their followers become better human beings. Consequently, all religions encourage the practice of kindness, generosity and concern for others.

This is why I find conflicts based on religious differences to be so sad and futile.

It is my belief, for the world in general, that compassion is more important than "religion". The population of our planet is over five billion. Of these, perhaps one billion actively and sincerely follow a formal religion. The remaining over four billion are not believers in the true sense. If we regard the development of compassion and other good qualities as the business only of religion, these over four billion, the majority, will be excluded. As brothers and sisters, members of our great human family, every one of these people has the potential to be inspired by the need for compassion. And compassion can be developed and nurtured without following or practising a particular religion.

Today, we are faced with many global problems such as poverty, overpopulation and the destruction of environment. These are problems that we have to address together. No single community or nation can expect to solve them on its own. This indicates how inter-dependent our world has become. The global economy too is becoming increasingly integrated so that the results of an election in one country can affect the stock market of another.

In ancient times, each village was more or less self-sufficient and independent. There was neither the need nor the expectation of cooperation with others outside the village. You survived by doing everything yourself. The situation now has completely changed. It has become very old-fashioned to think only in terms of my nation or my country, let alone my village. Universal responsibility is the real key to overcoming our problems.

Modern India is confronted by many problems. New initiatives and ideas will be required to deal with them. Because of its respected stature and ancient heritage, India has a responsibility not only to ensure the future happiness of its own people, but also to provide leadership in the world. When India was struggling for freedom, individuals who really cared for the welfare of the people came forward at enormous personal sacrifices to take the lead.

They possessed the courage and determination to face hardship. Now, may be more than in the past, there is great need for such kinds of dedicated and honest people. It is not a time for such individuals to retire in search of their own narrow happiness. India needs people who can integrate its rich heritage with the modern world, and who have the courage to forgo immediate personal concerns for the greater good. This would indeed be a fitting expression of universal responsibility.

4

HUMAN RIGHTS AND THE FUTURE OF TIBET

The promotion of human rights is of universal interest because it is in the inherent nature of all human beings to yearn for freedom, equality and dignity. All people are born into this increasingly interdependent world as part of one great human family. Regardless of class, education, ethnicity, religion or ideology, each of us is ultimately a human being like everyone else. Each of us, therefore, has the right to pursue the happy, fulfilling life that human rights protect.

It is often the most gifted, dedicated and creative members of society who are the targets of human rights abuses. Human rights violations, therefore, obstruct a country's political, social and cultural development. Both individuals and society as a whole suffer from these human rights violations. Members of the academic world understand and appreciate how freedom is necessary if humans are to use their unique intelligence to understand themselves, their society and their environment. Their support is therefore needed not only for the Tibetan people, but for all human beings who are presently prevented from exercising the rights and freedoms that many take for granted.

The protection of fundamental human rights in all communities, by preserving the ability of different cultures to freely express themselves, should produce on the international level a rich diversity of cultures and religions. Underlying diversity are, therefore, basic principles that bind together all members of the human family. The mere maintenance of a diversity of traditions, however, does not justify violations of human rights. Although social, gender and class discrimination are traditional in some regions, these forms of behaviour must change if they are inconsistent with universally recognized human rights. The universal principle of the equality of human beings must take precedence over strict cultural preservation in this context.

Some governments contend that the standards of human rights defined in the Universal Declaration of Human Rights are Western concept, and therefore do not apply to Asia and other parts of the Third world, both of which have experienced different patterns of cultural, social and economic developments from the West. I do not share this interpretation of human rights, and I am convinced that the majority of the world's population does not support it either. General standards of human rights apply to the people of all countries because, regardless of their cultural background, all humans share an inherent yearning for freedom, equality and dignity. Democracy and respect for fundamental human rights are as important to Africans and Asians as they are to Europeans and Americans.

Moreover, there is no contradiction between the implementation of successful economic development programmes and the protection of human rights. In fact, the freedom of speech and association is vital in promoting a country's economic growth. In Tibet, for example, unsuitable economic policies are implemented by the Chinese authorities, and continue long after they have failed to produce benefits, because the people are not free to speak out against the government's programmes.

A lasting effort to protect human rights in a global democratic future also entails world wide demilitarization. Although this may sound idealistic, it is important to re-evaluate the concept of the military establishments for it is not only during times of war that military establishments are destructive. By design, military establishments are the single greatest violators of human rights and the most regular opponents of democracy. The existence of a powerful army increases the chance of military dictatorship. If we truly believe that a dictatorship is the most despicable and destructive form of government, and the very antithesis of democracy, then we must recognise that in the contemporary world, powerful military establishments can only contribute to the formation of tyranny. Many dictators in the developing world have only retained power because they controlled the weapons and armaments supplied by countries of the developed world. Tremendous amounts of money have been used to purchase guns rather than to feed people and meet basic human and environmental needs. It is tragic that in many countries there are no shortages of guns and bullets, but there are frequently severe shortages of food for people. Compared to its neighbouring countries in which the military plays a dominant role, Costa Rica (a country which was

demilitarized) had done very well in areas such as education and health.

It becomes incumbent upon us to support universal human rights once we accept three fundamental notions: all people have an equal right to live in peace and happiness; people can only be happy when able to realize their inherent human affinities for freedom, equality and dignity; and protection of human rights is a precondition for the expression of natural affinities. Moreover, since those deprived of their rights are often also those least able to speak up for themselves, the responsibility for the protection of universal human rights rests with those who already enjoy these freedoms.

Living in exile, I enjoy freedom of speech and movement. For over three decades, I have tried my best to work for the freedom of the six million Tibetan people who have been suffering under the yoke of tyranny. As a result of the Chinese invasion and the ensuing occupation, over one million Tibetans have died of unnatural causes and over 6,000 of our monasteries, the learning centres and repositories of our culture, have been destroyed. Tibetans have been detained merely for expressing their determination to be free. Moreover, the national and cultural identity of Tibet has been subject to attack and abuse and, due to an influx of Chinese settlers, Tibetans are becoming a minority in their own land. There is much in the rich Tibetan religious, cultural and medical traditions that can be of benefit to the wider world. The world would be poorer if these should be entirely lost. But, over and above that, the six million Tibetan people have a right simply to live as human beings.

Following the Chinese army occupation, I was forced to leave my homeland in 1959. Over 100,000 fellow Tibetans followed me into exile in India, Nepal and other parts of the globe. Since that time, I have pursued a course of non-violence and have tried in every way I know to find some reasonable accommodation with the Chinese government so that the Tibetan people can resume a life of peace with dignity.

In 1979, Deng Xiaoping stated that the People's Republic of China was willing to discuss and resolve with Tibetans all issues other than the complete independence of Tibet. We responded positively to the principles advanced by Deng in the hope that the Chinese government would be genuinely committed to negotiating on all other matters concerning the future of the six million Tibetans.

We were able to send four fact-finding delegation to Tibet to see the actual situation there. Our delegation members were greeted, welcomed

and even mobbed by thousands of excited Tibetans wherever they went. When the first delegation arrived in Lhasa, the capital of Tibet, in August 1979, Tibetans disobeyed an order to stay away and huge crowds filled the streets. A member of the Chinese cadre was reported to have said, "The efforts of the last 20 years have been wasted in the single day." Apparently, this show of support outraged the Chinese leadership which, since the return of our last official delegation in October 1980, has refused to permit any more delegations from our side to central Tibet.

Tibetans were given a glimmer of hope in 1980 when Hu Yaobang, the General Secretary of the Chinese Communist Party, launched a limited policy of liberalization. While visiting Tibet, he publicly expressed shock at the poverty he witnessed, asking in a historic speech, never publicly released in its entirety, whether all the money sent to Tibet had been thrown in the river. He promised the withdrawal of 85 per cent of the Chinese cadres stationed in Tibet.

After an initial period in which we were able to send two high-level delegations to Beijing in 1982 and 1984 to engage in exploratory talks with the Chinese leadership, the prospects for direct talks dwindled. The Chinese failure to show any seriousness in negotiating with us compelled me to make public my Five-Point Peace Plan[1], which I did in 1987 at the invitation of the US Congressional Human Rights Caucus. I proposed that Tibet become a demilitarized zone of peace, a notion that continues to be the basis of my future vision for Tibet. I have always envisioned the future of my country as a neutral demilitarized zone of peace where people live in harmony with nature. I have called this a zone of Ahimsa, or non-violence. This idea is not merely a dream, it is precisely the way Tibetans tried to live for over a thousand years before Tibet was ruthlessly invaded by China in 1949/50. For at least the last three hundred years, Tibet has had virtually no army; Tibet gave up war as an instrument of national policy.

In June 1988, I delivered what has come to be known as the Strasbourg Proposal during an address to members of the European Parliament in Strasbourg, France.[2] In an effort to initiate substantive negotiations, I proposed that Tibet become a self-governing political entity in association with China. Since then, there has been some confusion over my stand on negotiations with China. Recently, certain

[1&2]*Vide* "The Spirit of Tibet: Universal Heritage", pp. 156-62 and 163-7.

statements made by the Chinese government, reported in a section of the press, have misrepresented my stand. In October 1991, in an address at Yale University,[3] I made a fresh overture to the Chinese government by suggesting I make a personal visit to Tibet, in the company of senior Chinese leaders and journalists, to make an on-the-spot assessment of the actual situation. In this instance, as before, the Chinese made such a proposed visit conditional upon my acceptance of Tibet as "a part of China" and upon the cessation of activities which they regard as "separatist". According to the official Chinese media, Chinese President Jian Zemin said in Beijing this July that I was welcome to return to Tibet "at any time" once I abandoned visions of Tibetans Independence. While I very much want to visit Tibet, the main issue should never be centred around me. I have stated this repeatedly in response to the frequent attempts by Chinese government officials to reduce the issue to my "repatriation". My concern is the welfare of the six million Tibetans living in Tibet and the protection of their rights, freedom and distinct culture.

Tibet has a long history of independence. There is no doubt that the Tibetans constitute a distinct people with their own culture, language and religion. Even geographically, Tibet is distinct from China. However, because of the gravity of the current situation in Tibet—particularly the threat posed to the distinct Tibetan culture and national identity by the continued influx of Chinese into Tibet and because of the political constraints I face, I have adopted a middle-of-road approach of reconciliation and compromise in the hope that I may in this way secure a peaceful and negotiated resolution of the Tibetan problem.

It has always been my belief that the only way to achieve a lasting solution to the Tibetan-Chinese conflict is through earnest, substantive negotiations. While it is the overwhelming desire of the Tibetan people to regain their national independence, I have over the years repeatedly and publicly stated that I am willing to enter into negotiations and work from an agenda that does not include independence.

Ever since direct contact with the Chinese leadership was established in 1979, I have consistently and vigorously pursued this approach. My official statements on March 10, the anniversary of the Tibetan national Uprising, and the proposals I have put forward since 1979 clearly demonstrate our willingness to seek and facilitate a peaceful and negotiated settlement of the Tibetan issue based on Mr. Deng Xiaoping's

[3] Ibid. pp. 168-74.

statement to my personal emissary in 1979 that "except for the independence of Tibet all other questions can be negotiated".

In June 1988, in Strasbourg, I proposed a framework for negotiations. This proposal aims at securing the right for Tibetans to govern their own country while allowing China to retain responsibility for Tibet's foreign policy. China would maintain a restricted number of military installations in Tibet for defence purposes until a regional peace conference is convened and Tibet is eventually transformed into a neutral and de-militarized peace sanctuary. The Strasbourg proposal clearly seeks a "self-governing, democratic political entity" for the whole of Tibet consisting of the three provinces—U-Tsang, Kham and Amdo in association with China.

On many different occasions, I had conveyed these ideas to the Chinese leadership through both personal letters and my personal emissary and delegations, who travelled to Beijing before I made these views public. Having informed the Chinese government of my position on negotiations, I was hopeful that a forthright response would come from the Chinese so that we could enter into serious negotiations. Unfortunately, the Chinese government has yet to accept any of my proposals and initiatives and has yet to enter into any substantive negotiations with my representatives, who remain prepared to meet with Chinese representatives at any time.

I am deeply concerned about the Chinese government's real intentions with regard to Tibet. While repeating the official position that China is prepared to negotiate, the Chinese government refuses to hold any substantial discussion on the problem. Meanwhile, they flood Tibet with Chinese, reducing the Tibetans to an insignificant minority in their own country. Some of my friends call this the Chinese "final solution" to the Tibetan people. The magnitude and seriousness of the problems in Tibet have escalated. Recent developments have been marked by an intensification of Chinese suppression, the marginalization of the Tibetan people in their own country, and the undermining and destruction of Tibet's unique culture and religion.

With the appointment of a new Chinese party Secretary in the so-called Tibet Autonomous Region, a radical shift in political character of the Chinese presence in Tibet has taken place. The Chinese government has abandoned their publicly stated policy of progressively reducing the number of Chinese administrators in Tibet. They are now appointing

Chinese to all major departments including key positions at the county level, where for many years the policy had been to appoint Tibetans. They are thus enhancing the drive to assimilate and absorb the Tibetan region into China. The new party Secretary, Chen Kuiyuan, has already pursued a tough course in Inner Mongolia, where he acquired a reputation as an administrator with little regard and consideration for local autonomy, culture and sentiments. His appointment and the subsequent policy shifts in Tibet are clear reflections of the Chinese government's hardening position. Furthermore, these indications corroborate the contents of classified Chinese documents revealing their intent to transfer even larger number of Chinese into Tibet in order to make it demographically "impossible for Tibetans to rise up" and to create disunity and disruptions in the Tibetan Government.

Tibet—an ancient nation with its unique culture and civilization—is quickly disappearing. The mortal danger to the survival of Tibet and its distinct cultural heritage and national identity is increasing day by day. In my endeavour to protect my nation from this threat, I have always sought to be guided by realism and patience. I have tried in every way I know to find some reasonable accommodation with the Chinese government in a spirit of reconciliation and compromise.

By 1987, I had broadly outlined my vision for a future Tibet in the Five-Point Peace Plan, the concepts of which were further elaborated in my Strasbourg proposal in 1988 and later in a plan called, "Guidelines for the Future Policy of Tibet and the Basic Features of its Constitution".[4] In this last document, I proposed that Tibet should ultimately be governed by a multi-party parliamentary democracy. In line with this system, a duly elected citizen of Tibet would become the supreme head of the country, or self governing region, and would subsequently assume the ensuing responsibilities as head of state. The legislative, judicial and executive organs of the Tibetan government would be independent and vested with equal power and authority. As I have often stated, I am not concerned about labels—independence, self-governing, in association, etc. The most important thing is that Tibetans govern themselves, and be able to determine a form of government which provides real freedoms, openness and democratic processes.

Tibet belongs to the Tibetans, especially to those who have remained in Tibet. Therefore those within Tibet would bear the main responsibility

[4] ibid p.186.

for establishing a democratic Tibet, in particular, because of their experience and knowledge, those Tibetan officials who are presently serving under the Chinese occupation should in the beginning hold the responsibility for running the government. It is therefore important that these officials eschew all feelings of uncertainty and doubt over their role in a democratic Tibet so that they might dedicate themselves to regaining the freedom of Tibet while simultaneously making efforts to improve the quality of its administration. Some Tibetans have had to involuntarily say or do things under coercive Chinese influence. I see no purpose in inquiring into their past activities. What is vitally important is the happiness of the Tibetans as a whole. To this end, all must stand united. All Tibetans must assume the responsibility to transform the present totalitarian system, which denies essential freedoms to the people, into a genuinely democratic federal system that guarantees the participation by all Tibetans in their governance.

Once Tibet regains its freedom, I will not accept any political status in the future Tibetan government on the basis of the traditional system. I have not taken this decision lightly, since all Tibetans place great faith and hope in me. For my part, I have an unflinching determination to aid the Tibetans, both politically and religiously. However, in order for Tibet to be able to exist as an equal member in today's community of nations, it is extremely important that it not be dependent on a single person, but rather that it reflect the collective consciousness of the Tibetan people. This requires the Tibetan people to take full responsibility for their own political destiny. Hence, it is in both the immediate and future interest of the Tibetan people that I do not hold a political position in the government.

On our return to a free Tibet following the withdrawal of the Chinese regime, there will be a transitional period before the finalization of the Tibetan constitution. During the transition, the existing Tibetan administration would continue to function and a president would be appointed as the interim head of state. He or she would be vested with all the political powers I currently hold. Simultaneously, the Tibetan Government-in-Exile would renounce its existence. Each official of the dissolved administration would bear the same responsibility for the affairs of Tibet as any other Tibetan. Though members of the Tibetan Government-in-Exile would not be entitled to any special privileges by virtue of their previous positions, they may, according to their desire and qualifications, voluntarily accept positions assigned to them by the transitional administration.

The main responsibility of the transitional government would be to create a Constituent Assembly to finalize Tibet's constitution. The comprehensive draft of the democratic constitution for a free Tibet is under preparation. We are circulating guidelines for the framework of the constitution in order to create awareness and to encourage the formulation of opinions regarding the type of democratic government Tibet should have.

I will continue with my sincere efforts to resolve the crisis in Tibet through negotiations. However, it has now become obvious and clear that our efforts alone, based on a spirit of reconciliation and compromise, are not sufficient to bring the Chinese government to the negotiating table. Moreover, in light of alarming developments in Tibet, I cannot continue to simply hope and wait for a positive signal from Beijing when the continuation of the present situation only enables China to complete the colonization and absorption to Tibet. I have, therefore, called for concerted efforts by the international community to press the Chinese leadership to enter into substantive negotiations with us. If this approach does not bring about a positive result, then, as I declared in my statement of March 10, 1994,[5] to commemorate the thirty-fifth anniversary of the Tibetan national uprising day, I will consult my people over the future course of our struggle for freedom. My commitment to non-violence, however, is fundamental, and there will be no deviation from this path under my leadership.

[5]*Vide* the following item

5
MARCH 10 STATEMENT, 1994

Today, as we observe the 35th anniversary of our National Uprising Day, I wish to take stock of our 14 years' effort to find a peaceful and realistic solution to the Tibetan issue through honest negotiations with the Chinese government. In my endeavour to restore freedom, peace and dignity to our country and people, I have always sought to be guided by realism, patience and vision.

For the past 14 years, I have not only declared my willingness to enter into negotiations but have also made maximum concessions in a series of initiatives and proposals which clearly lie within the framework for negotiations as stated by Deng Xiaoping in 1979, that "except for the independence of Tibet, all other questions can be negotiated". The ideas put forward in Five Point Peace Plan for Tibet in 1987 and the Strasbourg Proposal 1988 envisage a solution which does not ask for the complete independence of Tibet. However, the Chinese government has even refused to enter into negotiations of any kind. It has also avoided discussing any question of substance, insisting that the only issues to be resolved are those pertaining to my personal return to Tibet. The issue is not about my return to Tibet. I have stated this time and again. The issue is the survival of the six million Tibetan people along with the protection of our distinct culture, identity and civilization.

I have made it clear that the negotiations must centre around ways to end China's population transfer policy, which threatens the very survival of the Tibetan people, respect for Tibetans' fundamental human rights and entitlement to democratic freedom, the de-militarization and de-nuclearization of Tibet, the restoration of the Tibetan people's control over all matters affecting their own affairs, and the protection of Tibet's natural environment. Moreover, I have always emphasized that any negotiation must comprise the whole of Tibet, not just the area which China calls the "Tibet Autonomous Region"

I have maintained this approach for the last 14 years in spite of the disappointment and criticism expressed by many Tibetans to my moderate stand. I have not forgotten that 1.2 million Tibetans have died and that Tibet has suffered immeasurably since the occupation of our country by Communist China. I also know that every Tibetan hopes and prays for the full restoration of our nation's independence.

Nevertheless, I had hoped that my middle-way approach would eventually create an atmosphere of mutual trust conducive to fruitful negotiations and exert a restraining influence on the repressive Chinese policies in Tibet. Here I appreciate the many Tibetans who have supported my initiatives and felt they were a practical necessity.

The Chinese government has rejected my overtures one after another and has consistently attempted to confuse the real issue. Meanwhile, the magnitude and gravity of the situation inside Tibet has dramatically escalated. Developments in Tibet have been marked by an intensification of the Chinese policy of suppression, the marginalisation of the Tibetan people in our own country, the gradual extermination of our unique culture and religion, and the destruction and exploitation of Tibet's environment.

I must now recognize that my approach has failed to produce any progress either for substantive negotiations or in contributing to the overall improvement of the situation in Tibet. Moreover, I am conscious of the fact that a growing number of Tibetans, both inside as well as outside Tibet, have been disheartened by my conciliatory stand not to demand complete independence for Tibet. Because of my statements, some Tibetans have come to believe that there is no hope at all of the Tibetan people regaining their basic rights and freedoms. This and the lack of any concrete results from my conciliatory approach towards Chinese government over the past 14 years have caused disillusionment and undermined the resolve of some Tibetans.

Internationally, my initiatives and proposals have been endorsed as realistic and reasonable by many governments, parliaments, and non-governmental organisations. But despite the growing support of the international community, the Chinese government has not responded constructively.

I have left no stone unturned in my attempts to reach an understanding with the Chinese. We have had to place our hopes on international support and help in bringing about meaningful negotiations, to which I still remain committed. If this fails, then I will no longer be able to pursue this policy with a clear conscience. I feel strongly that it would then be my responsibility, as I have stated many times in the past, to consult my people on the future course of our freedom struggle. Just as the late Indian Prime Minister, Jawaharlal Nehru, stated in the Indian parliament on December 7, 1950, I too have always maintained that the final voice with regard to Tibet should be the voice of the Tibetan people.[6] Whatever the outcome of such a consultation, it will serve as a guideline for our future dealings with China and the re-orientation of the course of our freedom struggle.

I continue to remain committed to finding a peaceful and negotiated resolution to the issue of Tibet with the Chinese government directly. But the Chinese are merely paying lip service to this approach. It is evident that only increased international political and economic pressure can bring a sense of urgency to bear on the Chinese leadership not merely to pay lip service but to resolve the problem of Tibet peacefully and amicably. The tragedy of Tibet can be relieved through the determined and concerted efforts of various governments and NGOs championing human rights, liberty and democracy the world over.

If the Tibetan issue can be resolved peacefully, through mutual openness and understanding, I am convinced that it will help alleviate the anxiety felt in the minds of the six million residents of Hong Kong. It will also have a positive effect on China's relationship with Taiwan and enhance its international image.

Today, we remember those brave Tibetans who fought and died for the cause of our nation and those who are languishing in Chinese prisons. We also pay our respects to our courageous brothers and sisters in Tibet who are continuing the struggle for the freedom of our people under extremely adverse conditions. The course of history and the present world atmosphere are favourable to the aspirations of our nation. Our cause is gathering momentum. Fearful of these developments, China has now formulated policies to undermine our Administration-in-Exile as well as to create discord and division in our community. Therefore, every one of us must be alert and renew our commitment to the just cause of our country.

I firmly believe that the day is close when our beloved Land of Snow will no longer be politically subjugated, culturally ravaged, and economically and environmentally exploited and devastated. Our dedication,

---

[6]*Vide* "The Spirit of Tibet: Universal Heritage" p. 19.

sacrifice and hard work will eventually lead our captive nation to freedom and peace in dignity. However, it is important that our struggle must be based on non-violence.

On behalf of all the Tibetan people, I want to take this opportunity to express our deep appreciation and gratitude to our many friends throughout the world for their support of our cause. I must also thank the many parliaments and governments that have started to take a serious look at the Tibetan problem. Another positive development of recent years is support for our cause even amongst the Chinese people. For example, a long letter written on October 5, 1992, by the well-known Chinese dissident Wei Jingsheng, to Deng Xiaoping, speaking out against his government's unjust claims over Tibet and their misguided policies there, has just become public. These expressions are the manifestations of genuine human respect for truth and justice. I take this opportunity especially to thank our Chinese brothers and sisters the world over for their support and encouragement. Finally, I wish to reiterate our immense gratitude and appreciation to all the countries where Tibetan exiles have been given asylum, particularly to the people and government of this country, which has become a second home for the majority of the Tibetan in exile.

My prayers for the peace and welfare of all sentient beings.

6
MARCH 10 STATEMENT, 1995

The world is today undergoing major changes. While there is a spirit of reconciliation and peace emerging in many troubled parts of the world, unfortunately new conflicts are also breaking out. We have endeavoured to find a peaceful resolution to the Tibetan issue and hoped that positive changes would also come to Tibet. But, as we commemorate the 36th anniversary of our people's uprising, I must state with sadness that little has changed in our homeland and our people continue to suffer. In fact, the Chinese government has intensified its repression in Tibet. Recent Chinese policies demonstrate more clearly than ever their intention to resolve the question of Tibet through force, intimidation and population transfer.

The Chinese authorities have lately adopted a series of new measures to tighten political control in Tibet. Under a programme of "investigation and scrutiny" tighter security measures were imposed and a new crackdown on advocates of human rights and independence has been launched. Victims of this new political persecution include Tibetans who work for the preservation of Tibetan culture, which includes teaching the Tibetan language and opening private schools. Tibetan cadres and members of the Chinese Communist Party are made to undergo political re-education, reminiscent of the days of the Cultural Revolution. Those suspected of harbouring religious and national feelings are being purged. Monasteries have been raided by the People's Armed police and the chain of political arrests has been extended to rural areas. The rebuilding and construction of new monasteries has been prohibited and the admission of new monks and nuns stopped. Tibetan travel agents and tourist guides have been dismissed in order to control the flow of information and Tibetan children are no longer permitted to study abroad. Those who are presently studying abroad have been ordered to return.

At a high-level meeting in Beijing last July these policies were sanctioned and 62 new "economic development projects" in Tibet were announced. As in the past, these projects are designed primarily to increase the immigration of Chinese into Tibet and ultimately drown the Tibetans in a sea of Chinese. Similarly, China's proclaimed intention to build a railway to Central Tibet is particularly alarming. Under the present circumstances this will enable a dramatic acceleration of China's population transfer policy. We only need to look at the large influx of Chinese who are arriving by train every week in different parts of Eastern Turkistan to understand the impact such a railway will have on the survival of the Tibetan people with its unique cultural heritage.

Over the past 15 years, I have tried to resolve the Tibet-China problem in a spirit of genuine friendship and co-operation, discarding any feelings of enmity towards the Chinese. I have consistently and sincerely made attempts to engage the Chinese government in earnest negotiations over the future of Tibet. Regrettably China has rejected my proposals for a negotiated resolution of our problem. Instead she has set the pre-condition that I formally recognise Tibet to be "an inseparable part of China" before any negotiations can start. The true nature of the historical relationship of Tibet and China is best left for Tibetan and Chinese historians to study objectively. I also encourage other scholars, as well as international jurists and their institutions, to study the history of Tibet and draw their unbiased conclusions.

In the past I have deliberately restrained myself from emphasising the historical and legal status of Tibet. It is my belief that it is more important to look forward to the future than dwell in the past. Theoretically speaking it is not impossible that the six million Tibetans could benefit from joining the one billion Chinese of their own free will, if a relationship based on equality, mutual benefit and mutual respect could be established. If China wants Tibet to stay with China, then she must create the necessary conditions. However, the reality today is that Tibet is an occupied country under colonial rule. This is the essential issue which must be addressed and resolved through negotiations.

In the past few years our cause has gained increasing international importance and support. This is reflected in the United Nation's debates on the situation in Tibet: in the General Assembly's Third Committee, in the Commission for Human Rights, and in the reports of the United

Nations' Rapporteurs. Last year I appealed to the international community for help in facilitating negotiations between my representatives and the Chinese government. A number of Asian and Western governments have supported my call for negotiations publicly and through diplomatic channels and have offered their good offices to bring them about. I take this opportunity to thank these governments for their support. It is important that the international community, and especially democratic countries, continue to send a clear message to China that their behaviour in Tibet is deplorable and that the question of Tibet must be resolved through peaceful negotiations without pre-conditions. The need to make real progress in resolving the problem of Tibet is urgent. The present lack of progress increases the danger of violent conflicts breaking out in Tibet.

Many Tibetans have voiced unprecedented criticism of my suggestion that we should compromise on the issue of total independence. Moreover, the failure of the Chinese government to respond positively to my conciliatory proposals has deepened the sense of impatience and frustration among my people. Therefore, I proposed last year that this issue be submitted to a referendum. However, as long as I lead our freedom struggle, there will be no deviation from the path of non-violence.

The referendum should seek to clarify the political course of our struggle. A thorough and honest discussion on the various options open to us must take place among the Tibetan people. I hope that this historic exercise will be carried out carefully and thoroughly. I realise that under the present conditions it would be impossible to hold a fair referendum inside Tibet. Nevertheless, we will be able to find ways to collect representative opinions from different parts of Tibet and to conduct the plebiscite among our exiled community.

While we prepare ourselves for this referendum, I also wish to state that I remain open to any Chinese overtures for negotiations. I am still committed to the spirit of my "middle way" approach, and I am hopeful that continued international efforts to persuade the Chinese government to enter into negotiations with us may eventually yield tangible results. Our negotiating team remains ready to resume talks any time at a mutually agreeable venue. Sooner or later, a flexible and open-minded Chinese leadership must realise the wisdom of resolving the issue of Tibet through negotiations in a spirit of reconciliation and compromise. This is the only proper way to ensure stability, which the Chinese leadership assert, is their primary concern. However, true stability must be based on the mutual trust, consent and benefit of all concerned, not on the use of force.

Tibet's geographic position in the heart of Asia gives it enormous strategic importance. For centuries Tibet acted as a buffer ensuring peace in the region. The implications of China's presence in Tibet go well beyond Tibet's borders. Over the last more than forty years Tibet has undergone an unprecedented militarisation. Coupled with the increased transfer of Chinese population into Tibet, this has changed the peaceful character of the Tibetan plateau. If this alarming trend continues, it will not only threaten the survival of the Tibetan people and their culture, but will have serious repercussions for the region as a whole.

Tibet's spiritual and cultural traditions have contributed to peace in Asia. Buddhism not only turned Tibetans into a peace loving nation following a period of great military might, but also spread from the Himalayas to Mongolia and other places in Central Asia and provided millions of people with a spiritual foundation of peace and tolerance. Buddhism is not alien to China, and I strongly believe that Buddhism can be of great service in providing spiritual values, peace of mind, contentment and self-discipline to millions of Chinese in the future.

With the occupation of Tibet, Tibetan Buddhism has been robbed of its cradle and homeland, not only violating the Tibet people's right to freedom of religion but also endangering the very survival of this spiritual and cultural tradition in Tibet and Central Asia. This is particularly true of China's policy of cutting Tibet up into many separate administrative units, most of which have been incorporated into neighbouring Chinese provinces. Historically, the contribution of Tibetans from these areas to Tibet's cultural and spiritual heritage has been immense. But as tiny minorities in Chinese provinces it will be very difficult for these Tibetans to preserve their Buddhist culture and distinct identity in the long term. The Tibetan entities outside the so-called Tibet Autonomous Region (TAR) comprise a larger portion of the Tibetan area and roughly four of the six million Tibetans. A solution to the question of Tibet cannot be found without all these parts of Tibet being incorporated into one Tibetan entity. This is essential to the survival of Tibetan culture.

Finally, I wish to pay homage to the brave men and women of Tibet, who have died for the cause of our freedom. I pray also for our compatriots who are enduring mental and physical suffering in Chinese prisons at this moment. Not one day passes without my fervent prayers for an early end to the suffering of our people. I believe that today the question is not whether Tibet will ever be free, but rather how soon.

With my prayers

The Dalai Lama
March 10, 1995

7

MESSAGE TO PEACE MARCHERS

February 22, 1995

Since the beginning of Tibet's tragedy, I have never wavered from my conviction in the ultimate triumph of our cause. This conviction is rooted in the justness of our cause and in the indomitable spirit of Tibetan people. Today, once again, hundreds of Tibetans have come forth to undertake a Peace March from Delhi to Lhasa risking possible arrest, beating and even one's life.

The Peace March has inspired many Tibetan supporters throughout the world. The initiative has infused Tibetans and friends with renewed vigour and determination.

I believe in and support non-violence and civil disobedience as a means to peacefully voice one's grievances. Tibetans in Tibet and in exile have a right to engage in non-violent activities to highlight the human suffering in occupied Tibet and to draw the attention of the world community to the threat to the survival of the Tibetan people with its unique cultural heritage.

The people of Tibet place tremendous trust in me and I am always conscious of the heavy responsibility I bear for the fate of our people and country. In fulfilling this responsibility, I have always sought to be guided in my approach by realism, practicality, patience and vision.

Many Tibetans feel a deep sense of impatience and frustration because of the lack of any real progress in finding a peaceful resolution to our problem. I have full understanding for this and I share with them the sense of urgency in our freedom struggle. But I cannot with a clear conscience let you embark on this initiative, before sharing my concerns with you. I particularly feel that the timing of this undertaking is politically inappropriate. When the right moment for such a movement comes in the future, I will myself participate in it.

Our freedom struggle has reached a critical juncture. Great changes are taking place in China and in many other parts of the world. Our activities need to take these changes into consideration. The effects and ramifications of our actions must ensure a positive impact—not just in terms of publicity but in creating a political environment conducive to achieving the aspirations of our people in the long run.

The spirit of the Peace March will surely inspire our people inside Tibet. There is little doubt that Tibetans in occupied Tibet will come forth in solidarity and support of the Peace March. This in turn will lead to another wave of "merciless repression". In recent times the repression and political persecution in Tibet have reached a new peak since martial law was lifted in May 1990. I feel that the Chinese authorities will have no hesitation to ruthlessly exploit this opportunity to destroy the Tibetan freedom movement inside Tibet.

Moreover, at this point of time any political unrest and instability in Tibet will have significant impact on events in China. Presently, China is in a state of transition and any such event in Tibet will be exploited by the hard-liners within the Chinese leadership to strengthen their position. This would be counter-productive to our endeavour to encourage a political environment conducive to a peaceful resolution of the Tibetan issue. I, therefore, feel this is not the right time for the Peace March.

Furthermore, despite the non-violent nature of the Peace March, confrontations with Indian and Nepalese authorities are bound to happen. The people and the government of India and Nepalese are sympathetic to the Tibetan people. They have sheltered, nourished and cared for the exiled Tibetans over the last 35 years. I strongly believe that these governments will come out in support of our cause when the right opportunity arises. It has always been my endeavour not to cause any unnecessary inconvenience and embarrassment to any third party, particularly to those that have been kind, generous and supportive of the Tibetan people.

I am happy that the organisers of the Peace March have considered positively my concerns and that they have now decided to postpone the Peace March to Lhasa and instead to undertake a march from Dharamsala to Delhi for peace in Tibet and the world.

                                                        The Dalai Lama

8
MARCH 10 STATEMENT, 1996

As we commemorate today the thirty seventh anniversary of the Tibetan People's uprising, we are witnessing a general hardening of Chinese government policy. This is reflected in an increasingly aggressive posture towards the peoples of Taiwan and Hong Kong and in intensified repression in Tibet. We also see rising fear and suspicion throughout the Asia-Pacific region and a worsening of relation between China and much of the rest of the world.

Within the context of this tense political atmosphere, Beijing has once again sought to impose its will on the Tibetan people by appointing a rival Panchen Lama. In doing so, it has chosen a course of total disregard both for the sentiments of the Tibetans in general and for Tibetan spiritual tradition in particular, despite my every effort to reach for some form of understanding and cooperation with the Chinese government. Significantly, the official Chinese media compares the present political climate in Tibet with that in Poland during the Solidarity years of the 1980's. This demonstrates a growing sense of insecurity on the part of the Chinese leadership as a result of which, through a continuing campaign of coercion and intimidation, Beijing has greatly reinforced its repression throughout Tibet. I am therefore saddened to have to report that the situation of our people in Tibet continues to deteriorate.

Nevertheless, it remains my strong conviction that change for the better is coming. China is at a critical junction: its society is undergoing profound changes and the country's leadership is facing the transition to a new generation. It is obvious too that the Tiananmen massacre has failed to silence the call for freedom, democracy and human rights in China. Moreover, the impressive democratization in process across the Taiwan Strait must further invigorate the democratic aspirations of the Chinese people. Indeed, Taiwan's historic first direct presidential elections later this month are certain to have an immense political and psychological impact on their minds. A transformation from the current totalitarian regime in Beijing into one which is more open, free and democratic is thus inevitable. The only outstanding question is how and when and whether the transition will be a smooth one.

As a human being, it is my sincere desire that our Chinese brothers and sisters enjoy freedom, democracy, prosperity and stability. As a Buddhist monk, I am of course concerned that a country which is home to almost a quarter of the world's entire population and which is on the brink of an epic change, should undergo that change peacefully. In view of China's huge population, chaos and instability could lead to large-scale bloodshed and tremendous suffering for millions of people. Such a situation would also have serious ramifications for peace and stability throughout the world. As a Tibetan, I recognize that the future of our country and our people depends to a great extent on what happens in China during the years ahead.

Whether the coming change in China brings new life and new hope for Tibet and whether China herself emerges as a reliable, peaceful and constructive member of the international community depends to a large degree on the extent to which the international community itself adopts responsible policies towards China. I have always drawn attention to the need to bring Beijing into the mainstream of world democracy and have spoken against any ideas of isolating and containing China. To attempt to do so would be morally incorrect and politically impractical. Instead, I have always counselled a policy of responsible and principled engagement with the Chinese leadership.

It became obvious during the Tiananmen movement that the Chinese people yearn for freedom, democracy, equality and human rights no less than any other people. Moreover, I was personally very moved to see that those young people, despite being taught that "political power comes out of the barrel of a gun" pursued their aims without resorting to violence. I, too, am convinced that non-violence is the appropriate way to bring about constructive political change.

Based on my belief in non-violence and in dialogue, I have consistently tried to engage the Chinese government in serious negotiations concerning the future of the Tibetan people. In order to find a mutually acceptable solution, I have adopted a 'middle-way' approach. This is also in response to, and within the framework of, Mr. Deng

Ziaoping's stated assurance that "anything except independence can be discussed and resolved". Unfortunately, the Chinese government's response to my many overtures has been consistently negative. But I remain confident that his successors will realize the wisdom of resolving the problem of Tibet through dialogue.

The Tibet issue will neither go away of its own accord, nor can it be wished away. As the past has clearly shown, neither intimidation nor coercion of the Tibetan people can force a solution. Sooner or later, the leadership in Beijing will have to face this fact. Actually, the Tibet problem represents an opportunity for China. If it were solved properly through negotiation, not only would it be helpful in creating a political atmosphere conducive to the smooth transition of China into a new era but also China's image throughout the world would be greatly enhanced. A properly negotiated settlement would furthermore have a strong, positive impact on the peoples of both Hong Kong and Taiwan and will do much to improve Sino-Indian relations by inspiring genuine trust and confidence.

For our part, we seek to resolve the issue of Tibet in a spirit of reconciliation, compromise and understanding. I am fully committed to the spirit of the 'middle-way approach'. We wish to establish a sustainable relationship with China based on mutual respect, mutual benefit and friendship. In doing so, we will think not only about the fundamental interests of the Tibetan people, but also take seriously the consideration of China's security concerns and her economic interests. Moreover, if our Buddhist culture can flourish once again in Tibet, we are confident of being able to make a significant contribution to millions of our Chinese brothers and sisters by sharing with them those spiritual and moral values which are so clearly lacking in China today.

Despite the absence of positive and conciliatory gestures from the Chinese government to my initiatives, I have always encouraged Tibetans to develop personal relationship with Chinese. I make it a point to ask the Tibetans to distinguish between the Chinese people and the policies of the totalitarian government in Beijing. I am thus happy to observe that there has been significant progress in our efforts to foster closer interaction amongst the people of our two communities, mainly between exile Tibetans and Chinese living abroad. Moreover, human rights activists and democrats within China, people like the brave Wei Jingsheng, are urging their leaders to respect the basic human rights of the Tibetan people and pledging their support for our right to self-rule. Chinese scholars outside China are discussing a constitution for a federated China which envisages a confederal status for Tibet. These are most encouraging and inspiring developments. I am, therefore, very pleased that the people-to-people dialogue between the Tibetans and Chinese is fostering a better understanding of our mutual concerns and interests.

In recent years we have also witnessed the growth of a world-wide grass-roots movement in support of our non-violent struggle for freedom. Reflecting this, many governments and parliaments have come forward with strong expressions of concern and support for our efforts. Notwithstanding the immediate negative reactions of the Chinese regime, I strongly believe that such expressions of international support are essential. They are vital in communicating a sense of urgency to the minds of leadership in Beijing and in helping persuade them to negotiate.

I would like to take this opportunity to thank the numerous individuals, also the members of governments, of parliaments, of non-governmental organisations and of religious orders who have supported my appeal for the safety and freedom of the young Panchen Lama, Gedhun Choekyi Nyima. I am grateful for their continued intervention and efforts on behalf of this child who must be the world's youngest political prisoner. I also wish to thank our supporters all over the world who are commemorating today's anniversary of the Tibetan people's uprising with peaceful activities in every part of the globe. I urge the Chinese government not to construe such support for Tibet as anti-Chinese. The purpose and aim of these activities is to appeal to the Chinese leadership and people to recognize the legitimate rights of the Tibetan people.

In conclusion, I am happy to state today that our exile community's experiment in democracy is progressing well without any major setbacks or difficulties. Last autumn, the Tibetans in exile participated in preliminary polls to nominate candidates for the Twelfth Assembly of the Tibetan People's Deputies, the Parliament-in-Exile. Next month, they return to the polls to elect the members themselves. This accords with my conviction that democracy is the best guarantee for the survival and future of the Tibetan people. Democracy entails responsibilities as well as rights. The success of our struggle for freedom will therefore depend directly on our ability to shoulder these collectively. It is thus my hope that the twelfth Assembly will emerge as a united, mature and dedicated representative of our people. This will ultimately depend on every franchised member of our community. Each one is called upon to cast his or her vote with an informed and unbiased mind, with a clear awareness of the need of the hour and with strong sense of individual responsibility.

  With my homage to the brave men and women of Tibet, who have died for the cause of our freedom, I pray for an early end to the suffering of our people.

The Dalai Lama

9

INTERVIEW TO "AUROVILLE TODAY"

Kottakarai Guest House,
December 24, 1993

Q. *In 1973 you met the Mother in Pondicherry. What are your recollections of that meeting?*

A. Yes, I remember that meeting quite clearly. She was sitting in her chair —it seemed it was difficult for her to speak—but the atmosphere around her was not only nice, but meaningful. There were two or three persons with me and I asked about the future. I can't remember her exact words but the meaning was that the future was hopeful and positive.

Q. *For Tibet or the whole world?*

A. For the whole world, for humanity.

Q. *Yesterday you visited the chamber of Matrimandir. What were your impressions?*

A. It's difficult to describe. The main hall which you have completed is very nice and inside it's very calm, very peaceful. I spent a few minutes in meditation.

Q. *Have you noticed any changes in Auroville since you were last here?*

A. One thing that has surprised me very much is that when I first came here the land was barren. I remember the Sun was out that day and I was wondering where the best place was to find some shade. Today you needn't worry about that!

It's full of trees, it's almost like a jungle! Now you're probably worried about snakes, and yesterday I even asked if there were any elephants here! Today in many parts of the world we're very concerned about deforestation. This type of project of restoration is really marvellous. If the people involved in this work here could use whatever experience they have gained, and find the opportunity to extend their work to a high altitude place like Ladakh, if it works there, we could adopt it in a future Tibet.

Also, I have found here a very good sense of community; you are a determined people, you have an objective, will and determination. I've also found you have an incredible relation with the local people and they participate fully. I feel this type of teamwork should spread to other places.

Q. *Do you see that we can help you in a future Tibet?*
A. Certainly. Your spirit of dedication, your vision and sense of community and your clear acceptance and realization of the value of spiritual things are very important. You see, there are many projects that are very good for material development but are often lacking in spiritual value or realization. In other cases, there is an emphasis on spiritual things but with a neglect of practical progress. Here I found a combination of the two. Certainly we can learn many things from you and the members of the community here can help us in many fields.

Q. *Do you feel that there is a new consciousness, a new force at work in the world?*
A. That's a difficult question. On the mysterious level sometimes I feel there may be some energies or forces, but it is difficult to be definite about it. One thing I believe is that if our mind remains calm when we are facing serious problems and difficulties, we have the ability to find different alternatives. We have such a wonderful human intelligence and imaginative power. So, therefore, when things become really desperate, it helps to open our mind. And today I think we are passing through exactly that kind of period of difficulty.

Q. *Is humanity at a crossroads?*
A. I think so, I think so.

Q. *What is the path that we should take?*
A. My basic belief lies in a combination of material and spiritual development. It is not necessary to be religious-minded, for even without religion there are many secular moral ethics and, I think, a secular spirituality. That means the basic human values such as compassion, love and a willingness to forgive. These I usually call the human spiritual qualities. I believe we learn these basic qualities from our parents, particularly from our mother, or anyone who shows love and compassion to you. We learn these deeper human values from that period, from birth. Religion comes later. Of course religion has a great potential to help humanity and these basic human qualities

can be strengthened by religious belief, but if we go deeper, even without religion there can be genuine spirituality.

Q. *Will traditional religions still have a role to play in the future?*

A. Sometimes I've described religion as a luxury item. Now for the survival of the individual or the survival of humanity or the world, religion has an important role to play. But we can also survive without religion, provided that the basic human qualities are there. Without these basic human qualities we cannot survive. Our whole future must be dependent on what I call these secular moral ethics. These are the foundations of human existence. In order to make clear these basic values and their importance I described religion as a luxury item. Many people consider that religion is not very relevant to their day-to-day life. Their attitude to religion is indifferent. Simultaneously these people don't care about human values such as love, compassion and forgiveness, and they confuse these values with religion. This is absolutely wrong. You can be a believer or an unbeliever, that is up to the individual, that's each person's right, but there is no choice between being a compassionate or non-compassionate person, as I believe that compassionate moderation is the basis of our happiness, our mental stability. And for our daily life as well as the world's future, mental stability and calmness of mind is a crucial factor for a good life, a positive life. World peace—peace with our fellow human beings, peace with animals, and peace with the environment—is much dependent on that kind of mental state.

Q. *How would you define the essence of Tibetan culture?*

A. Tibetan culture has developed due to many factors—environmental, climatic and others—but Buddhism is the major factor in the development of Tibet's unique culture, which I call a Buddhist culture. Even non-Buddhist Tibetans have adopted the mental attitudes and way of life of Buddhist culture. That culture is based on the practice of compassion and tolerance.

Q. *Is that culture under threat?*

A. Yes, of course. Quite strangely, outside Tibet, although we are not in our own country and are in a different environment, I think we've kept our Tibetan spiritual identity. Inside Tibet, because of the overall situation in Tibet which is very tense—but where of course the Buddhist faith as well as the feeling for freedom is very strong—the

Tibetan people's behaviour sometimes seems less tolerant, they immediately lose their temper and their emotional control over small incidents. This I feel is a clear indication of how much damage is happening inside of Tibet.

Q. *Can you re-transplant that essential Tibetan culture back into Tibet?*
A. Yes, of course, of that there is no doubt. Of course, unless the situation changes and becomes positive it is difficult to think of returning. At the moment in the bigger towns such as Lhasa the majority of the population is Chinese. So one major factor is the Chinese population influx. Because of the majority Chinese population the Tibetan minority is compelled to speak Chinese and act like Chinese. This is the major negative factor. When in the future things change, we can of course re-transplant. I keep saying that one of the main tasks for Tibetans outside is to keep the Tibetan deeper spiritual values, no matter what the difficulties. So that when things change and we return with freedom, then it is our responsibility to restart.

Q. *Your Holiness, your main reason for coming today is to lay the foundation stone of the Tibetan pavilion. What for you is the significance of a pavilion of Tibetan culture in Auroville?*
A. I think we have some potential to make a little contribution for the betterment of human beings. We have a legitimate right to participate with you!

Q. *Do you see this Pavilion as having a significance stretching beyond the boundaries of Auroville?*
A. A symbolic significance, yes. I was very moved, very happy, when I was told that some earth from Tibet was brought here.

Q. *It was an eight kilo brick!*
A. Sometimes this works on a mysterious level. For the human mind, when you know that there's something from Tibet here, you feel a special relation. I feel that Tibetan culture with its unique heritage— born of the effort of many human beings of good spirit, of its contacts with Chinese, Indian, Nepalese and Persian culture, and due to its natural environment—has developed some kind of energy which is useful, and very helpful, towards cultivating peace of mind and a joyful life. I feel that there is a potential for Tibet to help humanity, and particularly our Eastern neighbour, where millions of young Chinese have lost their spiritual values. In this way I feel very strongly that

Tibetan culture will have a future role to play in humanity. So therefore, wherever there are spiritual centres like Auroville, if Tibet can participate it can be a way or a channel to communicate Tibetan culture to other people.

I have dedicated the rest of my life to demilitarization on a global level. As a first step, Tibet should be a zone of peace and completely demilitarized, so that in the future we can help not only China and India but also the world community. This is my vision and hope for the future.

His Holiness being greeted on his sixtieth birthday (*Courtsey* : Ms.Francoise Guerin)

His Holiness speaking on his sixtieth birthday (*Courtsey* : Ms.Francoise Guerin)

Sixtieth Birthday Celebrations (*Courtsey* : Ms. Francoise Guerin)

Sixtieth Birthday Celebrations (*Courtsey*: Ms. Francoise Guerin)

His Holiness being greeted (*Courtsey*: Ms. Francoise Guerin)

Sections of the audience: (*Courtsey* : Ms. Francoise Guerin)

Sections of the audience: (*Courtsey* : Ms. Francoise Guerin)

Prof. S. Rinpoche with the Tibetan flag (*Courtsey* : Ms.Francoise Guerin)

Cultural performers (*Courtsey* : Ms. Francoise Guerin)

Cultural performers (*Courtsey* : Ms. Francoise Guerin)

Cultural performers (*Courtsey* : Ms.Francoise Guerin)

XI
Sixtieth Birthday Speeches

Chapter XI
60TH BIRTHDAY SPEECHES

Dishonest behaviour harms both ourselves and others, bringing unhappiness to many people. This is why we have legal structures to protect society from certain kinds of arbitrary and harmful activity. Even rigid totalitarian systems claim to provide security and protection for their citizens. But in such cases it is often the most gifted, dedicated and creative members of society, the intellectuals and artists who challenge the government, who are labelled deceitful and dishonest. Having been deprived of their rights, they are no longer able to speak up for themselves. In such societies regulation is achieved through the exercise of raw power, unnaturally rigid discipline and the threatened use of force. This inevitably trespasses upon many basic human rights.

Freedom of speech and the independence of the mass media are vital components of democracy. These freedoms should be used to expose politicians, bureaucrats and those employed in the service of the community who are duplicitous or dishonest. These standards should apply to people working in any field whose actions behind the scenes do not comply with what they say in public. We should have the courage to expose these shortcomings in society directly and clearly with sincerity and honesty, free of prejudice. In this way we can tackle those acts of corruption and exploitation that sap the public good.

When certain sections of the Press fall a prey to the influence of powerful groups, political parties or business interests, readers must be vigilant in using their power of judgement and discrimination. This is only a short-term solution, for the Press also have a responsibility to the truth. It is the media's job to be critical and highlight social ills, but they should also point out what is good and constructive in society. Drawing attention to positive achievements enhances their value in the public eye and encourages others to do likewise.

—Dalai Lama

1

NON-VIOLENCE AND COMPASSION

New Delhi,
July 5, 1995

One of the major challenges we continue to face at the close of the twentieth century is the achievement of genuine lasting world peace. In the past, the effects of war were limited, but today our potential for destruction is beyond imagination. In many parts of the world local and regional conflicts remain, which, besides causing misery to millions already, have potentially far-reaching global consequences.

Concerned groups and individuals everywhere have a responsibility to work for peace. We have an obligation to promote a new vision of society, one in which war has no place in resolving disputes among states, communities or individuals, but in which non-violence is the preeminent value in all human relations.

Many of the world's problems and conflicts arise because we have lost sight of the basic humanness that binds us all together as a human family. We tend to forget that despite the diversity of race, religion, ideology and so forth, people are equal in their basic wish for peace and happiness.

Nearly all of us receive our first lessons in peaceful living from our mothers, because the need for love lies at the very foundation of human existence. From the earlier stages of our growth, we are completely dependent upon our mother's care and it is very important for us that she expresses her love. If children do not receive proper affection, in later life they will often find it hard to love others. This is how a mother's love has a bearing on peace. Peaceful living is about trusting those on whom we depend and caring for those who depend on us. We receive our first experience of both these qualities in our relationship with our mother.

As the world becomes smaller and increasingly interdependent, a sense of universal responsibility in our approach to world problems seems the only sound basis for world peace. Everyone wishes to live in peace, but it is not achieved by merely talking or thinking about it, nor by waiting for someone else to do something about it. Each of us must take responsibility as best we can within our own sphere of activity. What does this mean? We can begin with the recognition that each of us is a human being like everyone else. Like us, others also desire happiness and do not want suffering. And we all have an equal right to avoid suffering and pursue happiness.

We have recently seen how new found freedoms, widely celebrated though they are, have given rise to fresh economic difficulties and unleashed long buried ethnic and religious tensions, that contain the seeds for a new cycle of conflicts. In the context of our newly emerging global community, all forms of violence, especially war, have become totally unacceptable as means of settling disputes. As forceful intervention tends to perpetuate conflict and its causes, we must explore and strengthen more truly peaceful approaches to peacemaking.

The threat of nuclear destruction is still the greatest single danger facing all living beings on this planet. Beside this, other problems, whose effects are more gradual, are secondary. At a time of concern for increasing democratic freedoms and human rights it is contradictory to continue to pursue policies that take little account of every living being's right to life. In the event of nuclear war no one will win, because no one will survive. Realising this danger, steps are being taken to eliminate nuclear weapons. This is a welcome sign. Nonetheless, in a volatile world, the risk remains as long as even a handful of these weapons continue to exist. The key to changing such policies is to increase awareness of the issue.

This year marks the fiftieth anniversary of the bombing of Hiroshima and Nagasaki, which, reminds us of the horrifying nature of nuclear destruction. It is instant, total and irreversible. Like our neglect and abuse of the natural environment, it has the potential to affect the rights, not only of many defenceless people living now in various parts of the world, but also those of future generations.

To ensure long-term peace and stability, our ultimate goal should be the demilitarization of the entire planet. With this in mind, I have envisioned that the entire Tibetan plateau, also known as the "roof of the world" should become a free refuge where humanity and nature can live in peace and harmonious balance. The key elements of my proposal for Tibet as a Zone of peace include, the demilitarization and prohibition of the manufacture, testing and stockpiling of nuclear weapons and other armaments on the Tibetan plateau. When I visited Costa Rica in 1989, I saw how a country can develop successfully without an army, to become a stable democracy committed to peace and the protection of the natural environment, with the added advantage of being able to use funds, that would usually be spent on arms and defence, on education, health and other developmental programmes. This confirmed my belief that my vision of Tibet in the future is realistic, not merely a dream.

If it were properly planned and people were educated to understand its advantages, I believe it is quite possible. Some of you may think I am over-optimistic, but I believe that millions of people feel the way I do, although they have no public voice. It is on behalf of those silent millions that I am speaking out. The widespread positive response to my receiving the Nobel Peace Prize revealed to me the degree to which people around the world support non-violence. Therefore, I feel obliged to carry on with my work and speak up on their behalf.

Although we may talk of achieving a global demilitarization, to begin with some kind of inner disarmament is necessary. The key to genuine world peace is inner peace and the foundation of that is a sense of understanding and respect for each other as human beings, based on compassion and love. Some may dismiss love and compassion as impractical and unrealistic, but I believe their practice is the true source of success. Compassion is, by nature, peaceful and gentle, but it is also very powerful. It is a sign of true inner strength. To achieve it we do not need to become religious, nor do we need any ideology. All that is necessary is for us to develop our basic human qualities.

Only a spontaneous feelings of empathy with others can really inspire us to act on their behalf. Nevertheless, compassion does not arise simply by ordering it to do so. Such a sincere feeling must grow gradually, cultivated within each individual, based on his own conviction of its worth. Adopting an attitude of kindness and universal responsibility is, then a personal matter. How each of us behaves in daily life is, after all, the real test of our compassion.

From the moment of birth, every human being wants happiness and does not want suffering. Neither social conditioning nor education nor ideology affects this. From the very core of our being, we simply desire contentment. Therefore, it is important to discover what will bring about the greatest degree of happiness. When we consider what we human beings really are, we find we are not like machine-made objects. If we were merely mechanical entities, then machines themselves could alleviate all of our sufferings and fulfil our needs. However, since we are not solely material creatures, it is a mistake to place all our hopes for happiness on external development alone.

Although we have no religion, ideology or culture at birth, I believe that no one is born free from the need for love. Even if the source of affection is an animal or someone we would normally consider an enemy, both children and adults naturally gravitate towards it. And this demonstrates that human beings cannot be defined as solely physical. No material object, however beautiful or valuable, can make us feel loved, because our deeper identity and true character lie in the subjective nature of the mind.

As I have already said, developing universal responsibility on the basis of such attitudes as compassion and love, patience and tolerance, and genuine understanding between human beings is not simply a religious matter, but a condition for survival. To be a good human being in day to day life, neither philosophy nor ritual is necessary. To be a good human being means to serve other people if you can, but otherwise to refrain from harming them.

The necessary foundation for world peace and the ultimate goal of any new international order is the elimination of violence at every level. Each day the news media report incidents of terrorism, crime and aggression. Yet the overwhelming majority of the human race does not behave destructively. Deep down the human character desires constructive, fruitful growth. We dislike things collapsing, dying or being destroyed. Destruction goes against our basic nature. For this reason the practice of non-violence surely suits us all. It simply requires determination, for by its very nature, non-violent action requires patience.

Ahimsa or non-violence is an ancient but powerful idea that Mahatma Gandhi made familiar throughout the world. He refined, adapted and implemented non-violence in his struggle for political freedom. After independence, in a world threatened by power blocs and nuclear weapons, India adopted a foreign policy of nonalignment. This was not mere pacifism, but an active commitment to perpetuating non-violence as an ideal on our planet. Non-violence does not mean the mere absence of violence. It is something more positive, more meaningful than that. The true expression of non-violence is compassion. Some people seem to think that compassion is just a passive emotional response instead of a rational stimulus to action. To experience genuine compassion is to develop a feeling of closeness to others combined with a sense of responsibility for their welfare.

Although violence is still rife, the trend of world opinion is to recognise that the future lies in non-violence. Today, there is a growing global awareness of the meaning of non-violence, but its application is not restricted merely to other human beings. It also has to do with ecology, the environment and our relations with all the other living beings with whom we share the planet. Non-violence can be applied in our day to day lives whatever our position or vocation. It is even relevant to medical procedures, education systems, legal procedures and so forth.

It may sometimes seem that a problem can be solved quickly by force, but often at the expense of the rights and welfare of others. War is violent, and violence is always unpredictable. War and large military establishments are the greatest sources of violence in our world. Whether their purpose is defensive or offensive, these vast powerful organisations exist solely to kill human beings. War is neither glamorous nor attractive. War is like a fire where human beings are used as fuel and its very nature is one of tragedy and suffering. And as long as there are powerful armies there will always be the danger of dictatorship.

Naturally, global peace cannot occur all at once. All of us, every member of the world community, has a moral responsibility to help avert the immense suffering which results from war and civil strife. We must find a peaceful, non-violent way for the forces of freedom, truth and democracy to develop successfully as peoples emerge from oppression.

Recent events have shown that the desire for both peace and freedom lies at the core of human nature and that violence is its complete antithesis. Until lately, people believed that war was an inevitable condition of mankind. Few now hold this view. Today people all over the planet are genuinely concerned about world peace. They are less interested in propounding ideology than in the benefits of coexistence.

Nevertheless, in the present circumstances, no one can afford to assume that someone else will solve our problems. Every individual has a responsibility to help guide our global family in the right direction. Democracy is not only about rights; but about responsibility and participation. Good wishes are not sufficient; we must become actively engaged. The twentieth century has been the most painful period in human history, when more people have fallen victim to violence than ever before. And yet personalities as diverse as Mahatma Gandhi, Martin Luther King and Aung San Suu Kyi have shown by their practice of non-violence that individuals can influence change for the good and so affect the whole global community.

2

SPEECH ON 60TH BIRTHDAY

New Delhi,
July 6, 1995

Brothers and Sisters,

I am honoured that you have all gathered here today to celebrate my sixtieth birthday. However, let us regard this not so much as a tribute to myself, as to my endeavour to fulfil the principal responsibilities of my life. When I was born sixty years ago, my country, Tibet, still deliberately closed itself off from the rest of the world. It might have been my destiny to have lived out my days in isolation too. But, as circumstances would have it, I had to leave my homeland and I have spent more than half of my life as a refugee. In some ways this is a source of sorrow, but the positive result is that I and many of my compatriots have had to become citizens of the world.

Of course, as a Buddhist monk I live the life of a religious person, as the Dalai Lama I have particular concern for the people of Tibet, but first of all, like all of you, I am a human being. Consequently, I feel I have a responsibility, whenever I have the opportunity, to share some of my fundamental beliefs. I believe that human nature is fundamentally gentle and creative and that it is important for us to recognise this. If we examine the nature of our lives, we find that from the moment of birth until we die, human affection plays a crucial role in ensuring not only that we feel satisfied, but even that we survive.

We humans have existed in our present form for about a hundred thousand years. I believe that if during this time the human mind had been primarily controlled by anger and hatred, our overall population would have decreased. But today, despite all our wars, we find that the human population is greater than ever. This indicates clearly to me that love and compassion predominate in the world.

Some of my friends tell me that my view of human nature is too optimistic and that human beings are essentially aggressive and destruc-tive. I don't think this is so. Human beings are social animals, we depend on each other's support simply to live and we have a deep-seated desire to communicate with one another, to express our feelings and share our experiences. On the one hand, our need to live together, like members of any family, requires that we show each other tolerance and mutual support. On the other, our very diversity is a source of strength and creativity.

Despite the recent advances made by civilisation, the principal cause of our present predicament is our undue emphasis solely on material development. We have become so engrossed in this pursuit that, almost without knowing it, we have neglected to foster the most basic human needs for love, kindness, cooperation and caring. But the development of human society is based entirely on people helping each other. If we lose this essential humanity, what is the point of pursuing only material improvement?

On a more mundane level, one major dangerous problem is the gap between the North and the South—the rich and the poor. Not only is this morally wrong but, even in practical terms, it is source of trouble resulting from the big gap and how the wealthy consume the resources of the earth that we all share. Unless the rich, industrialized countries take the initiative to change the present pattern there will be neither sufficient natural resources to continue feeding the present uneven consumption nor will the rest of the world be at peace.

We have all been born on this earth as part of one great human family whether we are rich or poor, educated or uneducated, whatever our nationality, colour, social status or ideology may be, each of us is just a human being like everyone else. We all desire happiness and do not want suffering. What is more, each of us has an equal right to pursue these goals.

Because the very purpose of life is to be happy, it is important to discover what will bring about the greatest degree of happiness. Whether our experience is pleasant or miserable it is either mental or physical. Generally, it is the mind that exerts the greatest influence on most of us. Therefore, we should devote our most serious efforts to bringing about mental peace. In my own limited experience I have found that the greatest degree of inner tranquillity comes from the development of love and compassion.

The more we care for the happiness of others, the greater is our own sense of well-being. Cultivating a close, warmhearted feeling for others automatically puts the mind at ease. This helps to remove whatever fears or insecurities we may have and gives us the strength to cope with any obstacles we encounter. It is the ultimate source of success in life.

I believe that at every level of society from the family up to international relations, the key to a happier and more successful world is the growth of compassion. We do not need to become religious, nor do we need to believe in an ideology. All that is necessary is for each of us to develop our good human qualities.

Our world is growing smaller, politically and economically more interdependent, and the world's people are becoming increasing like one community. In the circumstances we have an obligation to promote a new vision of society, one in which war has no place in resolving disputes among states, communities or religions, but in which non-violence is the preeminent value in all human relations.

On the human level, nobody actually wants wars, because it brings unspeakable suffering. Everyone wants peace. But we need a genuine peace that is founded on mutual trust and the realization that as brothers and sisters we must all live together without trying to destroy each other. Even if one nation or community dislikes another, they have no alternative but to live together. And under the circumstances it is much better to live together happily.

The necessary foundation for world peace and the ultimate goal of any new international order is the elimination of violence at every level. For this reason the practice of non-violence surely suits us all. It simply requires determination, for by its very nature, non-violent action requires patience. While the practice of non-violence is still something of an experiment on this planet, if it is successful, it will open the way to a far more peaceful world in the next century.

Throughout history, mankind has pursued peace one way or another. Witnessing the mass slaughter that has occurred in our century has given us the stimulus and opportunity to control war. To do so, it is clear we must disarm. Our planet is blessed with vast natural treasures. If we use them wisely, beginning with the elimination of militarism and wars, every human being will be able to live a healthy, prosperous existence.

The question of real, lasting world peace concerns human beings, so basic human feelings are also at its root. Through inner peace, genuine world peace can be achieved. Here the importance of individual responsibility is quite clear, for an atmosphere of peace must first be created within ourselves, then it will be created in our families, our communities and gradually across the whole planet. In order to create inner peace, what is most important is the practice of compassion and love, understanding and respect for human beings.

As a boy studying Buddhism, I was taught the importance of a caring attitude toward the environment and the beings who live in it. Our practice of non-violence applies not just to human beings but to any living thing that has a mind. Where there is a mind, there are feelings such as pain, pleasure and joy. No sentient being wants pain, all want happiness instead. In Buddhist practice we get so used to this idea of non-violence and the ending of all suffering that we become accustomed to not harming or destroying anything indiscriminately.

The way we studied in Tibet followed the Indian system that had been pursued in such centres of learning as Nalanda University. I also studied the major Buddhist texts in this way. The approach we adopted was based on the open-minded practice of hearing, contemplation and meditation. In brief, this meant that whatever we learned through study, hearing and contemplation was integrated into our mindstreams and, as far as possible, was applied in actual practice.

These are the circumstances, following the noble tradition of combining the teaching and practice of dharma, in which I have led my life. Over the years, even in the most difficult and confusing periods of my life, the principal source of my mental peace and strength has lain in what I have studied and what I have put into practice based on these studies.

For Buddhists the most important thing is in our mind, here and now, and the way we use that mind in daily life. If we can create our own positive mind, it will bring deep satisfaction. If we eliminate our negative mind, we can dispel those thoughts that bring uneasiness and discomfort. It is not that certain thoughts are holier than others, but whether or not they are useful for humanity and health of our planet. I am not interested in converting other people to Buddhism but how we Buddhists can contribute to human society according to our own ideas.

Now, as a Buddhist monk, I always try to bring about closer understanding and greater cooperation between the various religious traditions of the world. All the world's traditions are similar because they help us become better human beings. For centuries, millions of people have found peace of mind in their own religious tradition. Today, the world over, we can find followers of many faiths giving up their own welfare in order to help others. I believe that this wish to work for the happiness of others is the most important goal of all religious practice.

Human beings naturally possess different interests. So, it is not surprising that we have many different religious traditions with different ways of thinking and behaving. But this variety is a way for everyone to be happy. If we have a great variety of food, we will be able to satisfy everyone's different tastes and needs. When we only have bread, the people who eat rice are left out. And the reason those people eat rice is that rice is what grows best where they live.

While I do not believe that everybody should become religious minded, each of the various religions can contribute to the welfare of mankind. All the great teachers of the past gave their religious teachings for the benefit of humanity. They did not mean to gain anything for themselves nor to create more trouble or unrest in the world. Through their own examples they advocated contentment, tolerance, and unselfishly serving others. They lived saintly lives, not luxuriously like kings, but as simple human beings. While their inner strength was tremendous, the outer impression they gave was of contentment with a simple way of life.

For most of us, our religion depends on our family and where we were born and grew up. Usually I think it is better not to change that. However, the more we understand of each others' ways, the more we can learn from each other, and the more easily we can develop respect and tolerance in our own lives and in our behaviour towards one another. This will certainly help to increase peace and friendship throughout the world, which is one of the aims of all religions.

Because all the world's religions have a similar intent, harmony between them is very important. Nothing can be achieved through feelings of discrimination and prejudice. Although I am a Buddhist Bhikshu, I firmly believe that all religions have the same potential to help mankind despite differences in philosophy.

How can religious harmony be achieved? Religious scholars can meet together and discuss the similarities, differences and values of their different traditions. Followers of different religious traditions who have real inner experience should also meet to share these experiences. Occasionally, religious leaders can come together as we did when we prayed together in Assisi and other sacred places and as we have done several times in different parts of India.

Finally, as a Tibetan and especially as Dalai Lama, I have a special responsibility towards Tibet and its people. Because the people of Tibet have placed so much trust and hope in me, I have a moral responsibility to speak up for them. In this capacity I try to raise public awareness of the real situation inside Tibet and the true nature of our freedom struggle.

In recent times, unspeakable misfortune has overtaken my country, Tibet, because of which more than one hundred thousand Tibetan including myself have had to flee our homeland and now live in exile. Of these, the majority are living in India and this has created the opportunity for us to preserve the precious traditions of scholarship and spiritual practice that, like jewels, we received from Indian scholars in the past and kept alive in Tibet for so many centuries.

Despite its own many problems and constraints, the Indian government has provided us generously with facilities for our needs. When I visit Tibetan settlements in different parts of the country today, I am encouraged to see what developments my people have managed to achieve. India has helped us in the field of education, rehabilitation, and in the preservation of our culture, religion and identity, along with our self-respect.

On the other hand, the continued Chinese occupation of Tibet poses an increasing threat to the very existence of a distinct Tibetan national and cultural identity. Therefore, I consider that my primary responsibility is to take whatever steps I must to save my people and their unique heritage from total annihilation. This is not a struggle to preserve old institutions. It is a struggle for national survival and the preservation of Tibetan culture which has some potential to serve humanity and to keep the peace in this part of the world.

In endeavouring to protect my nation from the threat of extinction, I have always sought to be guided by realism, moderation and patience. I have pursued a course of non-violence and have tried in every way I know to find some mutually acceptable solution, in the spirit of reconciliation and compromise, so that the Tibetan people can resume a life in peace and with dignity.

If I look back on the sixty years of my life so far, I have no regrets. As a human being like any other, I can at least say that my life has not caused suffering to others. I feel I have been of some service to both my human brothers and sisters and to animals. As a Buddhist monk, although in my early years, which should be a time for study, I was a little lazy and was occupied with other responsibilities, later as a refugee I put a lot of effort into spiritual practice. I have done my best and despite my constraints have sincerely carried out my responsibilities in serving my people and my country.

It is my dream that all of Tibet become a sanctuary, a zone of peace, where humanity and nature live in harmonious balance. That is what it once was, although it was not generally recognised as such. Under difficult circumstances, I think I have made some contribution to keeping the Tibetan spirit and a sense of hope alive. However, it has now become clear that these efforts alone are not sufficient to bring about a positive solution. Therefore, I appeal to all of you on this occasion to support the Tibetan people, as human beings who are presently prevented from exercising the rights and freedoms that many of us take for granted.

3

RIGHTS AND DUTIES IN A FREE SOCIETY[1]

As human beings we naturally appreciate positive qualities like truth, justice and honesty, recognising them as good and beneficial. We all dislike falsehood and mistrust people who are deceitful. Animals too instinctively respond to genuine affection and sincerity. Sensitive to deception, they invariably react accordingly.

Dishonest behaviour harms both ourselves and others, bringing unhappiness to many people. This is why we have legal structures to protect society from certain kinds of arbitrary and harmful activity. Even rigid totalitarian systems claim to provide security and protection for their citizens. But in such cases it is often the most gifted, dedicated and creative members of society, the intellectuals and artists who challenge the government, who are labelled deceitful and dishonest. Having been deprived of their rights, they are no longer able to speak up for themselves. In such societies regulation is achieved through the exercise of raw power, unnaturally rigid discipline and the threatened use of force. This inevitably trespasses upon many basic human rights.

If you weigh up the benefits and the disadvantages of totalitarianism, the repression it represents cannot be justified. The tight discipline imposed by authoritarian regimes may seem attractive from a distance, but it does not accord with human nature. We cannot, therefore, regard such methods of control as signs of civilised progress or as in the spirit of human advancement. The democratic process, however, is fundamentally in tune with human aspirations.

Human Nature

It is human nature to yearn for freedom. Therefore, those systems of organisation which are based on democracy and individual liberty are

[1]This was published on the Dalai Lama's 60th birthday.

more suited to human needs. Nevertheless, the very conditions that allow for freedom in democracy are also open to abuse and provide greater opportunities for individual misdeeds. There is more chance of dishonest and deceptive behaviour. So, it is very important to find ways and means of preserving our democratic structures while at the same time devising strategies to curtail such harmful activities such as bribery and corruption.

Freedom of speech and the independence of the mass media are vital components of democracy. These freedoms should be used to expose politicians, bureaucrats and those employed in the service of the community who are duplicitous or dishonest. These standards should apply to people working in any field whose actions behind the scenes do not comply with what they say in public. We should have the courage to expose these shortcomings in society directly and clearly with sincerity and honesty, free of prejudice. In this way we can tackle those acts of corruption and exploitation that sap the public good.

When certain sections of the Press fall a prey to the influence of powerful groups, political parties or business interests, readers must be vigilant in using their power of judgement and discrimination. This is only a short-term solution, for the Press also have a responsibility to the truth. It is the media's job to be critical and highlight social ills, but they should also point out what is good and constructive in society. Drawing attention to positive achievements enhances their value in the public eye and encourages others to do likewise.

Wide Disparity

Another factor contributing to corruption and underhandedness across the world is the gap between the rich and the poor. When there is such wide economic disparity, it is not surprising if people in desperate conditions resort to deceitful means to solve their problems. Often they must fulfil their basic needs quickly or die. Severe inequality between the rich and the poor inevitably gives rise to many social problems. Addressing these difficulties will require complex, long-term solutions. In the meantime, we can each make a contribution to a more kind society by cultivating a real wish to help others and acting on it whenever we can.

As leaders, politicians have a duty to set a worthy example. Public servants too are respected in proportion to the degree that they are fair and public-spirited. They all have an obligation to root out bribery and corruption by refusing to give in to them. If everyone made the effort, bribery, corruption and injustice could gradually be eliminated from public life.

India, which we Tibetans have long regarded as a holy land, has a long and rich ethical tradition exemplified by self-sacrifice and non-violence. But it is not enough to tell admiringly about these qualities, we must incorporate them into our daily lives. We must apply them to our relations within our own families and communities. If we hope to overcome corruption and abuse of authority and look forward to greater peace, justice and honesty in society, we must start by applying these values ourselves.

The Times of India, 6-7-1995

INDEX